Lecture Notes in Computer Science 13770

Founding Editors

Gerhard Goos
Juris Hartmanis

The series Lecture Notes in Computer Science (LNCS), including its subseries Lecture Notes in Artificial Intelligence (LNAI) and Lecture Notes in Bioinformatics (LNBI), has established itself as a medium for the publication of new developments in computer science and information technology research, teaching, and education.

LNCS enjoys close cooperation with the computer science R & D community, the series counts many renowned academics among its volume editors and paper authors, and collaborates with prestigious societies. Its mission is to serve this international community by providing an invaluable service, mainly focused on the publication of conference and workshop proceedings and postproceedings. LNCS commenced publication in 1973.

Mitsuko Aramaki · Keiji Hirata ·
Tetsuro Kitahara · Richard Kronland-Martinet ·
Sølvi Ystad
Editors

Music in the AI Era

15th International Symposium, CMMR 2021
Virtual Event, November 15–19, 2021
Revised Selected Papers

 Springer

Editors
Mitsuko Aramaki 🆔
Aix Marseille Univ, CNRS, PRISM
Marseille Cedex 09, France

Keiji Hirata
Future University Hakodate
Hakodate, Hokkaido, Japan

Tetsuro Kitahara
Nihon University
Tokyo, Japan

Richard Kronland-Martinet 🆔
Aix Marseille Univ, CNRS, PRISM
Marseille Cedex 09, France

Sølvi Ystad 🆔
Aix Marseille Univ, CNRS, PRISM
Marseille Cedex 09, France

ISSN 0302-9743   ISSN 1611-3349 (electronic)
Lecture Notes in Computer Science
ISBN 978-3-031-35381-9   ISBN 978-3-031-35382-6 (eBook)
https://doi.org/10.1007/978-3-031-35382-6

This Springer imprint is published by the registered company Springer Nature Switzerland AG
The registered company address is: Gewerbestrasse 11, 6330 Cham, Switzerland

Preface

The 15th edition of the International Symposium on Computer Music Multidisciplinary Research CMMR 2021 "Music in the AI Era" took place on 15th-19th November, 2021. This edition of the conference was notable for two reasons: firstly, it marked the first time that Japanese universities organized the event, and secondly, it was the first CMMR conference to be held entirely online. Due to the Covid-19 crisis, the 2020 edition of CMMR, which was initially planned to take place in Tokyo, was postponed in the hope that 2021 would be a year where the routines of the conference would get back to normal. Unfortunately, things did not improve as fast as we hoped, which incited us to propose a fully online event for CMMR 2021. Despite the difficult conditions among students, researchers and artists during this period, CMMR 2021 received an excellent response from both scientific and artistic communities.

The conference was chaired by Keiji Hirata (Future University Hakodate, Japan) and Satoshi Tojo (JAIST, Japan) and co-organized by six local institutions, i.e. Future University Hakodate, JAIST, Nihon University, RIKEN, University of Tsukuba, and Tokyo University of Science in collaboration with the Laboratory PRISM ("Perception, Representations, Image, Sound, Music"), Marseilles, France. As for previous CMMR gatherings there was also a music program that was chaired by Shintaro Imai (Kunitachi College of Music, Japan).

The seven scientific sessions that took place during the conference dealt with both traditional CMMR topics such as music information retrieval, audio signal processing and music analysis, together with more recent topics linked to interactive systems for music and IA-related approaches. Three internationally renowned keynote speakers were also invited to the conference. Shuji Hashimoto, Waseda University, gave a lecture on "Music in the AI era". Tadahiro Taniguchi, Ritsumeikan University, gave a lecture on "Generative Models for Symbol Emergence based on Real-World Sensory-motor Information and Communication". Gaëtan Hadjeres, Sony CSL Paris Music Team, gave a lecture on "Developing Artist-centric Technology".

The videos of the paper (and music) program are available at the conference website (https://www.cmmr2021.gttm.jp/).

The post-proceedings edition of CMMR2021 is the 15th CMMR publication by Springer Verlag in its Lecture Notes in Computer Sciences Series and completes the previous editions: LNCS 2771, LNCS 3310, LNCS 3902, LNCS 4969, LNCS 5493, LNCS 5954, LNCS 6684, LNCS 7172, LNCS 7900, LNCS 8905, LNCS 9617, LNCS 10525, LNCS 11265 and LNCS 12631. This year's edition contains 24 peer-reviewed chapters divided in 4 sections related to music technology in the IA era, interactive systems for music, music information retrieval and modeling, and music and performance analysis.

We would like to express our gratitude to all the participants of CMMR 2021 who made this event possible. A special thanks goes to the local organizers at Tokyo universities, who managed the practical organization and insured smooth and efficient coordination despite the many challenges that arose due to the fully remote format. Additionally, we would like to thank the Program and Music Committee members for their indispensable work in selecting the content.

Finally, we would like to thank Springer for agreeing to publish the CMMR 2021 post-proceedings edition in their LNCS series.

April 2023

Mitsuko Aramaki
Keiji Hirata
Tetsuro Kitahara
Richard Kronland-Martinet
Sølvi Ystad

Organization

General Chair

Keiji Hirata   Future University Hakodate, Japan

General Co-chair

Satoshi Tojo   JAIST, Japan

Scientific Program and Proceedings Chairs

Tetsuro Kitahara   Nihon University, Japan
Aiko Uemura   Nihon University, Japan
Mitsuko Aramaki   PRISM, AMU-CNRS, France
Richard Kronland-Martinet   PRISM, AMU-CNRS, France
Sølvi Ystad   PRISM, AMU-CNRS, France

Scientific Program Committee

Mitsuko Aramaki   PRISM, AMU-CNRS, France
Gilberto Bernardes   INESC TEC, Portugal
Marco Buongiorno Nardelli   University of North Texas, USA
Marcelo Caetano   McGill University, Canada
F. Amílcar Cardoso   University of Coimbra, Portugal
Roger Dannenberg   Carnegie Mellon University, USA
Matthew Davies   University of Coimbra, Portugal
Georg Essl   University of Wisconsin - Milwaukee, USA
Satoru Fukayama   AIST, Japan
Masatoshi Hamanaka   RIKEN, Japan
Tatsunori Hirai   Komazawa University, Japan
Keiji Hirata   Future University Hakodate, Japan
Katsutoshi Itoyama   Tokyo Institute of Technology, Japan
Tetsuro Kitahara   Nihon University, Japan
Richard Kronland-Martinet   PRISM, AMU-CNRS, France
Sven-Amin Lembke   De Montfort University, UK

Luca Andrea Ludovico	University of Milan, Italy
Sylvain Marchand	University of La Rochelle, France
Eita Nakamura	Kyoto University, Japan
Charles de Paiva Santana	PRISM, AMU-CNRS, France
Charalampos Saitis	Queen Mary University of London, UK
Bob Sturm	KTH, Sweden
Satoshi Tojo	JAIST, Japan
Ryosuke Yamanishi	Kansai University, Japan
Sølvi Ystad	PRISM, AMU-CNRS, France

Steering Committee

Mitsuko Aramaki	PRISM, AMU-CNRS, France
Mathieu Barthet	QMUL, UK
Matthew Davies	INESC TEC, Portugal
Richard Kronland-Martinet	PRISM, AMU-CNRS, France
Sølvi Ystad	PRISM, AMU-CNRS, France

Contents

Music Information Retrieval and Modeling

Music and Performance Analysis

Music Technology in the IA Era

KANSEI Informatics and Music Technology in AI Era

Shuji Hashimoto[✉]

Waseda University, Tokyo, Japan
shuji@waseda.jp

Abstract. "KANSEI" is a Japanese word to express some subjective concept like "sensibility", "sensuality" or "emotion". It is also used as "sense" or "feeling". These words often appear when we talk about the artistic human activities including music. Music has grammatical structure and musical sound is characterized physically, which makes music suitable for modern computer technology. At the same time, music has an illogical or KANSEI aspect like the other arts. This paper first describes the trend of modern technology and the concept of KANSEI Informatics. Then the author's observations on recent and future AI in relation to music technology in AI era are introduced.

Keywords: Music · AI · KANSEI

1 Introduction

Ever since humans came to have music, music has evolved along with technology. Music and technology have long been involved in the production and improvement of musical instruments, the design of performance venues, and the diffusion of performed sound. In addition, computerized information processing not only supplied a powerful weapon for music analysis, but also greatly changed the nature of composition and arrangement. Furthermore, it has brought innovation to the performance style at the concert site.

Among the artistic activities human beings engaged in, music is the most logical and mathematically well-founded, which has made it suitable for the application of the signal processing and symbolic computation. While music has an illogical aspect like the other arts, which led computer science to the new frontier named "KANSEI Informatics". "KANSEI" is a Japanese word to express subjective concept in wide sense. The ambiguity of the definition makes KANSEI computing and evaluation difficult [2–4].

Recently remarkable improvement of the power of computers and the accumulation of huge amounts of data via networks made deep machine learning possible to open a new epoch on information processing. One of the major features of recent AI is that it is data-driven rather than logical theory based [1]. Considering the activities related to music that cannot be grasped by logical thinking in a sense, AI that goes beyond the framework of conventional science and technology seems to provide a way to approach KANSEI. AI seems a key to usher in a new era in music and computer science through KANSEI information processing. In this paper, I will introduce the concept of KANSEI and AI

M. Aramaki et al. (Eds.): CMMR 2021, LNCS 13770, pp. 3–8, 2023.
https://doi.org/10.1007/978-3-031-35382-6_1

that will bring about a revolution in technology and discuss about music technology in AI era.

2 New Trend of Technology Development

We notice the changing trend of technological development as shown in Fig. 1. In the history of technological development, the pursuit of efficiency has been the goal for a very long time. Faster, bigger, smaller, more flexible, more convenient, etc. have been pursued, and productivity improvements in factories and comfort in life have been realized. In other words, it can be said that it is a technology that transcends the limits of human ability and makes a superhuman. These research results are reported in academic societies and academic journals, and demonstrations at industrial exhibitions make people realize their usefulness. Such efforts will continue to be important for socio-economic development, but since the end of the last century research and development of new technologies with a different taste have become active. It is an amenity-based technology. We can see the direction of recent technology that pursues more freedom, peace of mind, and more fun, and realizes improvements in services and quality of life. Rather than going beyond human limits, it is a challenge to realize something more human. Although these achievements may be reported at academic conferences, more importantly they are recognized by people at concert halls and amusement parks. The technology of music and art originally belonged to this kind of typology and constitutes the driving force of human renaissance.

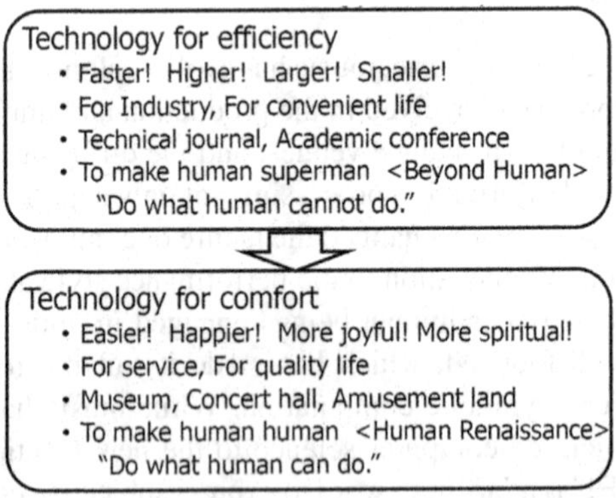

Technology for efficiency
- Faster! Higher! Larger! Smaller!
- For Industry, For convenient life
- Technical journal, Academic conference
- To make human superman <Beyond Human>
  "Do what human cannot do."

Technology for comfort
- Easier! Happier! More joyful! More spiritual!
- For service, For quality life
- Museum, Concert hall, Amusement land
- To make human human <Human Renaissance>
  "Do what human can do."

Fig. 1. New Trend of Technology Development

3 KANSEI Informatics

I would like to introduce "KANSEI" Informatics in relation to the new trend of technology."KANSEI" is a Japanese word to express some subjective concept like "sensibility", "sensuality", "intuition" or " emotion". It is also used as "sense" or "feeling".

We Japanese use the term in many different contexts in daily conversation as shown in Fig. 2. It is said that the postindustrial society will be the KANSEI society. KANSEI is sometimes a contrast to intelligence. It is another human ability of understanding. KANSEI includes psychological universality and individuality at the same time.

"Her KANSEI is excellent."
"He is a man of deep KANSEI."
"He has no KANSEI."
"Her KANSEI seems well suited to me."
"The Beatles expressed the KANSEI of the 60's."
"This tune stimulates my KANSEI."
"Polish up your KANSEI to be an artist."
"My KANSEI cannot accept this music."

Fig. 2. Example Sentences Using the Word "KANSEI"

Table 1 summarizes the three levels of information processing on music. The first is the signal processing. It is to create a physical system that transforms a signal represented by a physical quantity. The central issue here is how to shape the waveform according to the purpose within the scope of causality and physical laws. Secondly, with the advent of computers, we entered the age of information processing, and we can handle symbols and shapes rather than quantities. Moreover, any processing that contradicts the laws of physics is possible in this phase by manipulating symbols according to rules that are not logically inconsistent. The third is KANSEI level to treat artistic information. The object here is music itself, which is neither a physical sound nor a string of acoustic symbols arranged according to grammar. Kansei levels relate to personal and subjective perceptions of reality, whereas the first and second level perceptions of reality are universal and objective.

4 AI and Music Technology

In the circumstance that science and technology play a key role as the driving force of the industrial economy, we now have a new weapon, AI. The current development of AI appears to fundamentally change the nature of technology.

As soon as a digital computer appeared in the world, the term artificial intelligence came to be used among researchers [6]. For more than half a century, re-search on the principle, method and implementation of artificial intelligence has been conducted. So far, many times, we were declared "finally real artificial intelligence has been completed" and we were betrayed each time with various excuses. However, looking at recent progress in AI technology based on the deep learning, it seems that this time it may be true.

A key feature of modern AI is that it does not require theoretical knowledge about the object in order to obtain a solution. Instead, it accepts vast amounts of training data and adjusts the internal parameters to get the right output, but importantly, this adjustment

Table 1. Three Levels of Information Processing on Music

Level	Core objects	Key concepts
Physical level	Sound Frequency Amplitude Spectrum	"Physics" Explain Law of nature Causality >Accuracy
Logical level	Sound sequence Segment Structure Grammar	"Mathematics" Prove Logic Consistency >Correctness
KANSEI level	Music Melody/Harmony Expression Impression	"Humanities" Narrate Empathy Appreciation >Properness

mechanism is not problem-specific. Therefore, there is no way to prove the correctness of the path from the definition of the problem to the conclusion. Today, various of applications based on deep machine learning are presenting adequate answers to the different problems that could not be solved ever before. In most cases, the output of AI sounds like God's revelation. Similar situation is observed when we ask the Meister at violin workshop "why do you shave this part?" He will not give us any proof of validity to do so. Explainable AI only visualize what are happening in the system so far.

The role played by science in conventional technology development is receding in recent AI. Science and technology have been always considered in one set but now the current AI method to produce solutions directly from a huge accumulation of data on concrete facts has blown science away to change the traditional picture of science and technology. Therefore, the current AI seems to be suitable for dealing with KANSEI Informatics that cannot be fully explained scientifically. Especially, music is best for the studies to improve AI, because it has both a logical nature and a hyper-logical or illogical nature like KANSEI.

Another critical issue with AI and music concerns creativity. As the current AI is data-driven, it is inherently interpolative. We can expect good answers if the solutions are in the cloud of data, but interpolation is not creation. To create is to find answers outside the data cluster, that is, extrapolation. Current AI has great potential as a tool in the field of music but seems powerless for creation. In the same way as the Generative Adversarial Networks is used to generate photo images that are indistinguishable from the real one, it may be possible to generate music that is indistinguishable from Mozart or Bach's piece if enough data is properly prepared. Singing voices like Maria Callas or John Coltrane's performances and improvisations are also possible to generate. However, these are born from the imitated KANSEI based on the given data and cannot be said creative performances. The issue of creation is still ahead. Maybe, we need a much-advanced AI that has intention and consciousness. I don't know if it's possible by questing for music in present AI era, but at least it's worth trying.

There are a wide variety of activities related to music. There is an intellectual activity that deals with music from various angles along the sequence of composition, performance, and appreciation. The listed in Fig. 3 is one possible classification. Each of these is related to technology, but when considering the relationship between current AI and humans using AI as a tool for music, there are many things that are beyond the reach of current AI with the characteristics described above. While the basis of AI today is logic and mathematics, the next challenge is to make KANSEI the object of information processing, not only dealing with symbols or quantities. The goal is to realize a human-like information processing that fuses intelligence, intuition and will totally. How much spiritual fulfillment is given will be the criterion of the technology evaluation in this phase. Although "Affective computing" is proposed to treat emotional aspects of both human and machine [5], I would like to use "KANSEI" to express the broader meaning than "affective".

The term "human factor" has a close relation with KANSEI. However, in the KANSEI information processing, we intend to approach the human creativity more positively by applying computer technology to the affective and intuitive human communication including art and music. As the technology for music is a combination of Physics, Logic and KANSEI to have Universality and Individuality with Objectivity and Subjectivity in the same time. Music can be said a gateway to KANSEI informatics because Music technology is a technology of KANSEI. Or it is no exaggeration to say that music has become the central issue of new technology.

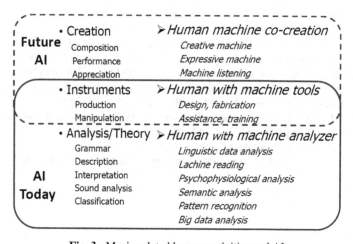

Fig. 3. Music-related human activities and AI

5 Conclusions

Music is fascinating field in elucidating true human intelligence and creativity as it contains philosophy and arts, science and engineering, logical and KANSEI aspect. Music can have a good relationship with AI. In particular, we can expect scientific elucidation of KANSEI. However, the current AI is not enough, AI is not yet in the final stage neither human intelligence is not.

AI today is a statistical method based on a large amount of data. Therefore, the averaging operation is at its essence. In other words, it results in leveling that dilutes the difference.

Creative music that appeals to KANSEI makes difference in many senses. Music in AI era has a potential to improve AI to shape another one that thinks different, and that makes, accepts and respects differences. In order to open up the possibility, it is important that music promotes the development of AI so that it will lead to the true elucidation of intelligence including KANSEI. I do not intend to make intelligent human artificially, but I hope to know what human intelligence through music in AI era is. Just as technology has advanced music, while music has driven technology since its birth, AI has the potential to advance music, and music can push AI to new horizons .

Acknowledgements. This article is based on the keynote talk delivered at the 15th International Symposium on Computer Music Multidisciplinary Research (CMMR) held online on 15 through 19 Nov. 2021. The author would like thank Prof. Keiji Hirata, the conference chair, and the organizing committee for the kind invitation.

References

1. Goodfellow, I.J., et al.: Generative Adversarial Networks (pdf)". arXiv:1406.2661v1. (2014)
2. Hashimoto, S.: Kansei as the third target of information processing and related topics in Japan. In: Proceedings of AIMI International Workshop on KANSEI, pp.101–104(1997)
3. Hashimoto, S.: Evaluation Issue of KANSEI technology and sound and music computing projects at Waseda university. J. New Music Res. **36**(3), 197–205 (2007)
4. Katayose, H., Takami, T., Fukuoka, T., Inokuchi, S.: Music interpreter in the Kansei music system. In: Proceedings of ICMC, pp. 147–150 (1989)
5. Picard, R.: Affective Computing. MIT Press, Cambridge (1997)
6. Strickland, E.: The turbulent past and uncertain future of AI. IEEE Spectr. **58**(10), 26–31 (2021)

On Parallelism in Music and Language: A Perspective from Symbol Emergence Systems Based on Probabilistic Generative Models

Tadahiro Taniguchi[✉]

Ritsumeikan University, 1-1-1 Noji Higashi, Kusatsu, Shiga 525-8577, Japan
taniguchi@em.ci.ritsumei.ac.jp
http://www.em.ci.ritsumei.ac.jp/

Abstract. Music and language are structurally similar. Such structural similarity is often explained by generative processes. This paper describes the recent development of probabilistic generative models (PGMs) for language learning and symbol emergence in robotics. Symbol emergence in robotics aims to develop a robot that can adapt to real-world environments and human linguistic communications and acquire language from sensorimotor information alone (i.e., in an unsupervised manner). This is regarded as a constructive approach to symbol emergence systems. To this end, a series of PGMs have been developed, including those for simultaneous phoneme and word discovery, lexical acquisition, object and spatial concept formation, and the emergence of a symbol system. By extending the models, a symbol emergence system comprising a multi-agent system in which a symbol system emerges is revealed to be modeled using PGMs. In this model, symbol emergence can be regarded as collective predictive coding. This paper expands on this idea by combining the theory that "emotion is based on the predictive coding of interoceptive signals" and "symbol emergence systems", and describes the possible hypothesis of the emergence of meaning in music.

Keywords: symbol emergence systems · probabilistic generative model · symbol emergence in robotics · automatic music composition · language evolution

1 Introduction

Symbol emergence in robotics (SER) is a constructive approach for symbol emergence systems [61]. Humans use symbol systems including language. To build an artificial cognitive system that can adapt to a society in which humans use symbols in an adaptive manner and understand human intelligence that can let symbol systems evolve, emerge, learn, and be used, we must understand the dynamics of symbol emergence systems in a constructive manner [61,66]. A series of studies on SER have attempted to reproduce cognitive behaviors

© Springer Nature Switzerland AG 2023
M. Aramaki et al. (Eds.): CMMR 2021, LNCS 13770, pp. 9–25, 2023.
https://doi.org/10.1007/978-3-031-35382-6_2

that enable humans to acquire language and form internal representations and external symbol systems with artificial robotic and computational models [61]. For example, researchers have developed cognitive developmental robots that perform multimodal object and place categorization and automatic phoneme and word discovery [2–4,17,26,36,54,59,62,64]. Importantly, many of these are performed through unsupervised learning using probabilistic generative models (PGMs) [11].

It is noteworthy that these studies are implicitly motivated by and appear to be related to parallelism in language and music. Studies on automatic lexical acquisition by robots in which the robots form object (or place) categories and discover words from multimodal sensorimotor information and speech signals by mutually segmenting and integrating them have been inspired by the "mutual segmentation hypothesis" proposed in relation to studies on songbirds [41–43]. Language models used in modeling phonemes or word sequences have been found to be naturally applied to automatic music composition. Importantly, the view analogy (or similarity) is concreted by reproducing the behaviors using computational models, that is, PGMs.

Considering this context, it will be worth revisiting parallelism in music and language from the viewpoint of SER and symbol emergence systems. Recently, a new computational model has been proposed that models symbol emergence systems and enables computation agents to emerge symbols as a decentralized Bayesian inference [25,27,68]. This is based on a new type of language game, namely, the Metropolis Hastings naming game. The model and its results suggest that symbol emergence in a society can be considered as collective predictive coding. In other words, we can hypothesize that the emergence of symbols and their meanings can be modeled from the viewpoint of predictive coding [28]. What will the findings and hypotheses suggest regarding the emergence of music and the meaning of music as a symbol system? It may be worth exploring the possible hypotheses suggested by symbol emergence systems and their PGM-based models.

The research question here is "How can the view of symbol emergence systems contribute to the discussion of the meaning of music?" This question is crucially related to "What is the meaning of music?" To answer this question, I would like to present a hypothetical argument based on studies on symbol emergence in robotics, which has been conducted based on a probabilistic generative model (PGM), and a recent understanding of "emotion". Recently, the idea of understanding "emotion" from the viewpoint of predictive coding has become prevalent [8,47]. By replacing the perceptual internal representations in symbol emergence systems with emotional ones and replacing the physical interaction with the external environment, that is, the world, using the sensorimotor system with interactions with the internal environment (i.e., body) via introspective systems, I hypothetically propose parallelism in music and language from the perspective of symbol emergence systems (Fig. 1).

The remainder of this paper is organized as follows. Section 2 reviews a series of studies on symbol emergence in robotics and automatic music composition in computers. Through this review, we will identify a type of parallelism in music and language from the viewpoint of PGMs. Section 3 briefly introduces the view of symbol emergence systems and the concept of collective predictive coding as an account of symbol emergence. Section 4 presents a hypothetical view of the "meaning of music" from the viewpoint of symbol emergence systems. Finally, Sect. 5 concludes the study.

2   Language Acquisition and Music Composition Using PGMs

2.1   Multimodal Concept Formation and Lexical Acquisition in Robotics

Language acquisition by infants is closely connected to their multimodal sensory-motor information. A series of studies on symbol emergence in robotics have attempted to reproduce the language acquisition process using machine learning models and robots [61]. By integrating multimodal information into a PGM, a computational model of language acquisition enables a robot to acquire grounded lexicons to some extent [34, 35, 37, 38].

Okanoya et al. focused on the articulate structure and grammar of songs sung by songbirds and proposed the "mutual segmentation hypothesis" of song phrases and song contexts [41–43]. The hypothesis is based on the idea that segmentation of context, which is also considered as a categorization of objects and situations, and segmentation of strings, for example, speech signals, are mutually dependent and indicate that the two weakly coupled processes are the basis of human language acquisition. This hypothesis motivated me to conduct a series of studies along with collaborators.

An important step in language acquisition is word discovery and phoneme acquisition. In artificial intelligence research, speech recognition typically means "text to speech", and usually, speech signals and their transcriptions are prepared. The speech recognition systems are trained using these systems. However, language acquisition in human infants is different. Infants cannot read transcriptions, that is, written texts, before acquiring spoken language.

The generative process of a spoken utterance y is described as follows:

$$w = w_{1:S} \sim p(w|z), \tag{1}$$

$$y = y_{1:T} \sim p(y|w) \tag{2}$$

where $y = y_{1:T}$ is the acoustic feature, that is, speech signals, corresponding to the word sequence, and z is a cause, that is, a state of the internal representation that generates the semiotic sign, that is, utterance. Here, conventional speech recognition is considered an inference of $p(w|y)$, assuming that the learning system can obtain both w and y in the training datasets, although this assumption cannot be applied to human child development.

Unsupervised simultaneous phoneme and word acquisition was achieved by modeling the generative process of speech signals with a PGM and inferring latent variables representing phonemes and words [62, 64]. Speech signals have a two-layer hierarchical structure called double articulation, which is also called the "duality of patterning". This means that a speech signal is grouped into phonemes, and the phonemes are segmented into words [18]. If we describe phoneme sequence l explicitly, the generative process shown in (2) becomes

$$y \sim \sum p(y|l)p(l|w). \tag{3}$$

The Bayesian double articulation analyzer is based on a nonparametric Bayesian PGM called the hierarchical Dirichlet process-hidden language model [62]. The generative process simply models a double articulation structure that represents (3) [18]. Based on the PGM, a Bayesian inference procedure for phoneme and word discovery, that is, the sampling procedure of $p(w, l|bmy)$, was developed. It is known that infants use not only distributional cues, which are sound sequence information, but also prosodic cues, which are prosody information (accent and silent intervals), and co-occurrence cues, which represent co-occurrence information with other stimuli, such as multimodal sensorimotor information, for lexical acquisition [46]. Models that integrate these two have also been proposed [36, 44, 57, 60].

Since 2015, unsupervised training of speech recognition systems has received considerable attention owing to the Zerospeech challenges [20, 40, 70]. The performance of unsupervised speech recognition systems has been significantly improved, especially in relation to representation learning based on self-supervised learning using neural networks (e.g., [7]).

There have also been a series of studies on object concept (or category) formation by robots based on multimodal information. By integrating multimodal information such as visual, haptic, and auditory information using a PGM, it has been shown that robots can form object categories at various levels in an unsupervised manner [2, 34, 35]. Similar studies have been conducted on place categories [26, 54, 59].It was also shown these concepts can be used for planning and active perception [55, 56, 69]. These studies have shown that predictive coding based on PGMs can represent the formation of internal representations based on physical interactions in symbol emergence systems.

In these studies on multimodal concept formation, the generative process of multimodal sensorimotor information is described as follows.

$$\{o_m\} \sim p(\{o_m\}|z) \tag{4}$$

where the generative process means that an agent, for example, a person or a robot, attempts to "predict" sensorimotor information. In this equation, o_m represents sensorimotor information of the m-th modality, and z represents the internal cause, that is, the perceptual state of the internal representations. Therefore, the learning process of concepts and categories corresponds to the inference of internal representations.

$$z \sim p(z|\{o_m\}) \tag{5}$$

This model is based on predictive coding in a broad sense. It is assumed that agents form concepts and categories to improve the prediction performance for multimodal sensorimotor information.

Furthermore, the PGMs proposed in these studies could be integrated. Grounded lexical acquisition from speech signals has been achieved by integrating models of unsupervised phoneme and word acquisition and multimodal category formation. Mutual learning between object categories and speech signals and between place categories and speech signals has been described [36,57,60]. Lexical acquisition from speech signals is achievable by integrating models of unsupervised phoneme and word acquisition and multimodal category formation[1].

Overall, several studies on symbol emergence in robotics have developed a wide range of learning methods assuming generative models representing

$$w, \{o_m\} \sim p(w, \{o_m\}|z), \tag{6}$$

$$y \sim p(y|w). \tag{7}$$

If we assume z is a discrete variable and iterative, i.e., mutual, inference of z and w can be regarded as mutual segmentation of strings and contexts mentioned in "mutual segmentation hypothesis [42]".

2.2   Automatic Music Composition in Computers

The similarity between music and language lies first in the fact that they are represented by a linear series of discrete sounds. Simply put, language is a series of phonemes or letters, whereas music is a series of sounds of a certain pitch or note. Many aspects of language and music are not bound by discreteness, such as the expression of emotion through prosody in spoken language and pitch bend in musical performance. However, especially in written documents and musical scores, the use of discrete letters or a series of notes is an acceptable approximation.

In linguistics and information science, "How do we model language?" is the major question. However, if we simply consider strings of letters or word sequences as simple arrays of discrete "symbols", it was a mathematically valid attempt to model them as stochastic processes of strings of letters or word sequences. This is a language model. This idea even goes back to Shannon's paper, which is a classic in information theory [48].

---

[1] Thus, integrating various predictive coding with PGMs is essential for modeling integrative human cognitive systems. As a framework for this purpose, SERKET was proposed [39,63]. Recently, the idea was extended to the whole-brain PGM, which aims to build a cognitive model covering an entire brain by combining PGMs with anatomical knowledge of brain architecture [67]. This approach is known as the whole-brain architecture approach [73]. Following this idea, the anatomical validity of the above NPB-DAA for spoken language acquisition and SLAM-based place recognition was also examined from the viewpoint of the brain [53,58].

When considering a word sequence (or string) $w_{1:S} = \{w_1, w_2, \ldots, w_S\}$, the language model is a statistical model that computes $P(w_{1:S})$. In many cases, $P(w_t|w_{1:t-1})$ is considered to generate a word sequence in time direction t. An approximation of $P(w_t|w_{t-n+1:t-1})$, which is censored at n, is called an n-gram model. Until the mid-2010s, the n-gram model was the standard approach for modeling $w_{t-n+1:t}$. However, since the success of deep learning in the 2010s,s, methods that directly approximate $P(\cdot|w_{1:t-1}) \approx f(w_{1:t-1}; \theta)$ using neural networks such as LSTM have become a new standard approach. Here, $P(\cdot)$ indicates that the probability of all random variables is output as a vector. In addition, f is a function represented by the neural network, where θ is its parameter[2].

The language model described above is a type of PGM. This represents the stochastic process by which a discrete series of words (or letters) is generated. The difference between music and language syntax has been discussed, but there is still a difference. There is a difference between music and language in that music does not have clear grammar, such as the double articulation structure and phrase structure grammar found in language. However, most language models do not explicitly consider these factors [5]. Therefore, the concept of the language model can be used equally well to capture the syntax latent in sound sequences in music. The language model is an important abstraction when discussing the parallelism between language and music.

In a musical performance, the actual sound y is generated by a performer. If we consider the generative process of music, including composition and performance, it can be described as follows:

$$w = w_{1:S} \sim p(w|z), \tag{8}$$

$$y = y_{1:T} \sim p(y|w) \tag{9}$$

where z is the cause of music generation, for example, the emotional state with which a player and composer attempt to generate the song. Interestingly, these equations are identical to those in (1) and (2), respectively. This correspondence apparently displays one parallelism between music and language.

Many statistical language models have been used to capture note sequences for automatic compositions. The bigram and trigram models of notes are not sufficient to capture the long-term dependency. Therefore, longer context-aware language models are required. A language model based on nonparametric Bayesian methods that consider a theoretically infinite number of contexts was proposed. Shirai et al. proposed a melody generation method using the variable-order Pitman-Yor language model proposed by Mochihashi et al. [33]. Another key point for automatic composition using the PGM is that "sampling from the posterior distribution" can be explicitly considered. In creative activities such as composing music, it is more important to propose a reasonably large number of candidates than to find the optimal solution. This means that rather than formulating automatic composition as an optimization problem, it is more appropriate

---

[2] Recently, this idea has been developed into a large-scale language model using transformers, and its generality and performance have become widely known.

to consider it as sampling from a posterior distribution. Shirai et al. considered melody generation as a sampling problem from the posterior distribution and derived Gibbs sampling and automatic composition based on it [49]. If we integrate constraints such as chord progressions and lyrics via PGMs, we can create an automatic composition model that considers various musical components [50].

Since the mid-2010s, recurrent neural networks have been actively used to model sound sequences in response to the success of deep learning. Recurrent neural networks can easily model time-series data without paying attention to context length in n-gram models. In particular, a variational autoencoder (VAE) is a probabilistic generative model that can use a variety of neural networks in its network architecture [1,19,32]. This is highly compatible with the PGM-based approach described previously. In recent years, many studies have used transformers, which have demonstrated high performance in natural language processing and image recognition [29,30].

Owing to the rise of deep learning, automatic composition has been gaining momentum [13]. However, rather than deep learning itself, the essential question in automatic composition is how to model the dependencies between the transition patterns of sound sequences, chord progressions, and other musical elements. Since then, the idea of generating music through sampling has remained unchanged.

In recent years, language models have moved in the direction of large-scale models called large-scale language models or foundation models [12,16]. Thus, their capabilities have become apparent. Applications for automatic composition have also been developed. However, there is no doubt that these are only generative models of the sound sequences themselves and are in line with the framework of the above discussion.

3   Symbol Emergence Systems and Emergence of Semiotic Meanings

3.1   Symbol Emergence Systems

Symbol emergence systems are schematic models that describe the process through which symbols acquire meaning in society [66]. The symbols used are arbitrary. The relationship between a sign and an object cannot be determined a priori. When another person utters a new sign (such as a sound sequence), because we cannot look into the mind of the other person, we cannot know with certainty what the speaker means, and we can only infer. If we accept such a reality in semiotics, how can we share the meaning of symbols in our society through an autonomous and decentralized adaptation of each agent?

A symbol emergence system is a multi-agent system consisting of multiple agents with the capability of learning generative symbols, that is, using signs for communication. Agents form internal representations based on their interactions with their environment. In the terminology of Piaget's genetic epistemology, this corresponds to the formation of a schema [22,65]. Barsalou's perceptual symbol

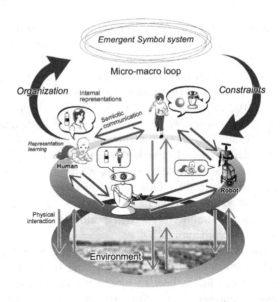

Fig. 1. An overview of a symbol emergence system [61,66]

system corresponds to the formation of symbols [9]. Based on the terminology of modern artificial intelligence, this can be called representation learning based on multimodal sensor information [52]. This allows the agent to form categories or concept-like objects independently. However, these internal representations are not "symbols" that can be used to communicate with others. According to Peirce's definition a symbol is a triadic relationship among signs, objects, and interpretants [18,45]. Letters in the written language and sound sequences in the spoken language are signs. The kind of internal representation in the brain related to the sound sequence as a sign is also arbitrary. If this can be coordinated through communication and interaction between agents, they will form a symbolic system and communicate symbolically. Consequently, an emergent symbol system was organized.

3.2 Collective Predictive Coding

How does an agent understand the meaning of the other's words without looking inside the other's head? Additionally, how can such a learning process lead to the emergence of stable symbol emergence systems in society? To answer this question, the author proposes the hypothetical idea that "symbol emergence in a society is a *collective predictive coding*". This can be regarded as a distributed Bayesian inference or social representation learning [68]. The author and colleagues introduced a language game called the *Metropolis Hastings Naming Game* and demonstrated that the emergence of word meanings and their sharing within a group can be regarded as distributed expressive learning by the entire group [68]. The algorithm for decentralizing the cognitive system is

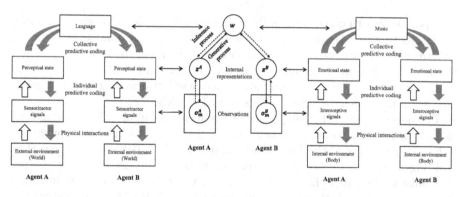

Fig. 2. (Left) Diagram of the process symbol emergence based on collective predictive coding. Each agent forms internal representations reflecting their perceptual state, and they use and form language through semiotic communications. The complete process is regarded as collective predictive coding [25,27,68]. (Center) A PGM for symbol emergence systems corresponding to Inter-DM, Inter-MDM, and Inter-GMM+VAE [25, 27,68]. Metropolis Hastings naming game becomes a decentralized Bayesian inference of the shared w and internal representations z^A and z^B. Note that in this graphical model, head-to-head connection across w is adopted [24]. (Right) Hypothetical diagram of the process of emergence of musical symbol systems. Instead of sensorimotor signals, emotional states are inferred through predictive coding of introspective signals [8,47]. Such internal representations may become the basis of the emergence of a musical symbol system, i.e., the source of the socially constructed meaning of music.

mathematically equivalent to the naming game, based on the idea of an integrated cognitive system that "combines the brains" of agents participating in communication using the same symbol system.

This suggests that the stochastic generative model is a framework that can express the "emergence of the meaning of symbols". In the discussion of "where does the meaning of a symbol come from?", people tend to consider cognitive and social perspectives. Although the answer is apparently "both", people in most scientific communities tend to focus on one of them depending on the academic community. However, the theory of symbol emergence systems emphasizes that considering both of them within one integrated model is important.

4   On Parallelism in Music and Language

4.1   Parallelism on Syntax, Brain and Evolution

It has long been argued that there is parallelism between music and language [14,21,31]. This relationship has been widely discussed from anthropological, cultural, semiotic, linguistic, and musicological perspectives. This discussion is not monolithic.

The structural similarities between music and language are often discussed, particularly with a focus on syntax [5]. From a musicological perspective, it has been pointed out that the grammatical structures latent in music are, in a sense, similar to those of language (although they do not have double articulation structures or phrase structure grammars, and their nature is very different). Syntactic parallelism is explained in Sect. 2 to a certain extent.

In neuroscience, the similarities and differences between language and music processing have been discussed and examined [6,15,51,72].

Furthermore, from the perspective of language evolution, it has been argued that an increase in vocalization complexity, that is, songs, may be a precursor to language evolution [42]. The influential hypothesis is based on evidence that birdsongs have a certain degree of grammatical structure [10,41].

Unlike syntax, little has been said about the semantics of music in terms of its parallelism with the meaning in language [5]. It is difficult to discuss the semantics of music. This difficulty seems to indicate a difference between music and language in semantics, that is, meaning. However, it is difficult to discuss the meaning on the linguistic side as well. In linguistics and natural language processing, the meaning of words can be discussed almost exclusively in terms of distributional semantics or relationships with other syntactic representations, that is, semantic parsing. This means that the meaning of a symbol is considered in terms of the relationship between symbols, not in terms of their relationship with sensorimotor experiences based on interactions with the external world.

In contrast, symbol emergence systems represent integrative system dynamics in which humans form concepts based on sensory-motor systems, and meanings are determined at the social level through social interactions, that is, semiotic communications. As a constructive approach to this end, a series of studies on symbol emergence in robotics have been conducted [61]. This approach attempts to reproduce the emergence of symbols by addressing both the cognitive and social dynamics in the system using machine learning and robot models. This was recently found to be related to predictive coding [28]. In addition, its relationship to the theory of self-organizational systems about neural and cognitive systems, such as the free-energy principle, has been gradually recognized [23].

4.2 Symbol Emergence Systems on Music, Emotion, and Interoception

The issue of the "meaning of music" is difficult to deal with. Unlike syntactic structure, which can be discussed based on observable acoustic units, the meaning itself is observable. Therefore, it is difficult to reach a consensus on the definition of "meaning" in music. However, "meaning" is also difficult to deal with in language. If we define "meaning" as a dyadic relation between a sign and an object, and if we assume that the symbol system we use is static, the picture becomes relatively simple. This view is often assumed in artificial intelligence studies such as image recognition. This may be referred to as Plato's idealistic worldview. However, such static pictures do not capture developmental language acquisition. This view cannot capture the language evolution in which the language itself emerges. From the perspective of symbol emergence systems, the question of the meaning of language is difficult. The author believes that the viewpoint of symbol emergence systems is necessary to answer the question "what is the meaning of language". If we assume the parallelism in music and language, we may be able to obtain some suggestions about the "meaning of music" from the perspective of symbol emergence systems.

If we have one of the most naïve viewpoints, the meaning of a word can be the speaker's internal intention or the object that the speaker means. In the model of symbol emergence systems, it is necessary for the listener to organize an internal representation system prior to communication to interpret it. Symbol emergence systems are adjusted (or emerged) through interactions between distributed agents. They coordinate the received signs with internal representations formed through their own sensory and motor experiences.

At this point, internal representation systems are formed based on physical interactions. The schematic representation of symbol emergence systems in Fig. 1 depicts the physical interactions as interactions with the external environment. In reality, however, the "world" is originally assumed to be *Umwelt*, i.e., the subjective world and not necessarily the external world [71]. Our experience is not only based on the interaction with the external environment, but also on the internal environment sensed by interoception.

As mentioned earlier, it is difficult to define the "meaning of music". However, if we view the "meaning of music" as a change in the mental state that the listener undergoes, or inference (or state updating) of internal representations, similar to the "meaning of language", and especially if we view it as an emotional impression (i.e., being moved, or its effect on the emotions), then through the discussion of predictive coding, we can connect it to the discussion of symbol emergence systems, which can be connected to the discussion of symbol emergence systems through the discussion of predictive coding.

In recent years, it has been argued that emotions are based on the predictive encoding of visceral sensations and introspective signals [8,47]. Based on this, we would like a hypothetical perspective on the correspondence between music and language, as shown in Fig. 2. The sign of music corresponds to the sign of language. The "perceptual" internal representation system that supports the interpretation of language corresponds to the "emotional" internal representation system in music. Perceptual internal representational systems are organized to predict sensorimotor information caused by an external environment. In contrast, emotional internal representational systems are organized to predict sensorimotor information caused by the internal environment. Language can also represent emotional states because it is a highly multifaceted system. This paper shows this comparative schema to give a clearer contrast, that is, parallelism, between music and language, assuming the argument that music does not have a function explicitly representing events in the external world, unlike human language. In this way, the discussion of symbol emergence systems on the emergence and acquisition of language can be mapped to the emergence of symbol systems such as music.

The central figure of Fig. 2 shows the PGM representing the symbol emergence system as a whole. This view was introduced in recent studies [25,27,68].

The symbol emergence between agents A and B can be described as a decentralized Bayesian inference.

$$w \sim p(w|z^A, z^B)p(z^A|\{o_m^A\})p(z^A|\{o_m^A\}) \tag{10}$$

where $p(w|z^A, z^B)$ can be sampled using a type of decentralized language game [68].

This correspondence provides an initial step in thinking about the meaning of music from the viewpoint of symbol emergence systems. This paper does not provide further details or evidence of this correspondence. However, the author believes that this perspective certainly has the potential to evoke new discussions about parallelism in music and language.

5   Conclusion

This article introduces generative models for symbol emergence based on real-world sensorimotor information and communication, which have been developed in a series of studies on symbol emergence in robotics. The paper also describes the symbol emergence systems that form the background of these models and the proximity of these models to models of automatic composition. Based on the above, this paper introduced the idea that symbol emergence systems can be regarded as a multi-agent system performing collective predictive coding. By combining this idea with the hypothesis that emotions can be explained by the predictive encoding of visceral sensory stimuli, I proposed a new view of "the meaning of music" as mediated by emotions and connected to symbol emergence systems.

There is one important difference between music and language from the viewpoint of symbol emergence. The sign of language has no direct influence on the external sensory systems that are directly related to the meaning of the linguistic sign. For example, the word "apple" does not give any direct sensation of a fruit "apple". The perceptual concept of an "apple" is based on visual, haptic, and taste sensory information. In contrast, music tends to have a relatively direct influence on the internal sensory stimuli. Peirce classified symbols as firstness, secondness, and thirdness [45]. A symbol with complete arbitrariness is given meaning by the arbitrary triadic relationship between the sign and object, i.e., thirdness. In contrast, firstness means that the sign itself has a reason for "meaning". For example, a sequence of sounds synchronized with the heartbeat affects the visceral senses on its own. This implies that music has many symbolic aspects of firstness. On the other hand, it is also true that music is a symbol of cultural aspects, as evidenced by the fact that musical trends change over time and that music reflects the time; for example, the '80s mood. Thus, we conclude the discussion of the parallelism of music and language by combining the viewpoints of semiotics and computational models, especially probabilistic generative models.

In the context of artificial intelligence research, the author pointed out the confusion in the view of symbols in the symbol grounding problem and how the symbol emergence problem is a problem to be discussed [66]. The picture of symbol emergence systems describes the process by which signs that previously had no meaning take on meaning as emergent phenomena within multi-agent systems composed of humans. The connection to the "meaning of music" discussed in this paper is a highly hypothetical picture that originates from outside research communities, such as music informatics and musicology, which are more closely connected to music. However, to discuss the elusive subject of "the meaning of music", interdisciplinary thinking will provide suggestions. In addition, thinking about the emergence of music will be beneficial for understanding symbol emergence in a general sense, e.g., cultural and historical symbol systems.

Acknowledgments. This paper was written as a post-proceedings paper for the keynote speech titled "Generative Models for Symbol Emergence based on Real-World Sensory-motor Information and Communication" presented at the 15th International Symposium on Computer Music Multidisciplinary Research (CMMR) 2021. This work was supported by JSPS KAKENHI Grant Numbers JP16H06569 and JP21H04904.

References

1. Akbari, M., Liang, J.: Semi-recurrent CNN-based VAE-GAN for sequential data generation. In: 2018 IEEE International Conference on Acoustics, Speech and Signal Processing (ICASSP), pp. 2321–2325. IEEE (2018)
2. Ando, Y., Nakamura, T., Araki, T., Nagai, T.: Formation of hierarchical object concept using hierarchical latent Dirichlet allocation. In: IEEE/RSJ International Conference on Intelligent Robots and Systems (IROS), pp. 2272–2279 (2013)
3. Araki, T., Nakamura, T., Nagai, T., Funakoshi, K., Nakano, M., Iwahashi, N.: Autonomous acquisition of multimodal information for online object concept formation by robots. In: 2011 IEEE/RSJ International Conference on Intelligent Robots and Systems (IROS), pp. 1540–1547 (2011). https://doi.org/10.1109/IROS.2011.6048422
4. Araki, T., Nakamura, T., Nagai, T., Nagasaka, S., Taniguchi, T., Iwahashi, N.: Online learning of concepts and words using multimodal LDA and hierarchical Pitman-Yor Language Model. In: IEEE/RSJ International Conference on Intelligent Robots and Systems, pp. 1623–1630 (2012). https://doi.org/10.1109/IROS.2012.6385812
5. Asano, R., Boeckx, C.: Syntax in language and music: what is the right level of comparison? Front. Psychol. **6**, 942 (2015)
6. Atherton, R.P., et al.: Shared processing of language and music: evidence from a cross-modal interference paradigm. Exp. Psychol. **65**(1), 40 (2018)
7. Baevski, A., Zhou, Y., Mohamed, A., Auli, M.: wav2vec 2.0: a framework for self-supervised learning of speech representations. In: Advances in Neural Information Processing Systems, vol. 33, 12449–12460 (2020)
8. Barrett, L.F., Simmons, W.K.: Interoceptive predictions in the brain. Nat. Rev. Neurosci. **16**(7), 419–429 (2015)
9. Barsalou, L.W.: Perceptual symbol systems. Behav. Brain Sci. **22**(04), 1–16 (1999). https://doi.org/10.1017/S0140525X99002149
10. Berwick, R.C., Beckers, G.J., Okanoya, K., Bolhuis, J.J.: A bird's eye view of human language evolution. Front. Evol. Neurosci. **4**, 5 (2012)

11. Bishop, C.: Pattern Recognition and Machine Learning (Information Science and Statistics). Springer, Heidelberg (2006)
12. Bommasani, R., et al.: On the opportunities and risks of foundation models (2021). https://doi.org/10.48550/ARXIV.2108.07258
13. Briot, J.P., Hadjeres, G., Pachet, F.D.: Deep learning techniques for music generation–a survey. arXiv preprint arXiv:1709.01620 (2017)
14. Brown, S.: Are music and language homologues? Ann. N. Y. Acad. Sci. **930**(1), 372–374 (2001)
15. Brown, S., Martinez, M.J., Parsons, L.M.: Music and language side by side in the brain: a pet study of the generation of melodies and sentences. Eur. J. Neurosci. **23**(10), 2791–2803 (2006)
16. Brown, T., et al.: Language models are few-shot learners. In: Advances in Neural Information Processing Systems, vol. 33, pp. 1877–1901 (2020)
17. Cangelosi, A., Schlesinger, M.: Developmental Robotics. The MIT Press, Cambridge (2015)
18. Chandler, D.: Semiotics the Basics. Routledge, Milton Park (2002)
19. Diéguez, P.L., Soo, V.W.: Variational autoencoders for polyphonic music interpolation. In: 2020 International Conference on Technologies and Applications of Artificial Intelligence (TAAI), pp. 56–61 (2020)
20. Dunbar, E., et al.: The zero resource speech challenge 2017. In: 2017 IEEE Automatic Speech Recognition and Understanding Workshop (ASRU), pp. 323–330 (2017)
21. Feld, S., Fox, A.A.: Music and language. Ann. Rev. Anthropol. **23**, 25–53 (1994)
22. Flavell, J.H.: The Developmental Psychology of Jean Piaget. Literary Licensing, LLC (2011)
23. Friston, K., Moran, R.J., Nagai, Y., Taniguchi, T., Gomi, H., Tenenbaum, J.: World model learning and inference. Neural Netw. **144**, 573–590 (2021)
24. Furukawa, K., Taniguchi, A., Hagiwara, Y., Taniguchi, T.: Symbol emergence as inter-personal categorization with head-to-head latent word. In: IEEE International Conference on Development and Learning (ICDL 2022), pp. 60–67 (2022)
25. Hagiwara, Y., Furukawa, K., Taniguchi, A., Taniguchi, T.: Multiagent multimodal categorization for symbol emergence: emergent communication via interpersonal cross-modal inference. Adv. Robot. **36**(5–6), 239–260 (2022)
26. Hagiwara, Y., Inoue, M., Kobayashi, H., Taniguchi, T.: Hierarchical spatial concept formation based on multimodal information for human support robots. Front. Neurorobot. **12**(11), 1–16 (2018)
27. Hagiwara, Y., Kobayashi, H., Taniguchi, A., Taniguchi, T.: Symbol emergence as an interpersonal multimodal categorization. Front. Robot. AI **6**(134), 1–17 (2019). https://doi.org/10.3389/frobt.2019.00134
28. Hohwy, J.: The Predictive Mind. OUP, Oxford (2013)
29. Huang, C.Z.A., et al.: Music transformer. arXiv preprint arXiv:1809.04281 (2018)
30. Huang, Y.S., Yang, Y.H.: Pop music transformer: beat-based modeling and generation of expressive pop piano compositions. In: Proceedings of the 28th ACM International Conference on Multimedia, pp. 1180–1188 (2020)
31. Jackendoff, R., Lerdahl, F.: A grammatical parallel between music and language. In: Clynes, M. (ed.) Music, Mind, and Brain, pp. 83–117. Springer, Cham (1982). https://doi.org/10.1007/978-1-4684-8917-0_5
32. Jiang, J., Xia, G.G., Carlton, D.B., Anderson, C.N., Miyakawa, R.H.: Transformer VAE: a hierarchical model for structure-aware and interpretable music representation learning. In: 2020 IEEE International Conference on Acoustics, Speech and Signal Processing (ICASSP), ICASSP 2020, pp. 516–520. IEEE (2020)

33. Mochihashi, D., Sumita, E.: The infinite Markov model. In: Advances in Neural Information Processing Systems, vol. 20 (2007)
34. Nakamura, T., Ando, Y., Nagai, T., Kaneko, M.: Concept formation by robots using an infinite mixture of models. In: IEEE/RSJ International Conference on Intelligent Robots and Systems (IROS) (2015)
35. Nakamura, T., Araki, T., Nagai, T., Iwahashi, N.: Grounding of word meanings in LDA-based multimodal concepts. Adv. Robot. **25**, 2189–2206 (2012)
36. Nakamura, T., Nagai, T., Funakoshi, K., Nagasaka, S., Taniguchi, T., Iwahashi, N.: Mutual learning of an object concept and language model based on MLDA and NPYLM. In: IEEE/RSJ International Conference on Intelligent Robots and Systems, pp. 600–607 (2014)
37. Nakamura, T., Nagai, T., Iwahashi, N.: Multimodal object categorization by a robot. In: IEEE/RSJ International Conference on Intelligent Robots and Systems (IROS), pp. 2415–2420 (2007). https://doi.org/10.1109/IROS.2007.4399634
38. Nakamura, T., Nagai, T., Iwahashi, N.: Bag of multimodal hierarchical Dirichlet processes: model of complex conceptual structure for intelligent robots. In: IEEE/RSJ International Conference on Intelligent Robots and Systems (IROS), pp. 3818–3823 (2012). https://doi.org/10.1109/IROS.2012.6385502
39. Nakamura, T., Nagai, T., Taniguchi, T.: Serket: an architecture for connecting stochastic models to realize a large-scale cognitive model. Front. Neurorobot. **12**, 25 (2018)
40. van Niekerk, B., Nortje, L., Kamper, H.: Vector-quantized neural networks for acoustic unit discovery in the zerospeech 2020 challenge. arXiv preprint arXiv:2005.09409 (2020)
41. Okanoya, K.: Language evolution and an emergent property. Curr. Opin. Neurobiol. **17**(2), 271–276 (2007). https://doi.org/10.1016/j.conb.2007.03.011
42. Okanoya, K.: Sexual communication and domestication may give rise to the signal complexity necessary for the emergence of language: an indication from songbird studies. Psychon. Bull. Rev. **24**(1), 106–110 (2017)
43. Okanoya, K., Merker, B.: Neural substrates for string-context mutual segmentation: a path to human language. In: Lyon, C., Nehaniv, C.L., Cangelosi, A. (eds.) Emergence of Communication and Language, pp. 421–434. Springer, London (2007). https://doi.org/10.1007/978-1-84628-779-4_22
44. Okuda, Y., Ozaki, R., Komura, S., Taniguchi, T.: Double articulation analyzer with prosody for unsupervised word and phone discovery. IEEE Trans. Cogn. Dev. Syst. (2022). https://doi.org/10.1109/TCDS.2022.3210751
45. Peirce, C.S.: Collected Writings. Harvard University Press, Cambridge (1931–1958)
46. Saffran, J.R., Newport, E.L., Aslin, R.N.: Word segmentation: the role of distributional cues. J. Mem. Lang. **35**(4), 606–621 (1996)
47. Seth, A.K.: Interoceptive inference, emotion, and the embodied self. Trends Cogn. Sci. **17**(11), 565–573 (2013)
48. Shannon, C.E.: A mathematical theory of communication. Bell Syst. Tech. J. **27**(3), 379–423 (1948)
49. Shirai, A., Taniguchi, T.: A proposal of an interactive music composition system using Gibbs sampler. In: Jacko, J.A. (ed.) HCI 2011. LNCS, vol. 6761, pp. 490–497. Springer, Heidelberg (2011). https://doi.org/10.1007/978-3-642-21602-2_53
50. Shirai, A., Taniguchi, T.: A proposal of the melody generation method using variable-order Pitman-Yor language model. J. Jpn. Soc. Fuzzy Theory Intell. Inform. **25**(6), 901–913 (2013). https://doi.org/10.3156/jsoft.25.901

51. Sternin, A., McGarry, L.M., Owen, A.M., Grahn, J.A.: The effect of familiarity on neural representations of music and language. J. Cogn. Neurosci. **33**(8), 1595–1611 (2021)

52. Suzuki, M., Matsuo, Y.: A survey of multimodal deep generative models. Adv. Robot. **36**(5–6), 261–278 (2022)

53. Taniguchi, A., Fukawa, A., Yamakawa, H.: Hippocampal formation-inspired probabilistic generative model. Neural Netw. **151**, 317–335 (2022)

54. Taniguchi, A., Hagiwara, Y., Taniguchi, T., Inamura, T.: Online spatial concept and lexical acquisition with simultaneous localization and mapping. In: IEEE/RSJ International Conference on Intelligent Robots and Systems, pp. 811–818 (2017)

55. Taniguchi, A., Hagiwara, Y., Taniguchi, T., Inamura, T.: Improved and scalable online learning of spatial concepts and language models with mapping. Auton. Robot. **44**(6), 927–946 (2020). https://doi.org/10.1007/s10514-020-09905-0

56. Taniguchi, A., Isobe, S., El Hafi, L., Hagiwara, Y., Taniguchi, T.: Autonomous planning based on spatial concepts to tidy up home environments with service robots. Adv. Robot. **35**(8), 471–489 (2021)

57. Taniguchi, A., Murakami, H., Ozaki, R., Taniguchi, T.: Unsupervised multimodal word discovery based on double articulation analysis with co-occurrence cues. arXiv preprint arXiv:2201.06786 (2022)

58. Taniguchi, A., Muro, M., Yamakawa, H., Taniguchi, T.: Brain-inspired probabilistic generative model for double articulation analysis of spoken language. In: IEEE International Conference on Development and Learning (ICDL 2022), pp. 107–114 (2022)

59. Taniguchi, A., Taniguchi, T., Inamura, T.: Spatial concept acquisition for a mobile robot that integrates self-localization and unsupervised word discovery from spoken sentences. IEEE Trans. Cogn. Dev. Syst. **8**(4), 285–297 (2016)

60. Taniguchi, A., Taniguchi, T., Inamura, T.: Unsupervised spatial lexical acquisition by updating a language model with place clues. Robot. Auton. Syst. **99**, 166–180 (2018)

61. Taniguchi, T., Nagai, T., Nakamura, T., Iwahashi, N., Ogata, T., Asoh, H.: Symbol emergence in robotics: a survey. Adv. Robot. **30**(11–12), 706–728 (2016)

62. Taniguchi, T., Nagasaka, S., Nakashima, R.: Nonparametric Bayesian double articulation analyzer for direct language acquisition from continuous speech signals. IEEE Trans. Cogn. Dev. Syst. **8**(3), 171–185 (2016). https://doi.org/10.1109/TCDS.2016.2550591

63. Taniguchi, T., et al.: Neuro-serket: development of integrative cognitive system through the composition of deep probabilistic generative models. N. Gener. Comput. **38**(1), 23–48 (2020)

64. Taniguchi, T., Nakashima, R., Liu, H., Nagasaka, S.: Double articulation analyzer with deep sparse autoencoder for unsupervised word discovery from speech signals. Adv. Robot. **30**(11–12), 770–783 (2016). https://doi.org/10.1080/01691864.2016.1159981

65. Taniguchi, T., Sawaragi, T.: Incremental acquisition of behaviors and signs based on a reinforcement learning schemata model and a spike timing-dependent plasticity network. Adv. Robot. **21**(10), 1177–1199 (2007)

66. Taniguchi, T., et al.: Symbol emergence in cognitive developmental systems: a survey. IEEE Trans. Cogn. Dev. Syst. **11**, 494–516 (2018)

67. Taniguchi, T., et al.: A whole brain probabilistic generative model: toward realizing cognitive architectures for developmental robots. Neural Netw. **150**, 293–312 (2022)

68. Taniguchi, T., Yoshida, Y., Taniguchi, A., Hagiwara, Y.: Emergent communication through metropolis-hastings naming game with deep generative models. arXiv preprint arXiv:2205.12392 (2022)
69. Taniguchi, T., Yoshino, R., Takano, T.: Multimodal hierarchical Dirichlet process-based active perception by a robot. Front. Neurorobot. **12**, 22 (2018)
70. Tjandra, A., Sakti, S., Nakamura, S.: Transformer VQ-VAE for unsupervised unit discovery and speech synthesis: zerospeech 2020 challenge. arXiv preprint arXiv:2005.11676 (2020)
71. Von Uexküll, J.: A stroll through the worlds of animals and men: a picture book of invisible worlds. Semiotica **89**(4), 319–391 (1992)
72. Vuust, P., Heggli, O.A., Friston, K.J., Kringelbach, M.L.: Music in the brain. Nat. Rev. Neurosci. **23**(5), 287–305 (2022)
73. Yamakawa, H., Osawa, M., Matsuo, Y.: Whole brain architecture approach is a feasible way toward an artificial general intelligence. In: Hirose, A., Ozawa, S., Doya, K., Ikeda, K., Lee, M., Liu, D. (eds.) ICONIP 2016. LNCS, vol. 9947, pp. 275–281. Springer, Cham (2016). https://doi.org/10.1007/978-3-319-46687-3_30

WaVAEtable Synthesis

Jeremy Hyrkas[(✉)]

University of California San Diego, La Jolla, USA
jhyrkas@ucsd.edu

Abstract. Timbral autoencoders, a class of generative model that learn the timbre distribution of audio data, are a current research focus in music technology; however, despite recent improvements, they have rarely been used in music composition or musical systems due to issues of static musical output, general lack of real-time synthesis and the unwieldiness of synthesis parameters. This project proposes a solution to these issues by combining timbral autoencoder models with a classic computer music synthesis technique in wavetable synthesis. A proof-of-concept implementation in Python, with controllers in Max and Super-Collider, demonstrates the timbral autoencoder's capability as a wavetable generator. This concept is generally architecture agnostic, showing that most existing timbral autoencoders could be adapted for use in real-time music creation today, regardless of their capabilities for real-time synthesis and time-varying timbre.

Keywords: Generative models · neural networks · sound synthesis

1 Introduction

A generative model can be broadly defined as a probabilistic method that learns a distribution based on a corpus of training data such that examples similar to the training data can be generated by sampling from the learned distribution [7]. Recently, the term has been largely associated with deep artificial neural networks that generate images, video, speech, or examples from a variety of other domains. Music researchers have utilized neural network generative models as a technology for sound synthesis in music (for example, the groundbreaking NSynth neural synthesizer [3]). One such approach is the *timbral autoencoder* (i.e. [2,4,9]). In this type of model, networks learn audio representations in the frequency domain, resulting in models that synthesize sounds based on a learned latent space of their training data, usually monophonic instruments. These timbral models target the problem of novel sound generation, particularly in a synthesizer setting [2]. Ideally, musicians can find sounds that interpolate the timbre of multiple instruments, or sounds that do not invoke any recognizable instrument at all. Recently, the variational autoencoder (VAE) [8] has been favored (an overview of VAEs for musical audio can be found here [7]). Once trained, a user may provide latent parameters to the VAE to generate new examples.

There are a number of benefits to training these models. The training data is represented in the frequency domain, which behaves better than time-domain representations with common loss functions that do not account for phase shift. Additionally,

© Springer Nature Switzerland AG 2023
M. Aramaki et al. (Eds.): CMMR 2021, LNCS 13770, pp. 26–31, 2023.
https://doi.org/10.1007/978-3-031-35382-6_3

some models render audio in near real-time [2] due to a sufficiently small architecture, as opposed to more complex audio models such as the NSynth autoencoder [3]. More recent efforts have shown that the models can learn the timbre of the training data in a way that sufficiently disentangles the pitch of the training examples, even when the training data does not contain pitch labels [9].

While integration of these models in music systems seems imminent, there are some practical drawbacks that remain unaddressed. Learning problems in the frequency domain largely concern magnitude spectra, meaning that phase reconstruction is necessary before the audio can be rendered in the time domain. Models that learn on magnitude Fourier transforms can use phase reconstruction algorithms that run in real-time [2]; however, models that use alternate spectral representations [4] rely on non-real-time algorithms such as the Griffin-Lim method [5]. Finally, recurrent connections are largely absent in timbral autoencoder models, meaning models are limited to generating a cyclic waveform per selection of latent parameters.

1.1 Motivation and Project Overview

This project aims to integrate a neural network synthesis engine implemented in Python with more general synthesis and composition engines in Cycling '74's Max software and SuperCollider (SC). While many of the aforementioned research efforts focus on improved synthesis in the form of fidelity, realism, or expressiveness, this project takes the philosophy that current synthesis methods are already usable in music creation when combined with existing and well understood computer music methods.

Because most timbral autoencoders produce inherently cyclic audio, we can conceptually treat them as oscillators. Many timbral autoencoders are not conditioned on pitch, precluding them from being used as oscillators in a traditional sense. Additionally, models that do not use real-time phase reconstruction cannot be used to synthesize audio in real-time like a traditional oscillator. Therefore, incorporating these models into real-time engines requires a method that utilizes pre-rendered cyclic audio signals.

The most straightforward candidate for such a synthesis system is wavetable synthesis [1], a scheme in which cyclic waveforms are stored and synthesized by reading and interpolating values at a given frequency. This project recasts timbral autoencoders as wavetable generators and provides methods for sampling and saving wavetables from their output. Proof-of-concept software is provided in Max and SC, demonstrating how timbral autoencoders as wavetable generators can be used in performance and composition, and can be sonically extended using methods such as wavetable interpolation and frequency-modulated playback. We refer to the process of incorporating timbral autoencoders, often VAEs, into a wavetable extraction framework and combining them with music synthesis software as WaVAEtable synthesis.

1.2 Related Methods

NSynth [3] is an early musically focused generative model for audio. NSynth's unique architecture allows it to iteratively create time-domain audio, resulting in audio with time-varying timbre. This result is arguably more musically useful than cyclic waveforms, but the model is expensive to train on most computers and slow to render audio.

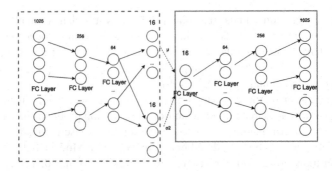

Fig. 1. Architecture of the basic VAE trained for this project. The *dotted blue rectangle* on the left contains the encoder and *solid-lined red rectangle* on the right contains the decoder. The *dotted line* between encoder and decoder represents a sampling operation. The input and output data are magnitude spectra extracted from the STFT of instrumental audio. (Color figure online)

Neural Wavetable [6] is perhaps the most similar project to the one presented here. The project uses an autoencoder to learn time-domain wavetables and interpolate between them. Interpolation is performed on the latent encoding of two target wavetables. This is conceptually similar to timbral autoencoders, with the exceptions that Neural Wavetable operates in the time-domain as opposed to the frequency-domain, and that the model is explicitly trained on wavetables. Because the method proposed here extracts wavetables from a broad collection of generative models, it is a more general method than the Neural Wavetable method. Neural Wavetable's underlying model cannot generate audio in real-time, so the associated plug-in uses pre-rendered wavetables for interpolation.

A more thorough survey of generative models for audio can be found here [7].

2   WaVAEtable Synthesis

2.1   Sample Neural Network Architecture and Training

This software exploits the architecture of timbral autoencoders, wherein user-provided encodings produce spectral audio that is converted to time-domain audio. To keep the design aimed towards utilizing existing models, this software uses a simple VAE (depicted in Fig. 1) implemented in PyTorch [11] that encapsulates the most basic generative capabilities shared by timbral autoencoder models. The data are positive frequency bins from Short-time Fourier Transform (STFT) frames of audio in the NSynth dataset [3]. The architecture model is shown in Fig. 1. After training, the 16 latent parameters are used to synthesize the magnitudes of the positive frequencies of an STFT frame. These frames are reflected and time-domain audio is added using the Griffin-Lim algorithm [5]. The decoder-to-audio process is detailed in Fig. 2. Adjusting the architecture and hyperparameters of this model could constitute a separate research effort, but are not critical to this project as this method aims to be as architecture- and model-agnostic as possible.

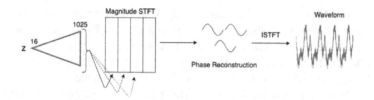

Fig. 2. Decoder to audio process: latent space parameters (z) are provided to the decoder, depicted as a *red triangle*. Output from the fixed z is used to create a *magnitude STFT*. The Griffin-Lim algorithm for *phase reconstruction* then yields in time-domain audio. (Color figure online)

2.2   Wavetable Generation

Many synthesis engines use a default wavetable size of 512 samples. If a given timbral autoencoder is conditioned on pitch, the model could generate output at a specific fundamental frequency f_0 such that the period of the waveform is 512 samples given the sampling rate f_s by setting $f_0 = \frac{f_s}{512}$. However, this setup is not always feasible. Many timbral autoencoder models, including the model used here, are not conditioned on pitch, resulting in a generative latent space that changes both timbre and fundamental frequency simultaneously. Even those models that disentangle pitch from timbre may be conditioned on discrete pitches (such as MIDI notes), and in general may not be able to generate the desired f_0. For example, the sampling rate of the NSynth data set is 16 kHz, so a waveform with period 512 samples has $f_0 = 31.25$ Hz, well below reasonable pitches in most music data sets.

Therefore, wavetables are created using a heuristic wavetable extraction algorithm that relies on f_0 estimation and resampling. Given a latent encoding from a user, the decoder is invoked to create a periodic waveform (see Fig. 2). We use the pYin [10] algorithm to estimate the fundamental frequency of each frame. The pYin algorithm is probabilistic and determines the likelihood of each frame containing a pitched sound. If a sufficient number of frames are found likely to be pitched, we predict the f_0 of the waveform to be the mean of the f_0 of the voiced frames; if this is not the case, it is likely that the provided encoding is very dissimilar from examples learned in the training data and the resulting sound may be noisy and therefore unpitched.

Given the f_s of a model and the predicted f_0 of the model's output based on the user's inputs, we resample the output to a new sampling frequency $round(f_0 * 512)$, which results in a waveform whose period is very close to 512 samples. Finally, samples are extracted from the new waveform starting from some position that is very near 0 to avoid an impulse at the beginning of the wavetable. Overall, the extraction method is subject to failures in f_0 estimation (usually octave errors) and resampling artifacts, but is architecture agnostic and can be adapted to any timbral autoencoder (or any generative model whose output is sufficiently periodic).

2.3   Synthesizer Implementations

Two prototype synthesizers were created as a proof-of-concept to demonstrate multiple musical uses for VAE wavetables. First, a simple polyphonic synth patch was created in Cycling '74's Max software. This patch assigns incoming MIDI notes to one of five voices. Here, random wavetables are pre-rendered using a Python script and can be regenerated by the user. Communication is done via the file system with wavetables saved and loaded from .WAV files. This patch also combines wavetable synthesis with FM synthesis, with MIDI CC controls controlling the wavetable assignment and FM controls of the wavetable playback speed. This patch, while simple, demonstrates the viability of using timbral autoencoder output in real-time performance.

A more complex system was constructed in SC with the goals of user interactivity with the underlying model, more complex synthesis methods and algorithmic composition. Users control the latent parameters of the VAE described in Sect. 2.1 using a custom GUI created in SC. The user can listen to a wavetable for a given setting, and if it is interesting for their compositional purposes, save it. All communication between Python and SC is performed locally using OSC, so no file system interaction is required. Figure 3 shows the interface for manipulating and storing wavetables.

Once stored, wavetables are played back using wavetable synthesis and wavetable interpolation. Users can also incorporate other SC generators to create complex synthesizer definitions (SynthDefs) with the generated wavetables at their core. We provide an example SynthDef that can be controlled by a MIDI controller, or used in algorithmic composition. A small etude is included in the provided software to demonstrate this capability. All Max, SC, and Python code, as well as the accompanying VAE model, are available at https://github.com/jhyrkas/wavaetable.

2.4   Incorporation of Existing Timbral Autoencoders

The neural network used in this project is not intended to be a standalone model, but acts as a basic stand-in for existing timbral autoencoder models (i.e. [2,4,9]), most of which have more complex architectures and are capable of more pleasing musical audio. To test the viability of the WaVAEtable synthesis approach, the Python script to interface with SC was adapted and added to a fork of the CANNe [2] synthesizer GitHub, available at https://github.com/jhyrkas/canne_synth. The only major changes to the script involved reinterpreting the latent space parameters sent from SC, as CANNe's latent space only contains 8 variables and expects a different range of values. With just these minor adjustments, the CANNe model can now be used as a wavetable generator

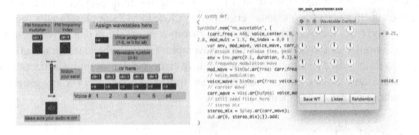

Fig. 3. Left: Max interface to playback wavetables, controlled via MIDI controller. Right: Super-Collider interface to control decoder parameters, listen to and store wavetables for playback.

in WaVAEtable synthesis. We posit that other timbral autoencoders can also be easily adapted, so long as they offer an encoding-to-audio synthesis method.

3   Future Work and Conclusion

This work offers a path towards incorporating an existing body of generative models into music systems. The proposed method allows for integrating models regardless of underlying architecture and real-time viability, and allows for a greater reuse of interesting latent parameters, which can be cumbersome to discover. Synth design and model improvement can thus be treated as complementary and orthogonal research avenues.

WaVAEtable synthesis may approach the practical limits of incorporating static generative models for audio in more traditional electronic music synthesis. Future timbral models that generate audio in real-time and are conditioned on pitch could function as a true oscillator in a synthesis system. Moving beyond these static timbral models to time-varying models allows for new combinations of generative models and synthesis methods, such as neural sample-generation and neural granular synthesis.

Acknowledgments. Special thanks to Karl Yerkes (MAT, University of California Santa Barbara) for his great help with SuperCollider and OSC implementations.

References

1. Bristow-Johnson, R.: Wavetable synthesis 101, a fundamental perspective. In: Proceedings 101st Convention of the Audio Engineering Society (1996)
2. Colonel, J., Curro, C., Keene, S.: Autoencoding neural networks as musical audio synthesizers. In: Proceedings of the 21st International Conference on Digital Audio Effects (2018)
3. Engel, J., et al.: Neural audio synthesis of musical notes with WaveNet autoencoders. In: Proceedings of the 34th International Conference on Machine Learning, vol. 70 (2017)
4. Esling, P., Chemla-Romeu-Santos, A., Bitton, A.: Generative timbre spaces: regularizing variational auto-encoders with perceptual metrics. In: Proceedings of the 21st International Conference on Digital Audio Effects (2018)
5. Griffin, D., Lim, J.: Signal estimation from modified short-time Fourier transform. IEEE Trans. Acoust. Speech Signal Process. **32**(2), 236–243 (1984)
6. Hantrakul, L., Yang, L.C.: Neural wavetable: a playable wavetable synthesizer using neural networks. In: Workshop on Machine Learning for Creativity and Design (2018)
7. Huzaifah, M., Wyse, L.: Deep generative models for musical audio synthesis. In: Miranda, E.R. (ed.) Handbook of Artificial Intelligence for Music, pp. 639–678. Springer, Cham (2021). https://doi.org/10.1007/978-3-030-72116-9_22
8. Kingma, D.P., Welling, M.: Auto-encoding variational bayes. arXiv preprint, arXiv:1312.6114 (2013)
9. Luo, Y.J., Cheuk, K.W., Nakano, T., Goto, M., Herremans, D.: Unsupervised disentanglement of pitch and timbre for isolated musical instrument sounds. In: Proceedings of the 2020 International Society of Music Information Retrieval Conference (2020)
10. Mauch, M., Dixon, S.: pYIN: a fundamental frequency estimator using probabilistic threshold distributions. In: Proceedings of the 2014 IEEE International Conference on Acoustics, Speech and Signal Processing (2014)
11. Paszke, A., et al.: Automatic differentiation in PyTorch. In: Proceedings of the 31st Conference on Neural Information Processing Systems (2017)

Deep Learning-Based Music Instrument Recognition: Exploring Learned Feature Representations

Michael Taenzer[✉], Stylianos I. Mimilakis, and Jakob Abeßer

Fraunhofer Institute for Digital Media Technology IDMT, Ilmenau, Germany
michael.taenzer@idmt.fraunhofer.de

Abstract. In this work, we focus on the problem of automatic instrument recognition (AIR) using supervised learning. In particular, we follow a state-of-the-art AIR approach that combines a deep convolutional neural network (CNN) architecture with an attention mechanism. This attention mechanism is conditioned on a learned input feature representation, which itself is extracted by another CNN model acting as a feature extractor. The extractor is pre-trained on a large-scale audio dataset using discriminative objectives for sound event detection. In our experiments, we show that when using log-mel spectrograms as input features instead, the performance of the CNN-based AIR algorithm decreases significantly. Hence, our results indicate that the feature representations are the main factor that affects the performance of the AIR algorithm. Furthermore, we show that various pre-training tasks affect the AIR performance in different ways for subsets of the music instrument classes.

Keywords: music instrument recognition · deep learning · representation learning

1 Introduction

Real world music recordings often consist of multiple music instruments that can be active simultaneously. Detecting individual instruments or instrument families is an important research problem in areas such as machine listening [29,30], music information retrieval (MIR) [23], and (music) source separation [28]. The problem of detecting and categorizing the active instruments is often referred to as automatic instrument recognition (AIR) [11,19]. Recent approaches to AIR are mostly based on deep convolutional neural networks (CNNs) [8,10,11,19,26, 31].

One commonality in deep learning approaches for AIR is that they consist of three modules [8,10,11,19,31], namely the pre-processing, embedding, and classification modules. The first module pre-processes and transforms the respective input music waveform into a compact signal representation. The most common

M. Taenzer and S. I. Mimilakis—Equally contributing authors.

M. Aramaki et al. (Eds.): CMMR 2021, LNCS 13770, pp. 32–46, 2023.
https://doi.org/10.1007/978-3-031-35382-6_4

transforms are the short-time Fourier transform (STFT) and related filter-banks such as Mel-bands [8,11,22,31] and the constant-Q transform (CQT) [15], and other spectral-analysis transforms such as the Hilbert and Hilbert-Huang transforms used in [17] and [20], respectively. Common operations as pre-processing steps are harmonic and percussive separation [8] as well as logarithmic magnitude compression and data normalization or standardization [31].

The second module, referred to as embedding, accepts as input the pre-processed and transformed music waveform from the first module. It yields a feature *representation* that is used to condition the last module, i.e., the classification module, which is responsible for computing the posterior, i.e., the label probability, of the corresponding instrument classes (e.g., "electric guitar" or "piano"). Most often, the embedding and classification modules are learned jointly during a training procedure that is based on supervised learning, in which the class labels for each recording are given from a curated dataset [11,31].

Regarding the embedding module, a common ingredient in the related literature is the usage of CNNs [8,11,20,31] and, more recently, CNN-based attention mechanisms [10,34]. The approaches employing attention mechanisms are experimentally shown to yield state-of-the-art results, and it is assumed that the attention mechanism is responsible for the success of the methods.

However, the studies presented in [10] and [34] condition the attention mechanism on a feature representation that is computed using a *pre-trained* CNN. In these cases, that CNN, in particular the VGGish network [13], is initially trained for audio event detection (AED) in a supervised way using general audio signals and classes obtained from Audio Set [6], before being applied on the task of AIR. This means that the attention-based approaches to AIR make use of transfer learning [21,25]. This differs from other approaches which learn the representations jointly for the task of AIR [8,11,31]. Therefore, it could be argued that the observed increase in classification performance of such attention-based models rather needs to be attributed to the discriminative power of the feature representations from the CNN, which was previously trained on more general audio signals instead of solely music signals [1,9].

In this work, we analyze the impact of the role of learning feature representations for an attention mechanism for music instrument classification performance. It must be noted that it is not our intention to conduct a comparative study on attention mechanisms [32] versus representation learning [1], as we believe that both are equally beneficial for the task at hand. Instead, we aim to show that deep learning approaches to AIR can substantially benefit from employing representations that are learned using reconstruction or alignment optimization objectives [4] as well as datasets that contain general purpose audio signals [6].

To answer our research question, we focus on the attention-based model presented in [10], which is trained and tested on the respective subsets of the OpenMIC dataset [14]. To investigate the influence of different feature representations, we experiment with various commonly used filter-banks, such as (log) Mel-spectrograms, and learned representations. For the latter case, different datasets and optimization objectives are used to pre-train the CNN that is responsible for yielding the feature representations. The datasets and objectives are described in Sects. 3 and 4.1, respectively.

The remainder of the report is structured as follows: Sect. 2 describes the applied method for the attention-based music instrument recognition. Section 3 describes the usage of the datasets. Section 4 provides details regarding the experimental procedure, followed by Sect. 5 that explains the evaluation methods. Section 6 presents and discusses the results from the experiments. Finally, Sect. 7 concludes this work.

2   Attention-Based Model

The attention-based model for AIR from the work presented in [10] is illustrated in Fig. 1. It is embedded into our general experimental pipeline as described in the following.

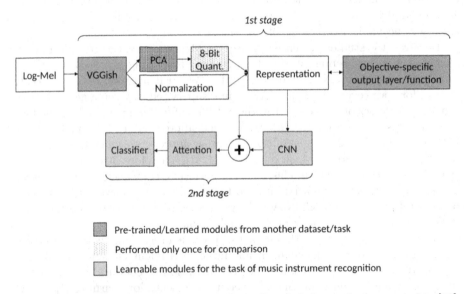

Fig. 1. An illustration of our experimental pipeline and the method presented in [10] that employs an attention mechanism (at 2nd stage) and a pre-trained CNN (the VGGish at 1st stage) for computing the feature representations.

2.1   Input Pre-processing

An input time-domain music signal is first resampled at a sampling frequency of 16 kHz and then transformed into a time-frequency representation using the short-time Fourier transform (STFT). The parameters for the STFT are a window size of 25 ms using the Hann window function and a hop-size of 10 ms.

Each windowed segment is zero-padded to 512 samples. From the magnitude of the STFT, a Mel-spectrogram with 64 mel bands is computed. Then we apply log-magnitude scaling to the Mel-spectrogram, yielding the final spectral representation denoted as "Log-Mel" in Fig. 1. This will be the input to the pipeline.

2.2   1st Stage: Post-processing and Representation

The Log-Mel is used to condition the VGGish network presented in [16]. This network comprises six convolutional (conv) blocks followed by three fully-connected feed-forward (dense) layers (FC). Each conv block consists of a two-dimensional conv layer (2Dconv), the rectified linear unit (ReLU) activation function [24], and a two-dimensional max-pooling operation. The numbers of kernels across the conv blocks are $\{64, 128, 256, 256, 512, 512\}$. The kernel sizes for the conv and max-pooling operations in all conv blocks are 3×3 and 2×2, respectively, and the stride size is set to 1. Furthermore, zero-padding is applied to preserve the size of the intermediate latent representations (activation maps), which are computed using the convolutions. The outputs of each kernel in the last conv block are concatenated to a vector and then given as input to the first FC. The number of output units in each FC is $\{4096, 4096, 128\}$, respectively. The ReLU activation function is used after each FC.

The output of the VGGish is a feature representation that summarizes approximately one second of spectral information into a single embedding vector [16]. This output representation is then subject to post-processing in two ways, before it is being fed to the 2nd stage of the pipeline:

- A whitening transform is applied on it using principal component analysis (PCA). The bases for the PCA are *pre-computed* from the audio signals' corresponding representation obtained by the VGGish [14, 16] using the training subset of Audio Set [6]. This yields a whitened feature representation. In a final step, it is 8-bit quantized and mapped to the range of $[0, 1]$. (See Fig. 1: 1st stage upper branch.)
- The features are simply scaled to the range of $[0, 1]$ (min-max normalization). (See Fig. 1: 1st stage lower branch.)

2.3   2nd Stage: CNN, Attention Mechanism and Classification

The above representation is processed by a block of 2D CNNs, which precede the attention module. It consists of three 2Dconv layers with unit stride and a group-normalization layer [35]. Each layer employs 128 1×1-kernels. The output of the group-normalization layer is then updated by means of residual connections [12] using the information of the post-processed representation.

The output of the residual connections is given to the attention module that consists of two 2Dconv layers, each with kernel size 1×1. The number of kernels in each 2Dconv layer is equal to the number of classes. The representation is fed to each 2Dconv layer in the attention module, followed by the application of the element-wise sigmoid activation function. The output of the conv layer responsible for decoding the attention embedding is normalized to unit sum with respect to the time-frame information. The output of the conv layer responsible for the class activity is used to gate the normalized output of the other conv layer.

Using this attention mechanism, the posterior can be computed by aggregating the time-information of the output of the attention mechanism. The aggregation is performed due to the weakly annotated labels contained in OpenMIC [10]. Finally, this is followed by the application of the hard-tanh function, which is linear in the range of $[0, 1]$, equal to 1 for values >1, and 0 for negative values.

3   Datasets

To optimize the overall model parameters contained in each module described in Sect. 2, a two-stage training scheme is employed. In the first stage, the modules that are used to compute the feature representation (i.e., as illustrated in green color in Fig. 1), are pre-trained on a task different from AIR. The second stage uses the pre-trained modules from the previous stage, and optimizes the rest of the modules (i.e., the yellow modules illustrated in Fig. 1), using the labels associated with the task of AIR. Tables 1 and 2 provide an overview of this.

For the first stage, we employ the already optimized VGGish embeddings [14][1] pre-trained on the Audio Set [6], and the NSynth [3] and Freesound [5] datasets. In this stage, various pre-training objectives are used, which depend on the dataset (see Sect. 4.1). For the second stage (training) and final evaluations (testing), we utilize only OpenMIC [14], with the respective subsets used in [10].

Audio Set comprises more than two million sound clips taken from Youtube videos, each with a length of 10s. It consists of >500 audio event classes with weakly-labeled annotations.

NSynth is a dataset of 305,979 annotated musical notes of 1,006 instruments. An audio example has a length of four seconds and consists of a single note.

Freesound is a weakly-labeled collaborative dataset of $>260,000$ audio examples covering >600 sound classes, spanning a large spectrum of all imaginable sounds (human, animal, things) at different lengths, including music.

OpenMIC contains 20,000 snippets of polyphonic music recordings from various music genres. Each snippet has a length of 10s and is weakly-labeled (i.e., no onset and offset times) for the presence and absence of 20 instrument classes.

4   Experimental Procedure

Since the PCA and 8-bit quantization steps in the post-processing of the feature representation from the VGGish (see Fig. 1: 1st stage upper branch) are irrelevant to the scope of our work, we have excluded them from our experiments. Instead, a simple normalization to $[0, 1]$ is applied to that representation (see Fig. 1: 1st stage lower branch) to avoid any crucial performance discrepancies due to the inductive biases of the attention-based method for AIR. The difference in performance of these two approaches are illustrated in Fig. 2 and Fig. 3.

---

[1] Publicly available under https://github.com/cosmir/openmic-2018.

4.1   1st Stage: Pre-Training Objectives

This section provides technical details regarding the experimental setup for each employed objective in the first training stage for optimizing the parameters of the VGGish. Tables 1 and 2 give a summary and overview of the detailed descriptions in the following paragraphs.

Table 1. Overview of the objectives and their purpose used for pre-training the VGGish in the first training stage.

Objective	Purpose and description
Textual description ("Textual")	Generate a textual description of the audio signal (audio captioning) → employs Word2Vec which yields a target vector
Signal recovery ("Denoising/Den +", "Denoising/Den ⊙")	Recovery of original Log-Mel from corrupted versions of the signal (additive noise and multiplicative noise) → employs Denoising Autoencoders
Audio & tag alignment ("Align")	Maximize agreement between audio and tag representations using contrastive loss → employs Co-Aligned Autoencoder as tag encoder

Table 2. Usage of different datasets for the respective stages, objectives, and evaluation. Signal recovery (Denoising) from additive noise is indicated by +, and from multiplicative noise by ⊙.

1st stage pre-training objectives	Datasets		
	1st stage training	2nd stage training	Evaluation
General purpose AED	Audio Set	OpenMIC	
Textual description; Denoising +; Denoising ⊙	NSynth		
Audio & tag alignment	Freesound		

For all pre-training learning objectives, the Adam optimizer [18] is used with a fixed learning rate of $1e^{-4}$. Furthermore, the batch size is set to 64 and an early stopping mechanism is active, which terminates the training procedure if the used criterion—validation loss—has not improved for five consecutive iterations throughout the entire training data. The maximum number of training epochs is 50. All parameters are initialized randomly with samples drawn from a uniform distribution and scaled using the method presented in [7].

Textual Description. One investigated pre-training objective is the prediction of the textual description of a music recording. This objective draws inspiration from the field of audio captioning [2], which aims at generating a textual description of an audio signal. Subject to the goal of this work, we employ the NSynth dataset [3] that contains the following textual descriptions of the musical notes for every recording in the dataset:

{"bright", "dark", "distortion", "decay", "presence", "multiphonic", "modulation", "percussive", "reverb", "rhythmic"}

Note that we replaced some of the original NSynth descriptions based on the additional description contained in the dataset. This was due to the fact that the original descriptions could not be fully encoded by the employed language model. See Table 3 for an overview of the descriptions in question.

Table 3. NSynth text descriptions for musical notes, and the adjustments applied to suit the encoding of the Word2Vec model.

NSynth description	Replaced by
"fast decay"	"decay"
"long release"	"presence"
"nonlinear env"	"modulation"
"tempo-synced"	"rhythmic"

For using the textual descriptions of the music files to train the VGGish, we employ the Word2Vec language model presented in [27] and pre-trained on an English vocabulary, to yield a vector representation of each description. The Word2Vec model encodes each input word, in our case the textual description, into a 300-dimensional vector embedding. That vector is used as the target to learn the parameters of the VGGish. To do so, the output of the VGGish is given as input to a trainable batch-norm layer and two fully-connected feed-forward (dense) layers (FC). The first FC employs the non-linear tanh activation function, whereas the second does not employ any element-wise non-linear functions. The number of units in the FCs is set to 300.

Feeding an audio example from the NSynth dataset to the VGGish network yields a single vector, because every NSynth example has a length of one second. Therefore, it is not necessary to aggregate over temporal information. The parameters of the VGGish and the following block of batch-norm and FCs are jointly optimized by minimizing the cosine loss between the predicted and target word-vector embeddings. The margin hyperparameter in the computation of the cosine loss is set to 0.5.

Signal Recovery. Another training objective we investigate is the recovery of the original Log-Mel spectrogram from a corrupted version of the signal. The goal of this objective is to enforce the representation from the VGGish to encode the relevant information contained in the Log-Mel. To do so, we employ denoising autoencoders (DAEs) [33] and corrupt the Log-Mel in two different ways before it is input to the VGGish: a) with element-wise additive noise (+) drawn from a Gaussian distribution with zero mean and 0.1 standard deviation, and b) with element-wise multiplicative noise ($\odot$). For the latter case, random values are drawn from a Bernoulli distribution with $p = 0.5$.

To decode the representation of the corrupted Log-Mel obtained by the VGGish, we employ a single block of conv layers containing four transposed one-dimensional conv (1Dconv) layers. We use transposed 1Dconv layers to be able to recover (upsample back to) the original dimensionality regarding time-frames, which the VGGish reduced. The number of kernels and their size in each layer are $\{128, 64, 64, 64\}$ and $\{10, 21, 31, 37\}$, respectively. No zero-padding is applied between each convolution. Furthermore, the first three 1Dconv layers employ the leaky ReLU activation function with a leaky-factor of $\{0.1, 0.25, 0.5\}$, respectively. The last conv layer uses a linear activation function. These hyperparameters are chosen experimentally so that a reasonable convergence is achieved using a random and smaller subset of NSynth.

Audio and Tag Alignment. We also explore the objective of aligning audio and associated tags. The alignment is achieved by maximizing the agreement of the computed audio and tag representations using a contrastive loss. We employ the tag encoder—based on Co-Aligned Autoencoders—and the corresponding hyperparameters following the method presented in [4], whose goal is to compute semantically enriched representations that reflect acoustic and semantic characteristics of audio signals. For the audio encoder, we use the VGGish as discussed above. To match the dimensionality used by the audio tag encoder, we apply an affine transformation after the VGGish. The optimization hyperparameters for this configuration are taken from [4].

4.2   2nd Stage: Downstream Instrument Recognition

After optimizing the parameters of the VGGish with one of the above pre-training objectives, the VGGish computes the representations of the audio files contained in OpenMIC. Together with the corresponding labels within Open-MIC, these are then used to optimize the parameters of the CNN and the attention mechanism. To that aim, we use the existing splits of OpenMIC for training and validation as described and employed in [10].

For training, we use the binary cross-entropy loss function. The hyperparameters for optimization are the Adam algorithm with a learning rate of $5e^{-4}$, a batch size equal to 128 data points and a total number of 350 training epochs, following [10]. After every iteration over the entire training subset, we evaluate the model performance on the validation subset. Once training has finished, we select the best set of parameters based on the obtained evaluation score calculated in every iteration.

5   Evaluation

While the total number of audio files per instrument in OpenMIC is balanced, the number of positive and negative examples varies from one instrument class to another. For this reason, we compute the macro-average F1-score (F1-macro) explicitly for positive and negative classes of every instrument class to evaluate both the parameters of the attention-based model and the pre-training stages, during both training and validation phases.

During evaluation, the outputs of the classifier are subject to a post-processing operation that thresholds to zero values below 0.5 and unity values otherwise. Finally, to determine the benefits of each objective, we test the attention mechanism on the test subset of OpenMIC each time it has been trained with a different feature representation.

To avoid any biases between the experiments using the attention-based model and various representations due to the random initialization, all experiments have been conducted using the same random seed.

6   Results and Discussion

6.1   Representation Post-processing: Impact on Performance

First, we examine the impact of the post-processing steps (see Sect. 2.2) versus normalization on classification performance, illustrated in Fig. 2 and Fig. 3. From the F-score, it can be seen that a simple scaling of the feature representation induces only a marginal performance drop. This allows us to omit further data-dependent post-processing stages that are irrelevant to our research question, yet might impose some performance discrepancies. It can also be observed from the barplot Fig. 2 that without the PCA and quantization steps the performance increases marginally for the banjo, clarinet, drums, mandolin, trombone, and voice instrument classes.

6.2   Learned Representations: Impact on Performance

To highlight the impact of the learned representations on the classification performance of musical instruments using the discussed attention mechanism, Fig. 2 shows the results from the attention-based model conditioned on four feature representations. These are computed from the VGGish pre-trained on Audio Set, a randomly initialized VGGish, and using the Log-Mel representation directly—i.e., the VGGish acts as an identity operator.

The boxplot Fig. 3 highlights two observations: First, regarding F1-macro, the discriminative power of the pre-trained VGGish is responsible for obtaining the best classification performance. Secondly, even an unoptimized (randomly initialized) VGGish can be used to compute a feature representation that yields a classification performance comparable to Log-Mel, which is a common feature

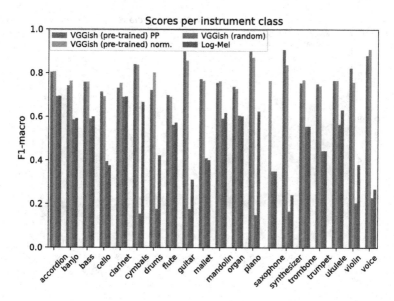

Fig. 2. F-scores per instrument class for the attention-based model [10], conditioned on four different feature representations. Note: marginal differences between post-processing and normalization; Log-Mel outperforms a randomly initialized VGGish.

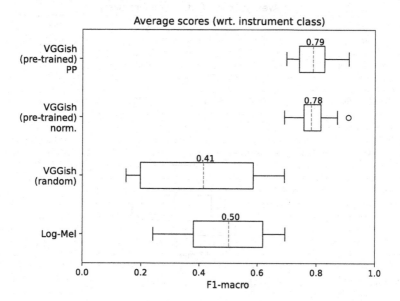

Fig. 3. Averaged F-scores over all instrument classes, complementary to Fig. 2.

representation for audio classification tasks. However, the barplot Fig. 2 demonstrates that Log-Mel outperforms the representation from the randomly initial-

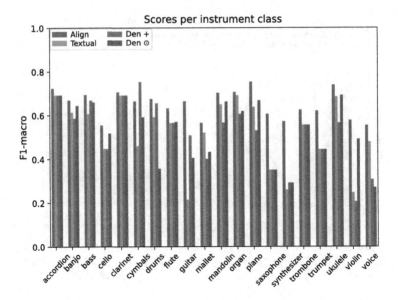

Fig. 4. F-scores per instrument class for the attention-based model [10], conditioned on feature representations obtained from pre-training the VGGish on the various objectives, using Freesound for Align, and NSynth for Textual, Den + and Den ⊙.

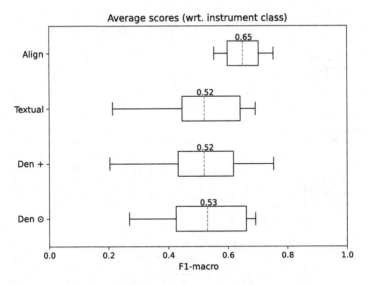

Fig. 5. Overall F-score averaged over all instrument classes, complementary to Fig. 4.

ized VGGish for a few musical instruments classes including cymbals, ukulele, violin, and voice.

These two tendencies suggest that the performance of the attention-based model may be accredited mostly to the discriminative power of the representation yielded by the VGGish. They also imply that different objectives or datasets may be used to pre-train the VGGish and yield different results.

Figure 4 and Fig. 5 further explore this observed direction with the results of the classification performance when using the various objectives as described in Sect. 4.1. As can be seen in the boxplot Fig. 5, the pre-training tasks of signal recovery and textual description provide significant improvements by 0.11 in the F-score over the randomly initialized VGGish. Compared to the Log-Mel features, marginal improvements of approximately 0.02 are observed. The barplot shows that each pre-training objective seems to be beneficial for different musical instrument classes. For example, Textual provides competitive results for the instrument classes mallet, mandolin, organ, ukulele, and voice, while Den ⊙ appears to work well for piano, ukulele, and violin. Den + provides improvements for percussive musical instruments such as cymbals and drums. In any case, the VGGish pre-trained on Audio Set (see Fig. 2 and Fig. 3) significantly outperforms the best performing models which employ NSynth.

Plausible explanations for these observed discrepancies lie in the amount of data and variability within Audio Set, and in the naiveness (in the sense of simple and not carefully devised) of the pre-training objectives, e.g. the signal recovery. This explanation is underlined when considering the results for the Align objective (see Fig. 4 and Fig. 5), which employs Freesound and uses a more sophisticated mechanism to exploit the information of the audio tags.

Figure 4 and Fig. 5 show that the usage of larger corpora in conjunction with a more sophisticated objective (Align) can lead to significant improvements in attention-based AIR compared to the signal recovery and textual description objectives. Nonetheless, it is still sub-optimal compared to VGGish pre-trained on Audio Set. The discrepancy in performance between the two may be accredited to the data availability. However, this finding highlights the trend that using more general purpose audio datasets can improve the downstream task of AIR.

7   Conclusions

In this work, we investigated the importance of the role of learning representations wrt. an attention mechanism in music instrument classification algorithms. To that aim, we focused on the attention-based model for music instrument recognition presented in [10], and experimentally explored the impact of various feature representations on the performance of the attention-based model. Our experimental findings highlight the following trends:

1. Discriminative objectives in conjunction with large scale and general purpose audio corpora are an important factor to be considered in AIR apart from the attention mechanism.
2. The usage of audio tags for computing representations is an attractive objective that yields competing performance.
3. Training objectives that take advantage of general audio and annotations or, respectively, the exploitation of multi-modalities in a self-supervised manner are emerging directions for future research.

Acknowledgments. This work has been supported by the German Research Foundation (AB 675/2-1).

References

1. Bengio, Y., Courville, A., Vincent, P.: Representation learning: a review and new perspectives. IEEE Trans. Pattern Anal. Mach. Intell. **35**(8), 1798–1828 (2013). https://doi.org/10.1109/TPAMI.2013.50
2. Drossos, K., Adavanne, S., Virtanen, T.: Automated audio captioning with recurrent neural networks. In: Proceedings of the IEEE Workshop on Applications of Signal Processing to Audio and Acoustics (WASPAA), New Paltz, New York, USA (2017)
3. Engel, J., et al.: Neural audio synthesis of musical notes with WaveNet autoencoders. arXiv preprint arXiv:1704.01279 (2017)
4. Favory, X., Drossos, K., Virtanen, T., Serra, X.: Coala: co-aligned autoencoders for learning semantically enriched audio representations. arXiv preprint arXiv:2006.08386 (2020)
5. Font, F., Roma, G., Serra, X.: Freesound technical demo. In: Proceedings of the 21st ACM International Conference on Multimedia, New York, NY, USA, pp. 411–412 (2013)
6. Gemmeke, J.F., et al.: Audio set: an ontology and human-labeled dataset for audio events. In: Proceedings of the IEEE International Conference on Acoustics, Speech and Signal Processing (ICASSP), pp. 776–780 (2017)
7. Glorot, X., Bengio, Y.: Understanding the difficulty of training deep feedforward neural networks. In: Proceedings of the International Conference on Artificial Intelligence and Statistics (AISTATS 2010), pp. 249–256 (2010)
8. Gomez, J., Abeßer, J., Cano, E.: Jazz solo instrument classification with convolutional neural networks, source separation, and transfer learning. In: Proceedings of the 19th International Society of Music Information Retrieval Conference (ISMIR), Paris, France, pp. 577–584 (2018)
9. Goodfellow, I., Bengio, Y., Courville, A.: Deep Learning. MIT Press, Cambridge (2016)
10. Gururani, S., Sharma, M., Lerch, A.: An attention mechanism for musical instrument recognition. In: Proceedings of the 20th International Society for Music Information Retrieval Conference (ISMIR), Delft, The Netherlands, pp. 83–90 (2019)
11. Han, Y., Kim, J., Lee, K.: Deep convolutional neural networks for predominant instrument recognition in polyphonic music. IEEE/ACM Trans. Audio Speech Lang. Process. (TASLP) **25**(1), 208–221 (2017)
12. He, K., Zhang, X., Ren, S., Sun, J.: Deep residual learning for image recognition. arXiv preprint arXiv:1512.03385 (2015)
13. Hershey, S., et al.: CNN architectures for large-scale audio classification. In: Proceedings of the IEEE International Conference on Acoustics, Speech and Signal Processing (ICASSP), New Orleans, LA, USA, pp. 131–135 (2017)
14. Humphrey, E.J., Durand, S., Mcfee, B.: OpenMIC-2018: an open data-set for multiple instrument recognition. In: Proceedings of the 19th International Society for Music Information Retrieval Conference (ISMIR), Paris, France, pp. 438–444 (2018)
15. Hung, Y.N., Yang, Y.H.: Frame-level instrument recognition by timbre and pitch. In: Proceedings of the 19th International Society for Music Information Retrieval Conference (ISMIR), Paris, France, pp. 135–142 (2018)

16. Jansen, A., Gemmeke, J.F., Ellis, D.P.W., Liu, X., Lawrence, W., Freedman, D.: Large-scale audio event discovery in one million YouTube videos. In: Proceedings of the International Conference on Acoustics, Speech and Signal Processing (ICASSP), pp. 786–790 (2017). https://doi.org/10.1109/ICASSP.2017.7952263

17. Kim, D., Sung, T., Cho, S., Lee, G., Sohn, C.: A single predominant instrument recognition of polyphonic music using CNN-based timbre analysis. Int. J. Eng. Technol. (UAE) **7**, 590–593 (2018)

18. Kingma, D.P., Ba, J.: Adam: a method for stochastic optimization. In: Proceedings of the 3rd International Conference on Learning Representations (ICLR) (2015)

19. Li, P., Qian, J., Wang, T.: Automatic instrument recognition in polyphonic music using convolutional neural networks. arXiv preprint arXiv:1511.05520 (2015)

20. Li, X., Wang, K., Soraghan, J., Ren, J.: Fusion of Hilbert-Huang transform and deep convolutional neural network for predominant musical instruments recognition. In: Romero, J., Ekárt, A., Martins, T., Correia, J. (eds.) EvoMUSART 2020. LNCS, vol. 12103, pp. 80–89. Springer, Cham (2020). https://doi.org/10.1007/978-3-030-43859-3_6

21. Long, M., Cao, Y., Wang, J., Jordan, M.I.: Learning transferable features with deep adaptation networks. In: Proceedings of the 32nd International Conference on Machine Learning (ICML), Lille, France, vol. 37, pp. 97–105 (2015)

22. Mimilakis, S.I., Weiss, C., Arifi-Müller, V., Abeßer, J., Müller, M.: Cross-version singing voice detection in opera recordings: challenges for supervised learning. In: Cellier, P., Driessens, K. (eds.) ECML PKDD 2019. CCIS, vol. 1168, pp. 429–436. Springer, Cham (2020). https://doi.org/10.1007/978-3-030-43887-6_35

23. Müller, M.: Information Retrieval for Music and Motion. Springer, Heidelberg (2007)

24. Nair, V., Hinton, G.E.: Rectified linear units improve restricted Boltzmann machines. In: Proceedings of the 27th International Conference on International Conference on Machine Learning (ICML), pp. 807–814. Omnipress, Madison (2010)

25. Oquab, M., Bottou, L., Laptev, I., Sivic, J.: Learning and transferring mid-level image representations using convolutional neural networks. In: IEEE Conference on Computer Vision and Pattern Recognition (CVPR), pp. 1717–1724 (2014)

26. Park, T., Lee, T.: Musical instrument sound classification with deep convolutional neural network using feature fusion approach. arXiv preprint arXiv:1512.07370 (2015)

27. Pennington, J., Socher, R., Manning, C.: GloVe: global vectors for word representation. In: Proceedings of the 2014 Conference on Empirical Methods in Natural Language Processing (EMNLP), pp. 1532–1543 (2014)

28. Rafii, Z., Liutkus, A., Stöter, F.R., Mimilakis, S.I., FitzGerald, D., Pardo, B.: An overview of lead and accompaniment separation in music. IEEE/ACM Trans. Audio Speech Lang. Process. **26**(8), 1307–1335 (2018)

29. Scheirer, E.D.: Music-listening systems. Ph.D. thesis, Massachusetts Institute of Technology (2000)

30. Smaragdis, P.: Redundancy reduction for computational audition, a unifying approach. Ph.D. thesis, Massachusetts Institute of Technology (2001)

31. Taenzer, M., Abeßer, J., Mimilakis, S.I., Weiß, C., Müller, M., Lukashevich, H.: Investigating CNN-based instrument family recognition for western classical music recordings. In: Proceedings of the 20th International Society for Music Information Retrieval Conference (ISMIR), Delft, The Netherlands, pp. 612–619 (2019)

32. Vaswani, A., et al.: Attention is all you need. In: Guyon, I., et al. (eds.) Proceedings of the 30th International Conference Advances in Neural Information Processing Systems (NeurIPS), pp. 5998–6008. Curran Associates, Inc. (2017)

33. Vincent, P., Larochelle, H., Bengio, Y., Manzagol, P.A.: Extracting and composing robust features with denoising autoencoders. In: Proceedings of the 25th International Conference on Machine Learning (ICML), Helsinki, Finland, pp. 1096–1103. ACM (2008)
34. Watcharasupat, K., Gururani, S., Lerch, A.: Visual attention for musical instrument recognition. arXiv preprint arXiv:2006.09640 (2020)
35. Wu, Y., He, K.: Group normalization. arXiv preprint arXiv:1803.08494 (2018)

Time-Span Tree Leveled by Duration of Time-Span

Masatoshi Hamanaka[1]($\boxtimes$), Keiji Hirata[2], and Satoshi Tojo[3]

[1] RIKEN, Wako, Japan
masatoshi.hamanaka@riken.jp
[2] Future University Hakodate, Hakodate, Japan
[3] JAIST, Nomi, Japan

Abstract. This paper describes a time-span tree leveled by the length of the time span. Using the time-span tree of the Generative Theory of Tonal Music, it is possible to reduce notes in a melody, but it is difficult to automate because the priority order of the branches to be reduced is not defined. A similar problem arises in the automation of time-span analysis and melodic morphing. Therefore, we propose a method for defining the priority order in total order in accordance with the length of the time span of each branch in a time-span tree. In the experiment, we confirmed that melodic morphing and deep learning of time-span tree analysis can be carried out automatically using the proposed method.

Keywords: generative theory of tonal music (GTTM) · time-span tree · time-span reduction melodic morphing · Transformer

1 Introduction

Our goal is to automate the system using a time-span tree of the Generative Theory of Tonal Music (GTTM) [11]. GTTM consists of grouping structure analysis, metrical structure analysis, time-span tree analysis, and prolongational tree analysis. A time-span tree is a binary tree with a hierarchical structure that describes the relative structural importance of notes that differentiate the essential parts of the melody from the ornamentation.

The time-span tree in Fig. 1 is the result of analyzing a melody (a) on the basis of GTTM. Reduced melodies can be extracted by cutting this time-span tree with a horizontal line and omitting the notes connected below the line (Fig. 1(b)–(f)). Melody reduction with GTTM is the absorption of notes by structurally important notes.

The problem with previous systems using time-span trees is that the priority order of branches of a time-span tree is not defined. The GTTM-based melodic-morphing algorithm we previously proposed was difficult to automate because it included a time-span reduction process [3,4]. We have been developing a GTTM analyzer using deep learning and have been able to automate grouping structure analysis and metrical structure analysis using deep leaning [7,8]. However, deep

M. Aramaki et al. (Eds.): CMMR 2021, LNCS 13770, pp. 47–58, 2023.
https://doi.org/10.1007/978-3-031-35382-6_5

learning of time-span tree analysis is difficult to automate due to the ambiguity of the reduction process.

Therefore, we propose a method for defining the priority order in total order in accordance with the length of the time span of each branch in the time-span tree, enabling melodic morphing and time-span analysis to be automated. Sections 2 and 3 describe problems with implementing our melodic-morphing algorithm and time-span analysis. In Sect. 4 we present our proposed method for the solving the above-mentioned problems. The experiments in Sect. 5, we show that melodic morphing and time-span analysis can be automating by prioritizing the branches of the time-span tree. We conclude in Sect. 6 with a brief summary and mention of future work.

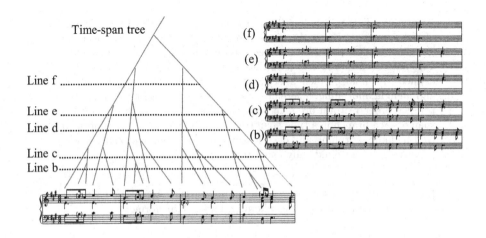

Fig. 1. Time-span tree and melody reduction

2   Implementation Problems of Melodic-Morphing Algorithm

The meaning of morphing is to change something, such as an image, into another through a seamless transition. For example, a method of morphing one face picture into another creates intermediate pictures through the following operations.

(a1) Link characteristic points such as eyes and nose, in the two pictures (Fig. 2a).
(a2) Rate the intensities of the shape (position), color, etc. in each picture.
(a3) Combine the pictures.

2.1   Ideas of Melodic Morphing

Similarly, our melodic-morphing algorithm creates intermediate melodies with the following operations.

(b1) Link the common pitch events of the time-span trees of two melodies (Fig. 2b).
(b2) Remove those notes that do not reside in the common part by using partial melody reduction, which is explained in the next subsection.
(b3) Combine both melodies.

Fig. 2. Examples of linking two pictures/melodies

By using the time-span trees σ_A and σ_B from melodies A and B, respectively, we can calculate the common events of $\sigma_A \sqcap \sigma_B$, which includes not only the essential parts of melody A but also those of melody B (Fig. 3(b1)). The *meet* operation $\sigma_A \sqcap \sigma_B$ is abstracted from σ_A and σ_B, and those abstracted notes that are not included in $\sigma_A \sqcap \sigma_B$ are regarded to be the difference between σ_A and σ_B.

2.2   Partial Melody Reduction

Music features contained in σ_A and σ_B should exist even in what is not included in the common part. To retrieve these characteristics, we need a method of smoothly increasing or decreasing the number of features. Partial melody reduction abstracts the notes of a melody by using reduction.

With partial melody reduction, we can first acquire melodies $\alpha_i(i = 1, 2, \cdots, n)$ from σ_A and $\sigma_A \sqcap \sigma_B$ with the following algorithm. The subscript i of α_i indicates the number of notes that are included in σ_A but not in $\sigma_A \sqcap \sigma_B$.

Step 1: Determine the level of abstraction The user determines the parameter L that determines the level of melody abstraction. Parameter L is from 1 to the number of notes that are included in σ_A but not included in $\sigma_A \sqcap \sigma_B$.

Step 2: Abstraction of notes This step involves selecting and abstracting a note that has the fewest dots, obtained from metrical analysis, in the difference of σ_A and σ_B. The numbers of dots can be acquired from the analysis results. If two or more notes have the fewest dots, we select the first one.

Step 3: Iteration Iterate step 2 L times.

Subsumption relations hold as follows for the time-span trees σ_{α_m} constructed with the above algorithm.

$$\sigma_A \sqcap \sigma_B \not\sqsubseteq \sigma_{\alpha_n} \not\sqsubseteq \sigma_{\alpha_{n-1}} \not\sqsubseteq \cdots \not\sqsubseteq \sigma_{\alpha_2} \not\sqsubseteq \sigma_{\alpha_1} \not\sqsubseteq \sigma_A \tag{1}$$

In Fig. 3(b2), there are nine notes included in σ_A but not included in $\sigma_A \sqcap \sigma_B$. Therefore, the value of n is 8, and we can acquire eight types of melody $\alpha_i (i = 1, 2, \cdots, n)$ between σ_A and $\sigma_A \sqcap \sigma_B$. Hence, melody α_i attenuates features that exist only in melody A.

In the same manner, we can acquire melody β from σ_A and $\sigma_A \sqcap \sigma_B$ as follows.

$$\sigma_A \sqcap \sigma_B \not\sqsubseteq \sigma_{\beta_j} \not\sqsubseteq \sigma_B \tag{2}$$

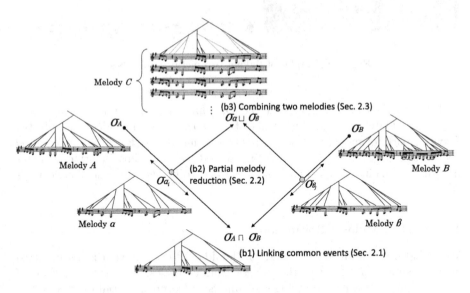

Fig. 3. Overview of melodic-morphing algorithm

2.3 Combining Two Melodies

We use the *join* operator $\sqcup$ to combine melodies σ_{α_i} and σ_{β_j}, which are the results of the partial reduction done using the time-span tree of melodies σ_A and σ_B (Fig. 3(b3)).

The simple *join* operator is not sufficient for combining σ_{α_i} and σ_{β_j}, because $\sigma_{\alpha_i} \sqcup \sigma_{\beta_j}$ is not always a monophony nevertheless σ_{α_i} and σ_{β_j} are monophonies.

In other words, the result of the operation may become polyphony (chords) when the time-span structures overlap and the pitches of the notes differ.

To solve this problem, we introduce a special notation, $[n_1, n_2]$, which indicates note n_1 or note n_2, as a result of $n_1 \sqcup n_2$. Accordingly, the result of $\sigma_\alpha \sqcup \sigma_\beta$ is all possible combinations of monophony.

2.4   Implementation Problems of Melodic-Morphing Algorithm

Although we have given priority to automating the morphing process, our melodic-morphing algorithm has the following two problems.

Problem 1: No order of abstract notes. The first problem has to do with the order of abstract notes in partial melody reduction. In Step 2 of Sect. 2.2, an abstraction is made from the notes with the fewest dots, but this is not always the case, for example, in a time-span tree where there is a structurally salient note on a weak beat. In addition, we have to consider whether it is appropriate to uniquely determine the partial reduction path, as in Eq. 1 in Step 3. If there are multiple paths for partial reduction, there is a possibility that more diverse melodies can be output.

Problem 2: Notes with overlapping times occur. The second problem is that the two notes overlapped temporally that may occur in the *join* of two time-span trees. In such cases, it is necessary to manually select one melody from among multiple generated melodies, and it is difficult to completely automate the morphing method. Further, the user remains in the dark as to the morphing process. In particular, it is difficult for the user to understand that the number of melodies output as a result of a number of melodic morphing changes. Even if the user understands the outline of the morphing method in Sect. 2, the outputs of multiple melodies may not match his or her expectations.

Our approach for automating melodic morphing is to define the order of notes abstracted by partial reduction and the order of notes selected by *join*. That is, when the time-span trees σ_A and σ_B of melodies A and B and the number of notes to be abstracted for each are determined, a unique melody, C, is obtained.

3   Implementation Problems of Deep-learning-based Time-Span Tree Analyzer

There are three problems in the deep learning of time-span tree analysis, as follows.

Problem 3: Low Number of Ground Truth Data Sets. As ground truth data of the time-span tree, 300 melodies and their time-span trees are published in the GTTM database [5]. However, the number of data sets (300) is extremely small for learning deep neural networks (DNNs). For a small amount of learning data, over-fitting is inevitable, and an appropriate value cannot be out-put when unknown data are input.

In the time-span analysis by musicologists, the entire time-span tree cannot be acquired at once but gradually analyzed from the bottom up. Therefore, the minimum process of analysis is set as one data set, then the number of data sets is increased. For example, if the DNN [1] directly learns the relationship between a four-note melody and its time-span tree, the number of data sets is only one. If we consider the process of reducing one note to one data set, the number of data sets will be three, as shown in Fig. 4a.

The trained DNN estimates the melody consisting of $n - 1$ notes that is reduced to one note when a melody consisting of n notes is input. A time-span tree for a melody consisting of four notes can be constructed by estimating four to three notes, three to two notes, and two to one note, and combining the results (Fig. 4b).

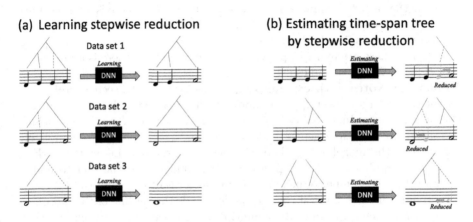

Fig. 4. Learning and estimating by stepwise reduction

Problem 4: Ambiguity of Reduction Process. Time-span reduction removes decorative notes by pruning from the leaves at the tip of the tree, leaving only structurally important notes in the melody. To implement the stepwise reduction described above, the priority of branches must be obtained in a total order. However, when it comes to GTTM, there are only a few examples of reduction using a time-span tree, and there is no detailed explanation on the reduction procedure [11]. For example, in Fig. 1, we can see five levels of reduction results, but it is not clear how many levels are necessary.

Marsden et al. [12] suggested a means of determining the salience of two note events a and b, neither of which are descendants of the other. They proposed defining the salience of an event as the duration of the maximum of the time spans of the two children at the branching point when the event is generated or where it is reduced.

To automate stepwise reduction, it is more important for the DNN to learn the relationship before and after the reduction than it is to reduce the order of the notes to close to that of human cognition. In Sect. 4, we propose a time-span tree leveled by the duration of the time span for a simple reduction order that is easy for the DNN to learn.

4 Solution: Time-Span Tree Leveled by Duration of Time Span

The *head* in a time-span tree is the top-most pitch event, that is, the most salient in the tree. When two adjacent subtrees are combined, one of the two heads of the subtrees becomes the head of the whole. This indicates that the head of a tree is most salient in the time interval the tree occupies. Since a tree is a hierarchical combination of sub-trees, the longest interval of each event in the tree is the most salient as the head of a subtree. Accordingly, we define the base case, when a subtree consists of a single pitch event, to be the duration of the event.

Maximum time span: We call the longest temporal interval when a given pitch event becomes most salient as the maximum time span for the event. In other words, the maximum time span of a pitch event coincides with the temporal duration of the subtree of which the event becomes the head, as a result of the time-span analysis.

The priority of each branch of the time-span tree is determined with a time-span tree drawn with the maximum time span used in the time-span segmentation carried out as the first step of the analysis of time-span reduction. The branch priority is determined in accordance with the following rules.

– Priorities are assigned to each level from the top of the time-span tree drawn with the duration of the time span.
– At the top level, the main branches take precedence.
– At the second and subsequent levels, the higher the priority of a branch X is, the higher the priority of the branch off of X becomes.

Figure 5 shows a time-span tree drawn with the duration of the time span. The branch priority is determined in order from the top in accordance with the first rule. Then, in accordance with the second rule, branch 1 has the highest priority in this time-span tree, and branch 2 has the second-highest priority. The second level in this tree is the double-note level. In accordance with the second rule, the branch off from 1 becomes 3, and that from 2 becomes 4. In the same manner, the priority is determined up to the 16th note level.

4.1 Automatic Melodic Morphing

For automatic partial reduction, we determine how much each melody is to be reduced and reduce the branches of the non-common part of the two melodies. If the non-common part of the melody of A is reduced by 30%, the reduction ratio of melody B is determined to be 70%, so that the total is 100%. Then, in the non-common part of each melody, the branches are reduced in order from the branch with the lowest priority. The number of notes is finite, so reducing them in accordance with a set reduction ratio is often impossible. In such cases, the branches are reduced to be closest to the reduction ratio.

As described in Sect. 2.3, when a melody is synthesized by a join operation, the branches of the time-span tree may overlap at the same time. For example, if the branches and notes overlap at the same time due to the join operation of melody A and B, the note with the lower reduction ratio is left. If both reduction ratios are 50%, the note of A is left.

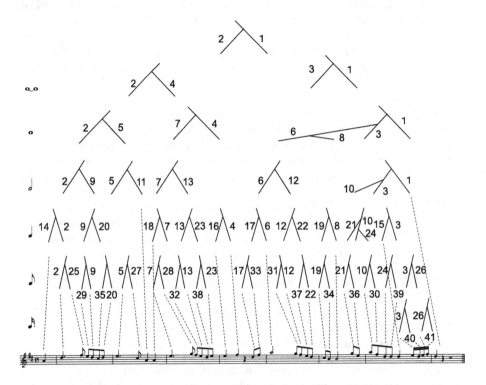

Fig. 5. Time-span tree leveled by duration of time span.

4.2   Automatic Time-Span Tree Analysis by Deep Learning

The melody is leveled by the duration of the time span, then it is reduced one note at a time from the lowest level. In the following explanation, when there is a branch, the child branch is called a "sub-branch," and the parent branch is called the "main branch". Since the ground truth data of the time-span tree are monophonic, the target is monophony in this paper.

In the time-span tree leveled by the duration of time span, the level of the main branch is always higher than that of a sub-branch. Therefore, if the reduction is carried out in order from the lowest level, the reduction process will proceed without contradiction. It is also important that the reduction process be simple when learning stepwise reduction with a DNN.

Previous time-span tree analyzers (ATTA [2] and σGTTMIII [6]) had low performance because they analyzed in a bottom-up manner using only local information. In contrast, we propose using the entire note sequence before and after step-wise reduction for learning the DNN.

When a recurrent neural network (RNN) [14] or long short-term memory (LSTM) [10] is used as the DNN, the DNN can learn using note sequence, but when a long note sequence is input, the DNN forgets the beginning of it, thus it cannot make use of all the information of the note sequence.

Seq2Seq [15] and Transformer [16] can learn and predict using the information of the entire note sequence. The difference between Seq2Seq and Transformer is the representation of position in the note sequence: Seq2seq uses relative positions by sequentially inputting sequence data into the RNN, while Transformer has an independent additional layer of position information and uses the absolute position.

Therefore, if the absolute position is important for stepwise time-span reduction, Transformer will have high performance, and if the relative position is important, Seq2Seq will have high performance. We evaluated which of the two has the higher performance, as described in Sect. 5.2.

5   Experiment and Results

As a verification of the usefulness of our proposed time-span tree leveled by the duration of time span, we conducted an experiment to confirm whether melodic morphing and time-span tree analysis can be carried out automatically.

5.1   Automating Melodic Morphing by Prioritization of Branches

After acquiring the time-span tree, there was no arbitrariness in the prioritization of the branches, partial reduction, and combination of melodies. Therefore, when the reduction ratio was determined, the morphed melody could be deterministically obtained. In Fig. 6, the notes included in melody A are displayed with stems up, and those included in melody B are displayed with stems down.

5.2   Comparison of Seq2Seq and Transformer in Stepwise Time-Span Reduction

Learning data and evaluation data were created from MusicXML, which are score data, and time-spanXML, which is the ground truth of a time-span tree by the following procedure. The proposed method was first used to reduce (in a stepwise manner) each of the 300 melodies by using the time-span tree, and data before and after the reduction were generated.

Fig. 6. Results of automatic morphing.

Next, the notes in the melodies were made into a one-character string with the pitch and duration concatenated. The pitch was represented as 12 types: C, C#, D, D#, E, F, F#, G, G#, A, A#, and B (excluding octave information). A key that was a major or minor key was then changed to C major or A minor. The duration was represented by multiplying the duration elements of MusicXML by 4. By multi-plying by 4, the duration of most notes became an integer, but since there were melodies containing only a few triplets, quintuplets, sextuplets, and septuplets, the duration was rounded up to an integer. Then, a space was inserted between the strings to represent notes. Finally, in the note sequence after the reduction, "r" was inserted at the position of the reduced note so that we would know which note had been reduced.

The Seq2Seq and Transformer models were both trained with 7362 stepwise time-span-reduction training data sets generated from 270 songs from a GTTM database consisting of 300 pieces, and 849 evaluating data sets were generated from the remaining 30 pieces. Table 1 shows the accuracy of matching the evaluation data and prediction data after 20,000 epochs of training. We can see that Transformer outperformed Seq2Seq in stepwise time-span reduction. Learning was carried out using Nvidia Quadro RTX5000 for laptops [13], and the learning time of Seq2Seq was six days, which is much longer than the seven hours taken by Transformer.

Table 1. Comparison of Seq2Seq and Transformer models.

	Seq2Seq	Transformer
Accuracy	0.90	0.99

6 Conclusion

We proposed the introduction of time-span tree leveled by the duration of time span to problems that are difficult to automate due to the lack of prioritization of time-span tree branches. Experimental results confirmed that melodic morphing and time span analysis based on deep learning can be automated.

We plan to develop various applications and content by using a time-span tree. Our morphing method has appeared in the smart-phone applications of Melody Slot Machine [9], which has a huge number of downloads. By using an automated morphing system, it is possible to build a system that facilitates the addition of content on Melody Slot Machine.

Acknowledgements. This work was supported by JSPS KAKENHI Grant number 21H03572.

References

1. Amari, S., Ozeki, T., Karakida, R., Yoshida, Y., Okada, M.: Dynamics of learning in MLP: natural gradient and singularity revisited. Neural Comput. **30**(1), 1–33 (2018)
2. Hamanaka, M., Hirata, K., Tojo, S.: ATTA: automatic time-span tree analyzer based on extended GTTM. In: Proceedings of the 6th International Conference on Music Information Retrieval Conference (ISMIR 2005), pp. 358–365 (2005)
3. Hamanaka, M., Hirata, K., Tojo, S.: Melody morphing method based on GTTM. In: Proceedings of International Computer Music Conference (ICMC 2008), pp. 155–158 (2008)
4. Hamanaka, M., Hirata, K., Tojo, S.: Melody extrapolation in GTTM approach. In: Proceedings of International Computer Music Conference (ICMC 2009), pp. 89–92 (2009)
5. Hamanaka, M., Hirata, K., Tojo, S.: Musical structural analysis database based on GTTM. In: Proceedings of the 15th International Conference on Music Information Retrieval Conference (ISMIR 2014), pp. 107–112 (2014)
6. Hamanaka, M., Hirata, K., Tojo, S.: σGTTM III: learning-based time-span tree generator based on PCFG. In: Proceedings of International Symposium on Computer Music Multidisciplinary Research (CMMR 2015), pp. 387–404 (2015)
7. Hamanaka, M., Hirata, K., Tojo, S.: deepGTTM-I: local boundaries analyzer based on deep learning technique. In: Proceedings of International Symposium on Computer Music Multidisciplinary Research (CMMR 2016), pp. 8–20 (2016)
8. Hamanaka, M., Hirata, K., Tojo, S.: deepGTTM-II: automatic generation of metrical structure based on deep learning technique. In: Proceedings of the 13th Sound and Music Conference (SMC 2016), pp. 221–249 (2016)

9. Hamanaka, M.: Melody Slot Machine. https://gttm.jp/hamanaka/en/melodyslotm achine/. Accessed 25 Oct 2022

10. Hochreiter, S., Schmidhuber, J.: Long short-term memory. Neural Comput. **9**(8), 1735–1780 (1997)

11. Lerdahl, F., Jackendoff, R.: A Generative Theory of Tonal Music. The MIT Press, Cambridge (1985)

12. Marsden, A., Tojo, S., Hirata, K.: No longer 'somewhat arbitrary': calculating salience in GTTM-style reduction. In: Proceedings of the 5th International Conference on Digital Libraries for Musicology (DLfM 2018), pp. 26–33 (2018)

13. Nvidia: Quadro for laptops. https://www.nvidia.com/en-us/design-visualization/quadro-in-laptops/. Accessed 25 Oct 2022

14. Pineda, J.F.: Generalization of back-propagation to recurrent neural networks. Phys. Rev. Lett. **19**(59), 2229–2232 (1987)

15. Sutskever, I., Vinyals, O., Le, V.Q.: Sequence to sequence learning with neural networks. In: Advances in Neural Information Processing Systems, vol. 27, pp. 3104–3112 (2014)

16. Vaswani, A., et al.: Attention is all you need. In: Proceedings of the 31st Conference on Neural Information Processing Systems (NIPS 2017), vol. 30, pp. 6000–6010 (2017)

Evaluating AI as an Assisting Tool to Create Electronic Dance Music

Niklas Bohm, Christian M. Fischer[✉], and Manuel Richardt

Hochschule Fulda/Academy of Applied Sciences, Leipziger Str. 123, 36037 Fulda, Germany
christian.fischer@ai.hs-fulda.de

Abstract. The demands on creatives to complete a jingle or a piece of music even under time pressure are growing. This paper analyzes Google's Magenta Studio to identify its possibilities for a more effective production of electronic dance music *(EDM)*, especially in terms of time, without a loss of subjective listening pleasure. For this purpose, the process of EDM music production, which includes artificial intelligence, was analyzed. With a subsequent survey, it was determined whether the music pieces produced in this way differ in their subjective listening pleasure and which of the approaches can be recommended for further production.

Keywords: Google Magenta Studio · Electronic Dance Music · AI · Music Production

1 Introduction

Artificial intelligence is used more and more in everyday life and therefore discussed controversially in everyday media. Its forms of application and areas of use are diverse. In this text AI is understood as a digital tool to support humans in their creative tasks. However, when one reads about AI in general, some authors find it obviously still difficult to think of AI in connection with creative tasks [6]. There are reservations of creative processes being mapped by a computer [8]. Music is one such creative construct. it is capable of triggering feelings in people and amplifying or even influencing moods. Interestingly, most listeners don't notice how much music composition in popular music is already influenced by AI and that nowadays many artists have already introduced AI into their creative production workflow [3]. AI can be applied in many areas of music, even in composing music itself. Still, it is not a question about whether AI will make the human composer obsolete, but how creative people use AI in their creative process [9]. Therefore, the aim of this work is to find out how the use of AI can affect the efficiency of the music production process and whether it has an influence on how the music is perceived. The focus was efficiency in time and to figure in which steps within the production, in the case of Electronic Dance Music (EDM), an AI can be particularly helpful.

M. Aramaki et al. (Eds.): CMMR 2021, LNCS 13770, pp. 59–65, 2023.
https://doi.org/10.1007/978-3-031-35382-6_6

2 Related Work

There is an area of application for artificial intelligence in almost every field. Among others, also in the creative areas of music and art. Because AI has so many forms, researchers divide it into the subfields of automation, machine learning, neural networks, and deep learning [2]. A common form of neural network is the Convolutional Neural Network (CNNs). In this paper, and the Magenta project respectively, Recurrent Neural Networks (RNNs) and the Long Short-Term Memory Network (LSTM), a type of RNN, are central [11].

While CNNs tend to be hierarchical, RNNs operate more sequentially [1]. Therefore, CNNs are often used for classification tasks such as text recognition, whereas RNNs are more flexible and are therefore increasingly used for language processing and creative tasks such as music generation [11]. The project "Magenta", placed under Open Source by Google is a project which explores machine learning in a creative context. Magenta Studio, basically a collection of music plugins, uses RNN and LSTM networks. To understand how a computer can utilize this to make music, it is important to take a closer look at these RNNs. An RNN is a class of neural networks used to model sequence data. In an RNN, the connections between artificial neurons form a circuit. For many applications such as speech and text, outputs can depend on previous inputs and outputs. The key concept of RNNs is to use sequential information. RNNs are thus given a "memory" in the form of the information and data that have been processed so far [1]. Related to the music context in this paper, this means that the neural network can, e.g., recognize which notes it has generated in previous measures and is able to adjust the next measure to sound coherent. The size of the "memory" determines how many notes, or even bars the neural network can look back. The goal is to have the generated sounds or musical sequences which contain repetition, as repetition is one core feature in music.

3 Environment Setup and AI-Created Music

Magenta is the name of several research projects by Google. The program Magenta Studio serves as AI support for digital music producers, as a standalone application or when used as a Plugin e.g., with the Digital Audio Workstation Ableton Live. Magenta has five different models, using different neural network types. In this study LSTM networks, a type of RNN, are used. An example of an LSTM network is the DrumsRNN model. Another example is the MelodyRNN model, which has the same structure but is programmed for melody generation [4]. Each model has different configurations that set the way in which it encodes the input data. For example, the DrumsRNN model has a one drum configuration, which stores a drum sequence in a class, and a drum kit configuration, which splits a drum sequence into nine different instruments (kick, clap, hi-hat, etc.) and adjusts the attention length [4]. Magenta provides many pre-trained models for download on its site. In this project, the models "DrumsRNN", "MelodyRNN" and "PolyphonyRNN" were used.

To structure the process of digital music production and to make the influence of AI in this process more comprehensible, we divided it into three levels. The higher the level, the less human involvement in the production process.

Level 1 - Inspiration: In this stage, the human producer is supported or inspired by the AI. For example: AI generated melodies are listened to. Being inspired, the human producer composes a new melody which contains no or hardly any parts of the original AI melody.

Level 2 - AI Assistance/Co-production: In AI assistance, one gets support from an AI in the creative process. Here, bigger parts of AI-generated music can be incorporated into the composition. The AI can be used to help, e.g., by suggesting subsequent notes. Since the AI and human are both working on the same piece, they can both inspire each other. An example of this would be Magenta's Continue function, where the producer passes a MIDI sequence to the program and then new sequences are created inspired by the input sequence. Conversely, using Magenta's Generate function, the AI would generate a melody and it would then be modified by the producer. The AI could make suggestions to improve the music and, in the best case, make it more versatile.

Level 3 - Automation: In automation, an AI generates new music on its own without input. The producer has no influence on the results. One of many examples of autonomous music generation would be Magenta's Generate function [10]. One other example is AIVA, which stands for Artificial Intelligence Virtual Artist. AIVA has already released self-produced albums in the EDM genre. It was created in early 2016 and has been under constant development ever since [7].

4 Test Structure and Efficiency Evaluation

4.1 Structure

First three simple EDM tracks, according to the three stages, each consisting of the three main components bass, chords, and melody, were composed. For the later evaluation, some measurement data had to be collected. Thus, the production duration and effort were measured based on mouse movement, mouse clicks and key usage, utilizing the free software Mousotron (Win; version 12.1; Black Sun Software 2017). In order not to confuse the participants of the later survey by different drums and drum patterns in the songs, an identical one was adopted here for all. For the music production itself the Digital Audio Workstation Studio FL (Win; version 20.8; Image-Line Software; 2020) was used.

One aim was to verify whether the introduction of AI into the production process is suitable for speeding up and simplifying music production. For this purpose, the individual steps of the production were calculated, and all mouse clicks made and the "mouse distance" were measured as the second and third measured values.

The evaluation (collecting data of mouse and keyboard usage) was carried out through the different phases to determine and track the highest increase in efficiency on specific production phases and production steps. In this way, phases for which AI is particularly suitable can be identified.

4.2 Evaluation

Preparation phase (Table 1): In the preparation phase, human production performed best. Preparation took just under a minute, with both AI automation and AI assistance at around three minutes.

Composition phase (Table 2): In the composition phase, the tendency of the first phase changes. Here, human production took by far the longest at around nine minutes. With the help of AI assistance and AI automation, up to 85% of the time used could be saved.

Editing phase 1 (Table 3, without mixing and sound design): In this phase, it is noticeable that the AI assistance has particularly high values. To adjust an AI given melody to one's own desires might take time. The duration of the production phase was therefore about four to five times longer for the AI assistance than for the other two production types.

Table 1. Measurements in Preperation Phase

	Duration	Mouse clicks	M. distance	Keystrokes
H. Production	01:12	22	3,51	24
Automation	03:20	64	18,56	76
AI Assistance	02:52	53	15,45	57

(Duration in mm:ss, mouse distance in cm)

Table 2. Measurements in Composition Phase

	Duration	Mouse clicks	M. distance	Keystrokes
H. Production	09:07	203	20,57	239
Automation	01:43	16	1,41	12
AI Assistance	01:23	16	1,56	14

(Duration in mm:ss, mouse distance in cm)

Table 3. Measurements in Editing 1

	Duration	Mouse clicks	M. distance	Keystrokes
H. Production	02:34	41	5,87	12
Automation	03:02	36	7,19	95
AI Assistance	13:01	227	30,28	433

(Duration in mm:ss, mouse distance in cm)

Editing phase 2 (Table 4, mixing and sound design): Great inspiration can come from sound design, as melodies can also sound very different depending on the sound. Since a producer usually creates a melody after the sound design, this phase also takes about twice as long as the other production types. With the support of AI, one comes to a time

Table 4. Measurements in Editing 2

	Duration	Mouse clicks	M. distance	Keystrokes
H. Production	07:48	141	21,34	78
Automation	03:47	67	12,17	67
AI Assistance	02:34	40	8,41	52

(Duration in mm:ss, mouse distance in cm)

saving of about 65% here. The AI assistance has the lowest effort in this phase, but this could change if the experiment is performed multiple times.

Human production took the longest in terms of total production time. However, this is closely followed by AI assistance. The use of AI automation reduced the duration of production by 40%. For composition only (without processing phase 2), there was even a 42% reduction. AI assistance took about 23% longer than a human production in the pure composition process.

5 Listening Evaluation

The second aim of this study was to find out how listeners like the generated songs and whether they can tell the difference between an AI-generated and a human production. To investigate these questions, 50 participants with different musical backgrounds and individual tastes (in balanced proportions) were asked to do an online questionnaire stating their opinions about the three generated songs.

After general questions (age, gender, knowledge/involvement in music and knowledge of EDM), the participants listened to the songs and were asked to rate the songs based on the following eight evaluation criteria.: Creativity, Recognition Value, Arrangement (of a song), Cohesiveness, Variety of Tones, Energy, Danceability, and Emotion. Through a study conducted by the University of California Irvine, these criteria were identified as crucial. The study found that songs are especially popular when they are more upbeat and danceable than other songs [7]. In addition, dynamics and the mood of the listeners play a role [7]. Other criteria such as the vocals or the genre are not considered in this paper it focuses exclusively on instrumental EDM music.

The participants could rate the different criteria from 1 to 5 points. One meaning low and five meaning high. All points from all 50 participants that were given for one song were added to an overall score for that song. (In the original questionnaire, there were more questions and tasks for the participants, for instance regarding AI generated melodies, which however did not find their way into this paper, as this would have gone beyond the scope.)

Song 1 - Automation: The first song was generated by the AI alone. The creativity of the song was rated an average of 3. The creativity is therefore exactly in the middle of the scale. The recognition score averaged 2.7 points, so it is in the bottom 50%. The arrangement was rated at 2.76 points on the scale. For the AI-generated song, energy got the highest score with an average of 3.8 points on the scale. This was followed by danceability with 3.4 points and cohesiveness with 3.22. Emotion was rated the worst with a mean of 2.62 points. Overall, Song 1 collected 1228 points in all criteria by all participants and thus achieved an average value of 3.08 points on the scale.

Song 2 - Human production: The second song was produced by humans. The arrangement scored best with an average of 3.8 points on the scale. This was followed by cohesiveness with 3.76 points and danceability with 3.65 points. Emotion was again rated the worst with a mean of 3.14 points. Overall, the song was rated with 1365 points and achieved an average value of 3.49 points on the scale.

Song 3 - AI assistance: The third song was produced in collaboration between a human and an AI. Creativity received the highest score here, with an average of 3.82 points on the scale. This is followed by energy with 3.66 points and recognition with 3.5 points. Emotion was again rated the lowest with a mean score of 2.98 points. Overall, the song was rated with 1368 points and achieved an average value of 3.42 points on the scale.

In comparison, the human-produced song, and the AI-human collaboration both scored about the same. The AI-generated song scored 1228 points, about 10% worse than the other songs (see Table 2). Creativity is rated the highest for the AI-assisted production, and the recognition value is also almost 30% higher. The human production was considered less creative, but the arrangement was easy for the listener to understand, and the song seemed cohesive. In the AI production, the rhythmic criteria such as danceability and energy stood out (Table 5).

Table 5. Results of Questionnaire

Song	Cr	ReVa	AoT	Co	VoT	En	Da	Emo
1	3	2.7	2.76	3.22	3.19	3.8	3.4	2.47
2	3.39	3.43	3.8	3.76	3.27	3.43	3.65	3.14
3	3.82	3.58	3.56	3.39	3.37	3.66	3.37	2.98

6 Summary and Conclusion

The experiment was designed to test whether the use of AI in digital music production can increase the time efficiency. In the experiment, three songs were produced with the same prerequisites, but each in a different production mode. Since AI can be used to different degrees in music production, three levels were developed: AI inspiration, AI assistance, and AI automation. As a result, it was expected that the producer will have significant savings in time and effort by using AI. However, some of the results differed from the assumptions. A digital music production was divided into four phases. The experiment showed that the use of AI in production increased efficiency especially in the composition phase and the second editing phase. There were no significant differences in the overall production ratio in the preparation phase, but this phase was slightly faster with human production. Overall, the AI automation was convincing with an efficiency increase of 41% on average. AI assistance decreased production efficiency by about 20% on average.

The created songs from the experiment were listened to, rated, and evaluated by 50 people. The result of the survey was that the computer-generated song was rated about 10% less, than the other two songs. It is concluded that although an AI can write songs and melodies on its own, they are perceived not as melodic and creative as productions that involved a human. Since AI assistance was rated 30% better in terms of melodic criteria, it can be stated that the introduction of AI into the production process can ex-ceed these very limits.

Thus, for the further development of AI-assisted programs for music production, it is important to develop AIs that see a song as a whole and when the "memory" (e.g., in LSTM) is large enough to remember a theme or idea in a song and repeat it at the right.

Evaluating AI as an assisting tool to create Electronic Dance Music 7.

places. For EDM producers, it should be noted that the introduction of AI as a tool into the right phase of the production process has many positive aspects such as saving time and effort and supporting the creative process of composing melodies.

References

1. Bisharad, D., Laskar, R.H.: Music genre recognition using convolutional recurrent neural network architecture. Expert Syst. **36**(4), e12429 (2019)
2. Dargan, S., Kumar, M., Ayyagari, M.R., Kumar, G.: A survey of deep learning and its applications: a new paradigm to machine learning. Arch. Comput. Meth. Eng. **27**(4), 1071–1092 (2020)
3. Deahl, D.: How AI-generated music is changing how hits are made. The Verge (2018). https://www.theverge.com/2018/8/31/17777008/artificial-intelligence-taryn-southern-amper-music. Accessed 15 Oct 2022
4. DuBreuil, A.: Hands-on Music Generation with Magenta (E-Book). Explore the Role of Deep Learning in Music Generation and Assisted Music Composition. Packt, Birmingham (2020)
5. Hewahi, N., AlSaigal, S., AlJanahi, S.: Generation of music pieces using machine learning: long short-term memory neural networks approach. Arab J. Basic Appl. Sci. **26**(1), 397–413 (2019)
6. Holeman, R.: Why A.I. Can't Replace Human Creativity. Modus Medium (2019). https://modus.medium.com/when-it-comes-to-creativity-is-it-game-over-for-humans-ef12907eb30d. Accessed 15 Oct 2022
7. Interiano, M., Kazemi, K., Wang, L., Yang, J., Yu, Z., Komarova, N.L.: Musical trends and predictability of success in contemporary songs in and out of the top charts. Royal Soc. Open Sci. **5**(5), 171274 (2018)
8. Müller, V.E.: Risks of Artificial Intelligence. In: Vincent, C., Müller (Hg.). Risks of Artificial Intelligence, pp. 1–8. CRC Press, Boca Raton, FL (2020)
9. Pennington, A.: Artificial Intelligence gets creative. IBC (2018). https://www.ibc.org/how-ai-is-being-used-to-boost-the-creative-process/2937.article. Accessed 15 Oct 2022
10. Roberts, A., et al.: Magenta Studio: Augmenting Creativity with Deep Learning in Ableton Live (2019)
11. Yin, W., Kann, K., Yu, M., Schütze, H.: Comparative Study of CNN and RNN for Natural Language Processing (2017)
12. Mousotron. https://mousotron.de.softonic.com. Accessed 15 Oct 2022
13. StudioFL. https://www.flstudioshop.de/fl-studio-/. Accessed 15 Oct 2022

Interactive Systems for Music

Suiview: A Web-Based Application that Enables Users to Practice Wind Instrument Performance

Misato Watanabe[✉], Yosuke Onoue, Aiko Uemura, and Tetsuro Kitahara

Nihon University, Tokyo, Japan
chmi19013@g.nihon-u.ac.jp,
{onoue.yousuke,uemura.aiko,kitahara.tetsurou}@nihon-u.ac.jp

Abstract. This paper presents a web-based application that enables users to check the stability of the pitches, intensities, and timbres of the sounds they play. Amateur musicians have opportunities to play wind instruments, at a brass-band club at school. To make sounds with the *stable* pitches, intensities, and timbres, players have to carefully control the shapes of their mouth and lips, the strength of the breath, and their vibration. But this is difficult for most amateur musicians, who rely on expert players to check whether they are appropriate and advise them how to improve them. To solve this problem, we have been developing a web-based application to enable amateur musicians to check whether the pitches, intensities, and timbres of their sounds are stable without help from an expert player (https://suiview.vdslab.jp/). In this paper, we describe its basic system design, the current implementation, and preliminary results of its trial use.

Keywords: Wind instrument · Musical practice · Stability · Web application

1 Introduction

Wind instruments are popular among amateur musicians. They are indispensable in brass-band clubs at junior high school and/or high school, and many people enjoy playing a wind instrument as a hobby. However, playing a wind instrument is not easy. To produce sounds with *stable* pitches, intensities, and timbres, players have to carefully control the shapes of their mouth and lips, the strength of the breath, and their vibration.

One problem in learning a wind instrument is a lack of appropriate instructors. In the case of the above-mentioned brass-band clubs at school, the responsible teacher at the club might not be a wind instrument expert. At such clubs, it is often common for novice-level players to teach freshman players. Also, there are fewer music schools that teach wind instruments than the piano.

Wind instrument performances have been investigated from different points of view such as acoustic, psychological, and physiological ones. Brown [1] investigated acoustic features for automatic identification of woodwind instrument sounds. Hirano et al. [3] analyzed muscular activity and related skin movement during French horn performances. Micheal [5] examined the effects of self-listening and self-evaluation in the context of woodwind and/or brass practice by junior high school instrumentalists, and found that self-evaluation was important for improving the instrument.

© Springer Nature Switzerland AG 2023
M. Aramaki et al. (Eds.): CMMR 2021, LNCS 13770, pp. 69–75, 2023.
https://doi.org/10.1007/978-3-031-35382-6_7

More recently, there have been attempts to develop systems that allow users to easily understand how their performances are good from visual feedback or computational assessment. Pati et al. [7] applied deep neural networks to automatic assessment of student musical performances. Giraldo et al. [2] developed a system that analyzes sound quality of violin performances and provides visual feedback to users in real time. Knight et al. [4] developed a visual feedback system of musical ensemble focusing on phrase articulation and dynamics. Morishita et al. [6] developed a system that gives novice practitioners (especially children) visual feedback of acoustic features in long-tone training of wind instruments. These systems have been aiming at a goal close to ours, but most of them are not designed to enable anyone to easily check his/her performances on his/her smartphone and/or tablet.

In this paper, we present a web-based application for practicing playing wind instruments by themselves. The important is to give users objective feedback. Because its target users are novice players, we consider that sounds should be stable, in other words, sounds should keep a close pitch, intensity, and timbre from the beginning to the end. Our app. analyzes the pitch, intensity, and timbre of sounds recorded on the app, evaluates their stability, and gives visual feedback to the user. It also provides a function that enables the user's teacher to give comments to the recorded sounds.

2 Basic Design and Functions

Our app aims to provide wind instrument practicers with useful information about the sounds performed by them. For novice-level players, as discussed in the Introduction, acquiring skills for sounding stably is important. Therefore, one of the important functions of our app. is therefore to visualize the stability of the acoustic characteristics (i.e., pitches, intensities, and timbres) of the sounds performed by the user.

Recognizing how well the user is incrementally improving such stability day by day is also important. Therefore, we implement a function for visualizing recording-by-recording variations in the stability of the pitches, intensities, and timbres as well as visualizing the acoustic characteristics of each recording.

Also, we implement a *teacher-to-student comment* function. Although objective visualization is useful for novice players, subjective evaluation and comments by their teacher is also important. By linking a teacher-mode user to student-mode users, the teacher-mode users can listen to the recordings of the linked student-mode users and give them his/her evaluations and comments.

2.1 Recording

Once the user opens and logs into our app., he/she can select what to play from a *long tone*, a *scale*, and an *arpeggio* (Fig. 1). The scores displayed are shown in Fig. 2. After selecting one from these three scores, the user starts recording his/her performance with a sampling rate of 48 kHz (Fig. 3). Recorded sounds are automatically stored on our web server with some metadata such as the user ID, and the recording date (Fig. 4).

Fig. 1. Screen for selecting what to play

(a) Score for a long tone

(b) Score for a scale

(c) Score for an arpeggio

Fig. 2. Three scores currently supported by our app.

2.2 Visualizing the Acoustic Characteristics

Once a recording is stored on the webserver, its acoustic analysis starts. The fundamental frequency (F0), amplitude, and spectral roll-off are extracted with a 512-point shift from the recorded sound. We use Librosa (https://librosa.org/) for extracting these features. Next, these features are plotted on the screen, as shown in Fig. 5(a) to (c). Features for multiple sounds can be plotted on the same screen, as shown in Fig. 5(d).

2.3 Visualizing the Recording-by-Recording Variations in the Stability

The stability of the pitch (F0), intensity (amplitude), and timbre (spectral roll-off) is calculated for each recording. The stability is defined based on the temporal standard deviation of each feature. Let $\sigma_{F0}, \sigma_{Amp}, \sigma_{Sp}$ represent the temporal standard deviations for the F0, amplitude, and spectral roll-off, respectively. Then, their stability s_i

Fig. 3. Screen for recording a sound

Fig. 4. Example of analysis results (A: self assessment, B: stability scores, C: chart)

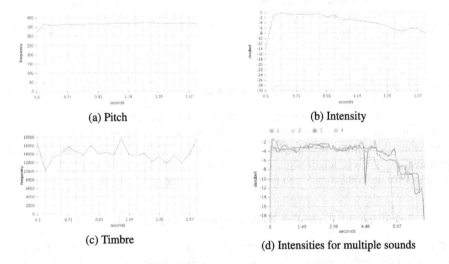

(a) Pitch

(b) Intensity

(c) Timbre

(d) Intensities for multiple sounds

Fig. 5. Examples of visualization of acoustic features of recorded sounds

$(i \in \{F0, Amp, Sp\})$ is defined as $s_i = 100 \exp(-\sigma_i/a_i)$, where a_i are pre-defined constants ($a_{F0} = 4, a_{Amp} = 70, a_{Sp} = 1500$). Thus s_i has a value between 0 to 100.

The stability is visualized in two ways to enable the user to check the stability for multiple recordings at a glance (Fig. 6). One is a stacked bar chart that represents the stability of each of the pitch, intensity, and timbre (Fig. 6(a)). The other is a line chart that represents overall stability scores (Fig. 6(b)).

2.4   Teacher-to-Student Comment

Logging in with the teacher mode, the user can listen to sounds recorded by the linked student-mode users and check the visualization of their acoustic features and stability scores. Also, using the teacher-mode, the user can write comments. The comments are automatically sent to the corresponding student-mode user (Fig. 7).

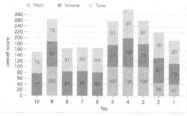

(a) Stacked bar chart (for each stability)

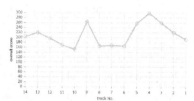

(b) Line chart (for total stability score)

Fig. 6. Examples of visualization of Recording-by-recording stability variations

Fig. 7. Screen for the teacher mode

3   Trial Use

Three participants used our app for a preliminary evaluation of the effectiveness of the app. Out of the three participants, one (P 1) was an active player with an intermediate-to-advanced level while the other two (P 2 and P 3) were novices, though they had experience in playing instruments in the past.

Logging in with the student mode, the participants played a long tone, a scale, and an arpeggio on the clarinet several times and recorded them on our app. They saw the visualization of their sounds made by our app. and were asked to answer the following questions on a four-level scale (4: agree, 1: disagree):

Q1 Do you think this app helps you produce stable sounds?
Q2 Did you get useful information from the visualization?
Q3 Are the stability scores close enough to your own impression?

Table 1. Results of the preliminary questionnaire (1 to 4)

	P 1	P 2	P 3
[Q1] Do you think this app helps you produce stable sounds?	3	4	3
[Q2] Did you get useful information from the visualization?	2	4	4
[Q3] Are the stability scores close enough to your own impression?	2	4	4

The results, listed in Table 1, imply that the participants comparatively highly evaluated our app. In fact, the two novice-level participants gave us comments such as:

- By listening alone, it was difficult to find what to improve to produce stable sounds.
- With graphical visualization, novice-level players could find what to improve.
- Line charts were easy to grasp which were good and which were not.

On the other hand, one participant answered that he/she could not understand what each graph means. More intuitive visualization should be explored. We also received an opinion that they wanted to see the analysis for sounds given by professional players.

4   Conclusion

In this paper, we presented a web-based application that enables users to recognize the stability of wind instrument sounds played by them by visualizing their acoustic features and stability scores. Once the user records his/her wind instrument sounds on the app, their acoustic features including the pitches, intensities, and timbres are analyzed as well as their stability is evaluated. Three participants in a preliminary experiment gave us comments that the visualization was useful to produce stable sounds.

Although we focused on the stability of pitches, intensities, and timbres, more complex expressions such as detailed dynamics would be important for more advanced players. We will extend the app to support such advanced level players' practice as well as systematic evaluation of our app.

Acknowledgments. This research was supported by JSPS Kakenhi Nos. JP-19K12288 and JP-20K19947.

References

1. Brown, J., Houix, O., McAdams, S.: Feature dependence in the automatic identification of musical woodwind instruments. J. Acoust. Soc. Am. **3**(109), 1064–1072 (2001)
2. Giraldo, S., Ramirez, R., Waddell, G., Williamon, A.: A real-time feedback learning tool to visualize sound quality in violin performances. In: Proceedings of MML 2017, pp. 19–24 (2017)
3. Hirano, T., Kudo, K., Ohtsuki, T., Kinoshita, H.: Feature dependence in the automatic identification of musical woodwind instruments. Mot. Control **3**(17), 256–272 (2013)
4. Knight, T., Bouillot, N., Cooperstock, J.: Visualization feedback for musical ensemble practice: a case study on phrase articulation and dynamics. In: Proceedings of VDA 2012 (2012)
5. Michael, P.: The effects of modeling, self-evaluation, and self-listening on junior high instrumentalists' music performance and practice attitude. SAGE J. **4**(49), 307–322 (2001)
6. Morishita, T., Oguchi, H., Kunimune, H., Kirihara, A., Honma, Y.: Development of a support system for beginners to practice long-tones in school wind instruments. Kyoiku Jissen Kenkyu, Shunshu University Higher Education System Center (in Japanese) (2018)
7. Pati, K., Gururani, S., Lerch, A.: Assessment of student music performances using deep neural networks. Appl. Sci. **8**(4), 507 (2018)

Continuous Parameter Control Using an On/Off Sensor in the Augmented Handheld Triangle

Marcio Albano H. Ferreira[1(✉)] and Tiago F. Tavares[2]

[1] School of Electric and Computer Engineering, University of Campinas (UNICAMP),
Campinas, Brazil
marcio.ahf@gmail.com
[2] INSPER, São Paulo, Brazil

Abstract. In this work, we present Triaume, an augmented musical percussion instrument based on the triangle. The augmentation proposal for this instrument is based on a capacitive thumb sensor, that allows controlling digital musical devices and at the same time, preserves the original instrument idiomatic inside the context in which it is inserted. Triaume's interaction proposals were built upon Brazilian music genres idiomatic, such as Forró, Xote, and Baião. The instrument invasiveness is further reduced through the use of an external device (an application running on a smartphone) for emulating faders related to sound parameter configuration. At first, we used the sensor as an on/off button able to trigger preprogrammed percussion samples, which can be synchronized with the triangle's acoustic sounds. This mechanism can be adjusted for triggering on pressing or releasing the sensor. Next, we convert the digital signals acquired by the sensor to continuous values by the on/off signal filtering. Such signal rectification and filtering system allows gradual change of continuous sound synthesis parameters, dealing with the on/off signal low robustness, turning it into a more controlled signal. Triaume can be inserted in the contexts of traditional and avant-garde music, also motivating further studies for applying the mechanism used on it in other percussion instruments.

Keywords: Triangle · Capacitive sensor · Pulse Width Modulation (PWM) · Augmented instrument · Brazilian music

1   Introduction

Traditional music instruments can be augmented with electronic sensors, which can acquire signals to control devices like synthesizers and effect processors. These sensors usually exploit the so-called spare bandwidth [4], that is, movements or limbs that are not used in the traditional playing techniques and, therefore, can be used for other purposes. Augmented instruments can provide new expressive possibilities when compared to their traditional counterparts.

This work presents an augmentation proposal for the triangle, a handheld non-pitched percussion instrument traditionally used in several regional Brazilian music genres such as Forró, Xote, and Baião [6]. The acoustic triangle is usually held with

M. Aramaki et al. (Eds.): CMMR 2021, LNCS 13770, pp. 76–93, 2023.
https://doi.org/10.1007/978-3-031-35382-6_8

one hand using the index finger and played with the other hand using a metal mallet. The instrument's sound can be damped by closing the holding hand's palm around the triangle's side.

Our augmentation proposal uses a single capacitive sensor [10–13,17,25] placed on the instrument's upper corner. The sensor is isolated from the instrument's body and is activated with the holding hand's thumb independently of the damping or mallet striking actions. This placement allows an interplay between the traditional techniques and the augmented possibilities.

This minimalistic augmentation barely impacts the use of the traditional techniques but brings other challenges of its own. The first one is to allow the musician to configure the instrument's parameters during performance without bringing a computer to the stage. We mitigate this problem using a smartphone, which provides all necessary faders for this configuration. The second challenge is to provide a diversity of interactions that can be creatively explored.

To tackle this challenge, we use mapping strategies inspired in the common (even if not traditional) technique of playing other instruments, such as hi-hats (triggered with a pedal), or sets of cowbells or carillons [7,20], together with the triangle in Brazilian regional music. In our proposal, we investigate the possibilities of triggering events on sensor touch or on sensor release, inspired by the damp (close hand) and release (open hand) gestures typically used in Forró music. They can be used to play virtual instruments, in special percussive sounds, allowing the musician to play with more instrumental layers.

Additional control possibilities can arise from encoding the sensor information through time [19]. In our proposal, we use a low-pass filtering technique to convert a sequence of on/off acquisitions to a continuous control signal, similarly to a Pulse Width Modulation motor control [16,23]. This allows using the capacitive sensor as an interactive fader that can be controlled using rhythm.

2   Instrument Design

The triangle augmentation consists of three blocks, as shown in Fig. 1. The first is Triaume itself, which is a regular acoustic triangle with an attached capacitive sensor and an ESP32 microcontroller [1]. The second is a smartphone that runs a MobMuPlat [15] patch and controls the digital configurations. Both of these blocks send Open Sound Control (OSC) [9] packets to the third one, a computer that executes sound synthesis and control in a Pure data (Pd) patch [18]. Each of these blocks is discussed next.

2.1   Triaume Body

The augmented triangle has one single sensor, which is a capacitive sensor attached to the triangle's upper corner. As shown in Fig. 2, the sensor is isolated from the instrument's body using insulating tape. A distance was kept between the insulated tape covered area and the region that is normally stroke by the triangle mallet when applying techniques used in the context of Brazilian music. Mounting the sensor close to the triangle's tip reduces the sensor's impact on the sound's quality.

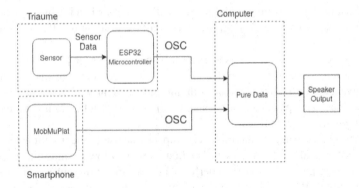

Fig. 1. System overview. The computer receives OSC packets both from the Triaume and from a smartphone.

We used the Capacitive Sensor library created by Paul Badger [2, 22], which allows to build high sensitivity sensors using only a resistor, a microcontroller, and an electrode, which can be made of any conductive material. Our electrode was made using copper tape and it was connected to a 1MΩ resistor, linked to ESP32 input/output pins. The library continually yields capacitance readings, which are disturbed by touching the copper tape.

Both the sensor type and microcontroller model are chosen based on the idea of developing a low-cost instrument since the acquisition of imported products in Brazil is expensive due to taxes. In some cases, the final cost of imported products can reach even twice the value of the original cost [24]. Therefore, using low-cost components is desirable for allowing easy access to the instrument.

The microcontroller is attached to the musician's body, reducing its impact on the instrument's sound and playability. It sends the measured capacitance values to the computer using OSC packets, which can use a RS-232 connection with serial line internet protocol (SLIP) [3] or UDP packages over a Wi-Fi connection. The RS-232 connection provides a lower delay, but requires a connection cable; conversely, the Wi-Fi connection allows a greater mobility for the musician, but tends to have longer and more unstable delays [21]. This simple setup is barely invasive to the instrument but requires an additional device to provide configuration faders for performance usage, as described next.

2.2 Smartphone

It is often desirable that control-to-sound mapping proposals allow on-site adjustments, either during soundcheck or to change sonorities in different parts of a performance. Our system provides this functionality using a smartphone application, shown in Fig. 3. The application is based on MobMuPlat and sends the computer configuration parameters using OSC over WiFi. Similarly to the knobs in a guitar effects pedal, the application can be used intermittently on stage.

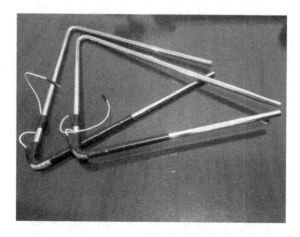

Fig. 2. The capacitive sensor is attached to the triangle's tip and isolated from the instrument's body using insulating tape.

The advantage of using a software application is that it can be easily configured and expanded as to match different sound processing proposals that might be built using Pd. Moreover, because it is external to the triangle, it can be left in a safe place during performance. Henceforth, this design option contributes to reduce the invasiveness and flexibility of Triaume's setup when compared to the idea of having physical knobs attached to the triangle.

2.3 Computer

The final block in the augmentation system is a computer, which executes a Pd patch responsible both for converting the capacitive sensor's continuous values to on/off information and for synthesizing audio to be played in a loudspeaker.

It is important to note that the conversion from continuous to on/off values could be performed in the microcontroller. However, this conversion depends on a threshold that changes depending on the sensor's materials, electric noise, the instrument's shape, and the size of the musician's hands. Therefore, this conversion is performed in the computer, and the threshold is configured using the smartphone, as described in the previous section.

The on/off sensor information is used to control sound synthesis using two different strategies, as shown in Fig. 4. For the first strategy, the sensor touch and release gestures are immediately mapped into on/off information for sound activation. In the second one, the on/off information is low-pass filtered, thus providing a continuous sound parameter control. Each of these strategies is discussed next.

Using On/Off Information for Sound Activation. A simple, immediate control strategy is to map the on/off sensor to a synthesizer's ADSR envelope controller. This allows using the sensors as a key that triggers and sustains a particular sound. The sensor (and,

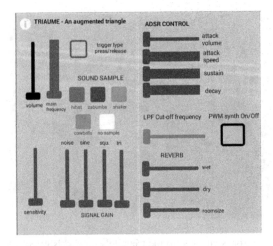

Fig. 3. Smartphone app graphical user interface.

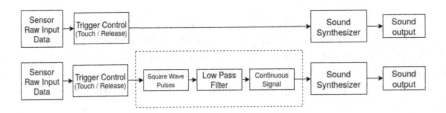

Fig. 4. Mapping strategies. The on/off sensor can be used either on touch or on release (left). Also, a low-pass filtering technique can convert the on/off information to a continuous signal (right).

consequently, the related sound) can be played independently of the triangle's damping because it uses the thumb while the damping process uses the hand palm.

Although the sensor can provide the musician with another sound layer, it can be hard to physically combine it with muting the triangle with the hand palm. For some rhythmic patterns, it can be easier to play sounds when the sensor is released. It is possible to reach a myriad of rhythmic possibilities by combining the different activations (on touch/on release) with sound synthesis configurations.

Figures 5 and 6, respectively, illustrate both of these activation modes, showing the on/off sensor data (upper panel) and the corresponding synthesized waveform. In both cases, the parameters for attack speed and sustain were adjusted for minimal values, which highlights the synchrony between the input signal and the sound output. Next, we present our proposal to generate continuous control with the sensor.

Continuous Parameter Control: A PWM-Like Approach. Continuous controls can be used in expressive sound control in important parameters that can not only be driven

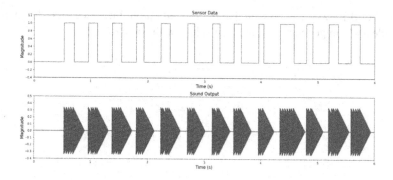

Fig. 5. Sensor data and sound output using trigger on touch.

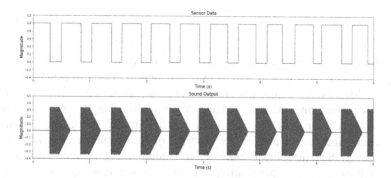

Fig. 6. Sensor data and sound output using trigger on release.

directly by a binary event logic, like wet/dry levels, gains, and filter cut-off frequencies. These parameters are usually controlled using faders, knobs, or sensors such as accelerometers. In this section, we describe how to use the on/off sensor to provide continuous control values.

The technique employed obtains continuous values from digital inputs using low-pass filtering, similarly to using Pulse Width Modulation (PWM) [16,23] control. In PWM, the input signal is a square wave, which is filtered so that the output signal level is proportional to the fraction of time in which the input is high (that is, the duty cycle). Equation 1 shows the relationship between the output signal level (Vout), the value corresponding to high level signal (A), and the duty cycle (d).

$$V_{out} = A \times d \tag{1}$$

In the on/off sensor, we can generate duty cycle variation by intermittently touching and releasing the capacitive sensor. Low-pass filtering generates a smooth, continuous signal, whose level is proportional to the duty cycle. Lower filter cut-off frequencies lead to smoother signals but also to slower responses.

Figure 7 illustrates a demonstration of this technique. It shows an acquisition of the on/off signal and the corresponding output after using a low-pass filtering with cut-off frequency of 0.1 Hz. It can be seen that the filtered output increases accordingly to the duty-cycle and can generate intermediate values with some ripple.

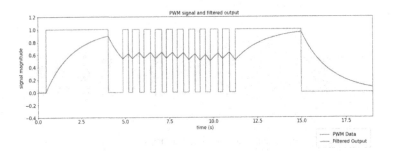

Fig. 7. Data acquired while playing the augmented instrument and low-pass filtered output.

This technique allows controlling effect or synthesizer parameters using a rhythmic input generated by touching and releasing the sensor. This is especially desirable because it allows using gestures that are close to those native to the Forró music repertoire, that is, playing rhythms with the hand. Moreover, touching and releasing parts of the instrument is also part of the traditional repertoire of many percussion instruments; hence this technique can be applied in other types of drums and other music genres.

Interestingly, both mapping techniques can be combined, generating a sound trigger that is simultaneous to a timbre control. This one-to-many mapping can generate new expression possibilities that do not necessarily fit the regional music genres Triaume was inspired in. The next sections will present tests made for instrument evaluation, followed by comments regarding the possibilities obtained by its use.

3   Instrument Evaluation

We qualitatively evaluated our instrument aiming to identify some of its musical possibilities. Triaume was evaluated from the author's viewpoint, using their own musical experience, first focusing on the on/off sensor, followed by some experiments made to evaluate the impact of the modifications made on the instrument body, then analyzing the PWM-like control mechanism.

3.1   On/Off Sensor

As a first experiment, we programmed Triaume synthesizer to play a sample of a percussive sound triggered by sensor release. A short track was recorded, and a part of its waveform can be seen in Fig. 8. The higher magnitude pulses correspond to the synthesized sound and the lower magnitude ones to the acoustic triangle.

In this test, the on/off trigger provided a quick response, which allowed playing rhythms without a perceptible delay. The capacitive sensors have shown a high sensitivity and were able to detect even more subtle touches. At the same time, the sensitivity control mechanism allowed rejecting false positives in this detection.

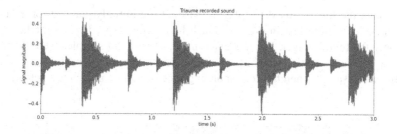

Fig. 8. Triaume sound record triggering a synthesized sound sample.

In order to illustrate another musical possibilities, an audio demo was recorded choosing different percussion sounds, and also synthesized sine, square and triangle waves. An interesting outcome was obtained when using an alternate toggle mechanism to play two different cowbell sounds[1,2]. Another experiment was made to evaluate the percussive sound samples speed activation with repeatedly triggers. For this scenario, Triaume's sensor was used initially to trigger some separate samples, increasing the trigger frequency over time, using the index and middle fingers alternately, as shown in Fig. 9.

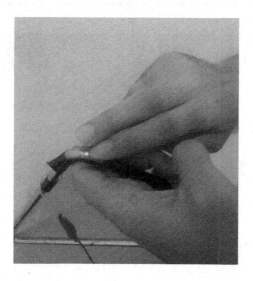

Fig. 9. Test for performing fast sound sample triggers, touching the sensor with two fingers alternately

---

[1] Audio demo with percussive sound samples available at: https://soundcloud.com/marcio-albano/triaume-test-samples/s-k7MKiggI4E2.

[2] Audio demo with synthesized waves available at: https://soundcloud.com/marcio-albano/triaume-demo-sine-triangle-square-waves/s-kzXDBiI6izr.

Although the method used for playing was not the initially planned for Triaume, this was an interesting test in order to reach high trigger speeds, even higher when using only the thumb finger. For this experiment, four sound samples were recorded, being one for each sample available in the smartphone app. Figures 10, 11, 12, and 13 show the audio samples and the corresponding spectrograms for each test performed.

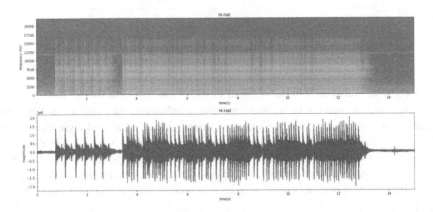

Fig. 10. Spectrogram (upper) and audio signal (lower) for *hihat* sample trigger test

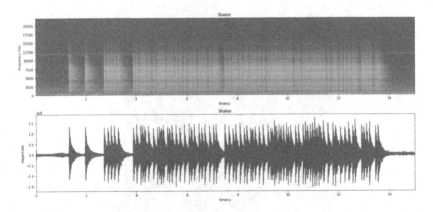

Fig. 11. Spectrogram (upper) and audio signal (lower) for *shaker* sample trigger test

The *zabumba* audio sample spectrogram shows smoother traces, since its components are associated to lower frequencies. However, an elevated number of triggers can be observed when looking at the sample audio signal, delimited by the waveform peaks, as shown in Fig. 12.

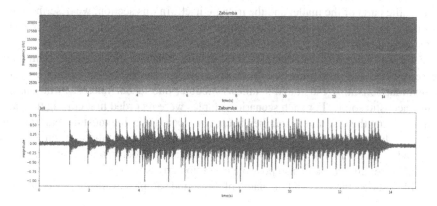

Fig. 12. Spectrogram (upper) and audio signal (lower) for *zabumba* sample trigger test

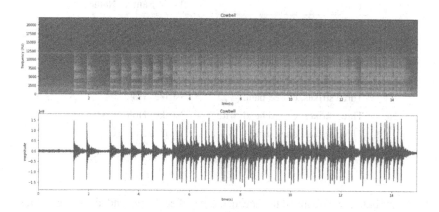

Fig. 13. Spectrogram (upper) and audio signal (lower) for *cowbell* sample trigger test

After observing each test, we can notice that in the faster scenarios the occurrence of ten triggers in a second. Within the context of Brazilian regional music and also considering the employed techniques for playing the triangle, this can be considered a satisfactory result.

3.2   Impact of Insulating Tape in the Acoustic Instrument Sound

Even though the proposed changes on the instrument body were little invasive for its handling, it is important to evaluate their impact on the acoustic instrument sound. When using the mallet to play any part of the instrument that is covered with insulating tape, sound differences are naturally expected, since there is no direct contact between the metallic parts of the mallet and the triangle itself. In this section, we describe some tests made to evaluate this impact through the analysis of the produced sounds in some scenarios.

First, we obtained sound samples from playing Triaume disassembled (removing the sensor and the insulating tape from the triangle), and next, assembling it again, but without activating the sound synthesis module, due to our interest in the instrument's acoustic sound. For each scenario, samples were recorded first closing the hand while handling the instrument and then keeping it open (releasing most fingers from the instrument body). Samples were recorded with a single strike and then for three strikes separated by an interval of approximately five seconds, in order to reduce any impact of external noise influence and also possible execution errors while playing.

Table 1 shows the tests and the name of the sound samples available for listening[3]:

Table 1. Sample Audio Description for insulating tape impact tests

Test	Audio Sample Name
One strike, closed hand	1strike Hold
One strike, open hand, with tape	1strike Hold Tape
One strike, open hand	1strike Release
One strike, open hand, with tape	1strike Release Tape
Three strikes, closed hand	3strikes Hold
Three strikes, closed hand, with tape	3strikes Hold Tape
Three strikes, open hand	3strikes Release
Three strikes, open hand, with tape	3strikes Release Tape

For more detail, we obtained the spectrograms of each test, and also the graphics for each audio sample (Figs. 14, 15, 16, 17, 18, 19, 20 and 21). Tests were performed aiming to execute the strikes with similar intensity and at the same recording time, reducing any changes in the results due to differences in each execution. Since the recordings were made in a place without proper acoustic insulation, some external noises can be noticed when observing the spectrograms.

Comparing the tests made for a single strike with closed hand between the disassembled Triaume (Fig. 14) and assembled with insulating tape (Fig. 15), a similar spectrogram signature can be noticed. Slightly differences can be observed in higher

---

[3] Insulating tape impact tests available in: https://soundcloud.com/marcio-albano/sets/testes-de-impacto-da-fita-isolante-no-som-do-triaume/s-pJrF9cby4SS?si=bea3fb1236db4e10a9217 aa1e29dcd04.

frequencies, appearing less in the test using the insulating tape. The waveform signature is also similar, with an small amplitude difference, that may be caused by different strike intensities in each test.

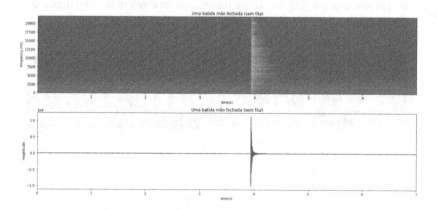

Fig. 14. Spectrogram (upper) and sound signal (lower) for test: one strike, closed hand, no insulating tape

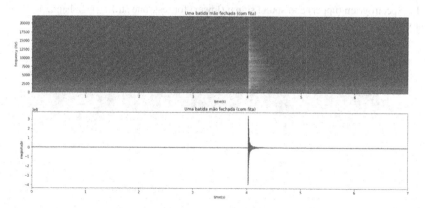

Fig. 15. Spectrogram (upper) and sound signal (lower) for test: one strike, closed hand, with insulating tape

For tests made with open hand (Figs. 16 and 17), we observe a spectrogram with persistent frequencies over time, since there is no damping hand action on the instrument. Again, it is possible to notice great similarity in the spectrograms form, but with loss in high frequencies in the test made with tape. When comparing the waveforms, we can also note the amplitude difference that was mentioned in the previous test.

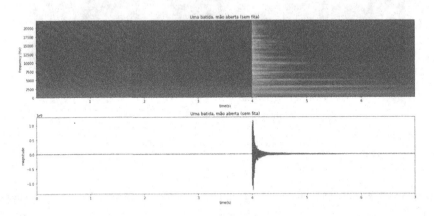

Fig. 16. Spectrogram (upper) and sound signal (lower) for test: one strike, open hand, no insulating tape

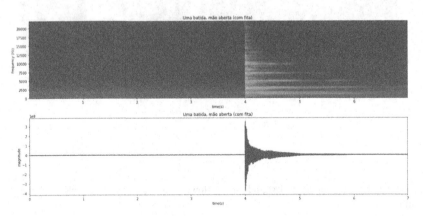

Fig. 17. Spectrogram (upper) and sound signal (lower) for test: one strike, open hand, with insulating tape

The tests performing three strikes (Figs. 18, 19, 20 and 21) did not show relevant differences when compared to its one strike counterparts: there are small losses on higher frequencies when using the insulating tape. Besides, the amplitude difference reinforces the influence of the strike intensity over the presence or absence of the tape.

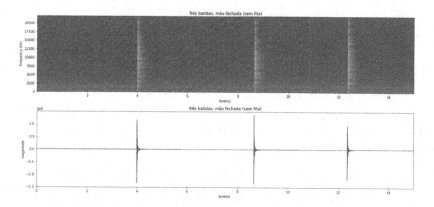

Fig. 18. Spectrogram (upper) and sound signal (lower) for test: three strikes, closed hand, no insulating tape

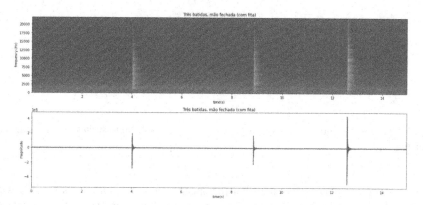

Fig. 19. Spectrogram (upper) and sound signal (lower) for test: three strikes, closed hand, with insulating tape

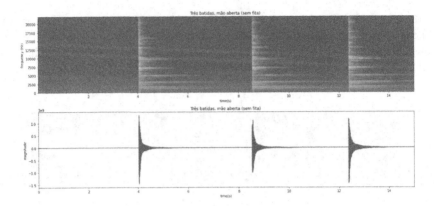

Fig. 20. Spectrogram (upper) and sound signal (lower) for test: three strikes, open hand, no insulating tape

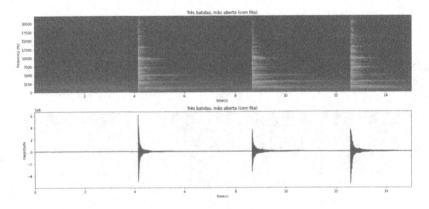

Fig. 21. Spectrogram (upper) and sound signal (lower) for test: three strikes, open hand, with insulating tape

Observing the results, we note that the spectrogram signature stays similar, with only small losses on higher frequencies when using the insulating tape. It is also important to notice that the amplitude variations for each test were not the same, which was expected as several factors may influence the final result: the location that the mallet strikes the triangle, the angle between the mallet and the instrument, and the strike velocity. Considering the playing techniques employed for the regional Brazilian music (opening and closing the triangle holding hand rhythmically while playing), the small differences noticed will not impact the instrument timbre, since the observed losses on higher frequencies are small.

3.3 PWM-Like Control

The PWM-like mechanism test consisted of linking the continuous control mechanism to a FM synthesis control module implemented in Pd. Continuous values control the modulating wave magnitude in the FM synthesis. Adjusting the low-pass filter cut-off frequency allows tuning continuous signal's change rate speed.

Mapping these continuous values directly into synthesizer fundamental frequencies would lead to an obvious one-to-one mapping strategy [14]. Using such a strategy can lead to results next to the ones obtained when playing the Theremin, but with an inevitable ripple (as suggested by Fig. 7).

For demonstration purposes, a song was composed and recorded by the authors in order to show the new instrument application context. This song, entitled "Forró do OSC", shows that the instrument can be used either inside the forró idiomatic, or for avant-garde music[4,5]. A demonstration video explaining the app features and with a short performance can be seen at [8].

4   Discussion

The results presented in this work demonstrate that Triaume can potentially bring new expressive possibilities to the triangle. Its interactions were designed aiming at a low invasiveness regarding the instrument's traditional techniques. Even though one of the authors plays Forró percussion, we could not perform any evaluation with external musicians due to the ongoing COVID19 crisis. However, the song composed by the authors shows an idiomatic Forró example, and at the same time, innovative possibilities for other music genres.

The idea of using low-pass filtering to convert on/off signals to continuous values is not novel per se, as it is a straight implementation of classic PWM control [5]. However, our proposal generates the input signal from a touch sensor placed so that it captures rhythms in the context of a handheld percussion. Henceforth, this process can be interpreted as a rhythm-to-control conversion, which can be applied in several other instruments.

5   Conclusion

This work presents an augmentation for the triangle, a handheld non-pitched percussion instrument used in several regional Brazilian music genres. The augmentation proposal uses minimalistic and low-cost hardware, comprised of a single capacitive touch sensor attached to the triangle's upper tip, which reduces its impact on using the traditional techniques to play the triangle. On-stage configuration possibilities are obtained by using an external mobile device to fine-tune all parameters.

---

[4] Song available for listening at https://soundcloud.com/marcio-albano/forrodoosc/s-Qty5RRE nsph.

[5] "Forró do OSC" music score available at https://1drv.ms/b/s!AnEYggKX1_PYkq4n8-k8xKsa44XXBA?e=Wc6mPG.

We use two mapping strategies. The first one uses the capacitive sensor as a key, which can operate either on touch or on release, making it possible to add another instrumental layer to the acoustic one. The second one uses a low-pass filtering technique to convert the on/off information to a continuous control, which allows reconfiguring synthesis or digital effect parameters by performing rhythms with the thumb.

Although the on/off to continuous signal conversion was inspired by the use of the triangle inside the Forró music context, it can be used also in other musical instruments and genres, e.g., using the gestures related to touching a drum's membrane or side to change its resonance. The main idea of the sensor is to convert rhythmic interactions to a continuous value, that is, it uses gestures that are native to playing percussions. Hence, the proposed augmentation is not only useful for Forró music itself, but also a potential path to augment other percussive instruments in other genres.

On a tecnhichal perspective, improvements can be made on the system robustness operating over Wi-Fi to reduce noise. It is also suggested evaluate the performance of modules that use radio transmittion coupled to serial communication instead of OSC via Wi-Fi. Finally, we also suggest ergonomy studies for the development of a structure for using an external battery along with the instrument on its wireless mode.

Additionally, another sound explorations can be made using the oscillations in the output signal filtered by the low-pass filter. This method can provide more expressiveness to the instrument, when used with proper mapping strategies. We also encourage new experiments by capturing the acoustic instrument sound as an additional control method for sound synthesis.

References

1. Espressif ESP32. https://www.espressif.com/en/products/devkits
2. Badger, P.: Arduino capacitivesensing library. https://playground.arduino.cc/Main/CapacitiveSensor/. Accessed 14 June 2021
3. CNMAT: OSC: arduino and teensy implementation of OSC encoding. https://github.com/CNMAT/OSC. Accessed 14 June 2021
4. Cook, P.R.: Principles for designing computer music controllers. In: Proceedings of the International Conference on New Interfaces for Musical Expression, Seattle, WA, pp. 3–6 (2001). https://doi.org/10.5281/zenodo.1176358, http://www.nime.org/proceedings/2001/nime2001_003.pdf
5. Dorf, R.C., Bishop, R.H.: Modern Control Systems. Prentice Hall, Upper Saddle River (2014)
6. Dreyfus, D.: Vida do viajante: a saga de luiz gonzaga. Editora 34 (2012)
7. Falamansa, B.: Sete meninas/forró do bole bole - Mtv Ao Vivo. https://www.youtube.com/watch?v=BzwqMciFc-s. Accessed 14 June 2021
8. Ferreira, M.A.H.: Triaume: an augmented triangle (2021). https://youtu.be/M-RomVwF37w. Accessed 14 Dec 2021
9. Freed, A., Schmeder, A.: Features and future of open sound control version 1.1 for NIME. In: Proceedings of the International Conference on New Interfaces for Musical Expression, Pittsburgh, PA, USA, pp. 116–120 (2009). https://doi.org/10.5281/zenodo.1177517, http://www.nime.org/proceedings/2009/nime2009_116.pdf
10. Gerhard, D., Park, B.: Instant instrument anywhere: a self-contained capacitive synthesizer. In: Proceedings of the International Conference on New Interfaces for Musical Expression.

University of Michigan, Ann Arbor (2012). https://doi.org/10.5281/zenodo.1178261, http://www.nime.org/proceedings/2012/nime2012_223.pdf

11. Gong, N.W., Zhao, N., Paradiso, J.: A customizable sensate surface for music control. In: Proceedings of the International Conference on New Interfaces for Musical Expression. University of Michigan, Ann Arbor (2012). https://doi.org/10.5281/zenodo.1178267, http://www.nime.org/proceedings/2012/nime2012_201.pdf

12. Guaus, E., Ozaslan, T., Palacios, E., Arcos, J.L.: A left hand gesture caption system for guitar based on capacitive sensors. In: Proceedings of the International Conference on New Interfaces for Musical Expression, Sydney, Australia, pp. 238–243 (2010). https://doi.org/10.5281/zenodo.1177783, http://www.nime.org/proceedings/2010/nime2010_238.pdf

13. Honigman, C., Hochenbaum, J., Kapur, A.: Techniques in swept frequency capacitive sensing: an open source approach. In: Proceedings of the International Conference on New Interfaces for Musical Expression, pp. 74–77. Goldsmiths, University of London, London (2014). https://doi.org/10.5281/zenodo.1178802, http://www.nime.org/proceedings/2014/nime2014_515.pdf

14. Hunt, A.D., Wanderley, M.M., Paradis, M.: The importance of parameter mapping in electronic instrument design. In: Proceedings of the International Conference on New Interfaces for Musical Expression, Dublin, Ireland, pp. 88–93 (2002). https://doi.org/10.5281/zenodo.1176424, http://www.nime.org/proceedings/2002/nime2002_088.pdf

15. Iglesia, D.: The mobility is the message : the development and uses of MobMuPlat (2016)

16. Lacamera, D.: Embedded Systems Architecture. Packt Publishing (2018)

17. Mathews, M.V.: The radio baton and conductor program, or: pitch, the most important and least expressive part of music. Comput. Music. J. **15**(4), 37–46 (1991)

18. Puckette, M.: Pure data. https://puredata.info/. Accessed 14 June 2021

19. Rocha, G.L., Araújo, J.T., Schiavoni, F.L.: Ha Dou Ken music: different mappings to play music with joysticks. In: Queiroz, M., Sedó, A.X. (eds.) Proceedings of the International Conference on New Interfaces for Musical Expression, pp. 77–78. UFRGS, Porto Alegre (2019). https://doi.org/10.5281/zenodo.3672872, http://www.nime.org/proceedings/2019/nime2019_paper015.pdf

20. de Rua, B.: Baião de rua no release showlivre. https://www.youtube.com/watch?v=JLg-c0ov7sI. Accessed 14 June 2021

21. Santos, G., Wang, J., Brum, C., Wanderley, M.M., Tavares, T., Rocha, A.: Comparative latency analysis of optical and intertial motion capture systems for gestural analysis and musical performance (2021)

22. Stoffregen, P.: Arduino capacitivesensor library (repository). https://github.com/PaulStoffregen/CapacitiveSensor. Accessed 14 June 2021

23. Valvano, J.W.: Embedded systems: real-time interfacing to Arm® Cortex™-M microcontrollers (2014)

24. Vieira, R.A., Schiavoni, F.L.: Fliperama: an affordable arduino based MIDI controller. In: Michon, R., Schroeder, F. (eds.) Proceedings of the International Conference on New Interfaces for Musical Expression, pp. 375–379. Birmingham City University, Birmingham (2020). https://doi.org/10.5281/zenodo.4813424, https://www.nime.org/proceedings/2020/nime2020_paper73.pdf

25. Young, D., Essl, G.: HyperPuja: a tibetan singing bowl controller. In: Proceedings of the International Conference on New Interfaces for Musical Expression, Montreal, Canada, pp. 9–14 (2003). https://doi.org/10.5281/zenodo.1176577, http://www.nime.org/proceedings/2003/nime2003_009.pdf

Networked and Collaborative Musical Play Amongst Humans and Virtual Biological Agents in Locus Diffuse

Rory Hoy(✉) and Doug Van Nort

DisPerSion Lab, York University, Toronto, ON, Canada
{hoy,vannort}@yorku.ca
http://dispersionlab.org/

Abstract. Locus Diffuse is a networked multi-user instrument populated by a simulated slime mold and four human players. Mimicking the biological behavior of slime mold and establishing a virtual living network between player nodes, the system sonifies interaction along these connections. Participants use a browser based interface to play the multi-user instrument, and access an accompanying stream for audio and visual output of the system. Player responses from various play sessions are reported, and discussed relative to the concept of sonic ecosystems. These responses demonstrate distinct frames of focus employed by participants in regard to human/machine and inter-human collaboration, including perceived interaction of sound sources and agent behavior, perceived interaction through personal connection to agents, and differing perceptions of an aural vs visual understanding of the system.

Keywords: agent-based musical systems · multi-user instruments · natural computing · slime mold

1 Introduction

Musical play has acted as a vessel for a communal engagement, identity, exploration, and expression throughout history [6]. While the style of play may vary from recital of composed works to free improvisation (and every permutation in between/beyond), a common thread is that emergent group dynamics are revealed through the complex interactions between each player [2]. This aspect of musical collaboration defines a social ritual in which participants are afforded a medium of aural communication beyond the verbal. We could imagine this as a kind of network in which players are represented as nodes within a network of participants that expresses interpersonal playing decisions; the resulting sonic landscape can then be seen as an emergent form of this established network. Viewed in this way, collective action results in a cumulative sound field that is the product of each node's (player's) input. An interactive instrument/environment, named *Locus Diffuse* was developed to investigate and facilitate such emergent

© Springer Nature Switzerland AG 2023
M. Aramaki et al. (Eds.): CMMR 2021, LNCS 13770, pp. 94–110, 2023.
https://doi.org/10.1007/978-3-031-35382-6_9

participatory network structures within collaborative musical play for four players. This is mediated by an instrument in which users can "play" a space through interaction both with its population of simulated agents and with each other. Situated at the crossroads of sonic ecosystem design, agent-based musical systems, multi-user instruments, and networked performance, *Locus Diffuse* draws on a network of practices to produce a system that is used to interrogate the outcome of their resulting collaborative human/machine interplay. The system was initially planned for a full scale room implementation within the DisPerSion Lab at York University, however due to social distancing restrictions caused by the global COVID-19 pandemic, the project was required to pivot to a distributed virtual performance space. Players and spectators access a live audio/visual stream as a collective hub for generated activity, while controlling their input within an additional browser window or mobile device. During this time of relative isolation, the project's aesthetic themes of connection and collaboration were heightened through this additional networking component, facilitating the communal play of all participants.

The behavior of the system's population of agents is modelled on networking structures found within the biological form of slime mold. Harnessing natural processes of emergent form and community, these organisms have been demonstrated to have repeatable emergent behaviors of aversion and attraction to environmental stimuli. Most notably their structure takes the form of thin physical networks between food sources, and through implementing approximations of this behavior, *Locus Diffuse* generates flowing and reactive networks of autonomous agents moving between player positions. We argue that these organisms are well suited as a metaphorical frame that mirrors the collaborative generative network-like structure found within musical performance, and that mapping various interaction responses can result in compelling ecosystemic behavior.

2 Related Works and Literature Review

Each of the disparate research areas addressed and employed within the development of *Locus Diffuse* point to a key aesthetic goal throughout various implementations of their themes and structures: Emergence. While "emergence" is a wide reaching term for a procedural creation or an unveiling of some kind [13], it will be demonstrated that each of these disciplines consciously involve the interplay of their own disparate components of various human/machine relationships, resulting in a whole. The rich explorative space of each of these processes results in behavioral, aural, and performative emergence culminating in dynamic and exciting artistic applications which in turn also facilitate communal musical play.

2.1 Harnessing Biology - Artistic and Computational Implementations

Natural Computing studies the application of natural phenomena within ecological systems and biological structure to a multitude of computational tasks [20].

These implementations can come in the form of mimicry, approximation, and inspiration from structures found within natural systems. Slime mold, specifically Physarum polycephalum, exhibits extraordinary behavior for an organism which contains no explicit sensory organs, capable of tactile, chemical, and photoreceptive sensing. The body consists of a single cell, but can produce many flexible space-searching tubules and can change their thickness to allow for a greater flow of cytoplasm in order to move. The body attempts to move in a direction towards food/positive stimulus or away from negative stimulus [5]. The slime mold is able to then retract, reinforcing a minimal path between all available food sources within even complex spatial layouts such as mazes [16]. Computational models of slime mold have resulted in creating logical gates, solving resource heavy computation, and achieving primitive memory [1]. Artistic applications of slime mold have been advancing in tandem with computational implementations. Miranda et al. [14] constructed a sound synthesis project which allowed for recordings of voltage at various locations through the electrical activity of a slime mold network across a series of food nodes. This data was then used within a granular synthesis engine to generate sonic events.

2.2   Sonic and Performance Ecosystems

Sonic ecosystems refer to interactive systems defined by the generation of a reactive audio environment in which self observing behavior and participant input result in audible dynamic feedback [4]. Such systems explore the relationships and outcomes established between human, machine, and ambient environment. A central question in the context of ecosystemic design is the role of human participation within an established work, and what constitutes "interaction". Some systems generate a sonic environment purely mediated by an established machine/ambience relationship, while others find room for human interaction to extend these interactions. Di Scipio [4] describes this ability of system self observation as "a shift from creating wanted sounds via interactive means, towards creating wanted interactions having audible traces", and claims that it is through these traces that compelling sonification can occur.

The original, in-person formulation of *Locus Diffuse* was initially planned to play off of the self-observing vocal & ambient feedback found within the design of the *dispersion.eLabOrate* project [9], a system exploring collaborative sounding within a Deep Listening-inspired sonic meditation [17] context. Within *Locus Diffuse*, self-observation occurs at the agent level. Each agent is only aware of its own state (vs a sense of other's or environmental current states) and acts according to its sensory input from the environment. Environmental changes and subsequent sonification are a result of the interplay between players and the system's agents.

2.3   Multi-user Instruments and Networked Music

Intended to promote close relationships between multiple players and resulting play techniques, multi-user instruments allow many participants to perform through a singular instrument. Designing for a multi-user instrument context requires explicit consideration of the intricacies and collaborative experiential content which the instrument/system needs to convey. Jordà [12] outlines key aspects of multi-user instruments that facilitate shared collective control within a musical system. These properties include number of users, user roles, player interdependencies/hierarchies, and the flexibility of each of these components.

Creation of mutual-influence via networked sound data has been explored by pioneering groups such as the League of Automated Music Composers and The Hub [8]. More recently, these networks have also been explored within the realm of telematics, employing the internet as a medium for musical collaboration [18]. Weinberg [23] presents the concept of an Interconnected Musical Network (IMN), live performance collectives in which player interdependencies result in dynamic social relationships and reactive playing. Weinberg states a successful musician network would promote "interpersonal connections by encouraging participants to respond and react to these evolving musical behaviors in a social manner of mutual influence and response", positioning the performance of group-based music as a social ritual. Additionally, exploring a biological metaphor of the established network, Weinberg [23] states: "Such a process-driven environment, which responds to input from individuals in a reciprocal loop, can be likened to a musical 'ecosystem.' In this metaphor, the network serves as a habitat that supports its inhabitants (players) through a topology of interconnections and mutual responses which can, when successful, lead to new breeds of musical life forms...". This parallels the key ecosystemic theme of *Locus Diffuse* and points back towards the culmination and amalgam of these disparate practices as viable in fostering a connected musical collaborative space.

3   Artistic Intention and System Overview

Locus Diffuse introduces a simulated biological agent that reacts to the movement of players, permeating the environment as a kind of traversable medium. Sonification of the system is achieved when interacting with this mediating entity as well as through participant movement in virtual space, and can therefore only exist/function through the symbiotic relationship of players to it and to each other. Control is neither centralized to one participant, nor surrendered to the simulated organism. Human action facilitates the musical composition of space, sculpting a form which the simulated organism populates spatially and aurally. This emergent structure and reactive behavior can be seen as a parallel to the social ritual of "musicking" [21], in that each player has a sensory experience of the whole while also contributing to it. Participating within the shared audio space means enacting this social ritual of musical play, thus the roles and capabilities of players along with the function of environmental agents were established such as to rely on all players. These inter-human and human-agent relationships are critical to exploring the resultant network structure. The simulation is contained within Max, employing JS for logic directing agent positions and control data for grain sonification, JWeb in Max is used for visual feedback in an HTML page, and audio synthesis control patches were additionally developed within Max.

3.1 Simulated Agents

Agent behaviour is modeled after the biological structures of Physarum poly-cephalum, but does not represent an exact scientific model of the organism. Player positions are represented as purple radial gradients within the simulation as shown in Fig. 2. Player positions act as food deposits for the simulated agents, and thus movement results in variations of the environmental structure sensed by the collective simulated slime mold. The simulation is informed by the research of Vogel et al. [22] and inspired by Jones [11], who outlines the mechanics of Physarum polycephalum.

An initial population of 500 agents spawn in the centre of the simulated environment and are given a random starting trajectory. Each agent is equipped with two sensors, which are positioned at an angular offset of 45° left and right, at a set distance ahead of the agent. The simulated world is quite large (1000^2 pixels) in relation to the size of the cellular bodies (2 pixels), necessitating sensors that have a far reach (default 350 pixels) and thus allowing them to "smell" food sources and trails from a reliable distance. As mentioned in Jones [11], this large distance would normally be considered a kind of remote sensing, separate from the body of an agent. However in this virtual environment, this distance also acts as the "overlapping actin-myosin mesh of the plasmodium gel system", allowing the cells to understand their position relative to each other and to nutrient sources.

Optimization of the agent network is achieved through a decaying chemoat-tractant trail, deposited and sensed by each agent. Trails are deposited when an agent senses either food or another trail, resulting in paths of deposits leading towards food. As trails diminish over time, an established network is strength-ened as searching agents either return from an unsuccessful search, or travel along a new path, continually depositing additional trails. Agent sensors work by checking for light values representing chemoattractant strength, averaging the data collected, and then determining the direction to face. Agents remember the last strongest "smell" they've sampled and choose what to do based on the current reading, always orienting towards the highest value. Agents are in search of energy to keep moving and find more food.

Globally, energy is a value held both by each agent as well as each player attractant node. This value in turn maps to qualities of the granular sonification, movement, and rotation speed. In the case of agents, losing energy will cause them to slow and eventually enter a hibernation-like state when approaching zero. Agents which gain energy again can be "revived" from this hibernation state if passed over by a player. Simulated agents actively gain energy while upon a player, while passively losing energy during movement or when wandering between nodes. Players, meanwhile, regain energy by being in close proximity to other players. Agents keep separate energy values as opposed to distributing energy, allowing for unique individual sonifications, based on the amount of energy one contains (Fig. 1).

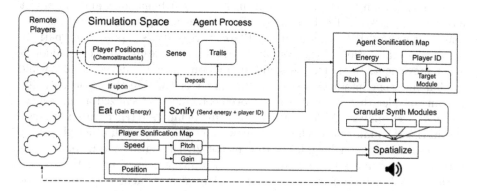

Fig. 1. Human and machine interaction with resulting data flow to sonification

3.2 Sonification

Unique sound source material was used to ensure an identifiable timbre for each player. Play sessions were done in two waves and audio sources were edited between waves both for refinement of sonification aesthetics, and to gauge any changes in the play experience due to these varied timbres. Wave 1 sources were textural in nature, using viscous drips, synth drones, running water, and a filtered conversation as audio material. Wave 2 sources were chosen to result in crisp textural sonification - timbrally in line with clicking, dripping, droning, and swarming noises. Sonification of a given audio grain is triggered by an instance of an agent "eating" at a particular player location, at the moment when an agent takes energy from the player's representational chemoattractant. The probability of a grain triggering is randomized to a 1 in 500 chance upon an agent eating in order to avoid continuous audio output from a single agent, while also mimicking the variance in time needed to break down and process energy from food sources.

Within Max, messages are sent from the logic script running in a JWeb object. These are routed to one of four granular synthesis engines, each corresponding to a different player. The messages include the energy value of the agent, and the player ID corresponding to their source of energy. The granular synthesis patches contain a Petra buffercloud object [15], allowing for accurate single-grain firing (5–50 ms long). Energy values are mapped to both transposition of the source material and to gain level. As energy values range from 0–100, values are scaled to an appropriate pitch range multiplier between 0.5 ($\pm$ 0.2) and 1.7 ($\pm$ 0.2), and gain ranging from -30 dB to 0 dB. Granular synthesis output is then spatialized relative to the corresponding player position within the virtual space. In addition to the granular synthesis of agent-human interactions, player movement is sonified by high frequency sine tones. Unique frequencies are assigned per player, then modulated based on movement speed, with slower movements being modulated down (with higher gain), and faster movements modulated up (with lower gain), which may produce a beating depending on relational position/speed of multiple players.

All sonification (both granular output from agent behaviour, and movement based tones) is spatialized virtually using dispersion.spat [10], a custom system built around IRCAM's Spat [3]. Player verticality is represented spatially within the sonification of the system, but this has no result on the behavior of agent movement. In short, the sonic interaction space of players is 3D, while the human-agent interaction space is 2D, embedded within this. Conceptually, we can consider that vertical player movement maps to localized agent behavior at a given player's X/Y position, with this being "stretched" up and down within the 3D audio space while still allowing interactions with other players at their respective planar heights. In the current 2D simulation form, connections between player nodes can be thought of as projected down upon the surface of the virtual environment, while their spatialized placement may be above or below this location.

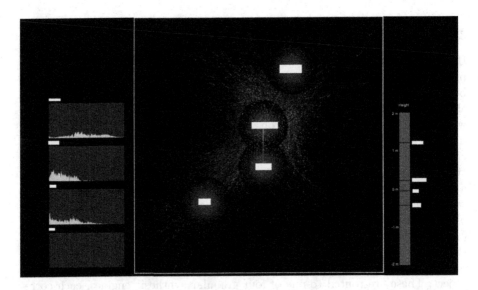

Fig. 2. Stream view of the simulated environment. Purple circles are human player positions, surrounded by the green bodies of the slime mold agents and trails. (Color figure online)

3.3 Networked Interaction and Visualization

Accommodating different devices and network connections was seen as essential to the project, in order for public accessibility to diverse groups of players and audience. As such, control of player movement occurs in the browser through a provided URL, and can be accessed with a browser or touch-enabled device.

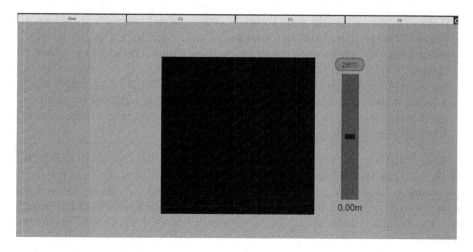

Fig. 3. Web interface for interaction with the system - a Max Mira multitouch surface

The interface contains a panel for each player consisting of identical controls, including a centre square for position input, and a right-hand slider for vertical movement (Fig. 3).

The accompanying stream view displays the visual output of the system, and spectroscope representations of current sonification (Fig. 2). As there is no depiction of agent activity within the online UI, the stream is situated as a centralized audio and visual hub for the experience both of the multi-user instrument and the resulting sonic ecosystem – with equal importance for both players and spectators of a play session.

4   Survey

Play sessions were held in two waves and consisted of open calls on set dates, as well as open-invite public exhibitions which followed the lab's weekly electro-acoustic improvisation series *DisPerSion Relations X*. The first wave of play sessions focused on a single behavior state of the agents, while the second wave presented players with four varied states. Sessions lasted roughly 25 min (with some lasting up to 60 min), allowing each player ample time to explore the sonic ecosystem and the results of their spatial interactions with other players and the simulated agents. Prior to play sessions, all participants were given information on the experience they were going to be taking part in to give some context for the behaviours they may experience:

> "The system is a multi-player instrument populated by a simulated slime mold which will attempt to reach all players and optimize networks between them. The simulation is a top down view, with the listening position located at the centre, facing the top. When an agent is upon you, it may take a "bite" where it attempts to draw energy from you. If successful

this will trigger an audio grain to fire in your personal voice. Each player's voice is unique. The pitch and loudness of this voice is tied to the agent energy. Personal player energy can be regained through proximity to other players. Agents with no energy die, and new agents can be born or old agents revived if alive agent energy is high enough. You'll be playing with 4 varied states that alter the behavior and simulated qualities of the simulated agents - try to be conscious of how each feels, noting key differences and how your playing differs".

Following play, participants were asked to complete an anonymous web form. As Wave 2 was centered around four different behavior states, the response form was updated to include questions on state comparisons. Questions focused on perception of the system from two perspectives: relations with other players and with the resulting sonification. The questions for Wave 1 (W1) were presented as follows:

1. What was your sense of playing in this virtual environment?
2. What was your sense of connection to the others in the virtual space? (Other players or agents)
3. How did you perceive your own "voice" while playing? (Location, timbre, relation to environment and others)
4. How would you describe your ability (or lack of) to perform expressive musical action?

Wave 2 (W2) introduced states which altered agent trail decay, sensory distance, "death" threshold, birth odds, and agent energy decay. Players were not primed on the behavior of each of these states. The transition between each state was announced over voice chat to prompt the players that they will be interacting with new behavior. This wave also allowed for participants to speak over voice chat to each other, allowing for live reaction and collaboration. States progressed sequentially through 1–4, but could be revisited following the session. The experienced states were:

- **S1 - Solitary:** Fast trail decay, low sensory distance, default death threshold, low birth odds, and default agent energy decay (Fig. 4)
- **S2 - Needy:** Slow trail decay, low sensory distance, lower death threshold, high birth odds, and very fast agent energy decay (Fig. 5)
- **S3 - Lively:** Fast trail decay, high sensory distance, default death threshold, high birth odds, and slow agent energy decay (Fig. 6)
- **S4 - Starving:** Slow trail decay, high sensory distance, lower death threshold, low birth odds, and very fast agent energy decay (Fig. 7)

The names provided before the description of each state were given by the first author through personal interpretation of their behavior and were not told to players. Questions from W1 were all asked again, including "For each state:" before a given question. One additional question was asked:

– How would you describe the behaviours of each state? (changes in response, characteristics, etc.)

Answer lengths were not prompted to be short or long, allowing players to provide as much detail as they wished. 10 player responses were recorded for both W1 and W2, and a thematic analysis was conducted on this data. Most players had little or no prior experience with participatory musical systems. A small amount had extensive prior experience with improvisational musical play.

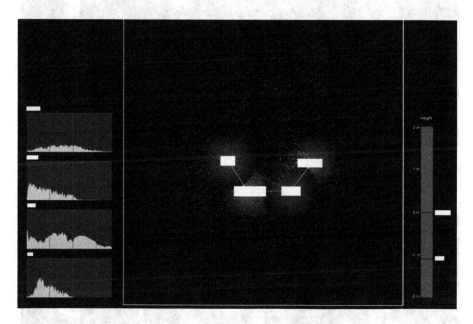

Fig. 4. Stream view of the simulated environment depicting State 1 - "Solitary" (participant names censored)

5   Responses and Analysis

5.1   Perception of the System

Participant responses outline a range of interpretations for *Locus Diffuse*, as various natural metaphors were attributed to the audio and visuals. One participant noted,

"I definitely had the sensation of being immersed in a medium - fluid. The dynamics of the particles, of course, were responsible for evoking this sensation, but so were the sounds and the way that they transformed".

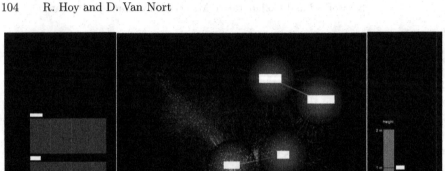

Fig. 5. Stream view of the simulated environment depicting State 2 - "Needy" (participant names censored)

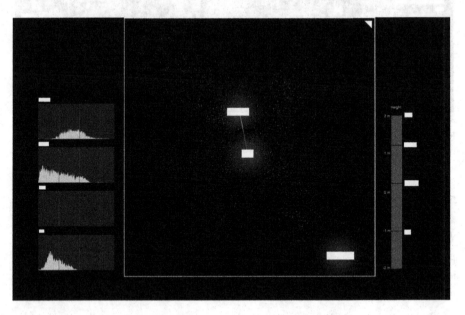

Fig. 6. Stream view of the simulated environment depicting State 3 - "Lively" (participant names censored)

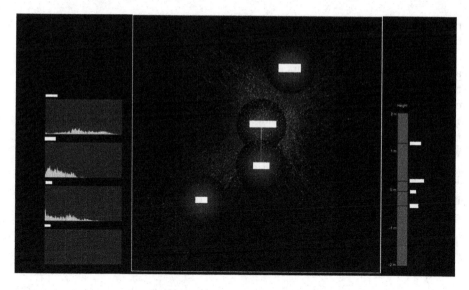

Fig. 7. Stream view of the simulated environment depicting State 4 - "Starving" (participant names censored)

While players were primed that the agent behavior was emulative of slime mold, their natural metaphors for the agent behavior tended towards more commonly encountered phenomena of the natural world, as seen by one participant who noted, "It felt like I was being swarmed by invasive digital bugs when the sound was present all around". Natural processes such as these swarms, flowing rivers, and immersion within a fluid substance were noted as a reaction to both the aural and visual content of the simulation. A mental image of a singular being or sound object was established through such auditory and visual complementaries. While similar audio sources were used as granular input across both waves, the sense of a natural process was far from 1:1 with source audio, and rather was in reaction to both timbre and agent behaviour. This points to the *perception of an emergent sonic ecosystem that is influenced both by variations of the sound source and by agent behavior.*

5.2   Narrative and Interaction

Interaction with agents, guided by personal connection/narrative, was also a key feature of participant responses. One player noted,

"There was a certain appeal to doing things like building 'bridges' between myself and other users, and seeing the cells speed up and slow down made it feel like we were almost taking care of the cells in a way".

This was exemplified within states S2 (Needy) and S4 (Starving) of Wave 2, where accelerated agent energy decay and earlier death resulted in huddles of player positions protecting a core population of agents. Multiple players stated to their collaborating players that they "can't let the agents die!", urgently coordinating with others to ensure their virtual collaborator would survive. Players attributed direct and/or implied characteristics towards agent and environmental behavior throughout each of the states. Players would alter the target of these characteristics, displaying that these changes were felt on *either an agent or environmental level*. Environmental-related characteristics tended to be a product of the visual aspects of the system, noting "busyness" and "growth" of agents within S2 & S4 when trail decay was reduced.

For agent behavior characteristics, S1 (Solitary (Fig. 4)) was perceived as "independent", resulting in localized areas of attraction with distant agents acting indifferent to the presence of energy. One response attributed 'interest' as a quality the agents possessed, stating that

> "Agents seem to be highly invested in the actions of players when they are sharing energy, but seem to actively avoid players who are not working together to share energy".

One player noted that these states "rewarded stillness", where one's interaction felt more impactful to the sonification by waiting and allowing the agents to move towards and through them. S2 (Needy (Fig. 5)) agent behavior was perceived as fragile and communal, reliant on close groups of players and agents to sustain life due to the very fast agent energy decay. This was compounded by high birth odds that resulted in tight birth clusters which would quickly die off if wandering away to look for more food. S3 (Lively (Fig. 6)) was observed as "chaotic" both audibly and visually. Due to the high sensory distance, high birth odds, and low agent energy decay, this state resulted in a high population which dispersed through the environment. This is echoed by another who attributed 'interest' as a quality the agents possessed, noting that "agents seem to be highly invested in the actions of players when they are sharing energy, but seem to actively avoid players who are not working together to share energy". Lastly, S4 (Starving (Fig. 7)) tended to be described environmentally as inhospitable or famine-like. Quick death threshold, low birth odds, and fast agent energy decay required players to focus on maintaining even closer networks of agents or else risk losing the population to energy decay.

5.3   Visual vs. Sonic Characterization of the System

Play sessions from Wave 2 which centred around the experience of four varying agent behaviors were enlightening in relation to the role that the collaborative agent behavior has upon the perception of the system's goals and player responsibility. As the players and simulated agents work symbiotically to establish the resulting sonic ecosystem, the audio and visual cohesion of the system is necessary for players to internalize a complete understanding of the culminating agent behaviors.

An trend is shown in some player responses to *lean towards a visual characterization of the system state vs an aural one*. A clear example of this reliance upon the visual is through changing the sensory distance of agents. Where Solitary (S1) has a short sensory distance and localized pockets of agent activity, Lively's (S3) large sensory distance results in loose clouds of agents that had trouble deciding which player or trail to orient themselves towards. While this allowed Lively (S3) agent behavior to sense and act towards players at a greater distance than Solitary (S1) agent behavior, these states were regarded as similar. Sonically this was not the case, where state 3 was clearly noted as more chaotic or busy, whereas state 1 was reserved and stable. Visually this was also not the case apart from the lack of residual trails, given the formations of agents that were observed. These states were seemingly deemed similar in contrast to the visual weight of states 2 & 4. Where Solitary (S1) & Lively (S3) had fast trail decay, Needy (S2) & Starving (S4) resulted in large static patterns of trails deposited by the slime mold agents due to the very slow trail decay. These lasting agent communication trails within the visualization of the environment state also resulted in participants noting their similarity, while 2 & 4 had varied sensory distances mirroring 1 & 3 which resulted again in tight and loose agent groupings. This depicts an interesting weighting of visual above sonic in terms of grouping similarity for performers.

It is clear through player responses within the second testing wave that the incorporation of fluctuating agent behavior through system states results in a more dynamic play experience, where each participant becomes more conscious about their action and its result between fellow players and the systems population of agents. Players were much more conscious of agent energy levels when these perceivably changed at a much higher rate. In these more volatile or fragile states (Needy (S2) & Starving (S4)), playing techniques required close coordination with others in order to ensure agents would survive and birth new agents. While the aural output of the system is pervasive throughout player responses, it is also apparent that the visual representation of the player positions and established networks between them are critical for the understanding of agent behavior for players and for contextualizing variances of behavior between states. While quite possible to navigate the sonic landscape "blind" by focusing completely upon audio, the visual representation of the system is clearly influential in understanding the network relations established between each player and agent within the social ritual of musical collaboration facilitated by *Locus Diffuse*.

5.4   Connection

Varied experiences of connectedness were reported, mainly falling into one of three categories:

i. a lack of connection
ii. connection mainly with the simulated agents
iii. connection to the meditative qualities of communal movement

Category (i): Reports of a lack of connection were attributed to a desire to have dialogue with fellow players (voice/text) in order to coordinate, or again due to a focus upon the visuals, noting "Being able to see where other players were going and patterns they were following made the connection much stronger across all states". Player responses pointed to a clear sense of a greater whole within which their interaction and presence resided. In some cases this may have come about through a potentially negative experience of feeling "lost" within a complex, blended sonic environment, as some responses noted their trouble at times in finding their own voice within the space, which could ultimately be perceived via subtle changes to their input. This process of sonic self-discovery, which is quite common for musical improvisers in ensemble settings, may have been foreign to participants who lacked this background.

Category (ii) was discussed above in Sect. 5.2.

Category (iii) responses focused on immersion within the system and attention to the sonification of player movements. Participants noted a distinct gravitation to the mediating agent system and its behaviours, with one participant stating "I could feel each of there positions in a unique way. It was as if they were taking up space in a room". They also focused on inter-performer, relational sonifications while immersed in the mediating virtual space, with one participant stating: "I found myself being more consciously aware of the other players' positions/motions, and adjusted my own motions in relation to theirs".

6   Conclusions and Future Work

Locus Diffuse blends aspects of sonic ecosystems, agent-based musical systems, multi-user instruments, and networked performance to establish a communal musical play contexts. Complementary aspects of these disparate fields of study are combined in order to establish compelling emergent behavior through various levels of interaction, sounding, group structure, and process. Employing natural computing for the mimicry of biological systems allows for flexible and dynamic collaborative musical agents by speeding up natural processes to allow them to be used in real-time musical computation tasks. We have provided a system overview that allows for detailed understanding of agent mechanism human/machine interplay and resultant sonification. Play sessions with *Locus Diffuse* resulted in four key observations from participant responses:

i. The qualitative perception of a sonic ecosystem was tied not only to variation in sound sources, but how these intersected with agent behavior.
ii. Narrative-based personal connection between players and agents mediated interaction characteristics.
iii. As one might expect for non-expert users, there was a bias towards a visual understanding of the system vs an aural one.
iv. The "locus" of experiences of connection organized into three categories: lack of systemic connection, a focus on inter-human collaborative sounding, and a focus on human-agent collaborative sounding.

Each of these outcomes is a product of the interaction between system behavior, player action, and aural & visual aesthetic decisions, constituting various networks at play between the project's amalgam of practices, communal musical goals, and telematic structure.

In order to explore how these perceptions of connection, agency and presence shift in different real vs. virtual and co-located vs. telematic contexts, we are working towards an in-person room scale version of the system, translating from the current network-based musical instrument design back into the originally-intended space. Moving to this physical space, we intend to further explore the perceptual implications of using embodied movement as the point of interaction within the established agent-based sonic ecosystem. Further research into emergent narratives focused on inter-human and human-agent-based collaboration in complex, distributed sonic ecosystems such as Locus Diffuse is also worth exploring. The performance ritual that this project affords merges aspects of ensemble electroacoustic musical improvisation and collaborative online gaming. It would be interesting to further explore how these two distinct communities, or those with high levels of experience in either, relate to these experiences of emergent narrative, navigation in the sonic environment and the nature of perceived connection within the performance space.

References

1. Adamatzky, A.: Physarum Machines: Computers from Slime Mould. World Scientific, Singapore (2010)
2. Borgo, D.: Sync or swarm: musical improvisation and the complex dynamics of group creativity. In: Futatsugi, K., Jouannaud, J.-P., Meseguer, J. (eds.) Algebra, Meaning, and Computation. LNCS, vol. 4060, pp. 1–24. Springer, Heidelberg (2006). https://doi.org/10.1007/11780274_1
3. Carpentier, T., Noisternig, M., Warusfel, O.: Twenty years of Ircam spat: looking back, looking forward. In: ICMC, Denton, pp. 270–277 (2015)
4. Di Scipio, A.: 'Sound is the interface': from interactive to ecosystemic signal processing. Organ. Sound **8**(3), 269–277 (2003)
5. Durham, A.C., Ridgway, E.B.: Control of chemotaxis in Physarum polycephalum. J. Cell Biol. **69**(1), 218–223 (1976)
6. Frith, S.: Music and identity. Questions Cult. Identity **1**, 108–128 (1996)
7. Gale, E., Matthews, O., De Lacy Costello, B. Adamatzky, A.: Beyond Markov chains, towards adaptive memristor network-based music generation. Int. J. Unconvent. Comput. **10** (2013)
8. Gresham-Lancaster, S.: The aesthetics and history of the hub: the effects of changing technology on network computer music. LMJ **8**(1), 39–44 (1998)
9. Hoy, R., Van Nort, D.: Augmentation of sonic meditation practices: resonance, feedback and interaction through an ecosystemic approach. In: Kronland-Martinet, R., Ystad, S., Aramaki, M. (eds.) CMMR 2019. LNCS, vol. 12631, pp. 591–599. Springer, Cham (2021). https://doi.org/10.1007/978-3-030-70210-6_38
10. Hoy, R., Van Nort, D.: A technological and methodological ecosystem for dynamic virtual acoustics in telematic performance contexts. In: Proceedings of Audio Mostly (2021)
11. Jones, J.: Characteristics of pattern formation and evolution in approximations of physarum transport networks. Artif. Life **16**(2), 127–153 (2010)

12. Jordà, S.: Multi-user instruments: models, examples and promises. In: NIME, Vancouver, pp. 23–26 (2005)
13. McCormack, J., Dorin, A.: Art, emergence, and the computational sublime. In: Proceedings of The Second International Conference on Generative Systems in the Electronic Arts, pp. 67–81. Monash University Publishing (2001)
14. Miranda, E.R., Adamatzky, A., Jones, J.: Sounds synthesis with slime mould of Physarum polycephalum. J. Bionic Eng. 8(2), 107–113 (2011)
15. Müller, M.W.: Petra for max (2016). http://circuitmusiclabs.com/projects/petra-for-max/
16. Nakagaki, T., Yamada, H., Toth, A.: Intelligence: maze-Solving by an Amoeboid Organism. Nature 407, 470 (2000)
17. Oliveros, P.: Deep Listening: A Composer's Sound Practice. iUniverse, Lincoln (2005)
18. Oliveros, P., Weaver, S., Dresser, M., Pitcher, J., Braasch, J., Chafe, C.: Telematic music: six perspectives. Leonardo Music J. 19 (2009)
19. Reid, C.R., Latty, T., Dussutour, A., Beekman, M.: Slime mold uses an externalized spatial "memory" to navigate in complex environments. Proc. Natl. Acad. Sci. 109(43), 17490–17494 (2012)
20. Rozenberg, G.: Handbook of Natural Computing. Springer, Berlin (2012). https://doi.org/10.1007/978-3-540-92910-9
21. Small, C.: Musicking: The Meanings of Performing and Listening. Wesleyan University Press, Middletown (1998)
22. Vogel, D., Gautrais, J., Perna, A., Sumpter, D., Deneubourg, J., Dussutour, A.: Transition from isotropic to digitated growth modulates network formation in Physarum polycephalum. J. Phys. D: Appl. Phys. 50(1), 014002 (2016)
23. Weinberg, G.: Interconnected Musical Networks - Bringing Expression and Thoughtfulness to Collaborative Group Playing. MIT, Cambridge (2003)

Towards an Aesthetic of Hybrid Performance Practice

Incorporating Motion Tracking, Gestural and Telematic Techniques in Audiovisual Performance

Iannis Zannos[1]($\boxtimes$) and Haruka Hirayama[2]

[1] Department of Audiovisual Arts, Ionian University, Corfu, Greece
zannos@gmail.com
[2] Hokkaido Information University, Ebetsu, Japan
hirayama@do-johodai.ac.jp

Abstract. This paper discusses the composition of works for interactive live performance based on the comparison between recent artworks and experimental work methods of the two authors. We compare the different interaction design strategies employed and discuss the factors which influenced the choice of methods for motion tracking and their influence on body movements when coupled with the generation of sound during the performance. We consider the resulting artworks as hybrid artforms that combine aspects of music composition, improvised sound performance, and stage performance or dance. A high-level comparison of the technical and practical aspects of said works is provided. We furthermore outline the principles of the system developed in SuperCollider by one of the authors o enable networked performance with sensors. It can be argued that the new expressive potential and the wealth of possibilities to be explored warrants further work in this direction, and that systematic comparison of the interactive characteristics and expressive affordances of the systems developed are useful in guiding further research in the development of novel hybrid performance forms.

Keywords: Interactive Music Performance · Audiovisual Art · Gesture Mapping · Telematic Art · Embodied Performance

1 Introduction

In acoustic music performance we can say that the actions or gestures of performers also provide visual cues conveying the character and shape of sound. At the same time, a performer's actions or gestures are directly coupled to the characteristics of produced sound and its musical expressive characteristics. Overall, we can say that instrumental music performance is a form of multimodal interaction synthesis [1].

The shapes of performer's gestures are dictated to a large extent by the physical properties of the instrument they are using, and appropriate techniques

© Springer Nature Switzerland AG 2023
M. Aramaki et al. (Eds.): CMMR 2021, LNCS 13770, pp. 111–121, 2023.
https://doi.org/10.1007/978-3-031-35382-6_10

of performance are required to play it functionally and effectively. In addition, performers' intentions with regard to musical expression influence the form of characteristic gesture shapes. Therefore, acoustic music performance creates a fairly strict framework within which performers must stay in order to interact with their instruments in a musically effective way. The actual shape of gestures is usually regarded as playing an auxiliary role in the experience of the performance.

However, in the context of interactive computer music composition we can create new relationships between performance gestures and sound and we can choose more freely both the types of movements and the degree and type of their influence on the resulting sound. This leaves greater margins of freedom to explore the expressive potential of performance gestures from the viewpoint of their visual expressive impact. This leads to a hybrid form of expressive art that lies between visual art and music or other types of stage performance.

This paper discusses composing works for interactive live performance based on the comparison between recent artworks and experimental work methods of the two authors. The works are: People in the Dunes, [2] and [3] created by Haruka Hirayama in collaboration with a visual artist and choreographer Bettina Hoffmann, and IDE- Fantasy, created by Iannis Zannos in collaboration with dancers Jun Takahashi and Asayo Hisai (Japan) and Tasos Pappas-Petrides, Vasiliki Florou, Natali Mandila and Mary Randou (Greece) [4].

We compare the different interaction design strategies employed in the above works and discuss the factors which influenced the choice of methods for motion tracking and their influence on body movements during the performance, when directly cou- pled with the generation of sound during the performance. We consider the resulting artworks as hybrid art forms that combine aspects of music composition, improvised sound performance, and stage performance or dance. We discuss the degree to which system design allowing dancers to develop their individual or intuitive style of perfor- mance, with reference to the affordances created by the technical characteristics of the systems employed. Several unresolved problems arise with regard to both performance practice and the aesthetic appreciation of such works.

The extent of possible couplings of body movement to sound forms is vast, and the task of choosing or designing interaction strategies is daunting. This problem is furthermore compounded by technical limits in the accuracy and response time of movement tracking devices and by the complex, at times almost entirely unpredictable behaviour of the couplings between movement and the resulting sounds, both in terms of the physical or mathematical behaviour and from the perceptual viewpoint. However, we argue that the new expressive potential and the amount of possibilities to be explored warrants further work in this direction, and that systematic comparison of the interactive characteristics and expressive affordances of the systems developed are useful in guiding further research in the development of novel hybrid performance forms. The present paper presents a simple methodology based on a classification of the interaction techniques used in the works mentioned, and evaluating their potential based on practical factors experienced during our work.

2   Performance Approach 1: People in the Dunes

The People in the Dunes project explores expressive potential of performance with real-time sound processing as a live audio-visual art that exists at the intersection of inter- active music performance and visual art involving human bodies. In this work, human body movement plays a theatrical role while at the same time working as a medium for sound conveyance and a form of music embodiment in a manner similar to instrumental performance in music.

The People in the Dunes project consists of three works: *People in the Dunes I, The Embodiment I - String*, and *People in the Dunes II* (See below photos from the performance: 1, and 2). The pieces were created and performed in Tokyo, Montreal, and Gatineau in Canada between 2018 and 2020 (see [4] and [5]). The title of the project is inspired by the novel The Woman in the Dunes by Kobo Abe, that de- picts the situation of a man trapped in the dunes fighting the ever flowing sand, reflecting about his life and in the end becoming aware of its essence and finding freedom: how human bodies and movements eventually find new directions under the influence of the forces acting from multiple directions between multiple individual actors, particularly under restricted circumstances? This project has been further developed by involving local dancers and instrumentalits working in Butoh and other contemporary styles.

Fig. 1. People in the Dunes II. Picture from Movement 1

Fig. 2. People in the Dunes II. Picture from Movement 5

3   Performance Approach 2: IDE-Fantasy

3.1   Preparation and Realisations

The objective of *IDE-Fantasy* is to create an interactive performance which can be realized in remote locations at the same time, through the collaboration of dancers in each location, and relying entirely on motion capture data from the dancers. The piece eschews any transmission of images or sounds between the locations of the performances. The presence of the performers is transmitted between the remote stages of the performances based solely on the influence of their tracked movements on the sounds which are produced locally at each stage. Both the performers and the audience must rely on the sounds locally created by sound synthesis software to reconstruct in their imagination the actions or states of the performers in remote locations. The objective is to explore the narrative and interpretive potential of strictly reduced means for rep- resentation and the capability for sensing the states and of the performers based on the data traces left by their body movements, but without having direct visual or auditory contact.

The subject matter of the performance is inspired by the story of *Izutsu*, a Japanese Noh Play by Zeami Motokyo, which talks of the encounter of a monk with the ghost of a woman that is longing for reunion with her lover and husband

from her previous life. Additionally, as a cultural reflection of the idea of correspondences between remote locations, symbolic correspondences between Izutsu
and the myths of *Echo and Narcissus* a poem from Ovid's *Metamorphoses* and
of *Daphnis and Chloe*, a novel by hellenistic author Longus are being explored
for future realisations of this work (see [2]).

The piece was developed through a series of rehearsals in Tokyo, Athens and
Corfu. A telematic performance between Stanford (USA), Athens and Corfu
was presented in March 2019 at the LAC19 conference, was combined with a
presentation of the software framework used to create the piece [7]. This was
followed by telematic performances between Ebetsu (Hokkaido) and Corfu, and
Lisbon and Corfu, as well as local performances in Tokyo, Japan and Elevsis,
Greece.

3.2 Software Architecture and Design Principles

When attempting to perform dance with sensors concurrently in different locations one faces the problem of exponentially growing complexity of control
parameters and coordination commands. The present project approached this
problem through the simple axiom of sharing all data and all code between the
performing locations in real time. In that way, the performers at each venue are
participating in one virtual performance, consisting of the shared data and control code. This virtual performance is physically translated into replicas at each
location. Thus, by definition the performers as well as the audience share a common experience independently of the actual physical venue space in which they
are located. The data sharing is implemented through the use of the open-source
software OscGroups by Ross Bencina. Fig. 3).

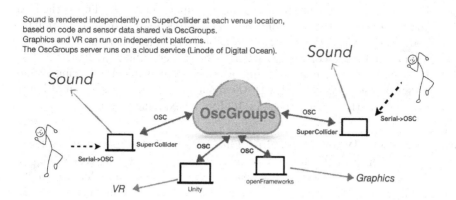

Fig. 3. Architecture of a Telematic Performance based on OscGroups

This is comparable to online game players sharing an experience in a virtual world, where the actions of each player are always transmitted to and
reflected in the local systems of all other players, thereby creating a virtual

space or game-universe shared by all players independently of their locations or gaming platform hardware. The performance is controlled by live-coding in SuperCollider who are responsible for configuring, mapping and routing the sensor input from the dancers to the various rendering modules. In practice, the system makes it possible for a single user to run a performance remotely with multiple dancers performing on multiple remote locations. This has been tried out recently also in educational settings, in performance classes directed by faculty at the Department of Audiovisual Arts of the Ionian University and the Department of Performing and Digital Arts of the University of the Peloponnese. However, increasingly complex challenges arise when one tries to use this system in settings that are not limited to a single user, type of sensor hardware or rendering software system. Thus, the software architecture must be designed in order to be capable of operating under the following 3 conditions:

1. Multiple live coders performing at the same time.
2. Multiple different types of sensors with different signal specifications and osc message protocols are in use in the same system.
3. Multiple different types of software for sound and/or graphics are operating at the same time in one performance setting.

At this stage, the system is being tested under the first 2 of the above conditions. We outline here the design principles that resulted from this research. Their implementation is found in the SuperCollider library on which this research is based, here: https://github.com/iani/sc-hacks-redux.

Use of a Separate Dictionary Environment for Each Sound Process. This principle follows one of the fundamental design patterns of *JITLib*, an early and widely used environment for live coding in SuperCollider [6]. This is the idea of a *ProxySpace*, that is an environment where objects are stored as dictionary entries, and accessible to the user as environment variables when the ProxySpace is made current by the command "push". The present library defines subclass of *EnvironmentRedirect*, called *Mediator* which responsible for storing sound processes and objects associated with them such as control busses, but behaves in a different way than ProxySpace in JITLib, as explained below.

Stop Processes When Replacing Them. One of the first obstacles faced by live coders in SuperCollider is keeping track of sound processes stored in variables. When such a process is replaced by a new one, the reference to the old one can be lost, resulting in a hanging sound which cannot be stopped. To help in this, Mediator automatically stops a sound process when something else is stored in its place.

Operators for Creating and Modifying Sound Processes. The library operator such as +> and ++> as shortcuts for commands that convert a function or a dictionary of type *Event* into a sound signal synthesis process or a stream generating many sound events, and for modifying the state of sound syntheses or event streams.

Operators for Accessing Control Busses and Buffers. The basic principle of interaction design in any system that uses input from sensors is to design a mapping between the values of the parameters input from the sensors into parameter changes of the sound synthesis processes. This becomes rapidly complicated when many sensors with many parameters of possibly different value ranges are involved, because each of these must be mapped into parameter changes in possibly many different parameters of different sound synthesis processes. Additionally, mapping strategies are not just limited to linear or exponential scaling between value ranges, but may also involve logical decisions denoting state changes such as *on* or *off*, or translation into trigger events that initiate event state changes (start or stop a sound event). It is therefore necessary to separate processes that operate on signals to produce control signals or triggers from the processes that produce sound in response to control signals. For this reason, the `sc-hacks-redux` library of this project defines operators and shortcuts for accessing control busses, mainly denoted by use of the @ mark (for example @>), and for defining signal processing processes operate on these. As a result of this distinction is possible to separate the design of control signal processing from the design of sound signal synthesis, and to combine these by using as keys the names of busses pointing to control signals. One future potential of this approach to be explored is the possibility to design information processing networks in a manner resembling artifiar neural networks.

Use of Observer Pattern Protocol. The Observer pattern is a widely used language pattern in Object Oriented Programming. It is based on the principle of a *notifier* object issuing a notification that it has changed, which is then received by any other objects that may need to respond to the changes in the *notifier*. The library of this project defines a new class *Notificaion* that implements this pattern along with an API that enables one to easily define custom responses of any object to *changed* messages received from another object. This patttern is almost ubiquitously used in the library and serves as basis for designing both Graphical User Interfaces and for designing and customizing the behavior of the system in response to OSC messages.

Dynamic Definition of Responses to OSC Messages. Based on the Observer pattern protocol of the *Notification* class, the library defines operators and methods which enable the user to modify on the fly the response of the language to incoming OSC messages. Prominent examples include the evaluation of a message argument as code - enabling remote code evaluation from any user, the writing of a messages argument values into control busses, and the display of received messages in various ways. This forms a core tool enabling customization of the behavior of the system by coders in general, and will therefore form the second future focus of the present research along with information processing networks.

Code Management. Making use of the basic tools mentioned above, the library provides a basic GUI framework for navigating a folder system holding SuperCollider code files, and for executing any of those files either as a whole, or in part based on a predefined separator syntax (//:). Furthermore, it is possible to play any such file as a score where each part or (*snippet*) has a predefined duration given in the comment header in the form of //: [duration]. This makes it possible to write scores as program files and to play these at any moment from the GUI.

Saving and Replaying of OSC Data. Since OSC is the defacto basis of communication both between sensor hardware and between live coders in a performance, the library provides a way to store all data in any performance session into a series of files as SuperCollider code and to replay these later for experimentation purposes. This feature is designed with view to help composers in designing sound and interaction strategies, and with the future prospect of employing machine learning algorithms to train the behavior of the system.

The library and the approach it implements are currently being evaluated through a series of performance projects making use diverse hardware systems with the participation of diverse live coders and performers. The results of this evaluation process will be documented in future research publications, and compared to other approaches to live coding.

4   Methodolody, Design Considerations, Discussion

From the perspective of an interactive music composer, the following research questions are addressed in both projects discussed: What are the expressive possibilities of music composition motivated by performance gestures? What is the theoretical framework required to create links between the shape formed by human bodies and sound, and between changes of shapes and sound transformations? Also, what are the technical means for linking physical body movement to sound production, and how can these influence the artistic process and its final outcome?

In the case of *People in the Dunes*, the experience of the composer's previous work *FRISKOTO* raised questions about the difference between performance gestures and control gestures in music. The hypothesis was posed, that the difference consists in the possibility of perceiving gestures as the animating force of music or not [1]. To make bodily movement perceivable as an animating force of music it is important to develop a system where sound can give an instant reaction to the movement, and vice versa. Furthermore, it is important to consider the correspondences between visual and auditory percepts. Visual and auditory sensations need to be properly coordinated or corresponded, in other words, their correspondences should be readily recognizable to performers as well as viewers. The following aspects guided the creative process and the design of the performances as a whole:

1. The availability of movement capture technologies and their technical performance characteristics (accuracy, reliability, temporal and measuring resolution, latency);
2. Affordances of the movement tracking devices for the performers (which movements are easy and comfortable for the performers to execute while using the tracking devices, and how do they understand the relationship between their movements and the resulting data when using the device);
3. Design of the mechanisms for influencing the sound produced based on the data received from the tracking devices;
4. Correspondence of the perceptual characteristics of the available or chosen sonic vocabulary to those of the gestural vocabulary developed by the performers;
5. Narrative effects of the sequential ordering of sequence of motions types and associated sound textures. The alternation of different motion types and types of sound textures produced by these can provide cues to the audience for understanding the causal relationship between movements and sounds, and thus aid their understanding of or identification with the performance. In addition, the ordering of motion types and sound textures can form a type of sequence of scenes that create the impression of a narrative, albeit of a fairly abstract and vague type. This plays an important role in capturing the attention of the audience, by offering hints for fabricating an interpretation of the events of the performance in their own imagination;
6. Subtle changes and minimalism. At certain parts of the performance, it is helpful to heighten the sensibility and awareness of the audience by purposely focusing on minute movements or changes of sound. This can intensify the sense of tension and the interpretive potential of the piece.

In the development of *IDE-Fantasy* we started with simple mappings between movement and synthesis parameters as few as 1 or 2, and gradually introduced more parameters. Even extremely simple parameter - sound mappings proved to be useful performance tools for dancers, providing them with instruments which they could explore very easily, but where nevertheless rich and responsive enough for short improvisations. In this approach, 3 or 4 parameters were already sensed as being hardly possible to handle or adapt to. 6 parameters per person were definitely outside the realm of feasible. We also experimented with 6-parameter chaotic algorithms cojointly performed by two dancers. These did capture the attention of the performers, even though they proved to be difficult to master. In Table 1 we summarise the techniques used in our works.

Table 1. Technologies used in People in the Dunes and IDE Fantasy.

Technology aspect	Heading level	Example	Font size and style
Movement tracking	Kinect	iPhone built-in sensors	a) 9-axis movement, b) 3-axis accellerometer
Sensors/person	–	2 iPhones/person	Up to 2/person
Sensors worn at	–	Left and right lower arms	Wrists
Magnitudes tracked	Horizontal boundary	Accelleration, Magenetic field, Gyroscope xyz	Accelleration, Magenetic field, Gyroscope xyz
Transmission Medium	USB	WiFi	WiFi, Xbee Mesh Network
Software	Max, Jitter	Max, ZIGSIM(iOS)	SuperCollider
Sound source	a) Boundary microphones b) Prerecorded voice	Prerecorded voice, cello, traffic, environmental sound, synthesisers	a) Prerecorded samples b) Simple or complex UnitGenerator graphs with or without feedback

5 Conclusions, Future Work

Overall, a common trait observable in both works discussed is the use of the technical affordances of motion tracking devices and sound generation or processing algorithms to design a sort of performance language which combines body movements and their assigned sound textures or events to create narratives of a more or less abstract type. In both pieces, concrete narratives of previously existing and well known works provided a reference framework in order to create the more abstract narrative of the pieces.

In conclusion, the main challenges confronting this kind of work stem from the abstract and indirect nature of digital mediation between bodily movement and generated audiovisual stimuli. The causal relationship between movement and generated sound or video tends to be difficult to recognise. In some cases it can be entirely absent, as is when employing chaotic synthesis algorithms. To counterbalance these obstacles, it is necessary to create interpretive or narrative links with the performers and the audience. Simple mappings and complex or chaotic correspondences both present advantages and disadvantages, and the decisive design criteria for developing a functioning performance seem to lie in semiotic domains such as the choice of sounds, images, and movements for their associative semantic charge, and the devising of narrative devices through trial and error during rehearsals. Currently we are interested in employing Machine Learning algorithms in order to devise improved methods for translating motion to sound, and in particular in experimenting with unsupervised learning and in adaptive techniques that modify their behaviour during the performance itself.

At the same time, the characteristics and affordances of motion tracking devices (shapes of sensors, kind of detecting data, mobility etc.) have a direct impact on the available movements and thereby on the kind of body movement language that the performers develop. We feel that a combination of different type of tracking method can enhance performance expression.

The body is capable of constantly adapting and changing shapes or forms [3]. We realised that there is an interdependence between isolated movements of individual parts of the body and the perception of forms created by movements of the body as a whole. This will serve as a guiding principle for the currently planned experiments for future work.

Acknowledgments. The research for the present paper was supported by funding from project HAL (Hub of Art Laboratories) at the Department of Audiovisual Arts of the Ionian University.

References

1. Collins, K., Kapralos, B., Tessler, S. (eds.): The Oxford Handbook of Interactive Audio. Oxford University Press, Oxford (2014)
2. IDE-Fantasy videos. https://ide-fantasy.tumblr.com/. Accessed 15 June 2021
3. Kobayashi, Y., Matsuura, H. (eds.): The Discourse of Représentation Skinship: The Rhetoric of the Body. University of Tokyo Press, Tokyo (2000)
4. People in the Dunes project page. https://www.facebook.com/peopleinthedunes/. Accessed 15 June 2021
5. People in the Dunes II videos. https://vimeo.com/user88406194. Accessed 15 June 2021
6. Rohrhuber, J., de Campo, A., Wieser, R.: Algorithms today: notes on language design for just in time programming. In: Proceedings of the 2005 International Computer Music Conference, ICMA (2005)
7. Zannos, I.: sc-hacks: a live coding framework for gestural performance and electronic music. In: Proceedings of the 2019 Linux Audio Conference, CCRMA, pp. 121–128. Stanford University (2019)

Development of Audio Descriptors Inspired by Schaefferian Criteria: A Set of Tools for Interactive Exploration of Percussive Sounds

Sérgio Freire(✉) [iD], José Henrique Padovani[iD], and Caio Campos[iD]

School of Music, Federal University of Minas Gerais, Belo Horizonte, Brazil
sfreire@musica.ufmg.br
https://musica.ufmg.br/lapis/

Abstract. Pierre Schaeffer's typomorphology (1966) proposes seven criteria of musical perception for the qualification of sound objects under reduced listening: mass, dynamics, harmonic timbre, melodic profile, mass profile, grain, and allure. These criteria form the basis of a theory (solfège) of musical objects fitted to musical contexts where pitch is not the most relevant feature. At the time of his research, Schaeffer was very skeptical about the contributions of the fields of physics and psychoacoustics to the explanation of the listening experience. While this gap still exists, two factors motivate us to bring Schaeffer's qualitative concepts closer to current quantitative methods focused on audio descriptors and machine listening: (1) the widespread availability of descriptor-related tools nowadays; (2) the correlations that can be drawn between the quantitative data retrieved by specific descriptor algorithms and the Schaefferian morphological criteria. We developed a real-time setup that uses low-level audio descriptors to identify and classify percussive sounds as bundles of features related to Schaefferian concepts. In this text, we shortly describe the background of our research and detail some tools which were the subject of former publications. Then we focus on three interactive uses of these tools, depicting the contexts and choices made for each one. Finally, we consider the achievements obtained so far and point to future steps of the project.

Keywords: Schaeffer typomorphology · Musical Interactive Systems · Percussion

1 Introduction

Pierre Schaeffer (1910–1995) devoted most of his research to the *solfège* of the sound object and proposed a framework based on seven criteria of musical perception. As a methodological starting point he raised the following question: "What elementary factors are we listening to in all music?" [10, p. 102]. Compared to traditional music theory, his approach is well-fitted to deal with

© Springer Nature Switzerland AG 2023
M. Aramaki et al. (Eds.): CMMR 2021, LNCS 13770, pp. 122–138, 2023.
https://doi.org/10.1007/978-3-031-35382-6_11

percussive sounds for different reasons. The first is the dynamic assemblage that characterizes different practices within this field. Further, some of these sounds do not bear a clear pitch and deserve a qualification based on other criteria. Finally, it is common to find sounds with complex patterns of variation in dynamics and timbre.

As we have a great interest in augmenting the resources of acoustic instruments through the analysis and processing of their sounds, it seems natural to bring the Schaefferian concepts closer to the interactive audio processing techniques. That is the central goal of a project developed in the last years. In recent works, we have already sketched a general framework to tackle this challenge using pre-recorded sounds and reviewed related works [4,6]. The present phase focuses on live musical practices.

The paper organizes as follows. First, we present the fundaments of Schaeffer's solfège; a central section deals with the selected audio descriptors, detailing diverse aspects of their implementation. Different applications of these tools come next, and a final section highlights the current achievements and future work.

2 Fundaments of Schaeffer's *Solfège*

In the sixth book of his *Traité des Objets Musicaux* (TOM), Pierre Schaeffer presents one of the most remarkable contributions of his research: a proposal of a generalized *solfège*[1], dedicated not only to the traditional musical notes, but also to any sound considered "potentially musical". This *solfège* entails seven typomorphological criteria of musical perception that have the purpose to guide the listening process that consciously attempts to detach the sonic characteristics from any referential or causal events that may generate sound objects themselves: a method that Schaeffer, borrowing the Husserlian concept of *epoché*, named *reduced listening*.

As a general method, *reduced listening* involves a conscious attitude that refrains the habitual curiosity towards the sound sources and their meanings in favor of addressing intrinsic features of the sonic phenomena.

Reduced listening is the listening attitude which consists in listening to the sound *for its own sake*, as a *sound object*, by removing its real or supposed source and the meaning it may convey.

[1] Traditionally, the French term *solfège*—from Italian *solfeggio*—refers to "to the singing of scales, intervals and melodic exercises to solmization syllables" like *sol, fa,* etc. [8]. Such term, strongly associated with the context of music conservatories and to music theory, is re-signified by Schaeffer assuming, in the context of his Treatise, an experimental attitude. Schaeffer defines this renewed notion of *solfège* as "the art of exercising to better hear", proposing a new and "generalized *solfège*": his Program of Musical Research (PROGREMU) [9,10]. While the English translation of the TOM uses the expression "the music theory" to refer to the Schaefferian concept of this term, in this text we employ the French word *solfège* to address, at the same time, its specificity in Schaeffer's work as well as its multiple connotations, in a broader context.

More precisely, it reverses the twofold curiosity about causes and meaning (which treats sound as an intermediary allowing us to pursue other objects) and turns it back on to the sound itself. In reduced listening, our listening intention targets the event which the sound object is in itself (and not to which it refers) and the values which it carries in itself (and not the ones it suggests) [1, 2, p. 33; p. 30].

In section 34.3, the TOM includes a Summary Diagram (*tableau général*), offering an overview of the whole method, where types, classes, genres, and species of sound objects are described according to seven criteria – mass, dynamic, harmonic timbre, melodic profile, mass profile, grain, and *allure* [9, 10][2]. The criteria help to locate the position and thickness (*site/calibre*) of sound object attributes in the three-dimensional space of a perceptual field formed by *pitches*, *durations*, and *intensities*.

In section 88 of the *Guide des Objets Sonores* [1], Michel Chion outlines the distinctive features of sound objects that each of the morphological criteria proposed by Schaeffer aims to evaluate.

- The *mass* details how the sound occupies the pitch perceptive dimension.
- *Harmonic timbre* describes the "diffuse halos" and "related qualities" that seem to be related to the *mass* and allow its qualification.
- *Grain*, in its turn, is related to the "micro-structure" of sound matter and is associated with rapid variations or reiterations of constituent sounds.
- While *grain* outlines the link between form and matter as one of the sustainment criteria, *allure* expresses the dynamism (mechanical, living, or natural) of what could be defined as a "generalized type of vibrato".
- *Dynamic* expresses the evolution of a sound in the perceptive dimension of *intensities*.
- *Melodic profile* describes the general contour of a sound in the perceptive dimension of pitches, a sort of trajectory in the tessitura.
- *Mass profile*, on the other hand, describes the "internal" variations of a sound in this same perceptive dimension: these changing shapes are responsible for "sculpting" the mass, making it to be more or less thick or thin, having thus a more or less complex or tonic quality, for instance [1].

While authors like Di Scipio [3] remark that the concept of *reduced listening* is ideologically and technologically circumscribed, ignoring the very audible traces of electroacoustic tools that enable us to focus on the 'sound itself', its relevance, since the Schaefferian seminal contributions, lies in the fact that the project of a "generalized *solfège*" has been successful in providing a rich theoretical framework that makes possible to describe different features, behaviors, and qualities of sound objects according to morphological criteria and perceptual dimensions.

Considering Pierre Schaeffer's well-founded warnings regarding the differences between the study of sound objects using perceptual-sensory criteria, on

---

[2] See, particularly, pp. 584–587 of the original edition; pp. 464–467 of the English translation.

the one hand, and physical-acoustic analysis of audio signals, on the other, it is relevant to underline the experimental nature of the present work. Thus, despite the differences between perceptual and signal-based evaluation, description, and categorization of sounds, our work is motivated by a common trait of low-level audio descriptors and the Schaefferian *solfège*: both focus on intrinsic qualities of sound phenomena, seeking to discriminate particular characteristics based on certain criteria, dimensions, or parameters. Indeed, Schaeffer himself, even warning to the differences between perceptual processes and what signals can represent, also recognized the usefulness of real-time visualization of signals using bathygraphs and sonagraphs [9,10].

> It is perhaps disconcerting to see us, after so many warnings, recommend-ing the use of the bathygraph and the Sonagraph to describe a piece of music.(...) On the physical level the bathygraph and the Sonagraph give two graphs of the signal in real time: its projection on the dynamic and the harmonic plane. Of course, these lines are not very intelligible because perceptions of sound differ so much (by anamorphosis) from the signal on the printout.
> But for giving a rough organization of events these two printouts will save hundreds of hours of painstaking, often impossible and probably prema-ture, work. [10, pp. 556–557]

3 Audio Descriptors: Selection, Implementation, and Parametrization

Our first challenge was to cover the variety of percussive sounds with a set of simple descriptors running in the interactive real-time environment *Max*[3]. From the start, it became clear that we needed to dedicate special attention to time-domain features like attacks, allures, and grains. In this way, we have used RMS curves with different window sizes and filtering parameters and also developed some tools acting directly on the sample level. Our frequency-domain descriptors rely on the spectral peaks and fundamental frequency estimation delivered by the [sigmund~] object and a native spectral centroid implementation.

Usually, there is no one-to-one correspondence between the Schaefferian cri-teria and the developed descriptors. To differentiate between different classes of mass, f. i., we use a combination of frequency domain descriptors and their possible variation in time. See details in [6].

In real-time interactive applications, one can not ignore background noise (and the expected leakage from loudspeakers on microphones). We use a graph-ical slide to set this value, from which thresholds for onset and offset derive. The analyses occur only between onsets and offsets. Offsets may occur in three different forms: through natural decay, slurred (a new onset condition occurs

---

[3] In addition to the *Max* implementation, we are working on a *Pure Data* version that will consist of a library of external abstractions and custom DSP objects/methods written in *C*.

before the expected level reduction), or forced (the user can determine a time delay or a decrease in amplitude to trigger it).

Figure 1 gives an overview of the audio flow in our program, mainly of time domain processes. Next, we discuss some elements of this flowchart.

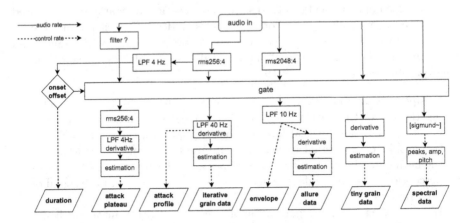

Fig. 1. Flowchart with the main audio processing blocks for audio analysis and descriptors. Source: [6].

Figure 2 depicts the waveform and different RMS curves for a guiro recording, where it is possible to observe the effects of the window size and filter parameters. We designate these curves with a couple of numbers, the first indicating the window size and the second the overlap rate used in these estimations. With the sampling frequency of 48 kHz, an RMS curve $rms256{:}4$ presents values calculated for time slices of 5.33 ms (256 samples) separated by intervals of 1.33 ms (64 samples). The $rms2048{:}4$ curve expresses the general envelope, the $rms256{:}4$ low-pass filtered 4 Hz is used for the estimation of the end of attack (which we prefer to call the first plateau), and the $rms256{:}4$ filtered 40 Hz is routed to routines dedicated to the attack profile and iterative grains.

A display of typical attack profiles from different percussive instruments can be seen in Fig. 3. In this selection, one of the $rms256{:}4$ curves was low-pass filtered 30 Hz.

Iterative grains are detected through derivation of the RMS curve (see Fig. 4), respecting two parameters: a minimum threshold and the maximal interval permitted between grains.

Tiny grains are trickier to handle since there is no objective definition for what Schaeffer calls resonant and friction grains. Given the nature of percussive sounds, we can not rely on audio processing dedicated to isolating harmonic and non-harmonic contents for this task. So we have chosen to analyze the proper audio signal, and indicate every change of direction as a tiny grain, aware of a significant warning to this option: are higher frequencies always more grainy than lower ones? We try to minimize this fact by calculating the abruptness of this

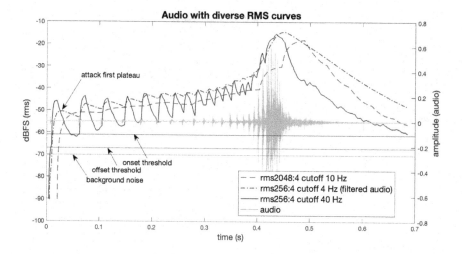

Fig. 2. Different RMS curves extracted from a guiro sound. Thresholds for background noise, onsets and offsets are also depicted.

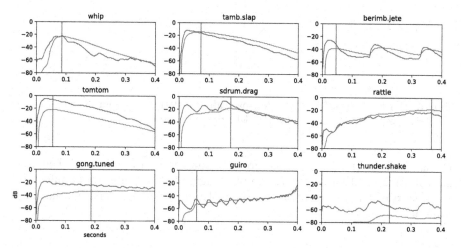

Fig. 3. Attack profiles and first plateau (vertical red mark) of nine percussive sounds. The smoothed light gray curve is a *rms256:4* low-pass filtered (4 Hz) envelope of the low-pass filtered input signal, and is used for the estimation of the plateau. The non-smoothed blue curve is a *rms256:4* low-pass filtered (30 Hz) envelope of the non-filtered input signal, and is used for the qualification of the attack profile. Filters and threshold parameters remained unchanged for all sounds. (Color figure online)

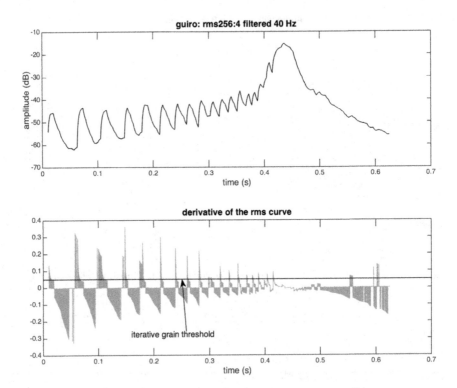

Fig. 4. Above: an *rms256:4* curve low-pass filtered 40 Hz from a guiro sound; below: its derivative, with a threshold for the detection of iterative grains.

change of direction. These two features–the number of tiny grains and their bend size–are estimated for every 512 samples. Figure 5 shows substantial differences in these two parameters between one stroke on a pandeiro and another on a tomtom.

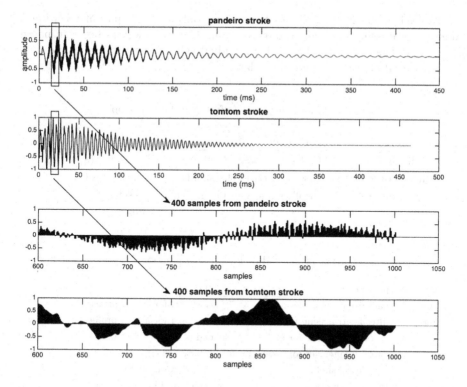

Fig. 5. Waveforms from strokes on a pandeiro and a tomtom, followed by a 400-sample zoom in their initial portion.

Since the developed spectral descriptors are well described in a former publication, we will just enumerate them here: (1) the number of spectral peaks needed to express 50 and 80% of the sound energy; (2) the percentage of the total energy expressed by 20 spectral peaks; (3) the most prominent peak (or peaks); (4) fundamental frequency (presence and value); (5) intrinsic dissonance; (6) spectral centroid; (7) difference between the highest and lowest spectral peaks; (8) spectral region; (9) spectral distribution in three or four ranges. All these descriptors are estimated with a window of 2048 points and an overlapping factor of 4, with a refresh rate of 10.67 ms in the chosen sampling rate.

Tables 1, 2, 3, 4 and 5 detail the inputs, outputs, and parametrization of different processing modules in our program. The small letters between parentheses after the outputs indicate (i) individual value per event; (s) sparse data; (c) control-rate data; (a) audio-rate data.

Table 1. Module for onset/offset detection envelopes.

inputs	parameters	outputs
audio in	background noise level	rms256:4 (a and c)
slurred onset/offset	onset and offset thresholds	rms2048:4 (c)
forced offset	cutoff frequencies for rms curves	onset (i)
		offset (i)

Table 2. Module for attack detection.

inputs	parameters	outputs
audio in	background noise level	rms256:4 for end of attack (a and c)
onset	filter for transient salience	rms256:4 for attack profile (a and c)
offset	cutoff frequencies for end of attack	end of attack - first plateau (i)
	cutoff frequencies for attack profile	attack size (i)
	attack thresholds	attack duration (i)
	re-attack interval	attack profile (i)
		slurred onset (i)

Table 3. Module for iterative and tiny grains.

inputs	parameters	outputs
audio in	cutoff frequencies for rms curves	iterative grain size (s)
onset	iterative grain thresholds	iterative grain duration (s)
offset	max iterative grain interval	iterative grain binary time series (c)
		tiny grain number in 512 samples (c)
		tiny grain bend in 512 samples (c)

3.1 Time Series Analysis

Different descriptors are represented by time series in the control rate, between onset and offset or, in the case of attack profiles, between onset and a maximal interval. Even for iterative grains and allures we estimate a binary time series (1 for occurrence, 0 for absence). In theory, all of these series can be considered profiles [4], and go through a simple statistical analysis. This analysis includes:

Table 4. Module for allures.

inputs	parameters	outputs
rms2048:4 (dB)	bend threshold	allure size (s)
onset	size threshold	allure bend (s)
offset		peak-peak interval (s)
		valley-peak interval (s)
		peak-valley interval (s)
		% p-v/v-p (s)
		allure binary time series (c)

Table 5. Module for spectral descriptors.

inputs	descriptor	output
audio in onset offset	percentage 50% of signal energy	number of spectral peaks (c)
	percentage 80%	number of spectral peaks (c)
	% energy 20 peaks	% (0–1) (c)
	spectral centroid	midicents (c)
	fundamental frequency	midicents (or −1 for unpitched frames) (c)
	most prominent peak (1 or more)	midicents (c)
	intrinsic dissonance	unitless value - typically 0 to 500 (c)
	difference between highest and lowest peak	midicents (c)
	spectral region*	1 to 7 (c)
	spectral distribution*	energy in each range (0–1) (c)

* These two descriptors requires frequency values dividing the spectrum in 3 or 4 regions.

- length;
- minimal and maximal values;
- average and standard deviation;
- mean value of 10 samples at the start, centre and end of the series;
- temporal centroid and spread;
- skewness and kurtosis;
- crest and flatness;
- allures (generalized to descriptors other than the amplitude envelope).

4 Practical Applications

In its current state, the program developed in *Max* has a modular structure including tools for parametrization and visualization of descriptors, and for mapping their outputs to (1) processing and synthesis processes; (2) to the machine learning software *Wekinator*; (3) to performance analysis; and (4) to interactive tools like transcribing excerpts in real time and playing variations on them. Lately, we have denominated this program *Obié*, a phonetic transcription into Portuguese of the French word *objet* that calls into play a bit of strangeness and humor for native speakers.

Although we developed *Obié* as a tool for dealing with the generality of percussive sounds, it is not our intention to feed a machine learning algorithm with a large amount of data, which would apply to any situation. On the contrary, we prefer to work with contextualized and "living" data. The contexts are crucial because they determine which perceptual criteria are the most important in each case. Schaeffer stresses the relativity of analyses, saying that "the application of the major distinctions in our typomorphology will depend in practice on particular applications and the listening criteria at the time."[10, p. 307]

We will describe three musical contexts in which selected features of *Obié* are employed for different goals. The first case is its integration into a composition for percussion and live-electronics; the second relates to its incorporation into the practice of a professional flutist. The last is a creative study exploring a simple, toy-like percussion instrument.

4.1 *Anesidora*, for Percussion and Live-Electronics

Composed for two percussionists and live-electronics[4], the piece's discourse is based on the sonic expectations produced/induced by percussionists corporal gestures while playing certain instruments. The piece tries to play with those expectations, composing certain musical gestures that relate with the expectation of the corporal ones in different forms.

Our program is used on the piece inside this multi-modal context, along with another *Max* patch developed specially for the piece. The real-time description of selected percussion sonorities opened certain interactive approaches to the electronics routed to the *pandoras* that amplified the possible multi-modal relationships of the piece.

The piece's patch uses mostly three types of data from *Obié*: the dynamic envelope, the size of iterative grains, and the number of tiny grains. Those values are used in different parts of the piece to (1) trigger filtered noises in certain rhythms (for example, following a roll) played by the instrumentalists (that activate the *pandoras* wires, as if playing them remotely), and (2) manipulate ring modulation processes, that try to emulate and compose with certain sonorities played on the bassdrum.

To exemplify this, we focus here on a certain timbre exploration: the activation/rubbing of the bassdrum membrane with a superball[5], exploring different harmonics. This is done towards the end the piece[6], as a contrasting approach to the percussionists corporal gestures, influencing the sonorities of a continuous gesture.

This approach consisted in using the tiny grains data to control a single-band ring modulation process done with the object [freqshift~]. The audio input

---

[4] The piece instrumentation is 2 *pandoras* (snare drums with speakers inside them), 2 tons, 2 floor tons, 2 woodblocks and a bassdrum. A video performance of the piece can be accessed here: https://musica.ufmg.br/lapis/projects/obie/.

[5] Superball refers to a type of mallet with a plastic or rubber ball on one end.

[6] See 08:20 to 09:15 of the mentioned recording.

came from the bassdrum microphone; during the experimentation processes, the number of tiny grains was scaled to certain ranges of values and used as the amount of frequency to be shifted. The result, routed to the speakers inside the *pandoras*, is a augmented superball rub sound, that has a direct relation to the musical and corporal gestures being made but is also filtered by the snare drums. This sonority is even more enhanced with the possibility to turn on or off the *pandoras* wires and activate them with the same gestures.

4.2   Differentiation of Attacks on the Flute

Not only sounds from percussion instruments can profit from the interactive analysis offered by our program. As an example, different attacks on the flute can be well described and discriminated by their profile. We have conducted an experiment using five attacks: regular, pizzicato, tongue ram, eolian, and voiced. A professional flutist, a member of our research team[7], played ten instances of each type using the note A4 (440 Hz). Analysis of their duration, shape, and amplitude can provide a crude differentiation, as shown in Fig. 6. If we add the spectral distribution to the process, it becomes clear that the eolian sounds have a large amount of high-frequency energy, followed by the pizzicatos (see Fig. 7). But there remains some similarity between regular and voiced attacks. In this case, we bring into play two more descriptors–the percentage of unpitched frames and the interval between the highest and lowest spectral peaks–to guarantee reliable discrimination, even when using different notes and octaves. Average values for these descriptors are depicted in Table 6.

Table 6. Percentage of unpitched frames and average interval between the highest and lowest spectral peaks for 5 different flute attacks.

Attack type	unpitched frames (%)	Δ peaks (midicents)
regular	0.02	56.2
pizzicato	0.59	44.1
tongue ram	0.37	60.6
eolian	0.53	34.9
voiced	0.1	51.2

---

[7] This musician also uses the *Obié* to practice specific sounds, including vibratos, bends, glissandos, multiphonics, timbral transitions, among others.

For interactive use of this recognition, we use machine learning software–
the *Wekinator*[8]. After sending a list with a few elements just after the offset
(natural or forced) to a previously trained *Wekinator* project, the estimation
and response occur within a short delay, between 3 and 5 milliseconds. This
process can help technical improvement, along with the visual cues given by our
program, but also shows potential for its use in creative musical situations.

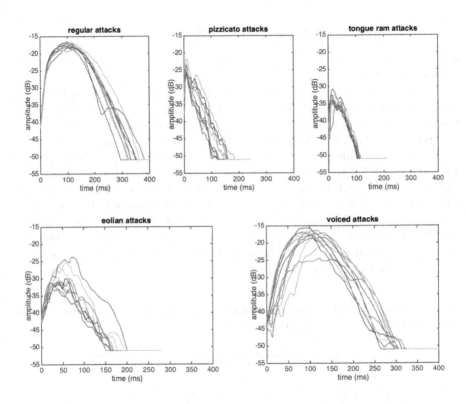

Fig. 6. Attack profiles of ten instances of 5 different attack types on the flute.

---

[8] See http://www.wekinator.org.

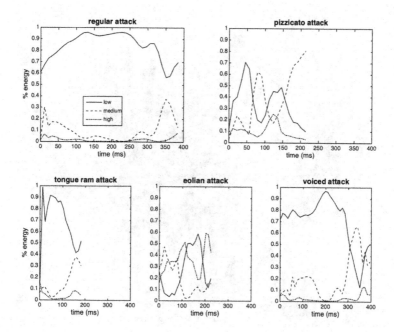

Fig. 7. Energy distribution in 5 different attack types on the flute. The regions are divided by the frequencies 523.25 and 1046.5 Hz, corresponding to the notes C5 and C6.

4.3   Improvisation with a Frog-Guiro

In order to explore the possibilities of interactive sonic expansion embeddded in *Obié*, we chose an instrument with limited resources: a small frog-guiro made from wood, with maximal dimensions of $10 \times 7 \times 5$ cm. It has five notches and a cut through the mouth that ends in a cylindrical cavity. It is played with a beater of the same material (see Fig. 8). The higher part of the mouth has a prominent resonance around 3400 Hz. Although less pronounced in the overall sound, the cylindrical hole has its own resonance, which becomes more evident when one side is closed (around 1800 Hz).

Fig. 8. A small wooden frog-guiro, with maximal dimensions $10 \times 7 \times 5$ cm.

We adopted a two-fold strategy: (1) recognition of seven different sound types and continuous transcription of excerpts, and (2) audio processing parametrized by audio descriptors. The seven sound types are: (1) stroke on the mouth; (2) stroke on the mouth with one end or the cavity closed; (3) stroke on the muffled mouth; (4) combination of 2 and 3; (5) stroke on the back side; (6) forward slide; and (7) backward slide through the notches. All these sounds present short durations, below 400 ms, the maximal duration of attack profiles in *Obié*.

For the differentiation between these types we have chosen the following descriptors to train *Wekinator*: normalized duration and crest of the attack profile, the number of iterative grains, percentage of unpitched frames, and energy in four spectral regions. These regions are delimited by the frequencies 2500, 3400, and 5000 Hz.

The continuous musical flow (played live) segments according to two criteria: a maximal number of events for each segment (13 as default) and a maximal allowed interval between two consecutive sounds (1500 ms). A transcription process switches between two constantly overwritten buffers. Stored data consists of a list of events, with onset time, duration, amplitude, and type.

Before playback, each excerpt can be varied rhythmically (shuffle of inter onset intervals–IOIs) or in the sequence of sound types. Each sound type can trigger selected excerpts–or their variation–if a gate is open and the former playback is over. The playback commands may be routed to synthesis routines inspired by the guiro sounds, or to Midi sound libraries (at this moment we use samples from woodblocks, tambourines, and bongos).

From the experimentation, we have developed five sound processing/synthesis modules to transform guiro sounds during a performance. The first is the control of the amplitude of a sinusoidal oscillator with the attack profile and its frequency with the scaled spectral centroid. The scaling occurs downwards since the centroid values are very high in frequency. The second process uses the detection and amplitudes of iterative grains to trigger pre-recorded and modified samples of the guiro. The third routine applies a variable delay line to the input sound, using the number of tiny grains to control the frequency of an oscillator and the percentage of energy expressed by 20 spectral peaks to control the depth of the modulation. The fourth process is a ring modulator (using only its negative sideband) in which spectral centroid values determine the multiplying frequency. Finally, we use a sound modulation based on FM synthesis parameters (see [5]). The modulation index is determined by the percentage of energy expressed by 20 peaks, inharmonicity is set by the ratio between the two most prominent spectral peaks, and the amplitude envelope is determined by the attack profile. Every incoming event can define new delay intervals for each of the five described processes.

The improvisation process relies on a cyclic counter of 60 events. As the counter increases, the number of simultaneous processes increases along. This option offers a cue to the player since an accumulating texture suddenly breaks at the counter reset. After a chosen number of resets, the gate for triggering recorded (and possibly varied) excerpts is open, the processing routines stop, and the improvisation takes another path, guided by the events played a few moments before. After another pre-defined number of resets, this gate is closed, and sound processing returns.

An improvisation instance is available at the website of our lab[9]. In this performance, processed and synthesized sounds are reproduced through one pandora, establishing a kind of dialogue between a soloist and a hidden virtual ensemble.

5   Final Remarks

Obié integrates analytical and interactive tools enabling direct applications in musical practices, from technical improvement to performance evaluation and creative situations. The concrete cases presented in this text have demonstrated not only the pertinence of our methodological starting point but also the importance of an interactive design for diverse musical applications. It is also important to point out that, despite being focused on percussion sounds, *Obié* adapts well to other instruments when sound objects are not exclusively pitch-oriented.

We intend to further explore these resources, increasing the number of participants and instruments in workshops and creative projects. The flexibility of

---

[9] https://musica.ufmg.br/lapis/projects/obie/.

our program still needs to be tested in more complex situations, where individual demands and collective coordination are equally important.

Presently we work on the integration of gestural data–delivered by portable IMUs[10]–into the system. A combined visualization and analysis of data from different media will certainly open new paths of exploration.

Concluding, it is worth mentioning that Schaeffer's solfège represented not only an inspiration and guide but also a constant source of ideas and insights regarding the choice, design, and combination of audio descriptors. In this way, *Obié* is not a substitute for human musical abilities but can be thought of as a partner capable of dialoguing with our strengths and weaknesses.

Acknowledgments. This work is supported by the Brazilian research agency CNPq (National Council for Scientific and Technological Development) and FAPEMIG (The Minas Gerais State Research Foundation). Our thanks to the percussionists Fernando Rocha and Douglas Rafael, and to the flutist Rodrigo Frade.

References

1. Chion, M.: Guide des Objets Sonores. Buchet/Chastel, Paris (1983)
2. Chion, M.: Guide to Sound Objects. English translation by John Dack and Christine North, London (2009). https://monoskop.org/images/0/01/Chion_Michel_Guide_To_Sound_Objects_Pierre_Schaeffer_and_Musical_Research.pdf
3. Di Scipio, A.: The politics of sound and the biopolitics of music: weaving together sound-making, irreducible listening, and the physical and cultural environment. Organised Sound **20**(3), 278–289 (2015). https://doi.org/10.1017/S1355771815000205
4. Freire, S., Padovani, J.H., Campos, C.: The profile concept in Schaeffer's solfège: discussion of its diverse meanings and proposal of a quantitative real-time approach. In: Proceedings of 12° Congresso Iberoamericano de Acústica, pp. 1–9. Florianópolis, Brazil (2022). https://musica.ufmg.br/sfreire/wp-content/uploads/2022/09/freire-padovani-caio-fia-2022.pdf
5. Freire, S.: Real-time audio processing by means of FM synthesis parameters: fundamentals and preliminary compositional applications. In: Proceedings of the International Computer Music Conference 2015, p. 4. University of North Texas (2015). https://hdl.handle.net/2027/spo.bbp2372.2015.015
6. Freire, S., Padovani, J.H., Campos, C.C.: Schaeffer's Solfège, percussion, audio descriptors: towards an interactive musical system. Vortex Music J. **10**(1) (2022). https://periodicos.unespar.edu.br/index.php/vortex/article/view/4693
7. Freire, S., Santos, G., Armondes, A., Meneses, E.A.L., Wanderley, M.M.: Evaluation of inertial sensor data by a comparison with optical motion capture data of guitar strumming gestures. Sensors **20**(19), 5722 (2020). https://doi.org/10.3390/s20195722
8. Jander, O.: Solfeggio. In: Grove Music Online. Oxford University Press, Oxford (2001). https://doi.org/10.1093/gmo/9781561592630.article.26144
9. Schaeffer, P.: Traité des Objets Musicaux. Éditions du Seuil, Paris (1966)
10. Schaeffer, P.: Treatise on Musical Objects: Essays Across Disciplines. University of California Press, Oakland, California (2017)

---

[10] An evaluation of the chosen IMU can be read here [7].

A Polytemporal Model for Musical Scheduling

Martin Fouilleul[✉], Jean Bresson, and Jean-Louis Giavitto

STMS – Sorbonne Université, IRCAM, CNRS, Grenoble, France
{martin.fouilleul,jean.bresson,jean-louis.giavitto}@ircam.fr

Abstract. This paper describes the temporal model of a scheduler geared towards show control and live music applications. This model relies on multiple inter-related temporal axes, called timescales. Timescales allow scheduling computations using abstract dates and delays, much like a score uses symbolic positions and durations (e.g. bars, beats, and note values) to describe musical time. Abstract time is ultimately mapped onto wall-clock time through the use of time transformations, specified as tempo curves, for which we provide a formalism in terms of differential equations on symbolic position. In particular, our model allows specifying tempo both as a function of time or as a function of symbolic position, and allows piecewise tempo curves to be built from parametric curves.

Keywords: Symbolic time · Time transformations · Tempo curves · Scheduling

1 Introduction

Timing is of utmost importance in performing arts. Among them, music has developed particularly fine-grained temporal constructs, using both continuous and discrete abstract representations of time. As such, it presents specific and interesting challenges with regard to the composition and interpretation of time at multiple scales, and across multiple independent time-flows.

In this paper we present the temporal model of a scheduler which is part of a programming environment for performing arts and interactive multimedia installations, called Quadrant [11]. Our temporal model allows scheduling computations along concurrent timescales organized in a temporal hierarchy. Timescales are related to their parent through time transformations. A time transformation can be specified by a tempo curve, either as a function of time or as a function of symbolic position. Piecewise tempo curves can be built from parametric curves such as Béziers curves, which are both versatile and intuitive. The scheduler exposes an interface based on fibers, that makes it easy to organize inter-dependant streams of related events.

We first highlight the importance of symbolic time in musical applications (Sect. 2). We then cover the notion of time transformations, and give a differential equation formulation to tempo curves (Sect. 3). We then show how we derive and solve tempo curves equations (Sect. 4). Finally, we present the symbolic time scheduler used by Quadrant (Sect. 6).

© Springer Nature Switzerland AG 2023
M. Aramaki et al. (Eds.): CMMR 2021, LNCS 13770, pp. 139–162, 2023.
https://doi.org/10.1007/978-3-031-35382-6_12

2   Abstract Timescales

Show controllers are programs used by sound and lighting engineers to create and run temporal scenarios synchronized to the actions of performers on stage. They allow users to launch sound and video samples, control mixing and lighting desks, operate motors for mechatronic stage props, and so on. Several approaches can be identified as to how they present and organize the temporal relations between the cues of the show:

- Timelines, which organize cues on a common, static time axis. Most sequencers, such as ProTools[1] or Cubase[2] fall in that category.
- Cuelists, which organize cues in nested lists with associated timing semantics. Notable examples are QLab[3] or Linux Show Player[4].
- Hybrid models offer both cuelists and timelines, either through separate modes of operation, as in Medialon[5] or Smode[6], or as dual views of the same cues, as in Ableton Live[7].
- Graphical planning environments that allow users to position cues in some abstract space, which maps to time through the use of trajectories, as in Iannix [8], or flow graphs, as in Ossia Score [7].

Despite its importance in music and other performing arts, most show controllers and computer music environments lack an abstract notion of musical time, and directly map cues to wall-clock dates or to external triggers. However, musical time is a symbolic notion that can have many different concrete, real time instantiations. For example, a musical score ascribes temporality to musical events using symbolic dates and durations (e.g. beats and notes values). Symbolic time is mapped to performance (real) time by the interpreter, following tempo indications, cultural conventions, and interpretative choices. Furthermore, is often deployed throughout a work at different scales (e.g. movements, phrases, cells, notes...), and not every scale is tied to the same global tempo, e.g. ornaments such as grace notes and *appogiatura* are not affected in the same way by a change of tempo as a main melody line. Hence, a temporal programming environment for live shows should allow encoding and performing streams of actions embedded within multiple symbolic musical times, or *timescales*.

The notion of abstract timescales has been tackled before by computer music environments or score followers. For instance, FORMULA [2] allows applying independent time deformations on groups of concurrent tasks. David A. Jaffe [16] proposed a recursive scheduler for hierarchical timing control, using explicit time maps. Antescofo [9] allows users to compose independent abstract times through the use of *time scopes* and tempo curves.

---

[1] https://www.avid.com/pro-tools.

[2] https://new.steinberg.net/cubase/.

[3] https://qlab.app/docs/QLab_4_Reference_Manual.pdf.

[4] https://linux-show-player-users.readthedocs.io/en/latest/index.html.

[5] https://medialon.com/wp-content/uploads/2019/07/M515-1-Medialon-Control-System-Manual.pdf.

[6] https://smode.fr.

[7] https://www.ableton.com/en/live/what-is-live/.

In Quadrant's scheduler, a timescale is a data structure used to maintain a notion of logical time, expressed as a rational number of *symbolic time units*[8], and to schedule events at specific logical dates. It is analogous in this respect to a score, which organizes musical events in terms of a musical time, that needs to be translated into wall-clock time by a musician according to tempo indications and interpretative choices.

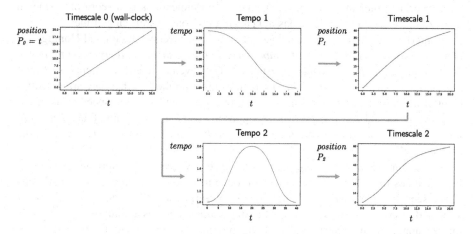

Fig. 1. Composing time deformations using tempo curves.

However, whereas the tempo indication of a score usually prescribes some idealized mapping from musical-time to wall-clock time, a timescale's logical time does not necessarily map directly to wall-clock time. Instead, each timescale has a *time source*, which can be either the wall-clock time or another timescale. A timescale is also associated with a *time transformation*, which maps its internal time to the time of its source. Thus, the scheduler can handle multiple notions of logical time and map dates to wall-clock time through a hierarchy of time transformations.

Figure 1 illustrates a time deformation between a timescale and its source. The time map plots for each timescale show the position of the timescale with respect to wall-clock time. The effect of the first tempo curve (tempo 1) is to warp the time map of timescale 0 (which represents wall-clock time) into that of timescale 1 (which represent some abstract musical time). Timescale 1 is then transformed by another tempo curve (tempo 2), to produces the time map of timescale 2.

---

[8] We deliberately avoid the term *beats* here. We think it would bring some confusion by conflating the notion of time unit with the notion of meter, and by suggesting that all beats are of equal conceptual length. This is, in fact, rather a Western exception than a universal norm.

3   Time Transformations

Quadrant's scheduler must be able to transform timescale-local positions to and from wall-clock time. These time transformations can be specified as *time maps*, which directly map the parent's timescale to the local timescale. The can also be expressed by the means of *tempo curves*, which describe the speed of a timescale's "playhead" with respect to the source time, much like tempo indications in a score prescribe an idealized conversion from durations in beats to durations in wall-clock time[9].

Tempo curves have been the subject of some controversy. Desain and Honing [10] claimed that there is *"no abstract tempo curve in the music nor is there a mental tempo curve in the head of a performer or listener"*. They even deemed tempo curves *"harmful"* and a *"dangerous notion"*, basing their opinion on the fact that they are not sufficient to accurately preserve musical timing of a piece under global speed transformations. Mazzola and Zahorka [18] firmly opposed this position, arguing that *"The problem is not the a priori concept of tempo curves, but rather its elaboration for realistic application"*.

From a practical standpoint, the debate on the existence of tempo curves seems a little dubious to us. Tempo curves have proven to be of practical use in virtually any music sequencing software. That they do not preserve musical timing when arbitrarily stretched or compressed is not a rebuttal of their adequacy as a compositional tool. In our opinion, a more interesting take on this problem is given by Honing in [15], where they suggest adjoining a time shift map to the tempo curve, in order to independently capture timings that do not react linearly to global tempo changes.

Several methods have been proposed to represent time transformations and to integrate tempo curves to map symbolic position to time. Jaffe [16] proposes to directly use time maps constructed from a collection of predefined time warping functions. Berndt [3] chooses to represent tempo curves by potential functions of symbolic position, matching some specified mean tempo condition. Timewarp [17] is a tool that uses regularized beta functions to define tempo curves satisfying polyrhythmic constraints. Antescofo uses a variety of tweening functions[10] to express tempo as a function of time, and uses closed form expressions to compute time transformation based on tempo curves. When there is no analytical solution to a tempo curve integration, Antescofo samples the curve to produce a piecewise linear approximation, which is then integrated analytically. Antescofo can also use arbitrary expressions to define tempo, although these expressions are not integrated: they are reevaluated each time a variable is updated, and considered constant between updates. As such, they can only represent tempo as step functions.

In Quadrant's scheduler, tempo curves can be specified either as a function of a timescale's parent time, or as a function of symbolic position (which is closer to the

---

[9] One difference, however, is that we use the word tempo here to refer to the ratio of internal symbolic time units over source symbolic time units, rather than the number of beats per minutes, since the latter could depend on the musical meter of the timescale.

[10] https://antescofo-doc.ircam.fr/Reference/compound_curve/.

way tempo is specified in a score). We use piecewise tempo curves where each piece can be defined by parametric curves. Instead of restricting tempo to predefined curves with known integrals, Quadrant uses a variable-step numerical solver to integrate tempo curves when simple analytical solutions are not readily available. This allows us constructing tempo functions from Bézier curves, which are more versatile than standard tweeners and allow easy tweaking of control points by a user through a graphical interface.

3.1 Differential Equation Formulation

In the following we will use the variable p to denote the position in a timescale, i.e. the logical time in this timescale's reference frame. The variable t will be used to denote the source time (or simply, *time*), i.e. the time in the timescale's parent reference frame (which could be the wall-clock time).

The function *position function*, $P(t)$, transforms the source time into the internal position of the timescale. The *time function*, $T(p)$, transforms the position into the source time. Obviously, $P = T^{-1}$.

A *tempo curve* $\boldsymbol{T}$ can be either a function of time or position. It maps its parameter to the value of the derivative of the position function at this instant. In the following we will refer to a tempo curve defined as a function of position as an *autonomous tempo curve*, whereas a tempo curve defined as a function of time will be referred to as a *non-autonomous tempo curve*. This naming stems from the formulation of the tempo curve as the right-hand side of an autonomous or non-autonomous differential equation:

$$\frac{dP}{dt}(t) = \boldsymbol{T}(P(t)) \quad \text{(autonomous)}, \quad \text{or} \quad \frac{dP}{dt}(t) = \boldsymbol{T}(t) \quad \text{(non autonomous)}, \tag{1}$$

with initial condition $P(0) = 0$.

4 Tempo Curves Integration

Tempo curves in Quadrant are defined as piecewise functions. For the sake of brevity, we may refer to an interval and its associated sub-function as a tempo curve *segment*, or simply as a *curve*, where the meaning should be clear from context. Each segment is defined by a start tempo and an end tempo, a duration, an interpolation mode and optional interpolation parameters. We implemented three interpolation modes, namely *constant*, *linear* and *parametric*.

4.1 Integration of Constant and Linear Tempo Curves

Constant and linear tempo curves can be solved analytically. We show below the differential equation of tempo, and the position and time functions for each case.

Constant Tempo

$$\boldsymbol{T}(p) = \boldsymbol{T}_0 . \tag{2}$$

$$T(p) = \frac{p}{\boldsymbol{T}_0} , \tag{3}$$

$$P(t) = t \times \boldsymbol{T}_0 .$$

Autonomous Linear Tempo

$$\boldsymbol{T}(p) = \boldsymbol{T}_0 + \alpha p , \text{ where } \alpha = \frac{\boldsymbol{T}_1 - \boldsymbol{T}_0}{L} . \tag{4}$$

$$P(t) = \frac{\boldsymbol{T}_0}{\alpha}(e^{\alpha t} - 1) , \tag{5}$$

$$T(p) = \frac{1}{\alpha} \log(1 + \frac{\alpha p}{\boldsymbol{T}_0}) .$$

Non-autonomous Linear Tempo

$$\boldsymbol{T}(t) = \boldsymbol{T}_0 + \alpha t , \text{ where } \alpha = \frac{\boldsymbol{T}_1 - \boldsymbol{T}_0}{L} . \tag{6}$$

$$P(t) = \boldsymbol{T}_0 t + \frac{\alpha}{2} t^2 , \tag{7}$$

$$T(p) = \frac{\sqrt{\boldsymbol{T}_0^2 + 2\alpha p} - \boldsymbol{T}_0}{\alpha} .$$

Numerical Considerations. Some of the above time and position functions are indeterminate forms for $\alpha \to 0$. To avoid that problem, we approximate these expressions by a series expansions in α when $|\alpha|$ is smaller than a given threshold. For instance, our approximation of the position function for the autonomous case when is $|\alpha| < 10^{-9}$ is:

$$P(t) \approx \boldsymbol{T}_0(t + \frac{\alpha}{2} t^2 + \frac{\alpha^2}{6} t^3 + \frac{\alpha^3}{24} t^4 + \frac{\alpha^4}{120} t^5) . \tag{8}$$

4.2 Parametric Tempo Curves

In this section we will give a definition of a parametric tempo curve, and show the differential equations that need to be solved in order to compute the time and position functions. These equations are then solved by a numerical solver.

An autonomous (resp. non-autonomous) parametric tempo curve segment is defined as a function $\mathscr{C}$ of the position p (resp. of the time t), which describes the same curve in the plane $(p, \mathbf{T})$ (resp. $(t, \mathbf{T})$) as a parametric curve $\mathbf{B}(s)$ with components $B_x(s)$ and $B_y(s)$[11].

Autonomous Parametric Tempo. The differential equation corresponding to an autonomous tempo curve can be written as

$$\frac{dP}{dt}(t) = C(P(t)). \tag{9}$$

Position function $P(t)$. The derivative of the position with respect to time is directly expressed by the autonomous tempo curve,

$$\frac{dP}{dt}(t) = B_y(s), \text{ where } s = B_x^{-1}(P(t)). \tag{10}$$

Time function $T(p)$. We operate the change of variable $s = B_x^{-1}(p)$ on Eq. 9. Finding the time function is then a matter of solving the differential equation[12]

$$\frac{d\tilde{T}}{ds}(s) = \frac{B_x'(s)}{B_y(s)}, \text{ with } \tilde{T}(s) = T(p). \tag{11}$$

Non-autonomous Parametric Tempo. The definition of the non-autonomous parametric tempo curves can be written as

$$\frac{dP}{dt}(t) = C(t). \tag{12}$$

Position function $P(t)$. Using the change of variable $s = B_x^{-1}(t)$ and the chain rule, we can write the differential equation for the position function as

$$\frac{d\tilde{P}}{ds}(s) = B_y(s)B_x'(s), \text{ with } \tilde{P}(s) = P(t). \tag{13}$$

Time function $T(p)$. Using the formula for the derivative of inverse functions on Eq. 12, we get

$$\frac{dT}{dp}(p) = \frac{1}{C(T(p))} = \frac{1}{B_y(s)}, \text{ where } s = B_x^{-1}(T(p)). \tag{14}$$

---

[11] Textbooks usually choose the letter t to denote the parameter of parametric curves. We instead choose the letter s to disambiguate it from time.

[12] Note that here we can find an equation in s. This is beneficial as it allows our numerical solver to find the parameter s once, and then evaluate the Bézier curve and its derivatives using only polynomials in s. The same change of variable is done in Eq. 13. It is unfortunately useless with Eq. 10 and Eq. 14, since s can't be computed directly from the independant variable.

4.3 Bézier Tempo Curves

The above formulation allows the use of any parametric curve, provided that it describes a derivable, non null function. Our specific implementation uses cubic Bézier curves, which are especially versatile, as they allow putting constraints on both endpoints and their first derivative, while ensuring that the curve remains contained inside its control points' convex hull. They are also intuitive to manipulate and map well to the curve-editing interfaces commonly used in animation, audio, and video applications.

An autonomous (resp. non-autonomous) Bézier tempo curve segment is defined by the parametric curve

$$B(s) = C_3 s^3 + C_2 s^2 + C_1 s + C_0,\tag{15}$$

where the C_i are the power basis coefficients computed from the Bézier curve's control points as follows:

$$\begin{aligned} C_0 &= P_0,\\ C_1 &= -3P_0 + 3P_1,\\ C_2 &= 3P_0 - 6P_1 + 3P_2,\\ C_3 &= -P_0 + 3P_1 - 3P_2 + P_3.\end{aligned}\tag{16}$$

Monotonicity. To ensure that the curve describes a function, the cubic function $B_x(s)$ must be monotonically increasing on $[0, 1]$. Given end points P_0 and P_1 with abscissae $P_{0,x} < P_{3,x}$, we want a condition on the abscissae of the intermediate control points $P_{1,x}$ and $P_{2,x}$ for this property to hold.

Let α and β be the respective ratios of the derivatives $B_x'(0)$ and $B_x'(1)$ at the end points over the slope of the line segment joining $B_x(0)$ and $B_x(1)$.

[12] derived the monotonicity region $\mathscr{M}$ of values (α, β) for which a cubic interpolant between two data points is monotonic (Fig. 2). It is the union of several sub-regions defined by the following equations:

$$\begin{aligned} &\alpha + \beta - 2 \leq 0,\\ &\alpha + \beta - 2 > 0 \text{ and } 2\alpha + \beta - 3 \leq 0,\\ &\alpha + \beta - 2 > 0 \text{ and } \alpha + 2\beta - 3 \leq 0,\\ &(\alpha - 1)^2 + (\alpha - 1)(\beta - 1) + (\beta - 1)^2 - 3(\alpha + \beta - 2) \leq 0.\end{aligned}\tag{17}$$

Remark 1. The first three regions are delimited by straight lines. The last region is the interior of the ellipse of center $(2, 2)$ which is tangent to the coordinates axes at points $(3, 0)$ and $(0, 3)$.

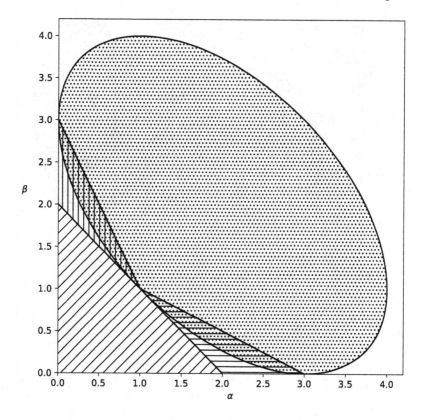

Fig. 2. Monotonicity Region $\mathcal{M}$ (Reproduced from [12]).

We now express α and β in terms of the Bézier control points:

$$\alpha = \frac{B'_x(0)}{B_x(1) - B_x(0)} = \frac{3(P_{1,x} - P_{0,x})}{P_{3,x} - P_{0,x}},$$

$$\beta = \frac{B'_x(1)}{B_x(1) - B_x(0)} = \frac{3(P_{3,x} - P_{2,x})}{P_{3,x} - P_{0,x}}. \tag{18}$$

without loss of generality, we can map the end points $P_{0,x}$ and $P_{3,x}$ respectively to 0 and 1. This gives us:

$$\alpha = 3P_{1,x},$$

$$\beta = 3(1 - P_{2,x}). \tag{19}$$

The corresponding monotonicity region for control points abscissae $P_{1,x}$ and $P_{2,x}$ is shown in Fig. 3. Note that the unit square is entirely contained within the monotonicity region. This means that as long as the abscissae of the intermediate control points lie between the abscissae of the end points, the Bézier curve can be used to specify a proper function. This fortunately lead to an intuitive user interface constraint: we can simply restrict the abscissae of control points to the temporal extents of the curve segment the user is editing.

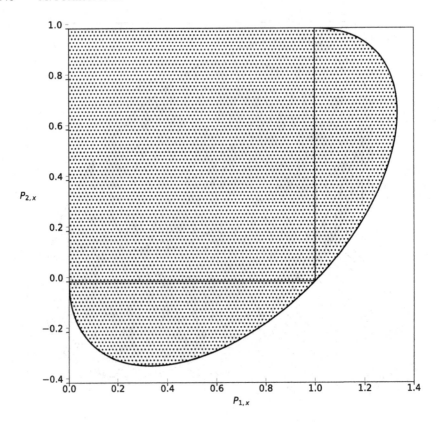

Fig. 3. Unit square and monotonicity Region $\mathcal{M}$ for control points $(P_{1,x}, P_{2,x})$.

Bézier Curves Evaluation. We should stress out that, although each coordinate of the parametric Bézier curve is cubic with respect to its parameter s, the second coordinate is *not* a cubic function of the first, i.e. the tempo is not a cubic function of position (resp. time). Analytically finding the tempo for a given position (resp. time) indeed requires solving a third order equation.

A faster method is to numerically find the parameter s for a given position (resp. time), up to some desired precision, and then compute the tempo from s. Our implementation first uses the Newton-Raphson root-finding method up to a fixed number of iterations, and falls back to a bisection algorithm if either the value of the derivative falls behind some threshold, or the desired precision is not reached within the maximum iteration count.

Numerical Resolution. Using Bézier curves, Eq. 13 poses no difficulty and can be analytically solved by integrating a 6th degree polynomial.

Bringing a symbolic calculus package to the rescue, one can find an analytical solution for Eq. 11, although it involves complex logarithms and require computing the roots of the third degree polynomial B_y. Despite the fact that these can be rearranged to involve only real logarithms, arctangents, and the (precomputed) roots, it is still quite impractical. Equation 10 and Eq. 14 on the other hand has no obvious analytical solution.

It is unclear at this point if there is a really compelling reason to favor the analytical solutions. A number of corner cases would have to be considered when finding (or numerically approximating) the roots, and special care would be necessary near singularities (much as discussed in Sect. 4.1).

On the other hand, using a numerical solver has the advantage of allowing us to control the tradeoff between accuracy and speed, and opens up the possibility of supporting other arbitrary functions to define tempo curves.

We use the Cash-Karp [6] method to numerically solve the Bézier tempo curve equations. It is an adaptive Runge-Kutta [5] solver with orders 5 and 4. We follow the general architecture proposed in [19], and adapt it to our needs.

Since the equations shown in Subsect. 4.2 are either autonomous or directly integrable, we wrote two specialized step routines, `autonomous_step()` and `integrate_step()`, that avoid much of the computation involved in a general Cash-Karp step. Given the value of the solution at the previous step, and a function pointer to compute the right-hand side of the equation, these routines advance the solution over a single step of given size, and return the result along with an estimation of the local error.

These routines are used in controlled-step routines which either accept the step, or adapt the step size and retry the step, depending on the local error estimate. These controlled-step routines are in turn called by driver routines that perform successive controlled steps across the desired interval. The drivers also adapt the error criterion at each step to the amplitude of the computed solution and its derivative, in order to achieve constant fractional errors.

4.4 Multi-segment Curves Implementation

Time transformation curves are created from a structure called a *curve descriptor*. This descriptor specifies the kind of curve (i.e. autonomous or non-autonomous tempo, or time map), and a list of *curve segments descriptors*. A *curve segment descriptor* is a structure containing the duration of the segment, the start value and end value, the interpolation mode and its optional control parameters.

At creation time, the list of segments descriptor is processed to produce a list of internal segments. These segments contain the precomputed values of the slope α of linear segments or the power basis coefficients C_i of Bézier segments. The value of the dependant variable (i.e. t for an autonomous tempo curve, or p for a non-autonomous tempo curve) at the end of the interval is also precomputed and stored in the tempo segment at creation time.

Queries on tempo curves are then handled as follows:

– The input position (resp. time) is checked against the precomputed positions (resp. times) at the breakpoints, in order to find the segment within which the input parameter lies.

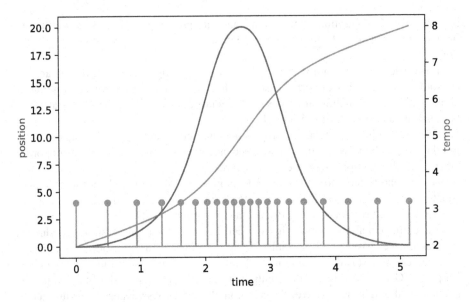

Fig. 4. Time map and beats trace for a tempo curve defined by two Bézier curves.

- If no segment is found, the tempo is curve is conceptually extended with constant tempos on the left and on the right, corresponding to the start tempo of the first segment, and the end tempo of the last segment.
- The output time (resp. position) is computed by solving the corresponding differential equation on the selected curve segment, using closed-form expression for constant and linear segments, or the numerical solver for Bézier segments.

An example of a time transformation produced by a tempo curve composed of two Bézier segments is shown in Fig. 4. The blue curve shows position as a function of time. The orange stems mark the timeline symbolic time units. The red curve shows the tempo curve, as a function of time. The figure is produced by computing the positions corresponding to a regularly spaced time grid.

5   Phase Synchronization

So far we only considered synchronizing relative clock frequencies (more formally called *syntonization*). However, when dealing with ensemble music, the notion of synchronization is really about the relative phase of each musician. It is also important to note that musical speed and phase are understood in the context of musical structure.

The musical structuration of time, at a very basic level, usually consists in a *meter*. Loosely speaking, a meter is a pattern describing a recurring grouping of pulses, and the relative lengths and accentuation of those pulses. The pulses are usually referred to as *beats*, and the groupings as *bars*. It is useful to keep in mind that not all beats are of equal nature within a bar, nor do they convey the same synchronization requirements.

To better highlight the fundamental difference between purely tempo-based synchronization and phase synchronization, let's imagine a DJ show based around samples of measured music. Although the sequencer can maintain virtually perfect tempo relations between the samples, and even presuming on the DJ's mastery, there are still many occasions where the samples will be slightly out of sync (input delay being the most obvious reason). Given enough information on the audio file, modern software such as Ableton Live [1] will already correct that asynchrony, by shifting and time-stretching the sample to align its beats on a predefined click track. They can even delay the triggering of a sample for it to happen on a bar boundary, a feature called *quantized launch* in Live's lingo.

Now, if our hypothetical show were to feature several DJs, there would be a need to synchronize multiple sequencers on shared beats and bars boundaries. Ableton Link [13] allows to share a common notion of playback transport and beat-based synchronization. Each connected software can control the transport and set its speed. Each application also chooses a beat quantum. Two applications sharing the same beat quantum value will be beat-aligned modulo that quantum. An application A with a beat quantum being a multiple of another application B's beat quantum will also be synchronized on B's boundaries.

Link offers an elegant model to select a subset of beats of A and a subset of beats of B to align. It certainly has the merits of being simple, easy to grasp from a user's point of view, and well-suited to regular meters. However, this model induces some limitations:

– This model implies a shared tempo. Pieces with multiple tempos, such as Charles Ives' *The Unanswered Question*, Stockhausen's *Gruppen*, or Steve Reich's *Piano Phase*, would be impractical to author and perform in such a model.
– Polyrhythms can also benefit from the ability to use several pulses, instead of the lowest common multiple of all groupings, which rapidly becomes difficult. For instance, exactly synchronizing a quintuplet over a septuplet would require counting 35 beats in this model, which would incur the use of an impractically high tempo.
– This model implies beats of equal lengths. Thus it is difficult to express additive meters without resorting, once again, to a common subdivision.
– The notion of a beat quantum implies that the only beats considered for boundary alignment are congruent to 0 modulo the beat quantum. In other word, alignment always happen at the beginning of the recurring group. But let's imagine a simple scenario, in which we have a kick sample K which must be aligned on 4 beat bars. Then we have a sample S of on-beats snare hits, that we want to shift by one beat in order to align it on the off-beats of K. This would call for the possibility of specifying arbitrary remainders in addition to the beat quantum: in our minimal example, the on-beats of S must be aligned to beats of K which are congruent to 1 or 3 modulo 4. One can certainly contemplate much more intricate scenarios, which would need manually specifying desired synchronization points altogether.

More generally, we think a meter-centric alignment model ala Link shouldn't be conflated with the more general notion of date alignment. In particular, the primitive of the system shouldn't be built around the assumption of congruent beat quanta, lest it be hampered by the shortcomings discussed above. Instead, at the most basic level, the synchronization system should only be concerned with aligning a future date and tempo of a process A to a given target, in a given amount of time. This goal can be stated as follow:

Given a processes A and date t_0 in its parent's timescale, corresponding to position p_0 in A's local timescale; Given $\boldsymbol{T}_0$ the tempo of A at t_0; We want to apply a time transformation to A such that at date $t_1 = t_0 + \delta$, A reaches a given position p_1 and a given tempo $\boldsymbol{T}_1$.

The target $(t_1, p_1, \boldsymbol{T}_1)$ can then be chosen to align some beats of A onto some beats of another measured process B. It can also be used to track a variably paced process B, such as the output of a score follower inferring position and tempo values from a human player. It can also be used to smear the timing of A based on irregular or punctual commands, such as *"skip two beats over the next 10 s"*. Note that this doesn't precludes the use of a simpler, meter-centric interface built *on top* of this basic capability.

5.1 Catch-Up Curves

Our scheduler itself doesn't directly handle date alignment. Instead, this is achieved by computing a catch-up time map curve and applying it to the task to be aligned. We want the time map to satisfy the following constraints:

$$\begin{aligned}
\mathscr{C}(t_0) &= P_0\,, \\
\mathscr{C}'(t_0) &= \boldsymbol{T}_0\,, \\
\mathscr{C}(t_1) &= P_1\,, \\
\mathscr{C}'(t_1) &= \boldsymbol{T}_1\,.
\end{aligned} \tag{20}$$

This ensure $\mathscr{C}$ is a smooth transition without sudden jumps or accelerations. Fortunately, Bézier curves allows us to control both endpoints and derivatives. The constraints implies the following equations on the Bézier curve control points:

$$\begin{aligned}
P_0 &= (t_0, p_0)\,, \\
P_1 &= (t_0 + \delta_1, p_0 + \boldsymbol{T}_0\delta_1)\,, \\
P_2 &= (t_1 - \delta_2, p_1 - \boldsymbol{T}_1\delta_2)\,, \\
P_3 &= (t_1, p_1)\,,
\end{aligned} \tag{21}$$

Remark 2. This means that P_1 (resp. P_2) must lie on the tangent to $\mathscr{C}$ at P_0 (resp. P_3).

Furthermore, the Bézier curve must define a monotonically increasing function. This means both $B_x(s)$ and $B_y(s)$ cubics must be monotonic. This can readily be enforced by applying the constraints shown in Subsect. 4.3, but this time both on the abscissae and ordinates of the intermediate control points P_1 and P_2.

6 Scheduler

Quadrant's poly-temporal model relies on concurrent tasks (implemented as stackful coroutines, or *fibers*) managed by a cooperative scheduler. Each task represents a sequence of interleaved computations and delays happening in a given timescale.

Computations are predictably ordered and are considered to happen instantaneously with respect to symbolic time. This makes Quadrant's model similar to that of synchronous languages [14], with a few differences that we detail below.

Strictly speaking, most synchronous languages don't have an inbuilt notion of time, and can only react to signals. This does not pose theoretical difficulties but does make some scenarios cumbersome, since one must rely on introducing and counting external "clock" signals. This downside is discussed in [22], which also proposes extending the host context of Esterel to allow a program to schedule its own wakeup time when returning from its `step` function. We use a somewhat similar approach in Quadrant, where tasks can pause for a requested amount of symbolic time.

We allow temporarily removing some task from the synchronous scheduling mechanism to have them executed in a background task pool. This permits graceful handling of blocking or asynchronous operations, such as input/output, without stalling the scheduler.

Finally, while most synchronous languages are concerned with providing hard real-time guarantees, we are mostly interested in providing a predictable yet flexible concurrency model, and only consider soft real-time goals on a best-effort basis.

API Design Discussion. The API of a scheduler essentially determines how a user will feed code fragments into the scheduler, to be executed later at a specified time. There are several important parameters to consider here: what constitutes a code fragment? How is a piece of data passed along with a fragment that operates on it? Are these fragments executed in the same context[13] as the code that provided them to the scheduler?

A common approach to that problem is to expose a callback mechanism, where the user can register functions to be called by the scheduler at a later date. This is the approach adopted, among others, by Max/MSP clock API[14], by the musical objects scheduler developed for OpenMusic in [4], or in a number of Web APIs such as [20,21]. In this model, the unit of code that can be provided to the scheduler is a function, and is usually executed in a different context that the code that registered it. Thus, the registering mechanism must also provide a way to capture some data for the callback.

Although this approach is relatively straightforward and well suited to the scheduling of independent actions, it has a number of shortcomings. In particular, when it comes to organizing streams of related actions in time, the callback model compels the user to break down the control flow of its code into lots of little distinct functions. Not only does it obfuscate the logical relationship of actions as well as their sequentiality, but it also puts on the user the unnecessary burden of passing a shared context around, ensuring its consistency and managing its lifetime. Sequential streams of actions would be better expressed by sequential code executed within the same context.

---

[13] The word *context* here is left intentionally broad. It could encompass the threading model, the data lifetime, the nature of the execution environment (e.g. native code scheduling interpreted code and vice versa), or even the machine on which the code is executed.

[14] See https://cycling74.com/sdk/max-sdk-7.3.3/html/chapter_scheduler.html.

Another approach is to design the scheduler to run user code in fibers[15]. The scheduler API then exposes functions to yield and reschedule the calling code to a future date, as well as functions to spawn other fibers. In this approach, the fragments of code provided to the scheduler by the user are not constrained to be functions, and sequential or logically related actions can be grouped within a straightforward control flow, and share the same local context.

A fiber-based scheduling API can feature mechanisms to wait for other fibers to complete, thus allowing to express dependencies between different workloads and execute them in the correct order, something which is impractical to implement with a callback API as it would require the construction of an explicit dependency graph beforehand. Another advantage of this model is that a fiber can easily be migrated between threads, which allows a very streamlined way to handle blocking calls without hanging the scheduler. Finally, callback semantics are readily emulated by spawning a new fiber that doesn't yield until it terminates. Hence, if considered strictly from the point of view of the usage code, this API design is strictly superior to the callback-based one. Its cost is a slightly higher complexity on the implementation side, which has to maintain and swap fiber contexts as needed. Another downside of fibers is the weaker support for visualization and line stepping of fiber code in most debuggers. That said, a callback-based API is also hard to debug due to the disrupted control flow and the non-obvious sharing of data across callbacks.

6.1   Scheduler API

Since our objective is to provide ways to specify and organize highly interdependent computations into complex temporal scenarios, we decided to base our scheduler architecture on the fiber approach. This is also the type of architecture adopted by FORMULA and Antescofo. However, FORMULA constitutes a whole operating system and its fibers are really more akin to system-level cooperative processes, while Antescofo is an interpreted language whose fibers are implemented at the interpreter level. On the other hand, Quadrant features user-level, native code fibers.

The API declaration is summarized in (Listing 1.1). The scheduler system is initialized by a call to `sched_init()` and shut down with `sched_end()`. User code can then interact with the scheduler by operating on *fiber* handles. A fiber represents the execution context of a piece of user code associated with a given timescale. Fibers are organized in a parent-children relationship.

Fiber Creation. User code can create and schedule a new fiber by calling one of the `sched_fiber_create_XXX()` functions. The default version creates a new fiber as a children of the fiber to which the calling code belongs. The `detached` version creates a new fiber synchronized to the clock-time. The third version creates a new fiber

---

[15] The notions of *fiber*, *coroutine*, or *green thread* are very closely related, and the distinction between them, if any, is amenable to debate. One could argue that *green thread* is more appropriate in the context of a virtual machine or runtime environment, while *coroutine* originates from programming language design. The term *fiber* may capture a more general view of the concept, but more importantly it happens to be shorter to type.

as a children of another fiber. Once the fiber is picked by the scheduler to be run, it will start executing the entry procedure passed in the `proc` parameter, passing it the value of `userPointer`. The fiber creation functions return a fiber handle, which can subsequently be used to operate on the fiber or query its properties.

Time Transformations.   The timescale associated with a fiber can be configured to apply a specified transformation to its source time, by using one of the `sched_fiber_timescale_set_XXX()` functions. The transformation can be specified as a simple tempo scaling or as a tempo curve (see Sect. 3).

```
// Initialization and shutdown
void sched_init();
void sched_end();

// fiber creation
sched_fiber sched_fiber_create(sched_fiber_proc proc, void* userPointer);
sched_fiber sched_fiber_create_detached(sched_fiber_proc proc,
                              void* userPointer);

sched_fiber sched_fiber_create_for_parent(sched_fiber parent,
                              sched_fiber_proc proc,
                              void* userPointer);

// fibers' timescales
void sched_fiber_timescale_set_scaling(sched_fiber fiber, f64 scaling);
void sched_fiber_timescale_set_tempo_curve(sched_fiber fiber,
                              sched_curve_descriptor* desc);

// Scheduling
void sched_wait(sched_steps steps);
void sched_suspend();
void sched_cancel();

void sched_fiber_suspend(sched_fiber fiber);
void sched_fiber_cancel(sched_fiber fiber);
void sched_fiber_resume(sched_fiber fiber);

sched_wakeup_code sched_wait_for_task(sched_object_handle handle,
                              sched_object_signal signal,
                              sched_steps timeout);
// Handles management
void sched_handle_release(sched_object_handle handle);
sched_object_handle sched_handle_duplicate(sched_object_handle handle);

// Background jobs
void sched_background();
void sched_foreground();
```

Listing 1.1. Quadrant's scheduler internal API.

Wait, Suspend, Resume, Cancel.   At any point in the execution of a fiber, user code can call `sched_wait()` to yield to the scheduler and reschedule the fiber in `steps` units of time. A call to `sched_suspend()` suspends the calling fiber, which can be resumed by a call to `sched_fiber_resume()`. A call to the function `sched_fiber_suspend()` suspends a fiber, which means that the timescale associated with the fiber is no longer updated and its playhead stops advancing. A suspended fiber can be resumed by calling the function `sched_fiber_resume()`. A fiber can be canceled by a call to `sched_fiber_cancel()`.

Fibers Lifecycles. Fibers can be running, retired, or completed. A fiber is running until it returns from its entry procedure or it is canceled, at which point it will be marked as *retired*. If it has no children, or all its children are completed, it will be marked as completed. Most resources associated with fibers are recycled as part of the retirement and completion stages, but a minimal set of resources is kept alive until all handles to the fiber are closed by a call to `sched_fiber_release()`. This is done so that handles can still be queried for some properties (such as status or exit codes) after the object they reference is completed. Handles can be duplicated by a call to `sched_handle_duplicate()`, should the object's lifetime be dynamically extended across multiple use-sites[16].

Waiting on Handles. A fiber can wait until another fiber is retired or completed, by calling one of the waiting functions on its handle. The most generic version waits on a handle for a specified `signal` (i.e. retirement or completion), or until a specified `timeout` has elapsed. All these functions return a wakeup code, which indicates the condition on which the wait was ended.

Background Jobs. A fiber should never hang the scheduler and prevent other fibers from progressing by failing to yield in a timely fashion. In fact we have plans for a watchdog mechanism that will interrupt and cancel such ill-behaved fibers. In order to comply with this rule, fibers that must call a blocking routine or perform untimed, lengthy computations, should request to be put on a background thread by calling `sched_background()`. Once their blocking work is done, they can reintegrate the normal scheduling flow by making a call to `sched_foreground()`.

6.2   Scheduler's Operation

Main Loop. Fibers are organized as a collection of trees corresponding to the synchronization relationships of their timescales: root fibers are synchronized on the real-time clock, and every other fiber is synchronized on its parent timescale. The scheduler also maintains a list of all running fibers, each associated with their date of next execution.

The scheduler's role is to execute actions at the clock-time corresponding to their logical date. In order to do so it must maintain the timescales's playheads consistent with the clock-time, through the time transformations, pick the next fiber to execute, sleep until its real time due date is reached, and execute it. It also has to handle control

---

[16] Although the use of shared or 'smart' pointers bears its share of problems and, in our opinion, usually warrants a reassessment of the architecture, handles to long-lived, reference-counted objects living behind an API boundary are usually fine: in this scenario, there can be no cycles across the boundary, objects memory can't be directly accessed by user code, and performance problems can be alleviated by the use of centralized memory management.

messages that may interrupt a sleep. The main scheduler algorithm is a loop whose general outline is given in Listing 1.2.

```
START:

FOR EACH timescale:
        Translate the date of the first event from logical time to
        clock-time. Set nextFiber to point to the event with the
        earliest date.

Store the distance between the date of the selected event and the current
clock-time in fiberDelay.

Compute how much time we can sleep before the next event.

Sleep during the amount of time computed above. The sleep can be
interrupted by an external message, e.g. to schedule new events.

Wakeup from the sleep. Advance the playheads over the duration slept,
applying the necessary time transformations.

IF the sleep was interrupted by a message:
        Handle this message.
ELSE:
        remove nextFiber from the queue and switch execution to this fiber.

Go back to START.
```

Listing 1.2. Scheduler algorithm outline

There is a subtlety in how the playheads are advanced: if the sleep was interrupted by an external message, the effective duration of the sleep timeSlept is used to advance the playhead. But if the process wakes-up due to the sleep's timeout, the duration used to advance the playheads is the logical duration of the sleep, i.e. the value of nextDelay. This could well be different from the effective duration of the sleep, but the scheduler maintains the illusion of a perfectly accurate sleep timing. This is done so to avoid accumulating errors when action results in the scheduling of new events, relative to the current date. To preserve the absolute timing accuracy, the scheduler maintains an accumulator of nextDelay - timeSlept, which is added to the timeout just before passing it to the sleep call.

Another measure that we take in order to improve timing accuracy is what we call *Zeno sleeping*. It stems from the observation that on our target operating systems, the accuracy of waiting calls is somewhat proportional to the timeout parameter. Thus, we wrap our sleep calls in a loop, with each iteration using a timeout equal to a fraction of the timeout residue from the previous iteration. The loop exits when the residue falls below the desired accuracy (or if the sleep duration is too small to be measured on the system). This allows us to achieve sub-millisecond accuracies with very few loop iterations even for long sleeps. Better accuracies can be achieved, but it is of course a tradeoff between desired accuracy and CPU usage.

Waiting Operations. A fiber whose user code calls `sched_wait()` simply yields back to the scheduler, and is put back into list of running fibers according to the duration passed to the waiting call.

Besides maintaining a list of running fibers, the scheduler also has a list of suspended fibers. When a fiber is suspended, it is simply moved from the running list to the suspended list. If the calling fiber happens to be the one that is suspended in the process, it also yields back to the scheduler. Resuming is simply a matter of moving the object back to the running list.

A fiber whose user code calls one of the "wait" functions is also moved to the suspended list. Additionally, the expected signal is stored inside the fiber structure, and the fiber is added to a list of waiting fibers inside the waited object. When a fibers is retired or completed, its list of waiting fibers is traversed and all fibers whose expected signal matches the current operation are put back to the running list, with their wakeup code set to the constant `SCHED_WAKEUP_SIGNALED`.

A special case is fibers which are waiting on a handle with a timeout. These are put in the running list like normal running fibers, but a status flag in the fibers structure indicates that it is in a `waiting` state. If the object is signaled before the timeout elapses, the status is simply set back to `running`. On the other hand, if the fiber is picked by the scheduler to be run before its waited object is signaled, it is first removed from the waiting list of said object, its status is set back to `running`, and its wakeup code is set to the constant `SCHED_WAKEUP_TIMEOUT`.

Background Jobs. The scheduler uses a thread pool to handle background jobs. The thread pool consists of a queue of fibers, a mutex M_{bg} and a condition variable C_{bg}, and a number of worker threads. In order for the job system to pass fibers back to the main scheduler thread, the scheduler also has a message queue protected by a mutex M_m and a condition variable C_m. Sleeping in the main scheduler loop is implemented by waiting on C_m, which allows the sleep to be interrupted by the arrival of messages posted by the job system.

A call to `sched_background()` sets the status flag of the running fiber to `background`, puts it in the suspended list, and yields back to the scheduler. The scheduler then detects the status change, locks the mutex M_{bg}, pushes the fiber in the job queue, signals the condition variable C_{bg} and unlocks the mutex.

Worker threads mostly sit idle waiting on the condition variable C_{bg}. When the condition variable is signaled, one worker thread wakes up, pops a fiber off the queue and switches to it. It continues executing fibers until there are no more fibers in the queue, at which points it goes back to sleep. When a background fiber calls `sched_foreground()`, it yields back to the main routine of the worker thread. This routine then locks M_m, puts a message containing the fiber in the message queue, signals C_m and unlocks M_m. This message will in turn be picked by the scheduler main loop, which will put the fiber back to the running list.

Buffered Actions. The goal of a computer music system or a multimedia show controller is ultimately to output some data to the outside world in order to provoke some action (e.g. audio samples to be converted into sound, or commands sent to external synthesizers, etc.). The operators are most concerned by the precise timing of the perceptible effects. However the system allows to specify the dates at which computations must happen, which is only a proxy for specifying the dates of actions: delay and jitter are induced by computations leading to the output. As such, it is useful to distinguish code that almost immediately result in an action (such as outputting an OSC packet), from code that actually computes the data to be sent out (such as computing the OSC parameters and formatting them into a well-formed message). The first category should always be strictly scheduled with respect to real time. Ideally, it should even be latency compensated to correct the delay between each individual system's output and its real-world effect. The second category can (and should) be scheduled as soon as feasible, in order to avoid delaying the actions that depend on their result.

The ability to make that distinction in the timing specification of the system is what FORMULA calls *action buffering* [2]. Processes in the system are executed ahead of time, and generate actions that are buffered and only executed when the real time clock reaches their due date. This prevents the timing variability of normal computation to create hiccups and jitter in the timed sequence of actions, because a computation running a little longer than usual will still be done in time to generate the desired action before its due date. However, the difference between the real time clock and the ahead-of-time clock induces an input delay, since inputs to the system can only modify the course of actions after the current ahead-of-time date. Thus there is a tradeoff between the stability of the output timings, and the reactivity of the system.

We explored the potential of action buffering in Quadrant by using a root logical clock that ran as fast as possible within a fixed look-ahead real-time window. Actions generated by internal computations were placed in a special real time queue and served at the specified real-time date. Sleeps only occur when the next event is outside the look-ahead window. The resulting scheduler loop is given in Listing 1.3 (compare with the simpler loop of Listing 1.2).

Although Quadrant's current implementation only schedules code within a single OS process, it is desirable to allow future synchronization of user code across multiple processes and machines, effectively implementing a form of distributed scheduling. In light of this objective, an additional nuance has to be made regarding the nature of outputs: some messages represent real outputs reaching outside the scheduler system, while others might be sent to remote parts of the (distributed) scheduler in order to influence its operations. The first category should be handled as before. However the second category shouldn't be buffered, and should in fact be timestamped with the logical, ahead-of-time clock, and sent as soon as possible.

A difficult problem arises when such an internal message is received by a local system whose ahead-of-time clock is already past the timestamp of the message. On the one hand, the system can overwrite the message's timestamp with the current date, at the cost of some internal inconsistency that might render the scheduling much less predictable. On the other hand, the system could prevent this situation from ever happening by mandating such interacting sub-systems to always work in lock-step, but this could create unnecessarily long latency chains, which would defeat the purpose of action buffering. A third avenue to attack this problem, would be to implement a form

```
START:
Get the next action and its delay from the action queue.
Store them in nextAction and actionDelay.

FOR EACH timescale:
    Translate the date of the first event from logical time to clock-time.
    Set nextFiber to point to the event with the earliest date.

Store the distance between the date of the selected event and the current
clock-time in fiberDelay.

Set nextEvent to nextFiber or nextAction, whichever comes first.

Compute how much time we can sleep before nextEvent.

IF nextEvent is a fiber:
    Increase the look-ahead to reach the fiber date. We only need to sleep
    if fiberDelay is outside the maximum look-ahead window.
ELSE:
    nextEvent is an action, we need to sleep until we reach the action
    real time due date.

Sleep during the amount of time computed above. The sleep can be
interrupted by an external message, e.g. to schedule new events.

Wakeup from the sleep. Advance the playheads over the duration slept,
applying the necessary time transformations. Decrease next action delay
by the time slept. Update the look-ahead depending on the time slept.

IF the sleep was interrupted by a message:
    Handle this message.
ELSE:
    IF nextEvent is an action:
        Remove it from the queue and execute its callback.
    ELSE:
        nextEvent is a fiber, remove it from the queue and switch
        execution to this fiber.

Go back to START.
```

Listing 1.3. Scheduler algorithm with buffered actions.

of selective backtracking when an old message that would have changed the flow of the local scheduler is received.

Regardless of the possible solutions to the above problems, their common flaw is to lock tradeoffs at a coarse grain level, without knowledge of the "semantics" of scheduled events. However, it is not unusual that within the same scenario, several strategies must be applied to deal with latency and jitter depending on the intended effects of the events being generated. Some events might need to be processed with very low latency, whereas some might need tight synchronization. Some might rely on strict ordering whereas some might be handled on a first-come first-serve basis. Some might be ignored altogether as soon as a new event comes in and over-rules previous events. It might also well be the case that in most situations, where the granularity of computational tasks is less than the accepted timing inaccuracy threshold, buffering is completely irrelevant.

As such, our opinion is that dealing with latency and jitter is much better left to ad-hoc, context-aware solutions. For that reason, with removed buffered actions from Quadrant's scheduler and stuck with the run loop shown in Listing 1.2.

7 Conclusion and Future Work

In this paper, we highlighted the need for symbolic time scheduling in show-control software and musical applications. We then described a temporal model based on time transformations expressed through tempo curves, and gave a formalism of such curves. We then described how these curves are implemented in the Quadrant scheduler, and presented the API of the scheduler.

In its current form, the scheduler is a local system, only maintaining proper time flow for its host process. Synchronizing timescales across multiple scheduler instances (potentially running on different machines) is the subject of ongoing work. This kind of synchronization implies some form of local speculation and catch-up. This involves both technical problems and user experience design decisions.

Another interesting problem is handling live modifications of tempo curves. Changing the tempo curve of a task while it is running is already possible, but creates a discrepancy between the actual (time, position) coordinates of the task and those same coordinates according to the tempo curve. This discrepancy could be resolved by silently offsetting either the new tempo curve or the current task's position so that those coordinates match. Another possibility would be to temporarily treat the new tempo curve as a synchronization source, and apply a catch-up curve to the task, as we describe in Sect. 5, until it matches the new curve. Allowing users to control these different strategies according to their use case and surfacing the resulting behaviour is another user interface challenge.

References

1. Ableton: Ableton Live. https://www.ableton.com/en/live/what-is-live/
2. Anderson, D.P., Kuivila, R.: A system for computer music performance. ACM Trans. Comput. Syst. **8**(1), 56–82 (1990). https://doi.org/10.1145/77648.77652
3. Berndt, A.: Musical tempo curves. In: ICMC (2011)
4. Bouche, D., Bresson, J.: Planning and scheduling actions in a computer-aided music composition system. In: Foundation, I.S. (ed.) Scheduling and Planning Applications Workshop (SPARK), pp. 1–6. Proceedings of the 9th International Scheduling and Planning Applications Workshop, Steve Chien and Mark Giuliano and Riccardo Rasconi, Jerusalem, Israel (2015). https://hal.archives-ouvertes.fr/hal-01163284
5. Butcher, J.C.: The Numerical Analysis of Ordinary Differential Equations: Runge-Kutta and General Linear Methods. Wiley, USA (1987)
6. Cash, J.R., Karp, A.H.: A variable order Runge-Kutta method for initial value problems with rapidly varying right-hand sides. ACM Trans. Math. Softw. **16**(3), 201–222 (1990). https://doi.org/10.1145/79505.79507
7. Celerier, J.M., Baltazar, P., Bossut, C., Vuaille, N., Couturier, J.M., Desainte-Catherine, M.: OSSIA: towards a unified interface for scoring time and interaction. In: First International Conference on Technologies for Music Notation and Representation (TENOR 2015). Paris, France (2015). https://hal.archives-ouvertes.fr/hal-01245957

8. Coduys, T., Ferry, G.: Iannix. Aesthetical/symbolic visualisations for hypermedia composition. In: Sound and Music Computing Conference (SMC) (2004)
9. Cont, A.: ANTESCOFO: anticipatory synchronization and control of interactive parameters in computer music. In: International Computer Music Conference (ICMC), pp. 33–40. Belfast, Ireland (2008). https://hal.inria.fr/hal-00694803
10. Desain, P., Honing, H.: Tempo curves considered harmful. Contemp. Music. Rev. 7(2), 123–138 (1993). https://doi.org/10.1080/07494469300640081
11. Fouilleul, M., Giavitto, J.L., Bresson, J.: A poly-temporal programming environment for live shows and interactive installations. Zenodo (2022). https://doi.org/10.5281/zenodo.6798287
12. Fritsch, F.N., Carlson, R.E.: Monotone piecewise cubic interpolation. SIAM J. Math. Anal. 17(2), 238–246 (1980). https://doi.org/10.1137/0717021
13. Goltz, F.: Ableton link – a technology to synchronize music software. In: Proceedings of the Linux Audio Conference (LAC 2018), p. 4 (2018)
14. Halbwachs, N.: Synchronous Programming of Reactive Systems. Kluwer Academic Publishers (1993). https://doi.org/10.1007/978-1-4757-2231-4
15. Honing, H.: From time to time: the representation of timing and tempo. Comput. Music. J. 25(3), 50–61 (2001). https://doi.org/10.1162/014892601753189538
16. Jaffe, D.: Ensemble timing in computer music. Comput. Music. J. 9(4), 38–48 (1985)
17. MacCallum, J., Schmeder, A.: Timewarp: a graphical tool for the control of polyphonic smoothly varying tempos. In: International Computer Music Conference (ICMC 2010), p. 4 (2010)
18. Mazzola, G., Zahorka, O.: Tempo curves revisited: hierarchies of performance fields. Comput. Music. J. 18(1), 40 (1994). https://doi.org/10.2307/3680521
19. Press, W.H., Teukolsky, S.A., Vetterling, W.T., Flannery, B.P.: Integration of ordinary differential equations. In: Numerical Recipes in C. The Art of Scientific Computing, 2nd edn., pp. 710–722. Cambridge University Press, USA (1992)
20. Roberts, C., Wakefield, G., Wright, M.: 2013: the web browser as synthesizer and interface. In: Jensenius, A.R., Lyons, M.J. (eds.) A NIME Reader. CRSM, vol. 3, pp. 433–450. Springer, Cham (2017). https://doi.org/10.1007/978-3-319-47214-0_28
21. Schnell, N., Saiz, V., Barkati, K., Goldszmidt, S.: Of time engines and masters an API for scheduling and synchronizing the generation and playback of event sequences and media streams for the web audio API. In: WAC. Paris, France (2015). https://hal.archives-ouvertes.fr/hal-01256952
22. Von Hanxleden, R., Bourke, T., Girault, A.: Real-time ticks for synchronous programming. In: 2017 Forum on Specification and Design Languages (FDL), pp. 1–8. IEEE, Verona (2017). https://doi.org/10.1109/FDL.2017.8303893

Interaction Strategies in Composition for Karlax and Acoustic Instruments

Benjamin Lavastre[1](✉) and Marcelo M. Wanderley[2](✉)

[1] DCS, IDMIL, CIRMMT, McGill University, Montreal, Canada
benjamin.lavastre@mail.mcgill.ca
[2] IDMIL, CIRMMT, McGill University, Montreal, Canada
marcelo.wanderley@mcgill.ca

Abstract. The Karlax is a gestural controller which arose substantial interest among composers since its inception in 2010 and continues to be commonly used in solo and group performances. One of the reasons for its longevity is the device's remarkable adaptability, especially in musical contexts involving acoustic instruments. This article analyses six chamber music pieces for Karlax and acoustic instruments by comparing performance videos, sounds generated, and the writing process (scores, sound synthesis, and mapping strategies in each piece). We further discuss the various composition strategies using interaction metaphor concepts from the computer music literature. These metaphors prove to be powerful analysis tools that allow describing the use of a digital musical instrument in a chamber music context. In the last part of this article, we discuss five such interaction strategies and their use in sketches of an original composition for Karlax and ensemble.

Keywords: Digital Music Instruments (DMI) · Mixed pieces · Computer Music · Electronic Music · Input Devices · Mapping · Interaction Strategies

1 Introduction

Though several hundred interfaces for musical expression have been developed and described in a variety of venues, most notably in the last two decades at the International Conference on New interfaces for Musical Expression (NIME)[1], relatively few articles discuss how these interfaces ares used in actual musical contexts, for instance [4,13,14] and [7]. Indeed, the use of DMIs is not often discussed from the perspective of artistic and musical composition. In other words, *the "M" in NIME*: why don't we talk more about music performance with musical interfaces, beyond sound control? In part, this is the consequence that most of the interfaces described in the literature have short life spans and/or are mainly used by their designers [5]. In this sense, the Karlax offers a vibrant subject of study with an existence of more than ten years, a community of regular users from different musical cultures, and several significant creations, notably with acoustic instruments, incorporating some form of music notation.

The Karlax is an input device in the shape of a clarinet or soprano saxophone that combines various sensors: ten continuous keys, eight velocity pistons, an inertial

---

[1] www.nime.org.

© Springer Nature Switzerland AG 2023
M. Aramaki et al. (Eds.): CMMR 2021, LNCS 13770, pp. 163–179, 2023.
https://doi.org/10.1007/978-3-031-35382-6_13

measurement unit, and several switches (Fig. 1)[2]. It also includes a rotary axis with bends at each end, allowing the performer to rotate controller's axis, a degree-of-freedom also explored in Cook's Hirn Controller [2]. Musicians have praised its "ability to detect subtle as well as larger gestures, continuous as well as event-based control, its low latency and high bandwidth, its reliability and portability" [10]. Like many musical interfaces that output sensor data but do not have a pre-defined sound, the Karlax is defined solely by its control characteristics, i.e., its gestural affordances, instead of a given sonic palette. This opens up unlimited musical possibilities but requires the composer to describe the sounds controlled and the mapping between sensor data and sound generation to be used in each context. A digital musical instrument (DMI) comprises the control interface + mapping + sound generation [12].

In a general way, we can define the "identity" of Karlax in three ways. First, *what remains unchanged for each project*: that is to say, the physical object, its control qualities, the types of data sent by the interface (MIDI mainly), and the basic gestures it allows. Secondly, *what concerns the writing of the Karlax instrument and which is specific to each project*: the choices of sound synthesis and mapping, gesture writing, notation, etc. Finally, *what has to do with the interactions with other instruments and devices*. Given that the Karlax is a controller, it allows us to consider many types of interaction, particularly in real-time, which are typically determined during the composition.

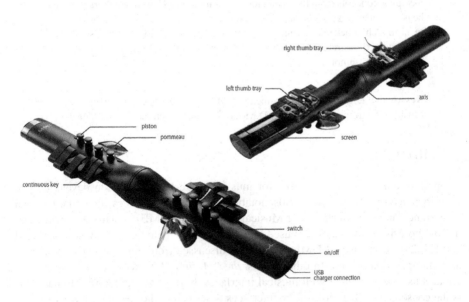

Fig. 1. Front and rear views of the Karlax (Source: www.dafact.com)

This study analyzes a corpus of six pieces for Karlax and acoustic instruments from audio and video recordings, scores, Max/MSP patches, presets, and information from published articles. We first identify three compositional models defining the main areas

---

[2] www.dafact.com.

of inspiration. In a second step, we discuss excerpts in the corpus by detailing the action of the Karlax and its interaction with the acoustic instruments, thanks to interaction metaphors from computer music. Finally, we comment on the use of interaction strategies in an original composition for Karlax and an ensemble of 14 acoustic instruments.

2 Analysis of the Pieces

We have selected six pieces written between 2013 and 2018 that combine the Karlax with one or two acoustic instruments, including a flute, a violin, and a cello.

1. *Fogg* by Lorenzo Bianchi for violin, cello and Karlax, 2013 (performed by *Fabrique Nomade* ensemble)
2. *Frottement, Bourdon, Craquement* by Francis Faber for cello, Karlax and electronic, 2013 (performed by *Fabrique Nomade* ensemble)
3. *Le Patch Bien Tempéré III* by Tom Mays, for flute, Karlax and real time electonic, 2013 (performed by *Fabrique Nomade* ensemble)(abbreviated *R.N.C.B.*)
4. *Ripples Never Come Back* by Michele Tadini for violin, cello and Karlax, 2013 (performed by *Fabrique Nomade* ensemble)(abbreviated *P.B.T.III*)
5. *Discontinuous Devices "In-between"* by Michele Tadini for cello and Karlax, 2015 (performed by *Fabrique Nomade* ensemble)(abbreviated *D.D.*)
6. *Le Violon, l'Oeillet et le Bambou* by Raphaël-Tristan Jouaville, for violin and Karlax, 2018 (abbreviated *V.O.B.*)

Five of the six pieces have been commissioned and performed by the *Fabrique Nomade* ensemble. This ensemble is an "electronic chamber music ensemble that wishes to rediscover the gestures and listening of classical chamber music"[3]. In this regard, "each musician is independent and has total control over their acoustic or electronic instrument" (each instrumentalist has their laptop and sound broadcasting system). It means acoustic instrument performers trigger their own electronic part, mostly real-time sound processing, thanks to a midi pedal. Furthermore, the Karlax does not process the acoustic sound of an instrumentalist in real time. This is not the case for the sixth piece, where the Karlax transforms the violin's sound in real-time in addition to having its own sound synthesis.

2.1 Sound Synthesis and Mapping Strategies

Table 1 indicates the main types of sound synthesis used in the pieces of the corpus. Tables 2, 3 and 4 indicate the mapping strategies for each Karlax sensor for the six pieces[4].

We can observe different trends in the use of the Karlax sensors. For example, the activation of the keys follows two main models. The first consists of associating to the keys the amplitude of different voices of the same type of sound synthesis as frequency

---

[3] www.fabriquenomade.com.

[4] P1 for piston 1, K1 for key 1 of the Karlax.

Table 1. Sound Synthesis types in the corpus pieces

Pieces	Sound synthesis type
Fogg	Additive synthesis and Sampling
R.N.C.B.	Subtractive synthesis and Sampling
P.B.T. III	Phase Aligned Formant Synthesis (PAF synthesis)
F.B.C.	Synthesized sounds from *Reaktor, Kontakt and Absynth* softwares
D.D.	Sampling
V.O.B.	Physical modeling from *String Studio* module

Table 2. Mapping strategies for keys and pistons

Pieces	Pistons	Keys
Fogg	– Trig sounds (velocity controls playback rate)	– Control volume parameter of 'voices' of the additive synthesis)
R.N.C.B.	– P1: Volume accent – P2–4: Trig sounds – P5–8: Change chords	– Control parameters of a stream of pitches (K1: Volume, K2: Note repetition, K3: Arpeggiation, K5: Random volume change, K6: Envelope, K7: Speed up, slow down, K8: Distortion, K9: Pitch Bend, K10: Filter)
P.B.T. III	– Trig sounds	– Control volume parameter of the voices of the "PAF" synthesis)
F.B.C.	– Synthesized sounds from *Reaktor, Kontakt and Absynth* softwares	– Control parameters of the synthesised sounds (K1: Oscillations, K2: Glide effect, K3: LFO, K4: Envelope, K5: Feedback, K9: Echo effect, K10 Acceleration)
D.D.	– Trig sounds	– K1: Reverb (Part I) – K1–10: Volume of looped samples (Part III)
V.O.B.	– Play and hold violin-like sounds (*String Studio*)	– K6: Activate Trill mode in *String Studio* – K7–8: Activate Damp mode in *String Studio*)

bands (*Fogg, P.B.T. III, D.D.*). In the second model, each key controls additional processing of the main sound stream (*R.N.C.B., F.B.C., V.O.B.*). Piston's use seems to follow a central model of activation and holding of sounds. We note a convergent mapping (described in [15]) type in *Fogg* where the indication of the velocity of the piston will be associated with the playback rate (the higher the velocity indication, the faster the sound is played). The axis is mainly used to modify the timbre of a sound flow (*P.B.T. III, Fogg, R.N.C.B., D.D.*), more rarely associated with the amplitude (*V.O.B., D.D.*). The bends are not used much and describe mostly accent-type sound morphology (*Fogg*). Motion sensors have different functions. They can control changes in timbre, pitch, or volume. We observe that the roll axis is privileged for pitch and volume control: upward gestures are associated with volume increasing or pitch shifting from the low to the high register.

Impulse/jab gestures are not used much. Finally, switches are rarely used because, for most of the pieces, the activation/deactivation changes are written in the program score (often in MAX/MSP environment). However, the use of switches will allow modifying specific characteristics in real-time, such as the activation of plug-ins (*V.O.B*). In rare cases, they are used to trigger sounds (*R.N.C.B.*).

Table 3. Mapping strategies for axis and bends and inertial units. Note that the mapping data for *F.B.C* concerning the axis bends and inertial unit are missing

Pieces	Axis and bends	Inertial Units
Fogg	– Comb-Filter (frequency), bend (accent)	– Inclin-roll axis: Comb-filter (volume)
R.N.C.B.	– Pitch center of the chord of the stream	– Pitch-axis: envelop and filter
P.B.T. III	– Variable speed tremolo	– Roll-axis (Acc-z): Volume and brightness – Pitch-axis (Acc-x): pitch glissandi
D.D.	– Volume (Part I) – Oscillation speed and resonance (Part II)	– K1: Reverb (Part I) – K1–10: Volume of looped samples (Part III)
V.O.B.	– Volume	– Mass parameter in Damp mode of *String Studio* plug-in – Parameter nodes in *GRM Tools* Plug-ins

In the corpus pieces, the data sent from Karlax are mapped without specific conditioning. The conditioning step transforms the raw data emitted by the Karlax into "cooked" data using algorithms. For example, Karlax contains two types of conditioning: signals from the inclinometer and impulses, both calculated from the accelerometer and gyroscope data. The piece *Ritual* (2015) by Andrew Stewart, for Karlax solo, has a significant conditioning phase of the raw Karlax signals, which provides essential insights into the composition of the Karlax, particularly in terms of gestural vocabulary. Even if this piece does not fit in with our study, its gestural approach elicits original interaction strategies.

The choices of synthesis and mapping have important consequences in the interaction strategies used, depending on whether the sound and gestural identity of the Karlax is close or not to the instrument with which it interacts.

Table 4. Mapping strategies for switches and impulses

Pieces	Switches	Impulses
Fogg	– Not used	– Not used
R.N.C.B.	– Trig sounds	– Not used
P.B.T. III	– Not used	– Not used
D.D.	– Volume (Part I) – Oscillation speed and resonance (Part II)	– K1: Reverb (Part I) – K1–10: Volume of looped samples (Part III)
V.O.B.	– Activation of Plug-Ins (*GRM Pitch Accum* and *GRM Delays*	– Mass parameter in Damp mode of *String Studio* plug-ins – Parameter nodes in *GRM Tools* Plug-ins

3   Composition Models

Among the corpus pieces, we have identified three compositional models representing three main sources of inspiration for the composers: model based on acoustic sounds, model based on electronic sounds, and Karlax as model. These allow describing the "role" of this controller in relation to the other instruments.

Model Based on Acoustic Instruments Sounds

For several pieces in the corpus, the acoustic sound of the instrument(s) with which the Karlax plays is used as the basic composition material. For example, in the piece *Fogg*, the sound synthesis of the Karlax is realized through an additive synthesis from the spectral analysis of several violin pizzicati with different "preparations" (addition of objects like pegs attached to the string). The Karlax triggers and controls processes related to the spectral content of pizzicato sounds by pressing continuous keys (control of the spectral envelope) (Fig. 2).

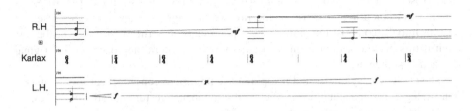

Fig. 2. "Shaping" of the spectral envelope with Karlax continuous keys in *Fogg* by Lorenzo Bianchi (mes. 68–69, karlax part) (with the permission of the composer). Each staff line represents the activation of a continuous key that will control the volume of a group of oscillators.

Other examples are pieces where the Karlax plays sounds very close to the sounds played by the instrument(s) it interacts with. In this way, the acoustic instrument is "augmented" by the action of the Karlax. For example, in the third part of *Discontinuous Devices*, the Karlax activates flautando and harmonics cello samples by pressing the continuous keys. The pistons also trigger shorter samples of the same type. It forms a harmonic environment for the cello, which performs more percussive figures like jettatti and glissandi, letting the open strings' natural harmonics resonate. With the same idea, in Jouaville's piece, the Karlax plays a physical model of a string by activating the pistons in a consecutive way whose pitches are previously set up (*String Studio* module). In most of the piece, the Karlax highlights and develops the melodic contour of the violin and creates a harmonic accompaniment (Fig. 3).

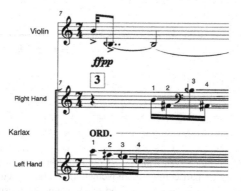

Fig. 3. Results of pitches played by the Karlax pistons with the corresponding fingerings in *Le Violon, l'Oeillet et le Bambou*, by Raphaël-Tristan Jouaville (mes. 7) (with the permission of the composer). See video from 00:30 to 00:32 www.youtube.com/watch?v=IrCmiwwFSUs

Model Based on Electronic Sounds
This type of composition model is the most common in the selected pieces. This category represents sound synthesis techniques and the treatments of the audio signal associated with electronic music, such as filtering, delay, granular synthesis, additive synthesis, etc. By assigning sound synthesis and digital sound processing parameters to different sensors, the Karlax can "drive" processes in real-time and bring an expressive dimension to the transformations. In this model, the sound of the Karlax is perceived as independent from the acoustic sound of the instruments.

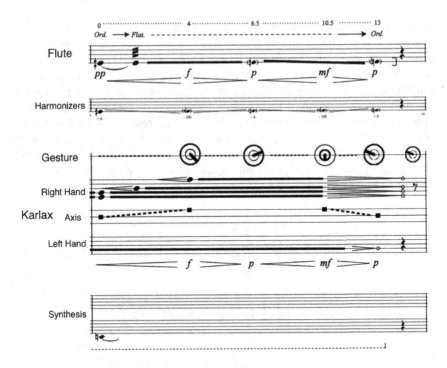

Fig. 4. General score of *Le Patch bien tempéré III* by Tom Mays (mes.6) (with the permission of the composer). The Karlax part combines -movements ("Gesture" staff with circle symbols) which control intensity, brightness, and pitch-bend of the sound synthesis, -rotation of the axis (dotted lines) which controls a speed tremolo and -continuous keys depression ("Right Hand" and "Left Hand" staves with thick lines) which activates "PAF" synthesis voices. The numbers at the top of the score represent the time in seconds. See video from 01:44 to 02:00 https://vimeo.com/80464641

For example, in *P.B.T. III*, the composer focuses on complementary electronic techniques such as harmonizers, delays, and "PAF" synthesis based on voice formants[5]. The input device activates different synthetic voices and modifies parameters in this piece. Generally, the accelerometer data corresponding to the forward-backward movements are associated with dynamics (brightness and intensity), and the left-right movements are associated with pitch (glissandi) (Table 3). At the same time, the central axis applies a speed tremolo [11]. In the score are noted the part of the flute, the Karlax movements laid out on four staves, and the acoustic results (Harmonizers and Synthesis staves) (Fig. 4).

Karlax as model
The design of the Karlax can also inspire the composition and constitutes a model in itself. Indeed, the conception of this controller is inspired by the keys system of wind and keyboard instruments (pistons and continuous keys) enriched with an axis (with bends) and movement sensors (accelerometer and gyroscope). For example, at the

---

[5] *Phase Aligned Formant* developed by Miller Puckette in 1995.

beginning of Faber's piece (*F.B.C.*), the instrumentalist executes a "call" thanks to the pistons, which remind one of trumpet playing. Indeed, the instrumentalist performs a "call" thanks to the pistons produced by short harmonic synthetic sounds (Fig. 5). Also, the possibilities of the Karlax can inspire the "trajectory" of the piece. For instance, *D.D.* starts with an extensive use of the pistons and then in the second section the Karlax triggers and controls long sequences through the accelerometer and gyroscope data, making the Karlax gestures more and more expressive.

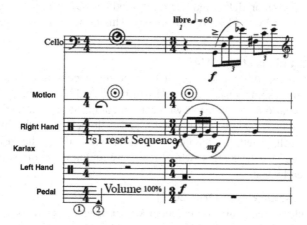

Fig. 5. "Call" played by the Karlax pistons in *Frottement, Bourdon, Craquement* (mes. 1-2) (with the composer permission). See video from 00:00 to 00:04 https://vimeo.com/118148219

4 Interaction Metaphors from Computer Music

In this part, we analyze excerpts of the corpus pieces thanks to metaphors from Computer Music. We have selected five metaphors from three articles: [1, 18, 20], for their relevance to describe the action of a gestural controller such as the Karlax (particularly in interaction with acoustic instruments) and for their capacity to give an overview of compositional strategies.

"Shaping" [Caramiaux et al., 2014]
Shaping "refers to scenarios where performers control sound morphologies by "tracing" in the air those salient sound features they desire to control" [1]. This metaphor is described as the "transfer of variations into a gestural morphology" and as synchronization of sound with movement. It is widely used in the analyzed pieces using Karlax's motion sensors but also with continuous keys. For example, in *P.B.T.III*, the Karlax imitates the distortions of the flute sound (created by harmonizers, flatterzunge, etc.) by "shaping" the "PAF" synthesis. At the same time, the ancillary gestures [19] of the flutist seem to imitate the gestures of the Karlax player (Fig. 4). With a more reduced gestural expression, the continuous key activation allows the Karlax performer in *Fogg* to "shape" the spectral envelope in a differentiated way to provide a harmonic accompaniment to the violin and the cello (Fig. 2).

"Catch and Throw" [Wessel & Wright, 2002]

This interaction strategy "involves the notion of selectively trapping musical phrases from an ongoing performance, transforming them in some way, and then sending these transformed materials back into the performance" [20]. This way of interaction, which could be defined as delayed real-time processing, was exploited in improvisational situations by Tom Mays in the early 2010s, where the direct sound of the acoustic instrument is captured, transformed by the Karlax and broadcast in real-time[6] Jouaville uses this type of interaction in the last part of *V.O.B.* where the acoustic sound of the violin is processed by resonator, delay, and pitch shift modules (*GRM Tools*) whose parameter nodes are controlled by the Karlax movements. This brings a sonic halo to the violin sound.[7]

"Fishing" [Caramiaux et al., 2014]

This metaphor is related to the learning stage in gesture recognition. When a dedicated program recognizes some gesture, a sound will be "fished" out to be played. One can compare this scenario of interactions with certain compositional strategies. For example, at the beginning of *Fogg*, several violin and cello actions with obvious gestural characteristics such as jettati, glissandi, strokes on the body of the instrument seem to be "recognized" by the Karlax, which reacts by imitating gestures, triggering and transforming nearby sounds.[8]

Musical tasks [Wanderley & Orio, 2002]

Related to the idea in the composition model *Karlax as model*, [18] proposes two levels of metaphors: *Musical Instrument Manipulation Metaphor* and *Control Metaphor*. In the first category are listed the interactions metaphors that refer to traditional instrumental playing (isolated notes, basic musical gestures like glissandi, vibrato, musical phrases, rhythmic playing, etc.) that appear for example in Faber's piece with the "call" (Fig. 5). In the second category, the authors evoke the actions of triggering of sequences but also their organization in time: synchronization, envelope control, continuous modulation features, etc.

"Space" [Wessel & Wright, 2002]

The purpose of using a control interface like Karlax in this type of strategy is to "suggest musically interesting trajectories for gesture", keeping in mind the "importance of proximity and timbre in the perception of these trajectories" [20].

Composers of the corpus employ various strategies to suggest movements and trajectories. For example, in *R.N.C.B.*, the composer evokes a distancing through repeated sequences where the violin and cello instruments begin a quasi homorhythmic figure "taken up" by the Karlax part in the form of arpeggios towards the high register. The input device controls a flow of notes produced by a subtractive synthesis: the axis controls the pitch of the arpeggio, the continuous keys control parameters like volume, filtering, or speed, while the inclination combined with a key activation control the amplitude envelope (Fig. 6 and Table 2).

---

[6] In this video, the Karlax controls the transformations of the acoustic sound of a Sheng, a mouth-blown free reed instrument: https://www.youtube.com/watch?v=fg9TgbI4gTM.

[7] See video from 05:43 to 06:42 https://www.youtube.com/watch?v=IrCmiwwFSUs.

[8] See video from 00:00 to 01:10 https://vimeo.com/67049071.

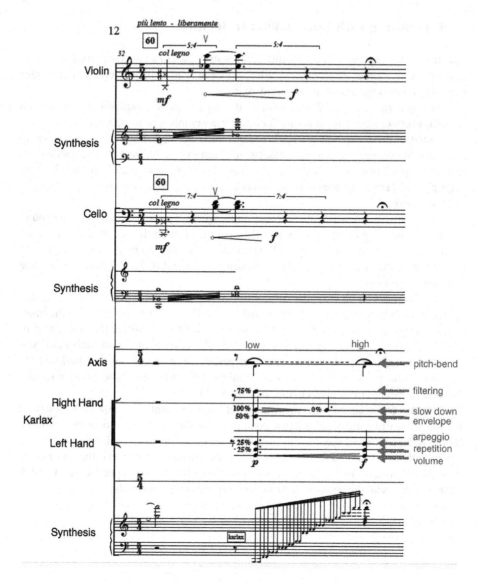

Fig. 6. Sequence that evokes a distancing in *Ripples Never Come Back* by Michele Tadini (mes. 32) (with the composer permission). See video from 00:48 to 01:00 https://vimeo.com/72995021

5   Composing with Interaction Strategies

The first author explored the use of interactions strategies in a new piece for Karlax and ensemble (*Instrumental Interaction*, 2022, ongoing work). Five interaction strategies were chosen through a perceptual-based approach.

The piece *Instrumental Interaction*, as its name suggests, explores the interaction strategies between the Karlax controller and the ensemble's instruments[9]. These strategies, noted in the score, tell the Karlax player the role they should play in relation to the ensemble (control of sound synthesis and gestures to be made). Some situations require the performer to be perceived prominently (using strategies "Imitating", "Borrowing", and "Transforming/Activation") or in the background (with strategies "Space" and "Shadowing").

Let us consider A and B as acoustic units, where A is associated with the sound synthesis controlled by the Karlax and B is associated with the acoustic sound of the instrument or instrumental group with which the controller interacts. Also, a and b are the respective musical proposals of the acoustic units A and B. Table 5 describes the five interactions strategies.

The composition process also allowed us to refine the definition of the predefined interactions. For example, we had previously elaborated a distinction between the interaction strategies "Transformation" which would describe a real-time transformation of the acoustic sound, and "Activation" which would describe a sensor activation type of interaction (Table 5). Given the angle of perception adopted and the conditions of creation of the piece where no real-time interaction was used, these two interaction strategies appeared to be challenging to differentiate.

Also, by focusing on perceptual and rhetorical elements, we establish situations not specific to playing with gestural controllers or DMIs. These, however, are more likely to adopt different roles due to their flexible sound identity. In this regard, we have experimented with interaction strategies presented in Table 5 between the ensemble's acoustic instruments or instrumental groups. Therefore, the perceptual units A and B are associated with the acoustic instruments' timbre of the ensemble.

---

[9] The ensemble is composed of 14 acoustic instruments (1111-1110-perc-pn-11111) + Karlax solo).

Table 5. Interaction strategies used in *Instrumental Interaction*

Interactions	Schema	Description
1. "Space"	Time → B — B → A	The sound synthesis controlled by the Karlax constitutes a kind of sonic environment. A is perceived in the background, while B is perceived in the foreground. This strategy is related to the "Space" metaphor, though not directly more concerned with the trajectory of a sound source.
2. "Imitating"	A — a1 → a2 → B — a'1 → a'2 →	A reacts to B's proposal (or vice versa) by imitating it. This type of interaction is close to the "Fishing" metaphor.
3. "Shadowing"	A — a ⟹ B — a' →	This interaction strategy consists of a quasi-synchronous imitation but a is perceived in the foreground while b (perceived as a') is perceived in the background. Also a' is slightly delayed compare to a (cf. Fig. 7).
4. "Transforming /Activation"	A — a → a → B ⋯▶ B' ⋯▶ B ⋯▶ B'	A's proposal modifies B's characteristics. This interaction strategy can be compared to a real-time transformation strategy (close to the "Catch and Throw" metaphor) or, in a broader sense, to the activation of a sensor. This must be repeated to perceive a's action on B more clearly.
5. "Borrowing"	A — c → B — b →	A interacts with B through sound and gesture behavior borrowed from a typical instrumental playing mode (c represents the borrowed proposition). This strategy contains, for example, the metaphor "Shaking" described in [11], where the performer imitates a kind of maracas playing.

Fig. 7. "Shadowing" interaction between the Karlax and the piano part of *Instrumental Inter-action* piece (mes.91–93). In this excerpt, the Karlax plays FM synthesis type of sounds that underline the high-pitched sound of the piano. The axis and the inclination of the Karlax control the modulation coefficients of the synthesis.

6   Discussion

The use of compositional models and Computer Music metaphors provide a framework and constitute powerful analytical tools to apprehend pieces that are, at first sight, complex. Generally speaking, they allow categorizing of specific roles of the Karlax and discussing typical situations of interaction.

For example, the piece *Fogg* by Lorenzo Bianchi seemed to us to belong to both the first and the second composition models, depending on whether one considers the process of composition or the sound result. Indeed, the process of additive synthesis and the fact that the "target" sounds are prepared (with the addition of pegs) make the sound synthesis played by the Karlax particularly distant from the acoustic sound of the violin. From a perceptual perspective, we would then need to determine whether or not the timbre of the sounds played by the Karlax "blends" with the sound of the instrument and determine what allows us to assert this. For the other examples given for the first model: *D.D.* (Part III) and *V.O.B.*, we can use the terminology of "timbral augmentation" as presented in [17].

The selected metaphors are thought in real-time interactions context. Though the composition process necessarily evolves in delayed time, we have seen that these metaphors are still appropriate to comment on typical situations of the pieces of the corpus. On the one hand, because they offer situations of real-time transformations and secondly because the composition strategies in terms of dramaturgy can be compared to situations of improvisations. Moreover, the setup chosen by the *Fabrique Nomade* ensemble influences these strategies. As the instrumentalists are independent and trigger more or less random processes (for example, delays), the composer tends to opt for "encompassing" strategies, highly describable by the metaphors [3]. On the other hand, these metaphors are limited to describe temporal and rhythmic aspects as specified in

[18]. In addition, metaphors that qualify the action of a controller such as "Shaping", or "Musical Tasks", facilitate the interaction with the instrumentalist(s) and the "reading" of the piece by the spectator/listener as they help to identify acoustically and gesturally the part played by the Karlax.

Furthermore, the description of the conditions of creation and the type of writing of the mixed pieces with Karlax seem fundamental to characterize the interaction strategies. Indeed, the venue's acoustics, the characteristics of the diffusion system (number of loudspeakers, spatialization), the existence or not of real-time processing of the acoustic instruments, and the freedom left to the performers will considerably influence the use and the perception of the interaction strategies. In *Instrumental Interaction*, we have opted for the ensemble's sound not to be used for typical real-time processing. Also, the venue for the premiere, a large rectangular box with 64 loudspeakers (the Music Multimedia Room at McGill University, Montreal), influences how we conceive the electronics and its spatialization and the poetic seeds of the piece. On the other hand, the idea that we wanted these interaction strategies to be perceptible also conditioned the writing.

Another critical aspect to qualify the action of the Karlax is its notation. Depending on the project of each piece, composers adopt a prescriptive (oriented on the action of the Karlax player) or descriptive method of notation (which reports the acoustic result) [8]. As a reference point, the composers of the corpus use the basics of Karlax notation presented in [10]. We can mention, however, the more pragmatic approach described in *V.O.B.*, which consists in assigning events in order of appearance to a simple range of fingerings and allows to visualize the pitches played by the Karlax and movements on a single staff (Fig. 3). Also, it is particularly interesting to relate to the approach of the composer D. Andrew Stewart in his piece *Ritual* for Karlax solo, based, among others, on gesture categorization and a spatial representation of space in the form of a grid [16]. In general, composers rarely add information related to mapping and sound synthesis, which would allow performers to appropriate the Karlax instrument further. Simultaneously, the notation must be practical and represent the composer's intention accurately and concisely. As such, an indication in the score of the metaphorical context, as presented above, would provide valuable information about how the Karlax is played and how it interacts with other instruments. In *Instrumental Interaction*, we opted for a hybrid approach by prescriptive (use of keys, pistons, axis, and inclination indications) and descriptive notation (main pitches, graphic description of the electronics). As for the mixed pieces with electronics, the composers can add audio files of the electronic part of the Karlax to communicate their musical ideas in the best possible way.

7   Conclusion and Future Work

In this article, we analyzed in detail six pieces for Karlax and acoustic instruments. We discussed how the Karlax was used by presenting the choices of synthesis and mapping in each piece. Three models of compositions have been identified, and five metaphors from the computer music literature have been proposed to characterize typical musical situations. Finally, we discussed the use of interaction strategies as main inspirations for a new piece for Karlax and ensemble of 14 acoustic musical instruments.

Several directions for future work arise from this research. Exploring interaction strategies in mixed compositions with a DMI contains many challenges from a creative, pedagogical, and perception point of view.

In the creative part of this project, we will further explore the interaction strategies with Karlax by diversifying the conditions for creating new pieces (types of instruments, types of diffusion, types of writing, etc.). Also, we want to focus on DMI-DMI type interactions, as with the T-Stick [9]. With these new inputs, we would like to propose new types of interactions and better qualify their use in the composition process.

Another follow-up to this research-creation project is to offer a workshop on writing mixed works with DMI to student composers. Pedagogical and demonstration activities are essential to understand the needs of DMI users, as shown with the Music Creation Project with the T-Stick [6]. The main objective of this workshop is to accompany the students in writing a mixed piece with DMI by experimenting with different interaction strategies. At the end of the workshop, students will be able to comment on the sound and gesture characteristics of the DMI and the interaction strategies they have chosen.

Finally, the study of perception between electroacoustic and acoustic components is generally not well explored, even less when the electroacoustic part is embodied with a gestural controller. As such, interaction strategies seem interesting tools to qualify these components.

Acknowledgments. The authors would like to warmly thank Rémi Dury, Francis Faber, Tom Mays, Andrew Stewart, Michele Tadini, Lorenzo Bianchi, Raphaël-Tristan Jouaville and Richard McKenzie for sharing their resources and their time.

References

1. Caramiaux, B., Françoise, J., Schnell, N., Bevilacqua, F.: Mapping through listening. Comput. Music. J. **38**(3), 34–48 (2014)
2. Cook, P.: 2001: principles for designing computer music controllers. In: Jensenius, A.R., Lyons, M.J. (eds.) A NIME Reader. CRSM, vol. 3, pp. 1–13. Springer, Cham (2017). https://doi.org/10.1007/978-3-319-47214-0_1
3. Dahl, L., Wang, G.: Sound bounce: physical metaphors in designing mobile music performance. In: Proceedings of International Conference on New Interfaces for Musical Expression, pp. 15–18 (2010)
4. Dobrian, C., Koppelman, D.: The E in NIME: musical expression with new computer interfaces. In: Proceedings of International Conference on New Interfaces for Musical Expression, pp. 277–282 (2006)
5. Ferguson, S., Wanderley, M.M.: The McGill digital orchestra: an interdisciplinary project on digital musical instruments. J. Interdisc. Music Stud. (2010)
6. Fukuda, T., Meneses, M., West T.J., Wanderley, M.M.: The T-stick music creation project: an approach to building a creative community around a DMI. In: Proceedings of International Conference on New Interfaces for Musical Expression (2021)
7. Hödl, O.: 'Blending dimensions' when composing for DMI and symphonic orchestra. In: Proceedings of International Conference on New Interfaces for Musical Expression, pp. 198–203 (2019)
8. Kanno, M.: Prescriptive notation: limits and challenges. Contemp. Music. Rev. **26**(2), 231–254 (2007)

9. Malloch, J., Wanderley, M.M.: The T-stick: from musical interface to musical instrument. In: Proceedings of International Conference on New Interfaces for Musical Expression, pp. 66–69 (2007)

10. Mays, T., Faber, F.: A notation system for the Karlax controller. In: Proceedings of International Conference on New Interfaces for Musical Expression, pp. 553–556 (2014)

11. Mays, T.: L'Harmoniseur augmenté: Le dispositif d'écriture mixte dans l'oeuvre Le Patch Bien Tempéré III. Proc. J. d'Inform. Musicale (2015)

12. Miranda, E., Wanderley, M.: New Digital Musical Instruments: Control and Interaction Beyond the Keyboard. A-R Editions, Inc. (2006)

13. Morreale, F., McPherson, A.: Design for longevity: ongoing use of instruments from NIME 2010–14. In: Proceedings of International Conference on New Interfaces for Musical Expression, pp. 192–197 (2017)

14. Palacio-Quintin, C.: Eight years of practice on the hyper-flute: technological and musical perspectives. In: Proceedings of International Conference on New Interfaces for Musical Expression, pp. 293–298 (2008)

15. Rovan, J., Wanderley, M.M., Dubnov, S., Depalle, P.: Instrumental gestural mapping strategies as expressivity determinants in computer music performance. In: Proceedings of the Kansei - The Technology of Emotion Workshop, pp. 68–73 (2007)

16. Stewart, A.: Karlax performance techniques: it feels like... In: Proceedings of International Computer Music Conference, pp. 83–89 (2016)

17. Touizrar, M., McAdams, S.: Aspects perceptifs de l'orchestration dans angel of death de roger reynolds: timbre et groupement auditif. In: Lalitte, P. (ed.) Musique et cognition: Perspectives pour l'analyse et la performance musicales, pp. 55–78. Editions universitaires de Dijon (2019)

18. Wanderley, M.M., Orio, N.: Evaluation of input devices for musical expression: borrowing tools from HCI. Comput. Music. J. **26**(3), 62–76 (2002)

19. Wanderley, M.M., Vines, B., Middleton, N., McKay, C., Hatch, W.: The musical significance of clarinetists' ancillary gestures: an exploration of the field. J. New Music Res. **34**(1), 97–113 (2005)

20. Wessel, D., Wright, M.: Problems and prospects for intimate musical control of computers. Comput. Music. J. **26**(3), 11–22 (2002)

Music Information Retrieval
and Modeling

Modelling Moral Traits with Music Listening Preferences and Demographics

Vjosa Preniqi[1(✉)], Kyriaki Kalimeri[2], and Charalampos Saitis[1]

[1] Centre for Digital Music, Queen Mary University of London, London, UK
v.preniqi@qmul.ac.uk
[2] ISI Foundation, Turin, Italy

Abstract. Music has always been an integral part of our everyday lives through which we express feelings, emotions, and concepts. Here, we explore the association between music genres, demographics and moral values employing data from an ad-hoc online survey and the Music Learning Histories Dataset. To further characterise the music preferences of the participants the generalist/specialist (GS) score employed. We exploit both classification and regression approaches to assess the predictive power of music preferences for the prediction of demographic attributes as well as the moral values of the participants. Our findings point out that moral values are hard to predict (.62 $AUROC_{avg}$) solely by the music listening behaviours, while if basic sociodemographic information is provided the prediction score rises to 4% on average (.66 $AUROC_{avg}$), with the Purity foundation to be the one that is steadily the one with the highest accuracy scores. Similar results are obtained from the regression analysis. Finally, we provide with insights on the most predictive music behaviours associated with each moral value that can inform a wide range of applications from rehabilitation practices to communication campaign design.

1 Introduction

Music played a fundamental role in the evolution of societies being tightly related to communication, bonding, and cultural identity development [17]. Influencing a wide range of cognitive functions such as reasoning, problem-solving, creativity, and mental flexibility [22], musical taste is also known to be strongly related to personality [9] and political orientation [8]. Musical sophistication is also shown to be related to personality traits regardless of demographics or musicianship level [12].

More recently, scientists aside from the traditional self-reported surveys [8], employed digital data and in particular online music streaming [2] and social media [25] data to assess music preferences. Employing data from the myPersonality Facebook project, Nave et al. [25], found that both people's reactions to unfamiliar music samples and "likes" for music artists predicted personality traits. Krismayer et al. [15] studied the Last.fm platform showing that the music listening behaviours can predict demographics, including age, gender, and nationality. More recently, Anderson et al. [2] presented evidence about the connection between personalities and music listening preferences studying Spotify music streaming data.

© Springer Nature Switzerland AG 2023
M. Aramaki et al. (Eds.): CMMR 2021, LNCS 13770, pp. 183–194, 2023.
https://doi.org/10.1007/978-3-031-35382-6_14

Building on comparable interactionist theories, we set to explore the less attended relation between moral values and music preferences. We operationalise morality according to the Moral Foundations Theory (MFT) [11], which defines five moral traits, namely *Care/Harm, Fairness/Cheating, Loyalty/Betrayal, Authority/Subversion*, and *Purity/Degradation*. These can further collapse into two superior moral foundations: of *Individualising*, compounded by fairness and care, that asserts that the basic constructs of society are the individuals and hence focuses on their protection and fair treatment, and of *Binding*, that summarises purity, authority and loyalty, and is based on the respect of leadership and traditions.

Moral values are considered to be higher psychological constructs than the more commonly investigated personality traits yet they have attracted less attention from music scientists. In recent literature there are indications that negative emotions enforced by types of music can worsen moral judgement [3] although that study did not rely on a psychometrically validated theory like the MFT. Kalimeri et al. [14] demonstrated the predictability of moral foundations from a variety of digital data including smartphone usage and web browsing. Their results showed that moral traits and human values are indeed complex, and thus harder to predict compared to demographics, nevertheless, they provide a realistic dimension of the possibilities of modelling moral traits for delivering better targeted and more effective interventions.

Here, we train classification and regression models which infer on self-reported survey data regarding the music preferences. We thoroughly assess the representativity of our data, not only in terms of sociodemographic attributes but also from music behavioural patterns comparing against the open access dataset of music learning histories dataset (MLHD). Our results show that moral values are indeed predictable from music preference information and in line with the findings of the related literature. Further, we discuss the most predictive music behaviours, contributing to an in-depth understanding of the moral profiles. Such insights are fundamental to the broader picture since moral values are a key element in the decision making process on several societal issues [13,14]. Modelling moral values from music represents a great opportunity for improving recommendation systems; designing online streaming applications with user well-being in focus [23]; increasing engagement to communication campaigns for social good applications.

2   Data Collection and Feature Engineering

Here, we employ data from a third-party survey administered online for a general scope marketing project. The survey consists of 2,003 participants (51% females) from 12 different regions in Canada. The participants filled in, among other items, information about basic demographic attributes, including age, gender, education, and political views. They also completed the validated Moral Foundations questionnaire [11], while stated their preferences on 13 music genres (on a 5-point Likert scale where 1 = strongly dislike and 5 = strongly like). The considered music genres were: alternative pop/rock, christian, classical, country, folk, heavy metal, rap/hip-hop, jazz, latin, pop, punk, R&B, and rock. These genres were set from the survey creators and were not further described to the respondents. Even so, they are commonly used to define general musical tastes

Table 1. Summary of the survey dataset (cleaned) with major demographic attributes utilised for this research work.

Attributes	Demographics	Sample size (N = 1062)
Age	18–24	80 (7.5%)
	25–34	154 (14.5%)
	35–44	205 (19.3%)
	45–54	205 (21.9%)
	55–64	187 (17.6%)
	65+	203 (19.1%)
Gender	Male	474 (44.6%)
	Female	588 (55.3%)
Education	Less than High School	35 (3.2%)
	High school graduate	195 (18.3%)
	Some College	154 (14.5%)
	Trade or professional school	115 (10.8%)
	College Graduate	349 (32.8%)
	Post Graduate work or degree	205 (19.3%))
Political Party	Conservative	328 (30.8%)
	Liberal	279 (26.2%)
	NDI (New Democratic Party)	184 (17.3%)
	Green Party	66 (6.2%)
	Party Quebecois	56 (5.2%)
	I don't vote	149 (14%)

among non-musician respondents. To justify these genres and observe if there is any affiliation between survey reported preferences and digital music listening patterns, we explored digital data of 1062 Canadian listeners extracted from the Music Learning Histories Dataset (MLHD) [28] with a similar age and gender distribution to our survey.

Moving on to our survey data, to make sure that participants were paying attention to the survey questions, two "catch questions" were included, which we later used to filter the data. After excluding these users we were left with 1,062 participants (55% females), a sample size substantially higher than previous survey-based studies [8,9]. Table 1 summarises the demographic features of our dataset.

We then applied a factor analysis using principal axis factoring with promax rotation to identify the major dimensions of participants' music preferences. A 5-factor solution was retained, which explained 67% of total data variance: {jazz, classical, latin}, {punk, heavy metal, rap/hip-hop}, {pop, R&B}, {country, Christian, folk}, and {rock, alternative pop/rock} (genres ordered by decreasing factor loading). These factors are in line with the ones obtained in related studies [9].

To quantify the respondents' diversity in music preferences, we employed an adapted version of the generalist-specialist (GS) score, inspired by the work of Anderson et al. [1]. The projections of the 13 genres onto the five factors were considered as that genre's vector representation in the "preference space". Intuitively, generalists

Table 2. Detailed list of the experiments we performed with the list of features employed as predictors in each one of them.

ID	Features Employed as Predictors
EX1	13 Music Genres
EX2	5 factors
EX3	GS score
EX4	13 Music Genres, Age, Gender
EX5	13 Music Genres, Age, Gender, Education
EX6	13 Music Genres, Age, Gender, Education, Political Views

versus specialists will have genre vectors spread apart versus close together in the preference space. We calculate the user centroid $\overrightarrow{ct_i}$ of genre vectors representing the loadings of genres on the 5 factors $\overrightarrow{l_j}$, weighted by the number of genre scores rated by each respondent w_j. The GS score is the cosine similarity between a genre vector and the preference-weighted average of a users' genre vectors:

$$GS(u_i) = \frac{1}{\sum w_j} \cdot \sum w_j \frac{\overrightarrow{l_j} \cdot \overrightarrow{ct_i}}{\| \overrightarrow{l_j} \| \cdot \| \overrightarrow{ct_i} \|} \quad , \quad \overrightarrow{ct_i} = \frac{1}{\sum w_j} \cdot \sum w_j \overrightarrow{l_j}$$

3   Experiments and Results

Exploratory Analysis. As a first step we assess the correlation between musical genres' preferences, demographics, political views and moral traits. We observed a positive Spearman correlation of age with Christian music, classical, country and folk music genres. While heavy metal, hip-hop/rap and punk were more preferred by younger ages, whereas older people expressed their dislike towards these genres (see Fig. 2 for all the correlations between demographics and genres). Education was positively related with classical music, jazz and latin music, indicating that people with higher education preferred these genres. Loyalty, authority and purity were positively correlated with Christian music and country music. Whereas Care and Fairness where slightly correlated with alternative pop-rock (see Fig. 1 for all the correlations between MFT values and genres). Looking at the political views of the respondents, conservatives were positively correlated with Christian genre and country, and negatively correlated with hip-hop-rap genre and punk.

Further, we assessed whether the obtained self-reported responses of the questionnaire are in line with digital music listening data. From the MLHD dataset [28] we extracted artists' genres using MusicBrainz identifiers. From the survey data we discerned that the top 10 most preferred genres were: rock, pop, alternative pop-rock, classical, r&b, country, jazz, folk, latin, and hip-hop/rap. Similar trends were encountered in the music listening histories of Canadian users in MLHD where the 10 most frequently listened genres were: rock, alternative rock, pop-rock, pop, electronic, folk, punk, jazz, heavy metal, and hip-hop.

	gender	age	education level	alternative-pop-rock	christian	classical	country	folk	heavy-metal	hip-hop/rap	jazz
Care	0.18	0.04	-0.10	0.10	0.11	0.00	0.04	0.04	-0.04	0.02	0.01
Fairness	0.06	0.09	-0.05	0.10	0.03	0.04	0.01	0.06	-0.04	0.02	0.04
Loyalty	-0.02	0.23	-0.14	-0.05	0.18	-0.07	0.17	0.00	-0.02	-0.01	-0.02
Authority	-0.05	0.23	-0.16	-0.11	0.26	-0.06	0.20	-0.02	-0.10	-0.08	-0.05
Purity	0.04	0.23	-0.19	-0.16	0.38	-0.02	0.21	0.02	-0.14	-0.07	-0.04
Individualizing	0.14	0.07	-0.08	0.11	0.08	0.02	0.03	0.05	-0.04	0.02	0.03
Binding	-0.01	0.26	-0.19	-0.13	0.32	-0.05	0.22	0.00	-0.11	-0.07	-0.04

	latin	pop	punk	r&b	rock	Conservative	Liberal	NDI	Green party	Party Quebecois	Non voter
Care	0.02	0.05	-0.01	0.01	0.02	-0.11	0.04	0.04	0.05	-0.03	0.04
Fairness	0.05	0.04	0.02	0.07	0.09	-0.15	0.05	0.10	0.09	-0.02	-0.02
Loyalty	-0.02	0.01	-0.09	0.02	-0.01	0.08	0.01	-0.01	-0.03	-0.03	-0.07
Authority	-0.05	0.01	-0.18	-0.02	-0.06	0.17	-0.01	-0.09	-0.07	0.00	-0.06
Purity	-0.02	-0.02	-0.21	-0.06	-0.16	0.17	-0.04	-0.09	-0.07	-0.04	0.00
Individualizing	0.04	0.05	0.00	0.05	0.05	-0.15	0.05	0.07	0.08	-0.03	0.02
Binding	-0.04	0.00	-0.19	-0.03	-0.10	0.17	-0.02	-0.08	-0.07	-0.03	-0.04

Fig. 1. Moral (MFT) values correlations with music genres, demographics and political leanings

Moral Values Classification. Our main research question is whether we can predict peoples' moral values from their music preferences. To answer this question, we postulate the task as a supervised classification one, developing a series of experiments to assess the predictive power of different variables (see Table 2). We assign the class label "high" to individuals with moral scores higher than the population median for the specific foundation, and "low", otherwise. We perform 5-fold cross-validation on shuffled data (to avoid dependencies in successive data points), with 70% of training and 30% testing data. We opt for the gradient boosting algorithm XGBoost (XGB) as it performed better than Random Forest (RF) and Support Vector Machine (SVM) in this task.

To take into account the effect of unbalanced class labels in the performance metric, we evaluate our models with the area under the receiver operating characteristic (AUROC) metric which is a performance measure for binary classifiers that employs a discrimination threshold to differentiate between a high and a low class [14]. The best model is then chosen as the one that maximized the weighted area under receiver operating characteristic (AUROC) statistic.

Initially, we compared the predictive power of the genre information against the features engineered by us (EX1, EX2, and EX3). We trained one model per moral foundation, and we present the cross validated results in Table 3. We notice that the information obtained directly about the music preferences (EX1) outperforms the features we developed. When comparing the scenarios, we observe that the 5 factors, and

	alternative-pop-rock	christian	classical	country	folk	heavy-metal	hip-hop-rap	jazz	latin	pop	punk	r&b	rock
gender	0.10	0.01	-0.08	0.01	-0.05	-0.04	0.18	-0.09	0.02	0.20	0.11	0.05	-0.04
age	-0.25	0.18	0.21	0.20	0.25	-0.22	-0.38	0.17	0.13	-0.13	-0.38	-0.04	-0.07
education level	0.01	-0.02	0.22	-0.11	0.06	-0.04	-0.01	0.13	0.13	0.00	0.04	-0.01	0.00
Conservative	-0.11	0.12	0.04	0.12	0.01	-0.08	-0.17	0.00	-0.03	-0.05	-0.15	-0.01	-0.06
Liberal	0.03	-0.02	0.00	-0.04	0.05	0.01	0.01	0.05	0.04	0.00	0.09	0.04	0.09
NDI	-0.01	-0.02	0.06	-0.01	0.07	0.01	0.03	0.01	0.02	-0.04	0.07	-0.02	-0.01
Green party	0.05	-0.06	-0.05	-0.04	-0.01	0.05	0.07	0.03	0.04	-0.04	0.06	0.04	0.05
Party Quebecois	0.06	-0.05	0.02	-0.03	0.02	0.02	0.01	0.01	0.10	0.04	0.02	-0.04	0.00
Non voter	0.04	-0.05	-0.10	-0.05	-0.15	0.04	0.08	-0.09	-0.08	0.00	0.07	-0.02	-0.07

Fig. 2. Demographic correlations (including participants political leanings) with music genres.

Table 3. Moral traits classification with XGBoost for music preference features (see Table 2): average weighted AUROC and standard deviation over 5-fold cross-validation (baseline is .50).

	EX1	EX2	EX3
Care	**.57 (3.7)**	.54 (2.1)	.52 (1.5)
Fairness	**.56 (2.9)**	.52 (1.1)	.48 (2.7)
Authority	**.63 (0.8)**	.60 (1.1)	.49 (1.7)
Purity	**.69 (2.8)**	.65 (3.0)	.57 (2.3)
Loyalty	**.61 (2.4)**	.56 (1.9)	.48 (3.1)
Individ	**.55 (3.5)**	.51 (0.8)	.50 (1.6)
Binding	**.67 (2.4)**	.63 (2.2)	.52 (1.9)

the GS score accounting only for part of the variance in the data, did not manage to outperform the explicit information on music preferences. A question that emerges naturally, is whether including knowledge regarding the participants' basic demographic features (i.e. age, political views, education level) will improve the prediction of their moral values. Table 4 summarises the results when age, gender, education and political views are incorporated in the design. As expected, the more information we have about the participants the more precise our predictions become, however, the improvement is minimum. This shows us the importance of music behaviours alone in explaining the variability of our moral values.

Further, we employed SHAP (SHapley Additive exPlanations), a game theory approach developed to explain the contribution of each feature to the final output of any machine learning model [19]. SHAP values provide both global and local interpretability, meaning that we can assess both how much each predictor and each observation, respectively, contribute to the performance of the classifier. The local explanations are based on assigning a numerical measure of credit to each input feature. Then, global model insights can be obtained by combining many local explanations from the samples [18]. As mentioned by the authors, the classic Shapley values can be considered "optimal" in the sense that within a large class of approaches, they are the only way to

Table 4. Moral traits classification with XGBoost for music preference and demographic predictors (see Table 2): average weighted AUROC and standard deviation over 5-fold cross-validation (baseline is 50).

	EX1	EX4	EX5	EX6
Care	.57 (3.7)	.62 (3.2)	.62 (3.0)	**.63 (2.3)**
Fairness	.56 (2.9)	.58 (2.5)	.57 (2.3)	**.62 (4.3)**
Authority	.63 (0.8)	.64 (1.6)	.65 (2.0)	**.66 (1.6)**
Purity	.69 (2.8)	.71 (3.0)	**.71 (1.4)**	.71 (1.6)
Loyalty	.61 (2.4)	**.67 (3.5)**	.66 (2.2)	.66 (2.9)
Individ	.55 (3.5)	.59 (2.4)	.59 (3.3)	**.61 (1.8)**
Binding	.67 (2.4)	.71 (3.2)	.70 (2.2)	**.72 (2.9)**

measure feature importance while maintaining several natural properties from cooperative game theory [20]. SHAP's output helps to understand the general behaviour of our model by assessing the impact of each input feature in the final decision, thus enhancing the usefulness of our framework.

Figure 3 depicts the impact of each feature in the prediction of the two superior foundations, when including demographics, education level, and political views, together with the 13 music genres (EX6 in Table 4). Across all experiments, Christian music emerged as the most predictive genre. Yet we don't have any further information from the survey whether "Christian" is used as a universal term for both contemporary Christian music and gospel music [6]. The former is listened predominantly by White Americans, while gospel music is fostered primarily by African Americans. and is mainly defined by the meaning or the lyrics instead of musical style [7,16]. Although the two genres have similar goals, each has emerged and evolved from distinct social and cultural situations: gospel songs, holding roots in blues, underline opposition and overcoming, while contemporary Christian lyrics, rooted in the aftereffect of the Hippie movement, promote devotion and inspiration [6]. Because all survey respondents self-reported as "White/Caucasian," it is plausible that "Christian" here refers to the contemporary Christian genre. Regarding the demographics, the participants' age stands out both for Individualising and Social Binding foundations.

Moral Values Regression. Data binning is a common way to aggregate information and facilitate the classification tasks. However, there are known issues to dichotomisation of variables which often lead to misleading results [21]. Here, to ensure that the most predictive features as emerged from the classification process are indeed descriptive of the respective moral trait, we conducted a regression analysis. At this point, the aim is to understand whether we can estimate the original moral scores (predicting the quantity) based on our explanatory variables in disposition (i.e., music genres ad demographics).

To do so, we trained an XGBoost Regressor for each moral foundation. We maintained the same experimental designs and settings as in the classification task. For evaluation, we used Mean Absolute Error (MAE). These options allow for a direct comparison of the most predictive features with the ones emerged from the classification task

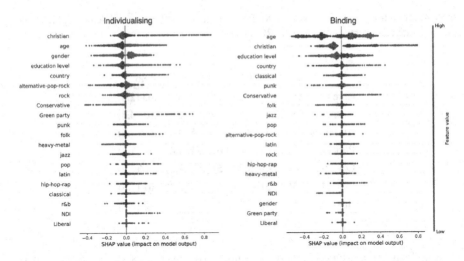

Fig. 3. Feature contributions (via SHAP values) based on XGBoost classification model. The higher the SHAP value (x-axis) the more the feature contributes to the moral prediction.

Table 5. Mean Absolute Error (MAE) and standard deviation over 5-fold cross-validation for XGBoost regression on music preference features (see Table 2).

	EX1	EX2	EX3
Care	3.86 (13.2)	**3.72 (10.9)**	3.89 (7.0)
Fairness	**3.27 (11.1)**	3.28 (9.6)	3.55 (8.7)
Authority	**4.19 (23.3)**	4.20 (16.7)	4.47 (13.9)
Purity	**4.86 (19.7)**	4.99 (25.0)	5.35 (21.0)
Loyalty	4.46 (12.1)	**4.33 (19.4)**	4.64 (11.6)
Individ	3.23 (9.5)	**3.17 (8.5)**	3.35 (9.9)
Binding	3.86 (15.1)	**3.79 (6.3)**	4.22 (18.5)

(Table 5). We noticed that as in the classification task, when adding information to the models, the MAE decreases indicating that the model fits the data better. Also in this case the gain of adding more information is relatively small with respect to the music genres alone. We visualised the most predictive features using again the Shap values (see Fig. 4). Interestingly, the christian music genre appears again as the most important predictor for both the Binding and Individualising traits. The feature importance for the output of the XGboost regressor, is in line with the feature significance obtained with the classification approach. The same holds for all the moral foundations which are not depicted here for spacing issues (Table 6).

Table 6. Mean Absolute Error (MAE) and standard deviation over 5-fold cross-validation for XGBoost regression on music preference and demographic features (see Table 2).

	EX1	EX4	EX5	EX6
Care	3.86 (13.2)	3.72 (6.2)	3.71 (9.3)	**3.60 (8.0)**
Fairness	3.27 (11.1)	3.25 (8.2)	3.19 (10.5)	**3.12 (13.4)**
Authority	4.19 (23.3)	4.14 (15.9)	4.10 (9.3)	**4.09 (11.0)**
Purity	4.86 (19.7)	4.86 (20.4)	4.74 (18.9)	**4.71 (15.8)**
Loyalty	4.46 (12.1)	**4.19 (22.8)**	4.20 (18.7)	4.21 (18.7)
Individ	3.23 (9.5)	3.17 (14.4)	3.17 (8.0)	**3.0 (8.9)**
Binding	3.86 (15.1)	3.80 (11.0)	3.76 (13.1)	**3.74 (5.4)**

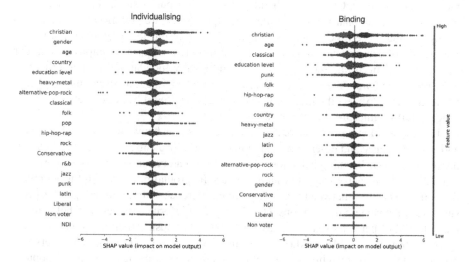

Fig. 4. Feature contributions (via SHAP values) based on XGBoost regression model. The higher the SHAP value (x-axis) the more the feature contributes to the moral prediction.

4 Discussions and Conclusions

Henry Wadsworth Longfellow wrote, "Music is the universal language of mankind". Contemporary research has found converging evidence that people listen to music that reflects their psychological traits and needs and help express emotions, cultures, values and personalities. In this paper, we analysed the less explored links between musical preferences, demographics (age, gender, political views, and education level) and Moral Foundations (MFT [11]). We applied both classification and regression models for moral traits prediction. From classification results, it was inferred that MFT Binding was best predicted with AUROC score 72%, whereas MFT individualising showed weaker results with AUROC score 61%. While, for the regression task the lowest MAE was 3.0 for the Individualising and 3.74 for Social Binding. In both approaches, the most impactful features on inferring morality were christian music and age.

Moral foundations are strongly tied to political views; despite that, the musical features are more predictive than political leanings. Social binding is related to conservative political views [10] - and in fact is predicted by christian, and country music. We notice that people naturally express their moral values through the music they listen to. We instinctively *categorize* objects, symbols, but also people, creating a notion of *social identity*. According to the social identity theory members of a group will seek to find negative aspects to other groups thus enhancing their self-image [27]. Such reasoning reflects on a broad range of attitudes related to stereotype formations [24] but also as we notice here to musical preferences. For instance, people higher in social binding foundations tend to listen to country music which often expresses notions of patriotism. Christian music is also a predictor of this superior foundation, which again fosters the notion of belonging to a group. Across all experiments, Christian music emerged as the most predictive genre. On the other hand, genres such as punk, and hip hop are known to challenge the traditional values and the status quo, hence are preferred by people who strongly value these aspects. Our findings suggest that musical preferences are quite informative of deeper psychological attributes; still there is space for improvement. For instance, we noticed that the care, fairness, and loyalty foundations are harder to predict. To this end we already started exploring musical content analysis, incorporating linguistic cues [26], and the moral valence scores as proposed by Araque et al. [4,5] on lyrics to further improve the performance.

In future work we aim to delve deeper into the relation between music and morality, and between music and other universal human values, by using passively collected digital traits of music listening behaviours outside a laboratory setting and over a period of time [2], while using self-reported surveys as a solid groundtruth. We will further investigate the association between music listening preferences other psychological aspects such as human values and emotions. Developing data-informed models will help unlock the potential of personalised, uniquely tailored digital music experiences and communication strategies [1,14]. Predicting the moral values from listening behaviours can provide noninvasive insights on the values or other psychological aspects of populations at a large scale.

Acknowledgments. This work was supported by the QMUL Centre for Doctoral Training in Data-informed Audience-centric Media Engineering (2021–2025) as part of a PhD studentship awarded to VP. KK acknowledges support from the "Lagrange Project" of the ISI Foundation, funded by the CRT Foundation. We would like to thank Dr. Robert Raleigh for providing the survey data, and the two anonymous reviewers for their thoughtful comments.

References

1. Anderson, A., Maystre, L., Anderson, I., Mehrotra, R., Lalmas, M.: Algorithmic effects on the diversity of consumption on spotify. In: Proceedings of the Web Conference 2020, pp. 2155–2165 (2020)
2. Anderson, I., et al.: "Just the way you are": linking music listening on spotify and personality. Soc. Psychol. Personal. Sci. **12**(4), 561–572 (2021)
3. Ansani, A., D'Errico, F., Poggi, I.: 'You will be judged by the music i hear': a study on the influence of music on moral judgement. In: Web Intelligence, pp. 53–62 (2019)

4. Araque, O., Gatti, L., Kalimeri, K.: Moralstrength: exploiting a moral lexicon and embedding similarity for moral foundations prediction. Knowl. Based Syst. **191**, 105184 (2020)

5. Araque, O., Gatti, L., Kalimeri, K.: The language of liberty: a preliminary study. In: Companion Proceedings of the Web Conference 2021, pp. 623–626 (2021)

6. Banjo, O.O., Williams, K.M.: A house divided? Christian music in black and white. J. Media Religion **10**(3), 115–137 (2011)

7. Cusic, D.: The Sound of Light: A History of Gospel and Christian Music. Hal Leonard Corporation (2002)

8. Devenport, S.P., North, A.C.: Predicting musical taste: relationships with personality aspects and political orientation. Psychol. Music **47**(6), 834–847 (2019)

9. Gardikiotis, A., Baltzis, A.: 'Rock music for myself and justice to the world!': musical identity, values, and music preferences. Psychol. Music **40**(2), 143–163 (2012)

10. Graham, J., Haidt, J., Nosek, B.A.: Liberals and conservatives rely on different sets of moral foundations. J. Personal. Soc. Psychol. **96**(5), 1029–1044 (2009)

11. Graham, J., Nosek, B., Haidt, J., Iyer, R., Koleva, S., Ditto, P.H.: Mapping the moral domain. J. Personal. Soc. Psychol. **101**(2), 366–385 (2011)

12. Greenberg, D.M., Müllensiefen, D., Lamb, M.E., Rentfrow, P.J.: Personality predicts musical sophistication. J. Res. Pers. **58**, 154–158 (2015)

13. Haidt, J., Joseph, C.: Intuitive ethics: how innately prepared intuitions generate culturally variable virtues. Daedalus **133**(4), 55–66 (2004)

14. Kalimeri, K., Beiró, M.G., Delfino, M., Raleigh, R., Cattuto, C.: Predicting demographics, moral foundations, and human values from digital behaviours. Comput. Hum. Behav. **92**, 428–445 (2019)

15. Krismayer, T., Schedl, M., Knees, P., Rabiser, R.: Predicting user demographics from music listening information. Multimed. Tools. Appl. **78**(3), 2897–2920 (2019)

16. Livengood, M., Ledoux Book, C.: Watering down Christianity? An examination of the use of theological words in Christian music. J. Media Religion **3**(2), 119–129 (2004)

17. Loersch, C., Arbuckle, N.L.: Unraveling the mystery of music: music as an evolved group process. J. Personal. Soc. Psychol. **105**(5), 777–798 (2013)

18. Lundberg, S.M., et al.: Explainable AI for trees: from local explanations to global understanding (2019)

19. Lundberg, S.M., Lee, S.I.: A unified approach to interpreting model predictions. In: Proceedings of the 31st International Conference on Neural Information Processing Systems, pp. 4768–4777 (2017)

20. Lundberg, S.M., Lee, S.I.: A unified approach to interpreting model predictions. In: Guyon, I., et al. (eds.) Advances in Neural Information Processing Systems, vol. 30, pp. 4765–4774. Curran Associates, Inc. (2017). http://papers.nips.cc/paper/7062-a-unified-approach-to-interpreting-model-predictions.pdf

21. MacCallum, R.C., Zhang, S., Preacher, K.J., Rucker, D.D.: On the practice of dichotomization of quantitative variables. Psychol. Methods **7**(1), 19–40 (2002)

22. MacDonald, R., Kreutz, G., Mitchell, L.: Music, Health, and Wellbeing. Oxford University Press, Oxford (2013)

23. Mejova, Y., Kalimeri, K.: Effect of values and technology use on exercise: implications for personalized behavior change interventions. In: Proceedings of the ACM Conference on User Modeling, Adaptation and Personalization (UMAP) 2019, pp. 36–45 (2019)

24. Miller, S.L., Maner, J.K., Becker, D.V.: Self-protective biases in group categorization: threat cues shape the psychological boundary between "us" and "them". J. Personal. Soc. Psychol. **99**(1), 62–77 (2010)

25. Nave, G., Minxha, J., Greenberg, D.M., Kosinski, M., Stillwell, D., Rentfrow, J.: Musical preferences predict personality: evidence from active listening and Facebook likes. Psychol. Sci. **29**(7), 1145–1158 (2018)

26. Preniqi, V., Kalimeri, K., Saitis, C.: "More than words": linking music preferences and moral values through lyrics. arXiv preprint arXiv:2209.01169 (2022)
27. Tajfel, H., Turner, J.C., Austin, W.G., Worchel, S.: An integrative theory of intergroup conflict. Org. Id.: Reader **56**(65), 33–47 (1979)
28. Vigliensoni, G., Fujinaga, I.: The music listening histories dataset. In: Proceedings of the International Society for Music Information Retrieval Conference (ISMIR), pp. 96–102 (2017)

Classification of 1950 to 1960 Electronic Music Using the VGGish Neural Network and Random Forest

Maurício do Vale Madeira da Costa, Florian Zwißler, Philip Schwarzbauer, and Michael Oehler[✉]

MTDML, Institute for Musicology and Music Pedagogy, Osnabrück University, Osnabrück, Germany
{madovalemade,florian.zwissler,philip.schwarzbauer, moehler}@uni-osnabrueck.de
https://www.mtdml.uni-osnabrueck.de

Abstract. This paper presents an approach to extend an ontological database concept aimed at the systematization of Electronic Music. Machine Learning techniques are used to test the significance of empirical investigations on the "output layer" of the production process, namely finished compositions of Electronic Music. As an example, pieces from the era of 1950 to 1960 are being examined, representing the aesthetics of Musique Concrète from Paris and Elektronische Musik from Cologne. The experiments performed using state-of-the-art techniques suggest the confirmation of measurable differences in the musical pieces from different studios for Electronic music that were motivated by aesthetically divergent approaches.

Keywords: Electronic music · musique concrète · Elektronische Musik · VGGish · random forest

1 Introduction

1.1 Analysis and Systematization of Electronic Music

Despite Electronic Music has existed for many decades, it is still lacking tools to reliably systematize it, the most striking being a shortage of a clear terminology capable of describing the phenomena themselves as well as the processes used to produce them. In most cases, analogies to the strong and established terminologies of instrumental music and sound production [11,14,17,18,20] are being taken as a solution to this problem, not facing the problem that electronic sound production implies a fundamentally different potential that needs to be addressed [12]. This issue is continued in the field of music analysis: only a few attempts have been made to present universally valid tools that allow musicologists to get significant insights into the structure of a piece of Electronic Music. The most valuable source of information at hand is represented by [3,9] and the

© Springer Nature Switzerland AG 2023
M. Aramaki et al. (Eds.): CMMR 2021, LNCS 13770, pp. 195–201, 2023.
https://doi.org/10.1007/978-3-031-35382-6_15

recently revised EMDoku Set (www.emdoku.de), a huge database of Electronic Music that gives insights into all the results of composing with electronically produced sound. A systematization that comprises the conditions of the production of these results is yet to be found. Recently, this topic has received more attention, for example, with regard to Musique Concrète [6].

The PRESET research project, which was presented at CMMR 2019, has set out to do basic work to make progress in this direction: a database is being put together collating information from an in-depth survey of several studios for Electronic Music. Exploring their informational resources and bringing them together will open new lines of insight into the nature and relations of the processes involved. To address this issue, it was decided to use a semantic web database with an underlying ontology as a structural and terminological foundation [1]. In connection with the methods of actor-network theory [13] and theories from the field of information systems [7,8], the working processes within the single studios as well as the connection between them will display a new perspective on the field.

1.2   Electronic Music in the 1950s: Musique Concrète and Elektronische Musik

The early period of Electronic music was characterized by a vivid debate between two quite different approaches to composing music within the context of an electronic studio. The Musique Concrète, which originated in Paris with its founder Pierre Schaeffer and since 1958 organised in the Groupe de Recherches Musicales (GRM), and the approach called Elektronische Musik (Electronic music), which was pursued at the West German Radio in Cologne, most prominently represented by its then leader Herbert Eimert and Karlheinz Stockhausen. The Musique Concrète originally set out their experiments from recorded sound, thus integrating the production medium (records and, later on, magnetic tape) within the very first steps of working on sound. The repertoire of sound to create a piece was gained by very simple means of manipulation such as cutting the tape, reversing it, changing its speed, and building loops to generate rhythmic structures. This results in an empirical approach to dealing with sound as a medium to work on, also leading to an elaborate theoretical concept of the nature of sounds that Schaeffer formulated in his Traité des objets musicaux [16]. In Cologne, on the other hand, the idea was rather to construct the sound following a pre-structured concept devised by the composer. This strategy, in turn, was strongly connected to the concept of serial music, which favoured a view on composition as a formal organization of sets of parameters [15]. It is evident that this view found a perfect fit in the new possibilities of sound creation and organization in an electronic studio. Here, the tape was used to build complex sounds by copying and assembling source material from synthetic sources, e.g. sine wave or impulse generators.

These two approaches, of course, did not exist separately from one another, and there was a vital interest in each other's musical results. On the other hand, the opposing views on concepts of composition led to an intense debate at the time. This debate has been broadly discussed [2, 4, 5] and displays the remarkable aesthetic difference between the positions represented by the studios in Paris and Cologne.

Without directly addressing these discussions, we decided to take the diverging concepts to an empirical test with the use of Machine Learning techniques.

1.3   Method

The methods presented in Sect. 1.1 basically represent a top-down model of systematisation. Connecting our efforts to the existing potentials of databases such as EMDoku, we decided to add a bottom-up method of information retrieval in analyzing datasets representing the actual "output" of the studios in Cologne and Paris within a time window ranging from 1950 to 1960 - a period where the aesthetically divergent approaches were most prominent [4]. In doing so, we will try to test methods of empirical analysis and check them for their significance. The experiment consists in using a pre-trained Deep Neural Network (DNN) to convert the audio samples into semantically meaningful embeddings and then training a classifier to learn to identify material from both classes (GRM and WDR) using such high-level embeddings as input features. This way, we propose to empirically assess the existence of differences between recordings of such groups in purely acoustic features. Although this approach does not indicate what those differences are, we intend to pursue an indirect demonstration of their existence, for the only information provided for classification is related to audio content.

The VGGish [19] model was used for the computation of the embeddings. This network is based on the VGG [10] model, which is one of the most used DNN architectures for image recognition, and produces embeddings of 128 samples. In order to prepare the audio data to be processed by this network, first, the audio input signal is collapsed to mono and band-limited to 8 kHz. Then, its spectrogram is computed using the short-time Fourier transform, with a Hann analysis window of 25 ms and a hop of 10 ms. Then, a mel-spectrogram with 64 frequency bands (125–7500 Hz) is obtained by remapping the spectrogram time-frequency bins. This mel-spectrogram is then framed into non-overlapping examples of 0.985 s, each example covering the 64 mel bands and 96 time frames of 10 ms each. Finally, this process produces the embeddings for all audio files available by computing the network's outputs and stores them in text files with the same names as their audio counterparts.

The random forest algorithm was used to classify the embeddings produced. To avoid having excerpts of the same musical piece both in the training and test sets by treating the embeddings as independent samples, all the embeddings of each piece were either assigned to the training set or to the test set. For this purpose, a random selection of the pieces was performed with a probability of 70% of each piece being selected as training data and 30% as test data. Since their variability in length is large (ranging from less than a minute to several minutes), considerable differences occur in the actual train/test proportion. This same classification experiment was repeated 10 times and both the average and the standard deviation of the results were computed to illustrate the classification performance. We used the implementation present in the "Scikit learn" framework for the random forest algorithm, set to train an ensemble of 400 decision trees and use its default settings. Smaller numbers of trees were tested and provided slightly lower performance. Nevertheless, yielding high classification performance and providing a detailed analysis regarding the classification problem itself is not the objective of this paper.

In order to assess the performance, the majority vote on the embeddings within each musical piece was taken to assign the piece's classification. This way, each piece accounted for one sample, instead of their group of embeddings, i.e. pieces from which more than 50% of the embeddings were correctly estimated are considered to be one correctly estimated sample, despite its duration.

The actual lists of pieces used for the analysis were determined through the following: As a first step, all output from both studios within the chosen time interval was identified following the data resources provided by EMDoku, which represents the most reliable resource available. After that, only works that purely consist of electronically produced sounds were selected, thereby excluding all pieces that use sound resources from outside the production processes under analysis. It was also decided to exclude all sorts of functional compositions (e.g. music for radio plays) within those lists to again ensure the validity of the data as examples of the two aesthetic directions. The next step was to retrieve the actual audio material of the pieces. From the list of pieces from the studio of the WDR, it was possible to obtain about 75% of the pieces in question (57 files), making up a total duration of 3.5 h. The examples available from the GRM made up a fairly larger amount, with 94 files, totalling roughly 6 h of audio material.

It should be noted that we only compared the audio content of these pieces with no regard to spatialization, so from all the pieces, also those that exist in multichannel versions, only mono-mixdown versions were used, due to the characteristics of the architecture adopted for the classification task.

1.4   Results

The results obtained from this procedure are summarized in Table 1, which shows the average and standard deviation for accuracy, precision, recall and F-measure. Despite the small dataset available, the results suggest that the classifier was capable of identifying differences in the acoustic features related to each aesthetic approach.

Table 1. Overall results.

Measure	Average	Std.
Accuracy	0.82	0.08
Precision	0.89	0.08
Recall	0.66	0.20
F-measure	0.74	0.14

Histograms that represent classification accuracy of the embeddings within each musical piece, i.e. the proportion of correct votes for each class within each piece, is illustrated in Fig. 1. As can be observed, the distributions obtained have different characteristics: the classifier was more successful in identifying excerpts from GRM, with voting proportion more concentrated towards 100% than from WDR, which had a more diluted classification of the embeddings. In total, the GRM pieces were classified as 82% GRM and 18% WDR, whereas the WDR pieces were estimated to be 47% WDR and 53% GRM.

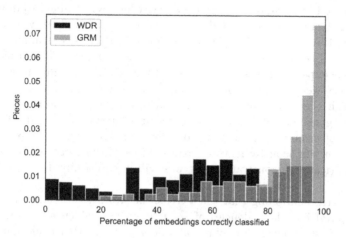

Fig. 1. Histograms of classification accuracy within each musical piece for the GRM samples.

The distributions obtained suggest that the classes may significantly overlap, as expected, but the classification system tended to have a bias towards the GRM class despite all data imbalancement compensation techniques. This may indicate that the GRM pieces might have less variation within the acoustic features of interest for the classification system. In contrast, the WDR pieces may show a wider variety in such dimensions. Besides, the pieces have a considerable amount of excerpts where audio material is present, like background noise or long reverb tails, which may severely interfere in this analysis. Nevertheless, the results are informative and serve the purpose of empirically assessing the differences present in sound.

1.5   Conclusion

The experiments presented in this paper served the initial goal to widen the focus of a database still under construction that aims at facilitating a valid and significant systematization of Electronic Music. The Machine Learning techniques employed to analyze the two specific sets of compositional results of studio work have displayed a specific difference within these sets. A possible consequence of this outcome in interaction with a future ontological database could be to check the technical equipment used within the specified time interval for correspondences and differences, as well as to investigate possible interdependencies of personnel involved. The inclusion of this "bottom-up"- method is therefore likely to provide valuable insights and to bring up crucial questions to constantly improve the structure of the database as a whole.

The experimental setup was comprised of two different Machine Learning techniques: a pre-trained deep neural network (VGGish), which uses as input mel-spectrograms of the audio signal and outputs a sequence of high-level embeddings, followed by a random-forest classifier, which was trained to differentiate embeddings from both classes under analysis. The musical pieces were then classified using the criterion of the majority vote of the classes estimated for their embeddings. The train and test sets were randomly generated from piece selection and the experiment was performed 10 times. No embeddings from the same musical piece were used for both training and testing.

Although the results are not particularly outstanding compared to a classical music genre classification task, with an accuracy of around 82% and an F-measure of around 74%, they demonstrate that, indeed, there exist tangible differences in the acoustic features extracted from the pieces of these groups, which empirically demonstrates what was only theoretically discussed in previous studies.

It is worth mentioning that the VGGish network does not encompass long-term temporal interdependencies of acoustic events, which are a fundamental part of music structure and may reveal hidden patterns that could improve this intricate classification task, if approached. For this purpose, we intend to expand this experiment in future work tackling this specific problem by considering the whole sequence of embeddings using a different downstream model, instead of purely classifying each one independently, or even using a deep neural network that takes into account the temporal dimension.

Acknowledgment. Supported by German Research Foundation (DFG).

References

1. Abdallah, S., Raimond, Y., Sandler, M.: An ontology-based approach to information management for music analysis systems. In: Audio Engineering Society. Audio Engineering Society Convention 120 (2006)
2. v. Blumrder, C.: Die elektroakustische Musik: Eine kompositorische Revolution und ihre Folgen. Der Apfel (2017)
3. Davies, H.: Répertoire International des Musiques Electroacoustiques: International Electronic Music Catalog. Groupe de Recherches Musicales de l'ORTF (1967)
4. Eimert, H., Humpert, H.: Das Lexikon der elektronischen Musik. Bosse (1973)
5. Frisius, R.: Musique concrète. http://www.frisius.de/rudolf/texte/tx355.htm. Accessed 03 Nov 2022
6. Godøy, R.I.: Perceiving sound objects in the musique concrète. Front. Psychol. **1702**, (12:672949) (2021)

7. Goldkuhl, G.: Design theories in information systems-a need for multi-grounding. J. Inf. Technol. Theory Appl. (JITTA), 2(6), 59–72 (2004)
8. Gregor, S., et al.: A theory of theories in information systems. Inf. Syst. Found. Build. Theor. Base, 1–20 (2002)
9. Hein, F., Seelig, T.: Internationale Dokumentation Elektroakustischer Musik. Pfau Verlag (1996)
10. Hershey, S., et al.: CNN architectures for large-scale audio classification. In: Proceedings of ICASSP 2017, pp. 131–135. New Orleans (2017)
11. Kartomi, M.J.: On Concepts and Classifications of Musical Instruments. The University of Chicago Press, Chicago (1990)
12. Kolozali, S., Barthet, M., Fazekas, G., Sandler, M.B.: Knowledge representation issues in musical instrument ontology design. In: ISMIR, pp. 465–470 (2011)
13. Latour, B.: Reassembling the Social: An Introduction to Actor-Network-Theory. Oxford University Press, Oxford (2005)
14. Montagu, J.: Origins and Development of Musical Instruments. Scarecrow Press (2007)
15. Morawska-Buengeler, M.: Schwingende Elektronen. Eine Dokumentation ber das Studio fr Elektronische Musik des Westdeutschen Rundfunks in Kln. PJ Tonger (1988)
16. Schaeffer, P.: Traite des Objets Musicaux. Essai Interdisciplines. Le Seuil, Paris, France (1966)
17. Simon, P.: Die hornbostel/sachs' sche systematik und ihre logik. Instrumentenbau-Zeitschrift-Musik International 46(7–8), 64–66 (1992)
18. Simon, P.: Die Hornbostel/Sachs' sche Systematik der Musikinstrumente: Merkmalarten und Merkmale. Verlag Peter Simon, Eine Analyse mit zwei Felderdiagrammen (2004)
19. Simonyan, K., Zisserman, A.: Very deep convolutional networks for large-scale image recognition. In: Proceedings of the International Conference on Learning Representations, pp. 1–14. San Diego (2015)
20. Von Hornbostel, E.M., Sachs, C.: Systematik der musikinstrumente. ein versuch. Zeitschrift für Ethnologie 46(H. 4/5), 553–590 (1914)

Knowledge Transfer from Neural Networks for Speech Music Classification

Christian Kehling[1,2]([envelope])[iD] and Estefanía Cano[3][iD]

[1] Institute for Digital Media Technology, Technical University of Ilmenau, Ilmenau, Germany
christian.kehling@tu-ilmenau.de
[2] Fraunhofer Institute for Digital Media Technology, Ilmenau, Germany
[3] Songquito UG, Erlangen, Germany

Abstract. A frequent problem when dealing with audio classification tasks is the scarcity of suitable training data. This work investigates ways of mitigating this problem by applying transfer learning techniques to neural network architectures for several classification tasks from the field of Music Information Retrieval (MIR). First, three state-of-the-art architectures are trained and evaluated with several datasets for the task of speech/music classification. Second, feature representations or embeddings are extracted from the trained networks to classify new tasks with unseen data. The effect of pre-training with respect to the similarity of the source and target tasks are investigated in the context of transfer learning, as well as different fine-tuning strategies.

Keywords: Deep Learning · Neural Networks · Audio Classification · Speech Music Classification · Transfer Learning · Embeddings · Music Information Retrieval

1 Introduction

Detection of speech and music in audio signals has been investigated in the field of Music Information Retrieval (MIR) to automatically enrich audio archives with metadata. In addition to binary classification where only one of the classes is assumed to be present at time more complex tasks like segmentation of speech or music as well as multi-label classification where multiple classes can be present at time gained popularity. Despite the vast amount of research in this field [2, 5, 8, 14–16, 20, 23, 24], speech/music classification (SMC) remains challenging in the presence of noise, the involvement of chanting, or under low-quality recording conditions [17]. SMC was first addressed with algorithms based on audio features (e.g., pitch, zero crossing rate) [14, 16, 23]. Recent approaches almost entirely focus on deep neural networks (DNN) that directly learn to detect desired audio properties from input signals and its corresponding annotations [3, 5, 15, 20]. In an attempt to make audio classifiers more robust to varying signal conditions and data scarcity, pre-trained feature representations (embeddings) from related

© Springer Nature Switzerland AG 2023
M. Aramaki et al. (Eds.): CMMR 2021, LNCS 13770, pp. 202–213, 2023.
https://doi.org/10.1007/978-3-031-35382-6_16

tasks are transferred to new tasks to avoid exhaustive training from scratch. These so called Transfer Learning techniques (TL) aim at taking advantage of the task-related knowledge learned during pre-training [3,4,6,8,11].

This work is divided in two stages. First, we analyze three state-of-the-art neural network architectures for SMC and evaluate their robustness to varying signal conditions by using a diversity of datasets. Here we aim to understand whether any of the three architectures is more robust to varying signal charac-teristics when trained under comparable conditions. In the second stage of our work, audio embeddings are computed from the three pre-trained architectures. These embeddings are then transferred to different MIR tasks. In this stage, we aim to understand how pre-trained models compare to baseline networks trained from scratch, and whether a close relation of the downstream task and pre-training task exhibit higher learning effects than general audio embeddings like OpenL3 [4] that were not trained on a related MIR task at all.

The remainder of this paper is organized as follows: a brief overview of the related work is presented in Sect. 2. Section 3 introduces the datasets used, Sect. 4 describes the training procedures and embedding creation, and results are pre-sented in Sect. 5. Conclusions and final remarks are discussed in the last Sect. 6.

2   Related Work

Current approaches for SMC mostly rely on deep neural networks (DNN) trained and optimized using raw audio data or its time-frequency transform. The most popular networks for this task are convolutional neural networks (CNN) [5,14,15, 20]. In 2015 Lidy et al. [15] used a CNN approach consisting of one convolutional layer followed by a fully connected layer achieving 99.7% accuracy on binary classification of speech and music at the MIREX competition [9]. The separate detection of both classes still achieved 88.5% accuracy. The model proposed by Marolt [17] obtained an accuracy of 98% for SMC, and 92% for a 4-class classification for speech, solo singing, choir, and instrumental music. This model uses a combination of convolutional layers followed by residual layers. Besides the GTZAN [25] and MUSAN [24] datasets, additional field recordings and traditional music from various libraries were included. In [2], different architectures including DNNs, CNNs and recurrent neural networks were evaluated for speech music detection. According to their findings, a model with six CNN layers performed best on AudioSet [21] with 86% accuracy for speech or music detection. SwishNet [8] uses a set of one-dimensional convolutions with multiple skip connections on Mel-Frequency Cepstral Coefficients (MFCCs). This model achieved 93% accuracy on a 3-class detection task with speech, music, and noise and 99% accuracy for speech detection using the MUSAN [24] dataset for training and GTZAN [25] for verification. For performance comparison Hussain et al. used a Gaussian Mixture Model, a fully connected neural network (FCN), and a transfer learning approach of the MobileNet architecture [7]. The MobileNet embeddings worked best throughout the paper followed by the proposed SwishNet architecture.

Complementing the findings of Hussain et al. also Choi et al. [3] showed that transfer learning can outperform traditional feature based methods in many different MIR tasks as well as audio event detection (AED). In [4] OpenL3 embeddings were trained on the task of audio-video correspondence in a self-supervised manner inspired by [1] and subsequently transferred to the task of environmental sound classification. On several AED datasets this approach outperformed other TL embeddings based on VGG-like and SoundNet architectures. Grollmisch et al. [6] verified the potential of OpenL3 for different MIR and industrial sound analysis tasks. The embeddings consistently resulted in good classification performance while other embeddings highly varied depending on the task. Kong et al. [13] proposed pre-trained audio neural networks (PANN) for transfer learning. The authors introduced an input representation called Wavegram, a neural network based time-frequency-transformation. A multi-layer CNN is connected to this input network and trained for audio tagging on the AudioSet [21]. Subsequently, these embeddings were augmented by trainable classifiers and applied to six different classification tasks including genre and acoustic scenes classification, among others. In most of these tasks, the embeddings performed better or similar to state-of-the-art approaches. The authors compared multiple networks and depths as well as different positions for unfreezing of the pre-trained embeddings concluding that a complete fine-tuning of all network parameters results in the highest accuracy. To overcome the overfitting to one particular task Kim et al. [11] proposed multi-task learning. During training, a CNN network structure is split at one stage in the model into multiple branches, one for each task. All branches consist of the same network architecture and where trained simultaneously. The last layers before the classifiers of each branch are concatenated and used as combined embeddings. Initially the system was trained on the Million Song Database [18] for tempo estimation and song similarity. The embeddings were evaluated on target tasks like genre classification or music recommendation. Different branch positions in the network were evaluated concluding that earlier branching results in better performance for the target tasks but also in bigger networks with more computational costs.

Table 1. Characteristics of the datasets used for training on speech/music classification (source task) and for transfer learning tasks (target tasks).

Application	Dataset ID	Classes [Number of Files per class]	Sample Rate	Bit Depth	Duration [min]
Training	MUSAN	Music [660], Speech [426], Noise [764]	16 kHz	16	6483
	GTZAN	Music [64], Speech [64]	22 kHz	16	64
	Marolt19	Solo Singing [1512], Choir [1618], Instrumental [2960], Speech [1284]	44 kHz	16	577
	ACMusYT	Speech [40], Music [35], A Cappella [40]	48 kHz	16	88
Transfer	S&S	Music [101], Speech [80]	22 kHz	16	45
	ACMusVF	Male [46], Female [24]	96 kHz	24	26
	ACMusIF	1 [43], 2 [42], 3 [43], 4 [21], 5+ [36]	96 kHz	24	65

3 Datasets

To get a better understanding of the performance of the evaluated architectures, four datasets were used during training as depicted in Table 1. The MUSAN dataset [24] and the GTZAN dataset [25] consist of clearly distinguishable broadcast material of western music and speech. In addition, two more challenging ethnomusicology datasets are included. The Marolt19 dataset was first introduced in [17]. Apart from the speech class, choir, solo singing and instrumental music are combined into the 'music' class for training. Marolt19 includes material from archives such as the British Library world & traditional music collection, the French Centre of Scientific Research (CNRS), or the Slovenian sound archive Ethnomuse. The ACMus Youtube Dataset (ACMusYT)[1] was collected as part of the ACMus research project.[2] It consists of audio excerpts of traditional Colombian music from the Andes region. The subset used in this work consists of two classes: speech and music with vocals. The 'vocal-only' class is not used in these experiments for better separation during training. For TL experiments, the pre-trained networks are subsequently fine-tuned with separate datasets. An established set for speech music tasks is the Slaney & Scheirer dataset (S&S) [23] with content taken from broadcast material. All 64 files of noise and mixed (speech/music) content are excluded before the evaluation. From the ACMus-MIR dataset [19], the Instrumental Format Set (ACMusIF) was used. This set was created from traditional Andean music recordings for the purpose of ensemble size classification. The goal of this task is to classify music tracks as solo, duo, trio, quartet, and larger ensembles. Finally, the ACMus Vocal Format Set (ACMusVF) is included.[3] It comprises Andean vocal music (male and female singers) partly with accompaniment.

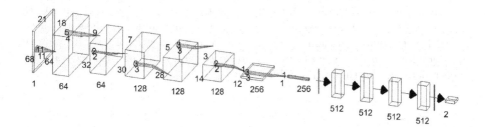

Fig. 1. INA network architecture [5]. The green line indicates the freezing point of the intermediate fine-tuning strategy. The red line indicates the output point of the embedding vector. (Color figure online)

---

[1] https://zenodo.org/record/4870820.
[2] ACMus project page: https://acmus-mir.github.io/.
[3] https://zenodo.org/record/4791394.

4   Methodology

4.1   Network Architectures

The INA (Institut National de l'Audiovisuel) approach [5] is a CNN-based network that uses patches of 68 frames of 21 MFCCs with a maximum frequency of 4 kHz as input representation to four 2D-convolutional layers followed by four dense layers with dropout. Each of these layers are followed by batch normalization and a *ReLU* activation. The output layer uses *Softmax* activation (see Fig. 1 for details). INA achieved an average accuracy of 92.6% at the 2018 MIREX [10] competition on music detection and 96.2% on speech detection.

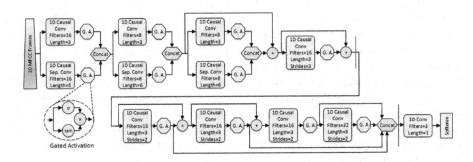

Fig. 2. SwishNet network architecture. The green line indicates the freezing point of the intermediate fine-tuning strategy. The red line indicates the output point of the embedding vector. Refer to [8] for more details on the architecture. (Color figure online)

SwishNet is an architecture based on one-dimensional convolutional layers in combination with residual and skip connections [8] (see Fig. 2). As input, 16 frames of 22 MFCCs are extracted from one second audio snippets and used as 2D feature representation. Classification results range from 93% frame-wise accuracy for 3 classes (speech, music, noise) to 99% segment-wise accuracy for speech detection in the initial publication [8].

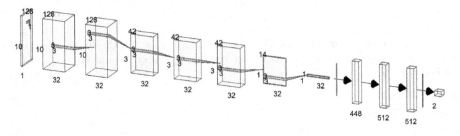

Fig. 3. VGG-like network architecture. The green line indicates the freezing point of the intermediate fine-tuning strategy. The red line indicates the output point of the embedding vector. (Color figure online)

VGG-like architectures are commonly used networks in many fields of deep learning [3,4,17]. The network illustrated in Fig. 3 is inspired by [22]. The logarithmic Mel-Spectrogram (MelSpec) representation is used as input from audio sampled 22050 Hz. Frames of 2048 samples with 512 samples hop size are transformed to 128 mel band representation. A patch of 10 frames is fed to four convolutional layers with 32 kernels of size 3×3. Each layer is followed by batch normalization and ReLU activation. After every second convolutional layer, Max-Pooling is applied with a 3×3 window. Two fully connected layers are added after flattening followed by the classifier with a *Softmax* activation.

OpenL3 embeddings are included as a state-of-the-art baseline. The 512 unit feature vectors are extracted from the audio data with default parameters from [4]. These vectors are normalized between 0 and 1 and used as input for a trainable neural classifier consisting of a 128 unit dense layer followed by the final classifier with *Sigmoid* activation. As a second baseline, a simple DNN architecture is used. MelSpecs with equal measures as for SwishNet and VGG-like models are input and passed through one dense layer with 128 units and the output layer. *Adam* is used as optimization and *Softmax* as activation function. This represents the same structure as the appended classifiers of the computed embeddings in Sect. 4.4 but instantly applied to the MelSpec input. Hence this will give an insight into the learning effects of the embedded architectures.

4.2 Input Representation

All datasets were normalized in a range of $[-1, 1]$ in time domain and unified to a sampling rate 22050 Hz and 16 bit sampling depth. The MelSpec representation with 128 bands and 512 samples hop size is evaluated as input representation for all networks. Additionally the original MFCC input representations of the SwishNet and INA approaches are included to check for side effects of the input adaption. The original VGG-like approach already used MelSpecs. The OpenL3 network creates batches of embeddings with a feature size of 512 samples (see Sect. 4.1) for each 100 ms of raw audio.

4.3 Implementation Details and Metrics

In all experiments, 10% of the data is used for testing, 10% for validation and the remaining data for training. All experiments are repeated using five-fold cross-validation. All data is balanced by random down-sampling. After transforming the input to MelSpec, it is normalized feature-wise to zero mean in the range from -1 to 1 and concatenated to batches of 64 frames. Each network is trained for 200 epochs with the option for early stopping if the validation accuracy does not increase for 50 epochs. The *Adam* optimizer [12] with a learning rate of 10^{-3} is used for all architectures for best comparability to the original implementations. Results are presented as the mean accuracy over 5 cross-validation folds with its standard deviation.

4.4   Transfer Learning Networks and Tasks

For transfer learning, the models are trained with a balanced combination of all four training sets 3. Afterwards the output layers are removed from the trained networks (see Sect. 4.1) and the remaining layers are fixed and used for embedding calculation. A trainable classifier is appended consisting of a 128 unit dense layer and a dense output layer matching the number of the target task classes.

Three different freezing positions for the trained models are evaluated. In the first strategy, only the classifier is trained while the network weights remain fixed. The second strategy unfreezes the networks in an intermediate position so the classifier and parts of the networks are fine-tuned. These positions are illustrated green in Figs. 1, 2, and 3, respectively. In a third strategy, all network weights are unfrozen and fine-tuned along with the classifier. These strategies do not apply for OpenL3 because of its baseline function.

As transfer learning tasks, we evaluate the following target tasks: (a) SMC with S&S dataset, (b) accompaniment detection with ACMusVF dataset. The goal of this task is to distinguish music pieces with instrumental accompaniment from vocal-only performances, (c) female vs male singer classification on the ACMusVF dataset. We refer to this task as gender classification in singing, (d) ensemble size classification on the ACMusIF set.

5   Results

5.1   Network Architectures Comparison

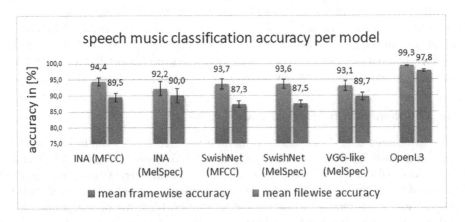

Fig. 4. Comparison of the mean frame-wise accuracy per architecture for speech/music classification averaged over all training sets (MUSAN, GTZAN, Marlot19, ACMusYT).

Figure 4 shows the mean file-wise and frame-wise results for each architecture. All four training sets were trained separately so the presented accuracy numbers represent averaged values over these sets. Results show that OpenL3 embeddings performed best on all datasets for SMC. Looking at the frame-wise accuracy, SwishNet is slightly below the remaining two CNN-based architectures by around 3%. The mean file-wise performance is comparable for all three network architectures regardless of the input representation.

Figure 5 presents results for binary SMC and a three-class task which includes noise as the third class. This is performed for the MUSAN and Marolt19 datasets where noise samples are included. Marolt19 data appears to be the most challenging set due to the fact that it does not only consist of broadcast material unlike MUSAN. As expected, the accuracy drops for a more complex task of three classes. The highest drop of 24.3% occurs for INA in connection with Marolt19 and MelSpec input followed by the VGG-like model. For MUSAN dataset the most significant drop can be observed for the INA model in connection with MFCC input. The varying results indicate that the INA architecture might not be well suited for alternative tasks in contrast to OpenL3 which shows best robustness.

Regarding the input representation no significant performance differences can be observed in Fig. 4. Only a slight improvement for MelSpecs on frame level is visible. Figure 5 confirms this trend for the INA architecture as MelSpecs maintain better performance on MUSAN data. Apart from that a high fluctuation can be observed for Marolt19 giving no clear indication of a a preferred input representation. In conclusion MFCCs can increase performance for specific tasks but MelSpecs have a more robust behavior in general. Hence, for better comparability only MelSpec is used for further experiments.

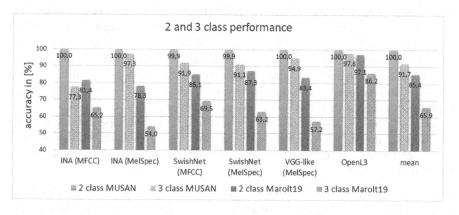

Fig. 5. Comparison of frame-based accuracy for binary classification versus 3-class classification. Results are shown for MUSAN (yellow) and Marolt19 (blue) datasets.

5.2   Transfer Learning

Results for all transfer experiments are presented in Table 2. Besides the three network architectures (INA, SwishNet, and VGG-like), results for OpenL3 embeddings and the DNN are added as baselines. In general, most of the resulting models tend to overfit during fine-tuning due to the small training data.

Speech Music Classification with S&S: In this experiment, the target task for TL was kept the same (SMC) so models are only transferred to an unseen dataset. In Table 2 a learning effect from the pre-training can be observed for the Slaney & Scheirer dataset. In detail embeddings from INA and VGG-like models can make better use of pre-training and gain up to 3% classification accuracy while the performance of SwishNet remains at almost the same level. OpenL3 embeddings outperform all other models for this dataset-task combination.

Accompaniment Detection on ACMusVF: For this task OpenL3 again shows best results and is followed by the VGG-like embeddings with a performance gap of around 11%. Despite the close task relation to SMC no architecture overcomes the accuracy of the plain DNN and hence no learning effect from TL is achieved in connection with this task. This is reinforced by the fact that for SwishNet and VGG-like architectures, the original models perform better than their embedding counterparts.

Female/Male Singer Classification on ACMusVF: For this task Swish-Net embeddings show best results closely followed by OpenL3 embeddings. The original networks for each model show comparable or better performances compared to the fully frozen embeddings indicating that no clear learning effect of pre-training is visible. Again the DNN performs comparable to the best model refuting a benefit of the knowledge transfer.

Ensemble Size Classification on ACMusIF: All created embeddings perform similar with nearly 50% accuracy in the fully frozen variant. The baseline architectures of VGG-like and SwishNet show better results when trained from scratch excluding the idea of a possible learning effect. This is confirmed by the plain DNN baseline that outperformed the embeddings by around 12%. The usage of embeddings results in a inverse effect for this task. Furthermore this experiment engages the most unrelated task relative to SMC in the set of transfer tasks. The best results with 76.2% are achieved using the OpenL3 embeddings which by their origin have no close relation to this target task. A file-wise evaluation of OpenL3 results in 84% accuracy which confirms the outcome from Grollmisch et al. [6].

Freezing Strategies: Inspecting the last two rows of each embedding in Table 2 gives insights to freezing strategies for the pre-trained networks. With more degree of freedom, meaning more trainable layers, the accuracy tend to increase in most cases. This trend is highly network-dependent and mainly applies to SwishNet models while INA tends to be more unstable showing a higher fluctuation. VGG-like models perform best in intermediate state.

Table 2. Transfer learning results. Mean frame-wise accuracy values are presented for fully frozen (Acc_{FZ}), partly trainable (intermediate) (Acc_{IN}), and the fully trainable embeddings (Acc_{FT}). Listed are the results for each architecture using their pre-trained embeddings (Emb) as well as their original network trained from scratch on the according task ($Orig$). In addition OpenL3 embeddings and the two-layer DNN (see Sect. 4.1) are listed as baseline.

Task-Set-Combination	Model	Acc_{FZ} [%]	Acc_{IN} [%]	Acc_{FT} [%]
Speech Music Classification on S&S	INA_{Emb}	98,8 ± 1,4	97,6 ± 2,1	85,1 ± 4,8
	INA_{Orig}	-	-	93,8 ± 3,0
	$VGG-like_{Emb}$	97,4 ± 1,5	97,9 ± 1,9	88,9 ± 1,6
	$VGG-like_{Orig}$	-	-	95,1 ± 2,1
	$SwishNet_{Emb}$	92,3 ± 2,7	93,0 ± 2,4	95,0 ± 1,7
	$SwishNet_{Orig}$	-	-	92,9 ± 1,5
	$OpenL3_{Emb}$	**99,2 ± 0,4**	-	-
	$DNN_{baseline}$	-	-	92,9 ± 1,9
Accompaniment Detection on ACMus VF	INA_{Emb}	85,2 ± 5,6	82,5 ± 9,1	90,8 ± 5,2
	INA_{Orig}	-	-	80,2 ± 6,6
	$VGG-like_{Emb}$	88,5 ± 7,4	94,9 ± 3,2	92,7 ± 5,8
	$VGG-like_{Orig}$	-	-	92,7 ± 4,9
	$SwishNet_{Emb}$	81,5 ± 4,6	85,1 ± 4,6	93,6 ± 3,2
	$SwishNet_{Orig}$	-	-	94,0 ± 3,7
	$OpenL3_{Emb}$	**99,6 ± 0,5**	-	-
	$DNN_{baseline}$	-	-	96,5 ± 1,7
Female/Male Singer Classification on ACMusVF	INA_{Emb}	70,0 ± 7,7	47,3 ± 7,9	59,3 ± 7,6
	INA_{Orig}	-	-	67,4 ± 7,0
	$VGG-like_{Emb}$	71,8 ± 5,2	75,8 ± 9,1	73,5 ± 6,2
	$VGG-like_{Orig}$	-	-	73,6 ± 8,1
	$SwishNet_{Emb}$	72,6 ± 5,0	73,1 ± 5,1	**78,3 ± 8,9**
	$SwishNet_{Orig}$	-	-	74,9 ± 9,5
	$OpenL3_{Emb}$	72,3 ± 9,6	-	-
	$DNN_{baseline}$	-	-	72,6 ± 10,3
Ensemble Size Classification on ACMusIF	INA_{Emb}	49,8 ± 5,6	52,1 ± 10,2	56,7 ± 4,5
	INA_{Orig}	-	-	48,8 ± 7,2
	$VGG-like_{Emb}$	49,7 ± 5,0	51,3 ± 6,8	47,1 ± 3,9
	$VGG-like_{Orig}$	-	-	57,9 ± 5,3
	$SwishNet_{Emb}$	46,7 ± 5,7	48,7 ± 6,3	54,3 ± 5,4
	$SwishNet_{Orig}$	-	-	56,3 ± 5,6
	$OpenL3_{Emb}$	**76,2 ± 4,4**	-	-
	$DNN_{baseline}$	-	-	61,4 ± 5,3

6   Conclusions

This work examines the idea of transfer learning (TL) by creating new feature representations from one source task (pre-training), to use them as embeddings for several target MIR tasks. Three network architectures (INA, SwishNet, VGG-like) were initially trained for SMC, and subsequently applied to four new classification tasks. Our experiments show a slight dominance of the MelSpec as input representation over MFCCs during training. No significant performance difference between the three architectures is visible for the source task while OpenL3 embeddings consistently showed best SMC accuracy. SwishNet shows the highest potential of adaption to new tasks when all network parameters are fine-tuned. In comparison to the networks trained from scratch, pre-training results in a slight improvement when used with an additional DNN classifier for the source task. In the TL experiments, the direct combination of MelSpec input and the DNN classifier surpasses the embedding performance in some cases. These results suggest that the learning effect of pre-training is not consistent over all experiments. This might indicate that only the appended classifier may adapt to the downstream tasks while the embedded network does not improve the semantic value of the processed data. To exclude such effects in future work the use of direct classifiers like support vector machines might be beneficial to compare the pure performance of the created models.

Furthermore, creating embeddings with tasks closely related to the target tasks show no evident benefit compared to general audio embeddings such as OpenL3, which performed best in most of the cases and were created on a very different and not music-related task. A possible cause can be the self-supervised creation of this embedding network which inhabits limitless availability of training data. However, the amount of training data used for pre-training the different embeddings is not considered in these experiments and is left for future work. For the created models even slight domain shifts as accompaniment detection already cause a significant performance drop. This trend continues the lower the relatedness of the target task becomes as can be seen for ensemble size classification.

Further experiments using different source tasks might give a more general insight on the relevance of task relatedness. Moreover, it would be beneficial to partly adapt learning strategies from OpenL3 to inspect which aspects have the strongest impact on its domain-agnostic behaviour.

References

1. Arandjelovic, R., Zisserman, A.: Look, listen and learn. In: IEEE International Conference on Computer Vision, pp. 609–617 (2017). https://doi.org/10.1109/ICCV.2017.73
2. de Benito-Gorron, D., Lozano-Diez, A., Toledano, D.T., Gonzalez-Rodriguez, J.: Exploring convolutional, recurrent, and hybrid deep neural networks for speech and music detection in a large audio dataset. EURASIP J. Audio Speech Music Process. **2019**(1), 1–18 (2019). https://doi.org/10.1186/s13636-019-0152-1
3. Choi, K., Fazekas, G., Sandler, M.B., Cho, K.: Transfer learning for music classification and regression tasks. In: Cunningham, S.J., Duan, Z., Hu, X., Turnbull, D. (eds.) Proceedings of the 18th International Society for Music Information Retrieval Conference, ISMIR 2017, Suzhou, China, 23–27 October 2017, pp. 141–149 (2017). https://ismir2017.smcnus.org/wp-content/uploads/2017/10/12_Paper.pdf
4. Cramer, J., Wu, H.H., Salamon, J., Bello, J.: Look, listen, and learn more: design choices for deep audio embeddings. In: ICASSP 2019–2019 IEEE International Conference on Acoustics, Speech and Signal Processing (ICASSP), pp. 3852–3856 (05 2019). https://doi.org/10.1109/ICASSP.2019.8682475

5. Doukhan, D., Lechapt, E., Evrard, M., Carrive, J.: Ina's mirex 2018 music and speech detection system. In: Music Information Retrieval Evaluation eXchange (MIREX 2018) (2018)
6. Grollmisch, S., Cano, E., Kehling, C., Taenzer, M.: Analyzing the potential of pretrained embeddings for audio classification tasks. In: 2020 28th European Signal Processing Conference (EUSIPCO), pp. 790–794 (2021). https://doi.org/10.23919/Eusipco47968.2020.9287743
7. Howard, A.G., et al.: MobileNets: efficient convolutional neural networks for mobile vision applications (2017)
8. Hussain, M.S., Haque, M.A.: SwishNet: a fast convolutional neural network for speech, music and noise classification and segmentation (2018)
9. music ir.org: 2015:music/speech classification and detection results - mirex wiki. https://www.music-ir.org/mirex/wiki/2015:Music/Speech_Classification_and_Detection_Results
10. music ir.org: 2018:music and or speech detection results - mirex wiki. https://www.music-ir.org/mirex/wiki/2018:Music_and_or_Speech_Detection_Results
11. Kim, J., Urbano, J., Liem, C.C.S., Hanjalic, A.: One deep music representation to rule them all?: a comparative analysis of different representation learning strategies. Neural Comput. Appl. 32, 1067–1093 (2020)
12. Kingma, D.P., Ba, J.: Adam: a method for stochastic optimization (2017)
13. Kong, Q., Cao, Y., Iqbal, T., Wang, Y., Wang, W., Plumbley, M.D.: PANNs: large-scale pretrained audio neural networks for audio pattern recognition. IEEE/ACM Trans. Audio Speech Lang. Process. 28, 2880–2894 (2020). https://doi.org/10.1109/TASLP.2020.3030497
14. Kruspe, A., Zapf, D., Lukashevich, H.: Automatic speech/music discrimination for broadcast signals. In: Proceedings - Series of the Gesellschaft fuer Informatik (GI). Lecture Notes in Informatics (LNI) (2017)
15. Lidy, T.: Spectral convolutional neural network for music classification. Music information retrieval evaluation eX-change (MIREX) (2015)
16. Marolt, M.: Probabilistic segmentation and labeling of ethnomusicological field recordings. In: Proceedings of ISMIR (2009)
17. Marolt, M., Bohak, C., Kavcic, A., Pesek, M.: Automatic segmentation of ethnomusicological field recordings. Appl. Sci. 9, 439 (2019). https://doi.org/10.3390/app9030439
18. millionsongdataset.com: Welcome! — million song dataset. https://millionsongdataset.com/
19. Mora-Ángel, F., Gil, G.A.L., Cano, E., Grollmisch, S.: ACMUS-MIR: an annotated dataset of Andean Colombian music. In: In 7th International Conference on Digital Libraries for Musicology. Delft, The Netherlands (2019). https://doi.org/10.5281/zenodo.3268961
20. Papakostas, M., Giannakopoulos, T.: Speech-music discrimination using deep visual feature extractors. Expert Syst. Appl. 114, 334–344 (2018)
21. research.google.com: Audioset. https://research.google.com/audioset/
22. Sakashita, Y., Aono, M.: Acoustic scene classification by ensemble of spectrograms based on adaptive temporal divisions. Technical report, DCASE2018 Challenge (2018)
23. Scheirer, E., Slaney, M.: Construction and evaluation of a robust multifeature speech/music discriminator. IEEE International Conference on Acoustics, Speech, Signal Processing (ICASSP 1997) (1997)
24. Snyder, D., Chen, G., Povey, D.: MUSAN: a music, speech, and noise corpus (2015)
25. Tzanetakis, G.: marsyas.info GTZAN speech music dataset download. https://opihi.cs.uvic.ca/sound/music_speech.tar.gz

Predominant Instrument Recognition in Polyphonic Music Using Convolutional Recurrent Neural Networks

C. R. Lekshmi[✉] and Rajeev Rajan

Department of Electronics and Communication, College of Engineering Trivandrum,
APJ Abdul Kalam Technological University, Trivandrum, Kerala, India
clekshmir04@gmail.com, rajeev@cet.ac.in

Abstract. Automatic identification of lead instruments is a challenging task in the field of music information retrieval (MIR). In this paper, predominant instrument recognition in polyphonic music is addressed using convolutional recurrent neural networks (CRNN) through Mel-spectrogram, modgdgram, and its fusion. Modgdgram, a visual representation is obtained by stacking modified group delay functions of consecutive frames successively. Convolutional neural networks (CNN) learn the distinctive local characteristics from the visual representation and recurrent neural networks (RNN) integrate the extracted features over time and classify the instrument to the group to which it belongs. The proposed system is systematically evaluated using the IRMAS dataset. A wave-generative adversarial network (WaveGAN) architecture is also employed to generate audio files for data augmentation. We experimented with two CRNN architectures, convolutional long short-term memory (C-LSTM) and convolutional gated recurring unit (C-GRU). The fusion experiment C-GRU reports a micro and macro F1 score of 0.69 and 0.60, respectively. These metrics are 7.81% and 9.09% higher than those obtained by the state-of-the-art Han's model. The architectural choice of CRNN with score-level fusion on Mel-spectro/modgd-gram has merit in recognizing the predominant instrument in polyphonic music.

Keywords: predominant · Mel-spectrogram · modgdgram · convolutional gated recurring unit

1 Introduction

Predominant instrument recognition refers to the problem where the prominent instrument is identified from a mixture of instruments being played together [18]. In polyphonic music, the interference of simultaneously occurring sounds makes instrument recognition harder. Automatic identification of lead instruments is important since the performance of the source separation can be improved significantly by knowing the type of the instrument [18].

© Springer Nature Switzerland AG 2023
M. Aramaki et al. (Eds.): CMMR 2021, LNCS 13770, pp. 214–227, 2023.
https://doi.org/10.1007/978-3-031-35382-6_17

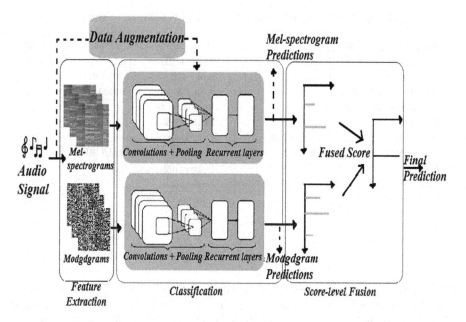

Fig. 1. Block diagram of the proposed method of predominant instrument recognition.

1.1 Related Work

Non-negative matrix factorization (NMF) model [19], end-to-end model [23], fusion model with spectral, temporal, and modulation features [20] can be referred to as initial attempts for the proposed task in a polyphonic environment. Han *et al.* [18] employed Mel-spectrogram-CNN approach for instrument recognition. Pons *et al.* [28] analyzed the architecture of Han *et al.* in order to formulate an efficient design strategy to capture the relevant information about timbre. Detecting the activity of music instruments using a deep neural network (DNN) through a temporal max-pooling aggregation is addressed in [17]. Dongyan *et al.* [39] employed a network with an auxiliary classification scheme to learn the instrument categories through multitasking learning. Gomez *et al.* [15] investigated the role of two source separation algorithms as pre-processing steps to improve the performance in the context of predominant instrument detection tasks. In [24], the Hilbert-Huang transform (HHT) is employed to map one-dimensional audio data into a two-dimensional matrix format, followed by CNN to learn the effective features of the task. In [21] an ensemble of VGG-like CNN classifiers is trained on non-augmented, pitch-synchronized, tempo-synchronized, and genre-similar excerpts of IRMAS for the proposed task.

1.2 Motivation

Conventionally, the spectrum-related features used in instrument recognition take into account merely the magnitude information, whereas the phase

Table 1. Model summary of CNN and CRNN architectures

	Mel-Spectrogram-CNN	Modgdgram- CNN		Mel-Spectrogram-CRNN	Modgdgram-CRNN
x4	2 X Conv2D $(3 \times 3),d_i$	Conv2D $(3 \times 3),f_i$	x3	2 X Conv2D $(3 \times 3),d_i$	Conv 2D $(3 \times 3),f_i$
	Leaky ReLU ($\alpha = 0.33$)	ReLU		Leaky ReLU ($\alpha = 0.33$)	ReLU
	3×3 Max-pooling, stride 1			3×3 Max-pooling, stride 1	
	Dropout(0.25)			Dropout(0.25)	
	Dropout (0.5)			Flatten(1024)	
	Dense (1024)	Dense(512)		Time Distributed layer	
	Leaky ReLU ($\alpha = 0.33$)	ReLU		2 X Bidirectional LSTM/GRU (32 units)	
	Dropout (0.5)			Flatten(1024)	
	Dense (11)			Dense(512)	
	Softmax Activation			Batch Normalization	
				Dropout(0.5)	
				Dense(11)	
				Softmax Activation	

information is mostly ignored due to complications related to its interpretation. The Fourier transform phase spectrum is generally available in a wrapped form. Due to the wrapping of the phase spectrum, group delay processing has been attempted effectively in numerous applications, such as speaker recognition, continuous-speech recognition [25], isolated instrument recognition [2] and musical onset detection [22]. Even though an end-to-end model is a good tool for solving a classification task, the study of the individual contribution of magnitude and phase information is not possible in such approaches.

The modified group delay feature (MODGDF) is proposed for pitched musical instrument recognition in an isolated environment in [2]. While the commonly applied mel frequency cepstral coefficients (MFCC) feature is capable of modeling the resonances introduced by the filter of the instrument body, it neglects the spectral characteristics of the vibrating source, which also, play its role in human perception of musical sounds and genre classification [13]. Incorporating phase information is an effective attempt to preserve this neglected component. Some preliminary works on predominant instrument recognition in polyphonic music using group delay functions are discussed in [1]. In [34] a multi-head attention mechanism is employed along with modified group delay functions for the proposed task. In [35] an ensemble of three visual representations and efficient transformer architectures are employed for the proposed task. In the proposed task, CRNN architecture with score level fusion of Mel-spectrogram and modgdgram is used for recognizing predominant instruments in polyphonic music. Similar approaches combining CNNs and RNNs have been presented recently in many music processing applications [6,8,26]. The idea of including modified group delay functions and GAN-based data augmentation strategy are the main contributions of the proposed scheme.

Section 2 explains the system description. Feature extraction is described in Sect. 3, followed by the model architectures in Sect. 4. The performance evaluation is described in Sect. 5. The results are analyzed in Sect. 6. The paper is concluded in Sect. 7.

2   System Description

The proposed scheme is shown in Fig. 1. In the proposed model, CRNN is used to learn the distinctive characteristics from Mel-spectro/modgd-gram to identify the leading instrument in a polyphonic context. We evaluate the proposed method on the IRMAS dataset and compare its performance to CNN and two variants of RNN-long short-term memory (LSTM) and gated recurring unit (GRU). The performance is also compared with a DNN framework. As a part of data augmentation, additional training files are generated using WaveGAN. During the testing phase, the probability value at the output nodes of the trained model is treated as the score corresponding to the input test file. The input audio file is classified into the node which gives the maximum score during testing. In the fusion framework, the individual scores of Mel-spectro/modgd-gram experiments are fused at the score-level to make a decision. The fusion score S_f is obtained by,

$$S_f = \beta S_{spectro} + (1 - \beta)S_{modgd} \tag{1}$$

where $S_{spectro}$, S_{modgd}, β are the Mel-spectrogram score, modgdgram score and weighting constant, respectively. The value of β has been empirically chosen to be 0.5. Each phase is explained in detail in the following sections.

3   Feature Extraction

Mel-spectrogram and modgdgram are the inputs used in the proposed scheme. Mel-spectrogram approximates how the human auditory system works and can be seen as the spectrogram smoothed, with high precision in the low frequencies and low precision in the high frequencies [27]. It is computed with a frame size of 50 ms and a hop size of 10 ms with 128 bins for the given task. Group delay features are being employed in numerous speech and music processing applications [31,32]. The group delay function is defined as the negative derivative of the unwrapped Fourier transform phase with respect to frequency. Modified group delay functions (MODGD), $\tau_m(e^{j\omega})$ are obtained by,

$$\tau_m(e^{j\omega}) = \left(\frac{\tau_c(e^{j\omega})}{|\tau_c(e^{j\omega})|}\right)(|\tau_c(e^{j\omega})|)^a, \tag{2}$$

where,

$$\tau_c(e^{j\omega}) = \frac{X_R(e^{j\omega})Y_R(e^{j\omega}) + Y_I(e^{j\omega})X_I(e^{j\omega})}{|S(e^{j\omega})|^{2b}}. \tag{3}$$

The subscripts R and I denote the real and imaginary parts, respectively. $X(e^{j\omega})$, $Y(e^{j\omega})$ and $S(e^{j\omega})$ are the Fourier transforms of signal, $x[n]$, n.$x[n]$ ((weighted signal with index), and the cepstrally smoothed version of $X(e^{j\omega})$, respectively. a and b ($0 < a, b \leq 1$) are introduced to control the dynamic range of MODGD [25, 30]. Modgdgram is the visual representation of MODGD with time and frequency in the horizontal and vertical axis, respectively. The amplitude of the group delay function at a particular time is represented by the intensity or color in the third dimension. Modgdgrams are computed with a frame size of 50 ms and hop size of 10 ms using a and b values of 0.9 and 0.5 respectively.

4   Model Architectures

CNNs and RNNs are specific instances of the CRNN architecture presented in this section: A CNN is a CRNN with zero recurrent layers, and an RNN is a CRNN with zero convolutional layers. CNN uses a deep architecture similar to [18] with repeated convolution layers followed by max-pooling. The detailed architecture for Mel-spectrogram and modgdgram CNN and CRNN are shown in Table 1.

RNNs are introduced to handle sequence and time-series data and are well suited for various speech and music-related applications [14,33]. RNN with sophisticated recurrent hidden units like long short-term memory (LSTM) and gated recurring unit (GRU) is used because such structures are capable of alleviating the vanishing gradient problem. They can memorize long sequences and are preferred over conventional RNNs. In the proposed experiment, LSTM and GRU models capture the predominant-specific traits from spectrograms and modgdgrams. The designed RNN consists of one input layer and two hidden layers which include two LSTM or GRU layers each with 32 nodes, and an output dense layer with eleven nodes for output classes. ReLU activation is used for hidden layers and softmax is used for the output layer.

An input gate, an output gate and a forget gate that avoids overfeeding the vanishing gradient are the building blocks of LSTM. LSTM architecture shown in Table 2 is effectively utilized to track the temporal pattern embedded in the modes of the music.

An LSTM can be formulated mathematically as follows:

$$u_t = tanh(W_{xu} \star x_t + W_{hu} \star h_{t-1} + b_u) : \tag{4}$$

$$i_t = \sigma(W_{xi} \star x_t + W_{hi} \star h_{t-1} + b_i), \tag{5}$$

$$f_t = \sigma(W_{xf} \star x_t + W_{hf} \star h_{t-1} + b_f), \tag{6}$$

$$o_t = \sigma(W_{xo} \star x_t + W_{ho} \star h_{t-1} + b_o), \tag{7}$$

$$c_t = i_t u_t + f_t c_{t-1}, \tag{8}$$

$$h_t = tanh(c_t o_t), \tag{9}$$

$$output_{class} = \sigma(h_t \star W_{outpara}) \tag{10}$$

where u_t, i_t, f_t, o_t, c_t, $output_{class}$ represents update equations for, input gate, forget gate, output gate, cell state and cell output, respectively. W terms represent weights, and b terms represent biases to be computed during training. h_t is the output of a neuron at time t. The input x_t is the features at time t. $output_{class}$ is the classification output and$\star$ represents the convolution operation.

As a variant of the RNN, GRU can process memories of sequential data by storing previous inputs in the internal state and planning from the history of prior inputs to target vectors. GRU is the newest entrant in sequence modeling techniques after RNN and LSTM. Hence it promises improvement over the other two in various sequential processing applications.

Table 2. LSTM architecture used for the experiment.

Sl no.	Output Size	Description
1	(128,100)	Input
2	(32)	LSTM, 32 hidden units
3	(32)	LSTM, 32 hidden units
4	(11)	Dense, 11 hidden units

GRU cell corresponds to a node of a recurrent network and has, in addition to the input and output, a forget gate that avoids overfeeding of the vanishing gradient [16]. The advantage of GRU cells is that they are computationaly more effecient even with small datasets [9]. The architecture given in Table 3 is employed for the proposed task.

Fully gated recurrent units are governed by the following equations [7] ;

$$z_t = \sigma_g(W_z.x_t + U_z.h_{t-1} + b_z) \tag{11}$$

$$r_t = \sigma_g(W_r.x_t + U_r.h_{t-1} + b_r) \tag{12}$$

$$\hat{h}_t = \phi_h(W_h.x_t + U_h.(r_t \odot h_{t-1}) + b_h) \tag{13}$$

$$h_t = (1 - z_t) \odot h_{t-1} + z_t \odot \hat{h}_t \tag{14}$$

where variables x_t, h_t, $\hat{h}_t$, z_t, r_t represent input, output, candidate activation, update gate and reset gate vectors, respectively. W, U, and b represent parameter matrices. σ_g and ϕ_h are activation functions. The operation $\odot$ denotes Hadamard product.

Table 3. GRU architecture used for the experiment.

Sl no.	Output Size	Description
1	(128,100)	Input
2	(32)	GRU, 32 hidden units
3	(32)	GRU, 32 hidden units
4	(11)	Dense, 11 hidden units

In order to benefit from both approaches, the two architectures can be combined into a single network with convolutional layers followed by recurrent layers, often referred to as CRNN. The CRNN makes use of the CNN architecture for the task of feature extraction while using LSTM and GRU placed at the end of the architecture to summarise the temporal information of the extracted features. The main drawback of CNNs is it lacks longer temporal context information. However, RNNs do not easily capture the invariance in the frequency domain, rendering high-level modeling of the data more difficult [6]. In the C-LSTM and C-GRU architectures, batch normalization is employed after convolutional layers to improve the training speed and performance. Two bidirectional LSTM/GRU units are connected after the time-distributed flattened layer. The bidirectional RNN is preferred rather than the unidirectional RNN since it considers the future timestamp representations also [10]. The CNN and CRNN networks are trained using Adam optimizer with a learning rate of 0.001.

The key equations of C-LSTM are shown below, where $\star$ denotes the convolution operator and $\odot$ is the Hadamard product [36].

$$i_t = \sigma(W_{xi} \star x_t + W_{hi} \star h_{t-1} + W_{ci} \odot c_{t-1} + b_i) \tag{15}$$

$$f_t = \sigma(W_{xf} \star x_t + W_{hf} \star h_{t-1} + W_{cf} \odot c_{t-1} + b_f), \tag{16}$$

$$c_t = f_t \odot c_{t-1} + i_t \odot tanh(W_{xc} \star x_t + W_{hc} \star h_{t-1} + b_c) \tag{17}$$

$$o_t = \sigma(W_{xo} \star x_t + W_{ho} \star h_{t-1} + W_{co} \odot c_t + b_o) \tag{18}$$

$$h_t = o_t \odot tanh(c_t) \tag{19}$$

Similarly, the equations for C-GRU have been modified as follows [4]:

$$r_t = \sigma(W_r \star_n [h_{t-1}; x_t] + b_r) \tag{20}$$

$$u_t = \sigma(W_u \star_n [h_{t-1}; x_t] + b_u) \tag{21}$$

$$c_t = \rho(W_u \star_n [x_t; r \odot h_{t-1}] + b_c) \tag{22}$$

$$h_t = u_t \odot h_{t-1} + (1 - u_t) \odot c_t \tag{23}$$

where $\star_n$ represents convolution with kernel size nxn and σ and ρ represents element-wise sigmoid and ReLU activation functions respectively.

A DNN framework on musical texture features (MTF) is also experimented with to examine the performance of deep learning methodology on handcrafted features. MTF includes MFCC-13 dim, spectral centroid, spectral bandwidth, root mean square energy, spectral roll-off, and chroma STFT. The features are computed with a frame size of 40 ms and a hop size of 10 ms using Librosa framework[1]. DNN consists of seven layers, with increasing units from 8 to 512. ReLU has been chosen for hidden layers and softmax for the output layer. The network is trained using a categorical cross-entropy loss function for 500 epochs using an Adam optimizer with a learning rate of 0.001. The approach attempted in [29] has been customized for multi-label classification and has been experimented with to analyze the role of machine learning techniques, especially using the MTF-SVM framework.

5   Performance Evaluation

5.1   Dataset

The performance of the proposed system is evaluated using the dataset, instrument recognition in musical audio signals (IRMAS) [12], comprising eleven

---

[1] https://librosa.org/doc/latest/tutorial.html.

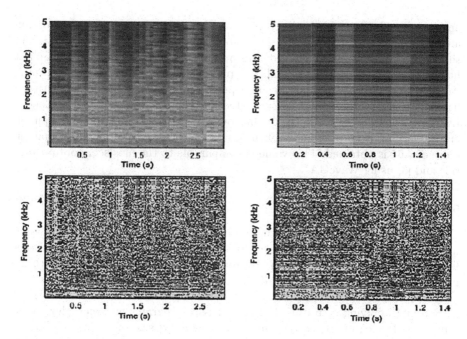

Fig. 2. Visual representation of an audio excerpt with acoustic guitar as leading, Mel-spectrogram of original and WaveGAN-generated (Upper pane left and right). Mod-gdgram of original and WaveGAN-generated (Lower pane left and right).

classes developed by the music technology group (MTG) of Universitat Pompeu Fabra (UPF). The classes include cello (Cel), clarinet (Cla), flute (Flu), acoustic guitar (Gac), electric guitar (Gel), organ (Org), piano (Pia), saxophone (Sax), trumpet (Tru), violin (Vio) and human singing voice (Voice). The training data are single-labeled and consist of 6705 audio files with excerpts of 3 s from more than 2000 distinct recordings. On the other hand, the testing data are multi-labeled and consist of 2874 audio files with lengths between 5 s and 20 s and contain the presence of multiple predominant instruments.

5.2   Data Augmentation Using WaveGAN

WaveGAN v2 is used here to generate polyphonic files with the leading instrument required for training. WaveGAN is similar to DCGAN, which is used for Mel-spectrogram generation, in various music processing applications. The transposed convolution operation of DCGAN is modified to widen its receptive field in WaveGAN. For training, the WaveGAN optimizes WGAN-GP using Adam for both the generator and discriminator. A constant learning rate of 0.0001 is used with $\beta_1 = 0.5$ and $\beta_2 = 0.9$ [11]. WaveGAN is trained for 2000 epochs on the three-sec audio files of each class to generate similar audio files and a total of 6585 audio files with cello (625), clarinet (482), flute (433), acoustic guitar (594), electric guitar (732), organ (657), piano (698), saxophone (597), trumpet (521), violin (526) and voice (720) are generated. The generated files are denoted by $Train_g$

and training files available in the corpus are denoted by $Train_d$. Mel-spectrogram and modgdgram of natural and generated audio files for acoustic guitar are shown in Fig. 2. The experiment details and a few audio files can be accessed at https://sites.google.com/view/audiosamples-2020/home/instrument. The quality of generated files is evaluated using a perception test. It is conducted with ten listeners to assess the quality of generated files for 275 files covering all classes. Listeners are asked to grade the quality by choosing one among the five opinion grades varying from poor to excellent quality (scores, 1 to 5). A mean opinion score of 3.64 is obtained. This value is comparable to the mos score obtained in [11] and [3] using WaveGAN.

5.3   Experimental Set-Up

The experiment progressed in three phases namely Mel-spectrogram-based, modgd- gram-based, and score-level fusion-based. Han's sliding window baseline model [18] is implemented for the given experiment with 1 s slice length for performance comparison[2]. We used the same aggregation strategy (S2) as that of Han's model, by summing all the softmax predictions followed by normalization and applying a threshold of 0.5. Mel-spectrograms and modgdgrams of input size $128 \times 100 \times 1$, corresponding to a window size of 1 s are applied to the corresponding network. The experiments are repeated for CNN, RNN with LSTM and GRU, CRNN with C-LSTM, and C-GRU respectively.

Since the number of annotations for each class was not equal, we computed precision, recall, and F1 measures for both the micro and the macro averages. The equations for computing accuracy, precision, recall, and F1 score is as follows:

$$Accuracy = \frac{TP+TN}{TP+TN+FP+FN} \tag{24}$$

$$Precision = \frac{TP}{TP+FP} \tag{25}$$

$$Recall = \frac{TP}{TP+FN} \tag{26}$$

$$F1score = \frac{2 \times Precision \times Recall}{(Precision+Recall)} = \frac{2 \times TP}{2 \times TP+FP+FN} \tag{27}$$

where $TP, FP, TN,$ and FN represent true positive, false positive, true negative, and false negative respectively. For the micro averages, we calculated the metrics globally, thus giving more weight to the instrument with a higher number of appearances. On the other hand, we calculated the metrics for each label and found their unweighted average for the macro averages.

6   Results and Analysis

Several studies [37,38] have demonstrated that by consolidating information from multiple sources, better performance can be achieved than uni-modal systems

---
[2] https://github.com/Veleslavia/EUSIPCO2017.

Table 4. F1 score for the experiments with data augmentation ($Train_d + Train_g$).

SL. No	Class	MTF DNN	Han's Model	Fusion CNN	Fusion LSTM	Fusion GRU	Fusion C-LSTM	Fusion C-GRU
		F1	F1	F1	F1	F1	F1	F1
1	Cel	0.15	0.55	0.55	0.15	0.36	0.42	0.50
2	Cla	0.26	0.18	0.36	0.13	0.36	0.48	0.39
3	Flu	0.27	0.43	0.55	0.32	0.62	0.34	0.31
4	Gac	0.43	0.72	0.63	0.44	0.54	0.51	0.70
5	Gel	0.36	0.69	0.67	0.50	0.49	0.62	0.74
6	Org	0.28	0.45	0.55	0.37	0.49	0.66	0.51
7	Pia	0.36	0.67	0.62	0.50	0.57	0.78	0.78
8	Sax	0.28	0.61	0.58	0.25	0.55	0.47	0.50
9	Tru	0.18	0.44	0.65	0.33	0.62	0.43	0.60
10	Vio	0.22	0.48	0.68	0.38	0.49	0.64	0.69
11	Voice	0.32	0.85	0.73	0.60	0.58	0.85	0.88
	Macro	**0.28**	0.55	0.60	**0.36**	**0.52**	0.56	0.60
	Micro	**0.32**	0.64	0.65	**0.43**	**0.55**	0.65	0.69

which motivated us to perform the score-level fusion. The F1 score of different fusion experiments is tabulated in Table 4. Fusion experiments using RNNs alone do not show improved performance over existing algorithms, however, GRU shows better performance than LSTM. Since we employed the same number of hidden units for both, GRU required fewer trainable parameters and makes faster progress, and reaches the convergence earlier than LSTM. Fusion experiments C-LSTM and CNN show similar performance, but C-GRU outperforms all the models. GRUs train is faster and computationally more efficient than LSTM because of fewer trainable parameters. Results of the experiments described in [9] suggest that GRUs perform better than LSTMs on small polyphonic datasets [9]. Fusion network C-GRU achieved micro and macro F1 measures of 0.69 and 0.60, respectively, which is 7.81% and 9.09% higher than those obtained for the state-of-the-art Han's model. Han employed Mel-spectrogram-CNN for the proposed task. The experimental results validate the claim that phase information contains additional information for instrument recognition [2]. Our Fusion-CNN with data augmentation reports a micro and macro F1 score of 0.65 and 0.60 respectively which is 1.56% and 5.26% higher than that obtained for our Mel-spectrogram-CNN with data augmentation. It is evident that the modgdgram added complementary information to the spectrogram approach and the importance of the fusion framework for the proposed task. Han's model and the proposed Mel-spectrogram-CNN approach show similar performance with better performance for the proposed architectural choice. Our C-LSTM for Mel-spectrogram requires

Table 5. Classification accuracy of all experiments.

No	Feature	Classifier	Class. Accuracy.(%)
1	MTF	SVM	**25.40**
2	MTF	DNN	**31.88**
3	Spectrogram	CNN	**64.43**
4	Spectrogram	LSTM	**42.56**
5	Spectrogram	GRU	**55.12**
6	Spectrogram	C-LSTM	**65.37**
7	Spectrogram	C-GRU	**69.22**

Table 6. Performance comparison on IRMAS dataset

SL.No	Model	F1 Micro	F1 Macro
1	Bosch *et al.* [5]	0.50	0.43
2	Han *et al.* [18]	0.60	0.50
3	Pons *et al.* [28]	0.58	0.52
4	Kratimenos *et al.* [21]	0.65	0.55
5	K.Racharla *et al.* [29] (MTF-SVM) $(Train_d + Train_g)$	0.25	0.23
6	**MTF-DNN** $(Train_d + Train_g)$	0.32	0.28
7	**Han Model** $(Train_d + Train_g)$	0.64	0.55
8	**Proposed Mel-spectrogram-CNN** $(Train_d + Train_g)$	0.64	0.57
9	**Proposed Modgdgram-CNN** $(Train_d + Train_g)$	0.54	0.53
10	**Proposed Fusion-CNN** $(Train_d + Train_g)$	0.65	**0.60**
11	**Proposed Fusion-C-LSTM** $(Train_d + Train_g)$	0.65	0.56
12	**Proposed Fusion-C-GRU** $(Train_d)$	0.62	0.53
13	**Proposed Mel-spectrogram-C-GRU** $(Train_d + Train_g)$	**0.66**	0.59
14	**Proposed Modgdgram-CGRU** $(Train_d + Train_g)$	0.55	0.53
15	**Proposed Fusion-C-GRU** $(Train_d + Train_g)$	0.69	0.60

100224 more trainable parameters compared to C-GRU. It reaches convergence faster without compromising accuracy. The experimental results validate the claim in [9]. The classification accuracy of our various experiments is shown in Table 5.

The results of various algorithms on the IRMAS dataset are listed in Table 6. Bosch *et al.* [5] algorithm used typical hand-made timbral audio features with their frame-wise mean and variance statistics to train SVMs with flexible audio source separation framework (FASST) in a pre-processing step. It reports a macro F1 score of 0.43, and it is evident that the proposed CNN approaches on visual representation outperform hand-crafted features. Multi-layer and single-layer approaches report macro F1 scores of 0.52 and 0.48, respectively [28]. The relevant time-frequency contexts for learning timbre are analyzed using log-Mel magnitude spectrograms through CNN in those approaches. The MTF-SVM approach [29] has not shown promising performance as claimed.

The state-of-the-art Han's model [18] reports micro and macro F1 score of 0.64 and 0.55, respectively. Our best-performing late fusion model achieved micro and macro F1 measures of 0.69 and 0.62, respectively, and these metrics are 7.81% and 12.73% higher than those obtained by the state-of-the-art Han's model. While the work proposed in [18] focuses only on Mel-spectrogram, we investigated the effectiveness of phase information using modgdgram and fusion of magnitude and phase information for the proposed task. It is evident that our proposed fusion techniques outperformed existing algorithms and the MTF-DNN and SVM framework for both micro and macro F1 measures. Our best model Fusion C-GRU, without data augmentation $(Train_d)$ reports micro and macro F1 score of 0.62 and 0.53 respectively. Fusion C-GRU $(Train_d + Train_g)$ reports micro and macro F1 scores of 0.69 and 0.60, respectively, with an improvement of 11.29% and 13.21% higher than that obtained by Fusion C-GRU $(Train_d)$. This shows the significance of data augmentation in the proposed task.

Our proposed CRNN technique outperformed existing algorithms on the IRMAS dataset for both the micro and the macro F1 measures. The analysis of the experimental frameworks shows the significance of CRNN architecture for the proposed task. Besides, the experiments show the potential of fusion of magnitude and phase information in the proposed task.

7 Conclusion

We presented a CRNN-based predominant instrument recognition system using Mel-spectro/modgd-gram. CRNN is used to capture the instrument-specific characteristics and then do further classification. The proposed method is evaluated on the IRMAS dataset. Data augmentation is also performed using Wave-GAN. The results show the potential of C-GRU architecture on the score-level fusion of Mel-spectrogram and modgdgram in the proposed task.

References

1. Ajayakumar, R., Rajan, R.: Predominant instrument recognition in polyphonic music using GMM-DNN framework. In: Proceedings of International Conference on Signal Processing and Communications (SPCOM), pp. 1–5 (2020)
2. Aleksandr, D., Rajan, P., Heittola, T., Virtanen, T.: Modified group delay feature for musical instrument recognition. In: Proceedings of International Symposium on Computer Music Multidisciplinary Research, pp. 431–438 (2013)
3. Atkar, G., Jayaraju, P.: Speech synthesis using generative adversarial network for improving readability of Hindi words to recuperate from dyslexia. Neural Comput. Appl. **33**, 1–10 (2021)
4. Ballas, N., Yao, L., Pal, C., Courville, A.: Delving deeper into convolutional networks for learning video representations. arXiv preprint arXiv:1511.06432 (2015)

5. Bosch, J.J., Janer, J., Fuhrmann, F., Herrera, P.: A comparison of sound segregation techniques for predominant instrument recognition in musical audio signals. In: Proceedings of 13th International Society for Music Information Retrieval Conference (ISMIR) (2012)

6. Cakır, E., Parascandolo, G., Heittola, T., Huttunen, H., Virtanen, T.: Convolutional recurrent neural networks for polyphonic sound event detection. IEEE/ACM Trans. Audio Speech Lang. Process. **25**(6), 1291–1303 (2017)

7. Cho, K., et al.: Learning phrase representations using RNN encoder-decoder for statistical machine translation. arXiv preprint arXiv:1406.1078 (2014)

8. Choi, K., Fazekas, G., Sandler, M., Cho, K.: Convolutional recurrent neural networks for music classification. In: Proceedings of IEEE International Conference on Acoustics, Speech and Signal Processing (ICASSP), pp. 2392–2396 (2017)

9. Chung, J., Gulcehre, C., Cho, K., Bengio, Y.: Empirical evaluation of gated recurrent neural networks on sequence modeling. In: NIPS 2014 Workshop on Deep Learning, December 2014 (2014)

10. Cui, Z., Ke, R., Pu, Z., Wang, Y.: Deep bidirectional and unidirectional LSTM recurrent neural network for network-wide traffic speed prediction. arXiv preprint arXiv:1801.02143 (2018)

11. Donahue, C., McAuley, J., Puckette, M.: Adversarial audio synthesis. In: Proceedimgs of International Conference on Learning Representations, pp. 1–16 (2019)

12. Fuhrmann, F., Herrera, P.: Polyphonic instrument recognition for exploring semantic similarities in music. In: Proceedings of 13th International Conference on Digital Audio Effects DAFx10, vol. 14, no. 1, pp. 1–8. Graz (2010)

13. Fuhrmann, F., et al.: Automatic musical instrument recognition from polyphonic music audio signals. Ph.D. thesis, Universitat Pompeu Fabra (2012)

14. Gimeno, P., Viñals, I., Ortega, A., Miguel, A., Lleida, E.: Multiclass audio segmentation based on recurrent neural networks for broadcast domain data. EURASIP J. Audio Speech Music Process. **2020**(1), 1–19 (2020). https://doi.org/10.1186/s13636-020-00172-6

15. Gómez, J.S., Abeßer, J., Cano, E.: Jazz solo instrument classification with convolutional neural networks, source separation, and transfer learning. In: Proceedings of International Society for Music Information Retrieval (ISMIR), pp. 577–584 (2018)

16. Gruber, N., Jockisch, A.: Are GRU cells more specific and LSTM cells more sensitive in motive classification of text? Front. Artif. Intell. **3**, 40 (2020)

17. Gururani, S., Summers, C., Lerch, A.: Instrument activity detection in polyphonic music using deep neural networks. In: Proceedings of International Society for Music Information Retrieval Conference (ISMIR), pp. 577–584 (2018)

18. Han, Y., Kim, J., Lee, K.: Deep convolutional neural networks for predominant instrument recognition in polyphonic music. IEEE/ACM Trans. Audio Speech Lang. Process. **25**(1), 208–221 (2017)

19. Heittola, T., Klapuri, A., Virtanen, T.: Musical instrument recognition in polyphonic audio using source-filter model for sound separation. In: Proceedings of International Society of Music Information Retrieval Conference, pp. 327–332 (2009)

20. Kitahara, T., Goto, M., Komatani, K., Ogata, T., Okuno, H.G.: Instrument identification in polyphonic music: feature weighting to minimize influence of sound overlaps. EURASIP J. Appl. Signal Process. **2007**, 155–175 (2007)

21. Kratimenos, A., Avramidis, K., Garoufis, C., Zlatintsi, A., Maragos, P.: Augmentation methods on monophonic audio for instrument classification in polyphonic music. In: Proceedings of 28th European Signal Processing Conference (EUSIPCO), pp. 156–160 (2021)

22. Kumar, P.M., Sebastian, J., Murthy, H.A.: Musical onset detection on carnatic percussion instruments. In: 2015 Twenty First National Conference on Communications (NCC), pp. 1–6 (2015)

23. Li, P., Qian, J., Wang, T.: Automatic instrument recognition in polyphonic music using convolutional neural networks. arXiv:1511.05520 (2015)

24. Li, X., Wang, K., Soraghan, J., Ren, J.: Fusion of hilbert-huang transform and deep convolutional neural network for predominant musical instruments recognition. In: Proceedings of 9th International conference on Artificial Intelligence in Music, Sound, Art and Design (2020)

25. Murthy, H.A., Yegnanarayana, B.: Group delay functions and its application to speech processing. Sadhana **36**(5), 745–782 (2011)

26. Nasrullah, Z., Zhao, Y.: Music artist classification with convolutional recurrent neural networks. In: Proceedings of International Joint Conference on Neural Networks (IJCNN), pp. 1–8 (2019)

27. O'shaughnessy, D.: Speech Communication: Human and Machine, pp. 1–5. Universities press, Hyderabad (1987)

28. Pons, J., Slizovskaia, O., Gong, R., Gómez, E., Serra, X.: Timbre analysis of music audio signals with convolutional neural networks. In: Proceedings of 25th European Signal Processing Conference (EUSIPCO), pp. 2744–2748 (2017)

29. Racharla, K., Kumar, V., Jayant, C.B., Khairkar, A., Harish, P.: Predominant musical instrument classification based on spectral features. In: 2020 7th International Conference on Signal Processing and Integrated Networks (SPIN), pp. 617–622. IEEE (2020)

30. Rajan, R., Murthy, H.A.: Two-pitch tracking in co-channel speech using modified group delay functions. Speech Commun. **89**, 37–46 (2017)

31. Rajan, R., Murthy, H.A.: Group delay based melody monopitch extraction from music. In: Proceedings of IEEE International Conference on Acoustics, Speech and Signal Processing (ICAASP), pp. 186–190 (2013)

32. Rajan, R., Murthy, H.A.: Music genre classification by fusion of modified group delay and melodic features. In: Proceedings of Twenty-third National Conference on Communications (NCC), pp. 1–6 (2017)

33. Rajesh, S., Nalini, N.: Musical instrument emotion recognition using deep recurrent neural network. Procedia Comput. Sci. **167**, 16–25 (2020)

34. Reghunath, L.C., Rajan, R.: Attention-based predominant instruments recognition in polyphonic music. In: Proceedings of 18th Sound and Music Computing Conference (SMC), pp. 199–206 (2021)

35. Reghunath, L.C., Rajan, R.: Transformer-based ensemble method for multiple predominant instruments recognition in polyphonic music. EURASIP J. Audio Speech Music Process. **2022**(1), 1–14 (2022)

36. Shi, X., Chen, Z., Wang, H., Yeung, D.Y., Wong, W.K., Woo, W.c.: Convolutional LSTM network: a machine learning approach for precipitation nowcasting. In: Advances in Neural Information Processing Systems, vol. 28 (2015)

37. Toh, K., Jiang, X., Yau, W.: Exploiting global and local decisions for multimodal biometrics verification. IEEE Trans. Signal Process. **52**, 3059–3072 (2004)

38. Wang, Y., Tan, T., Jain, A.K.: Combining face and iris biometrics for identity verification. In: Kittler, J., Nixon, M.S. (eds.) AVBPA 2003. LNCS, vol. 2688, pp. 805–813. Springer, Heidelberg (2003). https://doi.org/10.1007/3-540-44887-X_93

39. Yu, D., Duan, H., Fang, J., Zeng, B.: Predominant instrument recognition based on deep neural network with auxiliary classification. IEEE/ACM Trans. Audio, Speech, Lang. Process. **28**, 852–861 (2020)

The Matrix Profile for Motif Discovery in Audio - An Example Application in Carnatic Music

Thomas Nuttall[1]([✉]) [ID], Genís Plaja-Roglans[1] [ID], Lara Pearson[2] [ID], and Xavier Serra[1] [ID]

[1] Music Technology Group, Universitat Pompeu Fabra, Barcelona, Spain
{thomas.nuttall,genis.plaja,xavier.serra}@upf.edu
[2] Max Planck Institute for Empirical Aesthetics, Frankfurt am Main, Germany
lara.pearson@ae.mpg.de

Abstract. We present here a pipeline for the automated discovery of repeated motifs in audio. Our approach relies on state-of-the-art source separation, predominant pitch extraction and time series motif detection via the matrix profile. Owing to the appropriateness of this approach for the task of motif recognition in the Carnatic musical style of South India, and with access to the recently released Saraga Dataset of Indian Art Music, we provide an example application on a recording of a performance in the Carnatic *rāga*, *Rītigauḷa*, finding 56 distinct patterns of varying lengths that occur at least 3 times in the recording. The authors include a discussion of the potential musicological significance of this motif finding approach in relation to the particular tradition and beyond.

Keywords: Musical Pattern Discovery · Motif Discovery · Matrix Profile · Predominant Pitch Extraction · Carnatic Music · Indian Art Music

1 Introduction and Related Work

Short, recurring melodic phrases, often referred to as "motifs", are important building blocks in the majority of musical styles across the globe. The automatic identification and annotation of such motifs is a prominent and rapidly developing topic in music information retrieval [7,19,29,30], playing a significant role in music analysis [9,28, 34], segmentation [2–4] and development of musical theory [12,24,26]. No consensus exists on how this is best achieved, and indeed difficulty and differences in evaluation make it hard to contextualize the efficacy of a method outside of the task to which it is applied. A thorough review and comparison of approaches that handle symbolic music representations can be found in [30] and [19] however in this paper we focus on the much more common case of music without notation, extracting repeated motifs from audio.

Difficulty in working with raw audio for this task stems from the incredibly dense amount of information contained in audio signals, simultaneously clouding that which we might be interested in and providing a heavy workload for computational methods. A common method of reducing this complexity is to extract from the raw audio an object or feature set that captures the aspect of the music most relevant to the type of motif desired, and to subsequently compute some self-similarity metric between all subsequence pairs to group or connect similar sections [5,20]. This could take the form of

© Springer Nature Switzerland AG 2023
M. Aramaki et al. (Eds.): CMMR 2021, LNCS 13770, pp. 228–237, 2023.
https://doi.org/10.1007/978-3-031-35382-6_18

audio features such as Mel-frequency cepstral coefficients (MFCC) [22,33] or chroma [5,35], rhythmic onsets [8,21] or monophonic pitch [6,17]. When performed successfully, it is the latter that provides an abstraction with the most information pertaining to the melody in audio. And with more recent advances in both predominant pitch extraction [31] and time series motif detection [36], we are afforded the opportunity to revisit the approach of predominant pitch extraction/self-similarity in computationally feasible time on relatively large time scales.

Certain musical styles are particularly suitable for this type of analysis: for example, those for which automated transcription is not yet possible, and where the symbolic to sonic gap is such that musically salient units may sometimes be better characterised by segments of continuous time series pitch data than by transcriptions. This is the case in Indian Art Music (IAM), including Hindustani and Carnatic styles. Automated motif detection in these traditions is a limited but active area of research. In the case of Carnatic music, *svaras* (notes) are coarticulated (merged) through *gamakas* (ornaments) [25]. This characteristic provides particular challenges for processes involving automated segmentation, and can even mean that different Carnatic musicians' annotations of the same phrase may vary subtly in places, with different degrees of symbolic detail being possible. This leaves motif detection through time series pitch data as one of the most viable and popular approaches to finding meaningful melodic units in the style [14,23,27].

In this paper we demonstrate an approach for the automated discovery of repeated motifs in audio: state-of-the-art source separation [18], predominant pitch extraction using the Melodia algorithm [31] and ultra-fast means of time series motif detection via the matrix profile [36]. Owing to the appropriateness of this approach for the task of motif recognition in Carnatic music, and with access to the recently released Saraga Dataset of IAM [32], we provide an example application, applying these existing methods in this tradition. All code is available on GitHub[1] with a Jupyter notebook walk through of both the generalized and IAM-specific code.

2   Dataset

We demonstrate our approach on an example recording from the Saraga dataset [32]. Developed within the framework of the CompMusic project[2] and openly available for research, Saraga comprises two IAM collections, representing the Hindustani and Carnatic traditions. Both collections comprise several hours of music with accompanying time-aligned expert annotations and relevant musical (e.g. *rāga*, *tāla*, form) and editorial (e.g. artist, work, concert) metadata. In this work we focus on a performance taken from the Carnatic collection, 168 of which contain separate microphone recordings of: lead vocal, background vocal (if present), violin, mridangam and ghatam (if present). However, since these tracks are recorded from live performance, the multi-track audios in the dataset contain considerable background leakage, i.e., are not completely isolated from the other instruments.

---

[1] https://github.com/thomasgnuttall/carnatic-motifs-cmmr-2021/.
[2] https://compmusic.upf.edu/.

We access and interact with the Saraga dataset through the mirdata library [10]. This tool provides easy and secure access to the canonical version of the dataset, while loading and managing the dataset contents (audio, annotations and metadata) to optimize our research pipeline.

3   Methodology

The process consists of two stages (1) the extraction from audio of a vocal pitch track, which consists of a one-dimensional time series representing the main melodic line of the performance and (2) the use of self-similarity euclidean distance to identify likely candidates for repeated motifs in the main melodic line.

3.1   Predominant Pitch Extraction

The quality and consistency of the predominant pitch extraction is paramount. Given the shortage of training data and algorithms to extract the vocal pitch from Carnatic music signals, our raw audio recording is subject to three processing steps to arrive at a one dimensional time series of pitch values representing the main melodic line.

Isolating the Vocal Source. Where possible we use the vocal track recording for analysis (still containing leakage from other instruments). If this is not available, the mix is used. For the isolation of voice from the background instruments (both in mixed and vocal tracks), we use Spleeter, which is a deep learning based source separation library which achieves state-of-the-art results on automatically separating vocals from accompaniment [18].

Extracting the Predominant Pitch Curve. We use one of the most popular signal processing based algorithms for predominant pitch estimation from polyphonic music signals, the Melodia algorithm [31], applying an equal-loudness filter to the signal beforehand to encourage a perceptually relevant extraction. In the majority of studies attempting this task in IAM, Melodia has achieved consistent and viable results [11, 13–15, 27]. We use a time-step of 2.9 ms for the extraction.

Post-processing. Two post-processing steps are applied to the pitch track. (1) Gap interpolation, linearly interpolating gaps of 250 ms or less [16], typically caused by glottal sounds and sudden decrease of pitch salience in *gamakas* and (2) Gaussian smoothing with a sigma of 7, softening the curve and providing a more natural, less noisy shape. The final extracted pitch track is a time-series of n pitch values, $P = p_1, p_2, ..., p_n$.

3.2   Repeated Motif Discovery

To search P for regions of similar structure we look for groups of subsequences that have a low euclidean distance between them. The subsequence length to search for, m is a user-defined parameter of the process.

Matrix Profile. An efficient method of inspecting the euclidean distances between pairwise combinations of subsequences in a time series is the matrix profile [36]. Given a time series, T, and a subsequence length, m, the matrix profile returns for each subsequence in T, the distance to its most similar subsequence in T. The STAMP algorithm computes the matrix profile in impressive time by exploiting the overlap between subsequences using the fast Fourier transform, requiring only one parameter, subsequence length, m [36]. We use the *non-z-normalized* distance, since we are interested in matching subsequences identical in shape *and* y-location (i.e. pitch).

The matrix profile is therefore defined as $MP = ed_1, ed_2, ..., ed_{n-m}$ where ed_i is the regular euclidean distance between the subsequence of length m beginning at element i and its nearest neighbour in P.

Exclusion Mask. To ensure that only subsequences of interest are considered, a mask of subsequences in P to exclude is computed by applying a series of *exclusion functions* to each subsequence. These exclusion functions are informed by expert understanding of what constitutes a relevant motif in the tradition. Explicitly, the exclusion mask, $EM = em_1, em_0, ..., em_n$ where em_i is either 1 or 0, yes or no, does the subsequence satisfy any of the following:

- *Too silent* - more than 5% of the subsequence is 0 (i.e. silence)
- *Minimum gap* - subsequence contains a silence gap of 250 ms or more
- *Too stable* - in more than 63% of cases for a rolling window of 100, the average deviation of pitch from the average is more 5 Hz. This step is designed to exclude subsequences with too many long held notes - although musically relevant, not interesting from a motific perspective. A similar approach is taken in [14]

Subsequences that correspond to a mask value of 1 are not considered valid and not returned.

Identifying Motif Groups. The search for groups of repeated motifs begins by looking for a *parent* subsequence; those in P that have the lowest euclidean distance to another subsequence i.e. minimas in MP. The assumption being that if these subsequences have one very near neighbour, i.e. they are repeated once, then they are more likely to occur multiple times; a similar approach is used in [23].

For a candidate parent motif, we use the MASS similarity search algorithm [36] to calculate the non-normalised euclidean distance to every other subsequence in the pitch track, returning those that satisfy the requirements set by the parameters; $topN, maxOcc, minOcc$ and $thresh$. Algorithms 1 and 2 describe the process and parameters.

Output. The returned motif groups are arrays of start indices in P. The number of groups and occurrences in each is influenced by the $topN$, $minOcc$ and $maxOcc$ parameters.

Algorithm 1. Identify groups of motifs with low inter-group euclidean distance

```
 1: procedure GETMOTIFGROUPS
 2:     MP ← matrix profile array from Matrix Profile
 3:     P ← pitch sequence array from Predominant Pitch Extraction
 4:     EM ← exclusion mask array from Exclusion Mask
 5:     m ← pattern length
 6:     topN ← maximum number of groups to return
 7:     maxOcc ← maximum number of occurrences per group
 8:     minOcc ← minimum number of occurrences per group
 9:     thresh ← maximum length-normalised distance of occurrence to parent
10:
11:     MP[where(EM == 1)] ← ∞
12:     nGroups ← 0
13:     allMotifs ← array()
14:     while nGroups < topN
15:         ix ← argmin(MP)                              ▷ get parent index
16:         if MP[ix] == ∞                               ▷ entire sequence searched
17:             break
18:         motifs ← GETOCCURRENCES(ix, P, m, maxOcc, thresh, EM)
19:         if Length(motifs) < minOcc       ▷ discard, not enough significant matches
20:             continue
21:         for mtf in motifs                            ▷ motifs is an array of indices
22:             MP[mtf - m : mtf + m] ← ∞    ▷ clear part of array to avoid future discovery
23:         nGroups ← nGroups + 1
24:         allMotifs ← append motifs
25:     return allMotifs       ▷ array of motif groups, each motif group an array of start indices
26: end procedure
```

Algorithm 2. Identify other occurrences of parent motif in P using MASS

```
 1: procedure GETOCCURRENCES
 2:     ix ← index of parent sequence to query
 3:     P ← pitch sequence array from Predominant Pitch Extraction
 4:     m ← pattern length
 5:     maxOcc ← maximum number of occurrences to return
 6:     thresh ← maximum length-normalised distance of occurrence to parent
 7:     EM ← exclusion mask array from Exclusion Mask
 8:
 9:     parent ← P[ix : ix + m]
10:     stmass ← MASS(parent, P)    ▷ array of distances between parent and all subsequences
11:     stmass[where(EM == 1)] ← ∞
12:     nOccs ← 0
13:     allOccs ← array()
14:     while nOccs < maxOcc
15:         ix ← argmin(stmass)
16:         if stmass[ix]/m > thresh                    ▷ length normalised distance
17:             break                            ▷ cease search, no significant patterns remain
18:         stmass[ix - m : ix + m] ← ∞
19:         allOccs ← append ix
20:     return allOccs           ▷ array of occurrence start indices for this parent
21: end procedure
```

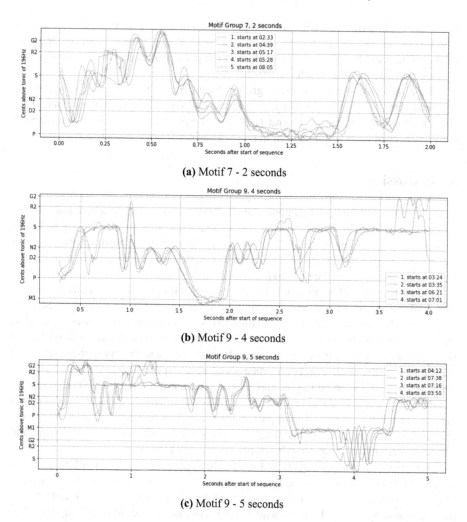

(a) Motif 7 - 2 seconds

(b) Motif 9 - 4 seconds

(c) Motif 9 - 5 seconds

Fig. 1. Overlaid pitch contour plots of three returned motif groups. The y-axis of each figure represents cents above the tonic (S) 196 Hz, divided into the discrete pitch positions defined in Carnatic music theory for this *rāga* - S, R2, G2, M1, P, D2, N2 [1]. R2 is two semitones (200 cents) above the tonic, S, and G2 is one semitone (100 cents) above R2, and so on. The oscillatory melodic movement that can be seen cutting across these theoretical pitch positions is typical of the style, illustrating the challenges of locating individual 'notes', either through expert annotations or automatically.

4   Results

We include the results of our process applied to a performance by the Akkarai Sisters of a composition titled Koti Janmani[3], by the composer Oottukkadu Venkata Kavi, which

---

[3] https://musicbrainz.org/recording/5fa0bcfd-c71e-4d6f-940e-0cef6fbc2a32.

is set in the Carnatic *rāga*, *Rītigauḷa*. The process is run for pattern lengths of 2, 3, 4, 5 and 6 s using parameters; $topN = 15$, $minOcc = 3$, $maxOcc = 20$. The parameter *thresh* is selected by subjective evaluation of the patterns returned in one motif group, choosing a value beyond which consistency is lost.

The number of significant motif groups found for 2, 3, 4, 5 and 6 s runs is 15, 15, 11, 11 and 4 respectively. For the code and full results we refer the reader to the GitHub repository. Figure 1a, 1b and 1c present the pitch plots associated with the top 5 occurrences of an example pattern in the 2, 4 and 5 s groups respectively.

5   Discussion

Due to the current lack of complete (i.e., saturated) ground truth annotations in the Saraga dataset, it is difficult to evaluate our application systematically. Creation of such annotations are ongoing as part of this project. In the meantime, however, the nature of the task and size of the results allow us to reflect on the coherency between patterns and their significance within the tradition.

The high degree of similarity between patterns returned within groups is obvious even to listeners who have no experience of the style, and can be appreciated from both the audio and pitch plots. This similarity is unsurprising, we choose a modest euclidean distance threshold and the process returns motifs that correspond to areas of pitch that are very similar by this measure. It is however a testament to the quality and consistency of the pitch extraction process and audio in the Saraga dataset [32], both resources not yet available in previous works. And more impressive still, also unseen in other works, is that these results can be achieved relatively quickly on a personal machine requiring little user input: pattern length, m and euclidean distance threshold, *thresh* (easily tuned in negligible time). This is due to the efficiency of the STAMP and MASS algorithms in computing the all pairs self-similarity [36].

Of course, we are more interested in whether the consistent results identified by a process like ours have the potential to contribute to ongoing musicological endeavours of pattern recognition, documentation and music analysis in the Carnatic tradition. Initial evaluation by the third author, who has expertise in the tradition [25], suggests that there is a high degree of musical similarity across the returned patterns in each group. At least the first few matches, and often all of the patterns, in each group would be considered by experts in the style to consist of the same motifs, or motif fragments. Some of the returned groups contain whole motifs that are particularly important for this *rāga*; *Rītigauḷa* is one of the Carnatic *rāgas* that is expressed through a number of characteristic motifs, sometimes referred to as *pidi* (catch-phrases), *sañcāras* or *prayogas* [1].

Two examples of particularly musically significant motifs returned can be seen in Fig. 1a and Fig. 1b. Figure 1a shows a frequently recurring phrase in this composition that includes the motif "npnn" (expressed here in *sargam* notation, which is used by practitioners to represent Carnatic *svaras*). The fact that 11 results are returned for this pattern (only five of these are illustrated for the sake of visual clarity) points to both the significance of the phrase in this composition, and also the importance of the motif "npnn" in the *rāga* [1]. Figure 1b consists of another recurring characteristic phrase "ssndmmnns", which is amongst the annotations of characteristic phrases identified by Carnatic musicians for the Saraga dataset [32].

The musicological applications of this process as it stands are limited to some extent by the fact that some of the matches returned are not full motifs, but rather are partial: for example, including part of one motif and then part of another (e.g., 5-s motif 0) or not returning the full motif (e.g., 5-s motif 1).[4] Segmentation at musically meaningful junctures such as silences or articulation of consonants should improve this. Another problem is that the process currently often returns multiples of the same motif, but with different top matches (e.g., 5-s motif groups 9 and 10). Lastly, it is clear that we need to evaluate the results against comprehensive annotations of all motifs in the performance,[5] to discover whether the process returns a good number of the total number of occurrences.

One interesting feature is that the process, in addition to returning precise matches of motifs, also identifies those that are similar but not identical. This could be particularly useful in a style such as Carnatic music which often employs a theme and variation structure, where phrases are repeated many times but with various elaborations. We can see an example of this returning of non-identical, but musically closely-related motifs in Fig. 1c where 4 motifs are returned, with two of them including a variation in the period between 0.5–1.5 s. Any process used to identify motifs in Carnatic music for musicological purposes would ideally show this degree of flexibility, in order to provide useful and meaningful results. Finally, considering the significance of recurring motifs in the vast majority of musical styles, it seems likely that this process would be musically relevant beyond the specific case of Carnatic music.

6 Further Work

Close scrutiny of the results offers potential lines of improvements; variable length motif detection could help capture full motifs rather than partial motifs, so too could more tradition-specific exclusion rules such as consonant onset detection, which should aid in further constraining the search to whole motifs due to the fact that the style is melismatic, with several *svaras* often sung to one syllable. An essential next step for the continuation of this work is the development of a more empirical evaluation framework of comprehensive ground truth motifs created in collaboration with expert performers of the tradition. We also recognize that to facilitate inter-recording discovery, a dynamic time warping distance measure or tempo normalisation might be necessary.

7 Conclusion

We hope to have demonstrated the effectiveness of predominant pitch extraction and matrix profile/self-similarity for the task of repeated motif identification and annotation in audio. We highlight its potential for these tasks in Carnatic music, a tradition where

---

[4] Please refer to the Github repository for results not plotted here.

[5] Although some motifs are annotated in the Saraga dataset, these annotations are not complete. Such annotating is extremely time consuming and must be done by practitioners of the style.

transcriptions into symbolic representation can show variance, and so where working directly with time series pitch data from audio is a more promising approach to motif identification. Alongside this document we provide the code and full results for the application to this tradition as well as to example audio from other musical styles.

Acknowledgments. This research was funded by the MUSICAL AI project (PID2019-111403GB-I00) granted by the Ministry of Science and Innovation of the Spanish Government. We also thank Rafael Caro Repetto for his continued guidance and input.

References

1. Bhagyalekshmy, S.: Ragas in Carnatic Music. CBHH Publications, Trivandrum (1990)
2. Boot, P., Volk, A., Bas de Haas, W.: Evaluating the role of repeated patterns in folk song classification and compression. J. New Music Res. **45**(3), 223–238 (2016)
3. Cambouropoulos, E.: Musical parallelism and melodic segmentation: a computational approach. Music. Percept. **23**(3), 249–268 (2006)
4. Conklin, D., Anagnostopoulou, C.: Segmental pattern discovery in music. INFORMS J. Comput. **18**(3), 285–293 (2006)
5. Dannenberg, R.B.: Pattern discovery techniques for music audio. J. New Music Res. **32**, 153–163 (2003)
6. Dannenberg, R.B., Hu, N.: Discovering musical structure in audio recordings. In: Anagnostopoulou, C., Ferrand, M., Smaill, A. (eds.) ICMAI 2002. LNCS (LNAI), vol. 2445, pp. 43–57. Springer, Heidelberg (2002). https://doi.org/10.1007/3-540-45722-4_6
7. Discovery of Repeated Themes & Sections - MIREX Wiki (2017). https://www.music-ir.org/mirex/wiki/2017:%20Discovery_of_Repeated_Themes_%26_Sections
8. Foote, J., Cooper, M., Nam, U.: Audio retrieval by rhythmic similarity. In: Proceedings of the 3rd International Society for Music Information Retrieval Conference (2002)
9. Forth, J.: Cognitively-motivated geometric methods of pattern discovery and models of similarity in music. Ph.D. thesis, Goldsmiths, University of London (2012)
10. Fuentes, M., et al.: mirdata vol. 0.3.0. Zenodo (2021). https://doi.org/10.5281/zenodo.4355859
11. Ganguli, K., Gulati, S., Serra, X., Rao, P.: Data-driven exploration of melodic structure in Hindustani music. In: Proceedings of the 17th International Society for Music Information Retrieval Conference (2016)
12. Gjerdingen, R.: Music in the Galant style. OUP USA (2007)
13. Gulati, S., Serra, J., Ganguli, K.K., Serra, X.: Landmark detection in Hindustani music melodies. In: International Computer Music Conference Proceedings (2014)
14. Gulati, S., Serrá, J., Ishwar, V., Serra, X.: Mining melodic patterns in large audio collections of Indian art music. In: International Conference on Signal Image Technology and Internet Based Systems (SITIS-MIRA), pp. 264–271. Morocco, 9, 87, 124, 148 (2014)
15. Gulati, S., Serrá, J., Serra, X.: Improving melodic similarity in Indian art music using culture-specific melodic characteristics. In: Proceedings of the 16th International Society for Music Information Retrieval Conference (2015)
16. Gulati, S., Serrà, J., Ganguli, K., Sertan, Ş., Serra, X.: Time-delayed melody surfaces for Raga recognition. In: Proceedings of the 17th International Society for Music Information Retrieval Conference, pp. 751–757 (2016)
17. Gulati, S.: Computational approaches for melodic description in Indian art music corpora. Ph.D. thesis, Universitat Pompeu Fabra, Barcelona (2016)

18. Hennequin, R., Khlif, A., Voituret, F., Moussallam, M.: Spleeter: a fast and state-of-the-art music source separation tool with pre-trained models. J. Open Source Softw. **5**(50), 2154 (2019)

19. Janssen, B., de Haas, W.B., Volk, A., van Kranenburg, P.: Finding repeated patterns in music: state of knowledge, challenges, perspectives. In: Aramaki, M., Derrien, O., Kronland-Martinet, R., Ystad, S. (eds.) CMMR 2013. LNCS, vol. 8905, pp. 277–297. Springer, Cham (2014). https://doi.org/10.1007/978-3-319-12976-1_18

20. Klapuri, A.: Pattern induction and matching in music signals. In: 7th International Symposium on Exploring Music Contents, CMMR, Málaga, Spain, pp. 188–204 (2010)

21. Krebs, F., Böck, S. Widmer, G.: Rhythmic pattern modeling for beat and downbeat tracking in musical audio. In: Proceedings of the 14th International Society for Music Information Retrieval Conferences (2013)

22. Lie, L., Wang, M., Zhang, H.: Repeating pattern discovery and structure analysis from acoustic music data. In: Proceedings of the 6th ACM SIGMM International Workshop on Multimedia Information Retrieval, MIR, pp. 275–282 (2004)

23. Murthy, H., Bellur, A.: Motif spotting in an Alapana in Carnatic music. In: Proceedings of the 14th International Society for Music Information Retrieval Conferences (2013)

24. Nuttall, T., Casado, M.C., Ferraro, A., Conklin, D., Caro Repetto, R.: A computational exploration of melodic patterns in Arab-Andalusian music. J. Math. Music 1–13 (2021)

25. Pearson, L.: Coarticulation and gesture: an analysis of melodic movement in South Indian raga performance. Music. Anal. **35**(3), 280–313 (2016)

26. Rao, P., Ross, J.C., Ganguli, K.K.: Distinguishing raga-specific intonation of phrases with audio analysis. Ninaad **26–27**(1), 59–68 (2013)

27. Rao, P., et al.: Classification of melodic motifs in raga music with time-series matching. J. New Music Res. **43**, 115–131 (2014)

28. Ren, I.Y.: Closed patterns in folk music and other genres. In: Proceedings of the 6th International Workshop on Folk Music Analysis, FMA, pp. 56–58 (2016)

29. Ren, I.Y., Volk, A., Swierstra, W., Veltkamp, R.C.: In search of the consensus among musical pattern discovery algorithms. In: Proceedings of the 18th International Society for Music Information Retrieval ISMIR, pp. 671–680 (2017)

30. Ren, I.Y., Volk, A., Swierstra, W., Veltkamp, R.C.: A computational evaluation of musical pattern discovery algorithms. CoRR (2020)

31. Salamon, J., Gomez, E.: Melody extraction from polyphonic music signals using pitch contour characteristics. IEEE Trans. Audio Speech Lang. Process. **20**, 1759–1770 (2012)

32. Srinivasamurthy, A., Gulati, S., Caro Repetto, R., Serra, X.: Saraga: open dataset for research on Indian Art Music. Empir. Musicol. Rev. (2020). https://compmusic.upf.edu/ [Preprint]

33. Thomas, M., Murthy, Y.S., Koolagudi, S.G.: Detection of largest possible repeated patterns in Indian audio songs using spectral features. In: 2016 IEEE Canadian Conference on Electrical and Computer Engineering (CCECE), pp. 1–5 (2016)

34. Volk, A., van Kranenburg, P.: Melodic similarity among folk songs: an annotation study on similarity based categorization in music. Music. Sci. **16**(3), 317–339 (2012)

35. Wang, C., Hsu, J., Dubnov, S.: Music pattern discovery with variable Markov oracle: a unified approach to symbolic and audio representations. In: Proceedings of the 16th International Society for Music Information Retrieval Conference, pp. 176–182 (2015)

36. Yeh, C.M., et al.: Matrix profile I: all pairs similarity joins for time series: a unifying view that includes motifs, discords and shapelets. In: IEEE 16th International Conference on Data Mining (ICDM), pp. 1317–1322 (2016)

A Rule-Based Method for Implementing Implication-Realization Model

Kaede Noto[✉], Yoshinari Takegawa, and Keiji Hirata

Future University Hakodate, Hakodate, Japan
{g3120002,yoshi,hirata}@fun.ac.jp

Abstract. We present an implementation method of a melodic analyzer based on the implication-realization (I-R) model, proposed by Eugene Narmour in 1990. The proposed method involves two stages; firstly, the triplet of notes to which an I-R symbol is assigned are identified based on note duration, beat structure, and pitch transition, and secondly, an I-R symbol is assigned to each triplet of notes identified in the previous stage. Since the rules provided by Narmour of the symbol assignment is incomplete, for all patterns of a triplet included in real melodies, an I-R symbol to be assigned is not defined; that is, the I-R symbol assignment map is partial. Then we make the total assignment map of the I-R symbol assignment by fixing I-R symbols in undefined areas repeatedly with varying the threshold for determining the boundary between small and large intervals. Comparing with the analysis results shown in the Narmour's book [9], our melodic analyzer achieves an F measure of 0.86 regarding the starting tone estimation of the I-R symbols.

Keywords: implication-realization model · music theory · music cognition

1 Introduction

We present an implementation method of the melodic analyzer based on the implication-realization (I-R) model proposed by Eugene Narmour [9,10]. The I-R analysis classifies the relationship between adjacent notes in accordance with how implications are satisfied or denied. The principles for determining these relationships is based on Gestalt theory, in which the perceptual elements are grouped and recognized in the cognition level [8,9]. Narmour claims that a similar principle works in the perception of melody and the smallest unit of a group is three adjacent notes, which are assigned *the I-R symbols* in accordance with the relationships among pitches of the three notes. Firstly, for two adjacent notes heard, people can perceive the characteristics of interval and direction of the movement that the two notes draw. Then, people usually have the implication or prediction of a third note which may satisfy some conditions regarding interval and direction. Next, when the third note is actually heard, the third note may or may not satisfy the implication; we say implication is *realized* or *denied*, respectively. Narmour provided the two principles regarding interval and direction for the third note to realize implication described below. For example, the I-R symbol P (process) is assigned to a sequence of notes that are implicated to be heard at the same interval in the same direction for the third note. In contract, when people have the same

© Springer Nature Switzerland AG 2023
M. Aramaki et al. (Eds.): CMMR 2021, LNCS 13770, pp. 238–250, 2023.
https://doi.org/10.1007/978-3-031-35382-6_19

implication from the first two notes as previous, the symbol IP (intervallic process) is assigned if only the implication of interval of the third note is satisfied, and the symbol VP (registral process) is assigned if only the implication of direction is satisfied.

The I-R analysis involves two stages. Firstly, according to Narmour, the starting tone of an I-R symbol is identified with checking *closures* as the clues one-by-one for estimating the starting tone. A closure is a note at which no implication arises from the sequence of notes occurring or where the implication is weakened; in other words, a closure is a pitch event that triggers a grouping boundary. Specifically, a closure can be detected by a change in pitch interval, direction or note value, or the occurrence of a strong beat, etc. As a result, some of closures are identified as starting tones of I-R symbols. The process described above corresponds to the operation to discover the cognitive boundary in a melody.

Secondly, the proper I-R symbols are assigned to a sequence of notes that is longer than three notes, starting with the note estimated in the first stage. The I-R symbol to be assigned is determined mainly on the basis of the following two principles, principle of intervallic difference (PID) and principle of registral direction (PRD). The PRD states that small (five semitones or less) intervals imply an interval in the same direction, and large (seven semitones or more) intervals imply an interval in the registral direction. The PID states that small intervals imply a similar interval (plus or minus two semitones), and large intervals imply a small interval. According to these two principles, eight types of the I-R symbols are derived: D, ID, P, IP, VP, R, IR, and VR.

The purpose of this study is to examine our implementation method for the melodic analyzer based on the I-R model and quantitatively evaluate the performance of the analyzer. Although several methods have been proposed to implement I-R model analyzers, there have been little studies in that the accuracy of the analysis results were not assessed in depth. Grachten et al. implemented the symbolic melodic similarity measures by computing the edit distance between the I-R analysis of melodies [4], and Yazawa et al. implemented the melodic analyzer with extension of I-R symbols to express melodic contours more precisely [12]. Since both studies employ the melodic similarity as the metrics to evaluate performance, the performances of the melodic analyzers are only measured indirectly. To clarify the usefulness of the I-R analysis in the context of the Music information retrieval (MIR) field, we conduct the quantitative performance evaluation by directly comparing with the ground truth that is the analysis results shown in the Narmour's books [9, 10].

2 Implementation Method of Melodic Analyzer

The flow of our method is as follows (Fig. 1). Firstly, we estimate the starting tone. This stage consists of two steps: closure estimation (Sect. 2.1, 2.2) and determining the order of symbol assignment (Sect. 2.3, 2.4, 2.5). Secondly, after the starting tone is estimated, we assign it a symbol (Sect. 2.6, 2.7).

2.1 Closure

We first explain a closure to estimate the starting tone of the symbol. We give examples of the I-R analysis by Narmour (Fig. 2) to explain the relationship between a closure

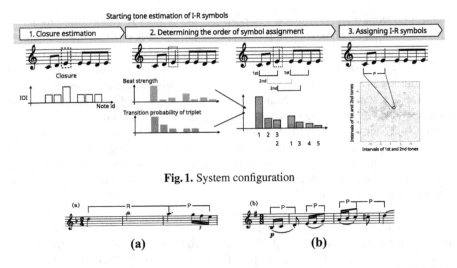

Fig. 1. System configuration

Fig. 2. The I-R analysis by Narmour. (a) W. A. Mozart: Piano Concerto No. 19 in F Major, Kv.459, 3rd mov., (b) L. v. Beethoven: Piano Sonata op.14-2, 3rd mov.

and starting tone. In the example in Fig. 2 (a), the note considered to be the closure is the first note of the third measure, i.e., "la," which has a strong beat and changing note value. In this case, the closure "la" is the end of symbol R, which starts in the first measure, and the beginning of symbol P, which starts in the third measure.

In the example in Fig. 2(b), the first and fourth notes of the first measure, third note of the second measure, and first note of the third measure are considered closures. In this case, the first, fourth, and third notes of the first measure are the end notes of symbol P, and the third note of the second measure is the start and end notes of the symbol. Thus, we define "closure" as the union set $A \cup B$ when the starting tone is represented by set A and the symbol-end note by set B.

2.2 Closure Estimation Based on Inter-onset Interval

Our proposed method uses a closure-estimation method that focuses on the change in the inter-onset interval (IOI). Researchers have attempted to estimate a closure by focusing on note duration. For example, with current closure-estimation methods, the closure is considered to be the point where the note duration increases [8] or rests occur [12]. The problem with these methods is that they estimate many closures for melodies that have alternating notes and rests. However, we integrate the above methods by focusing on the change in the IOI. Because the IOI is the difference between the times at which each note occurs, the IOI of any two notes will not change even if the note value changes or rests are inserted, unless the timing of onset is changed. Because time is handled differently for note value and IOI, it is necessary to develop a method for detecting changes in note duration when targeting the IOI. Current methods are based on the note value (quarter notes, eighth notes) in a score. It is reasonable that an increase in note value is defined as a factor of two or more compared with the previous notes. Therefore, we consider a note at which the IOI increases by a factor of two or more compared with the previous IOI as the closure.

Closure estimation can be used to limit the targets for symbol assignment. As above, because we define a closure to be the union set of the start and end notes of a symbol, we do not assign symbols across closures. However, if the symbols before and after the closure are identical, sometimes they may be regarded as symbols across the closure. The details are given later.

2.3   Transition of Pitch

We introduce transition of pitch on the basis of the hypothesis that the first note of a pitch-transition pattern that frequently occurs in a melody is likely to be the starting tone. Because the length of the I-R symbol is three, we calculate the probability of occurrence of a tri-gram in a melody. In addition, the first two notes in the I-R symbol are those that generate an implication. The third note will satisfy or deny the implication. Thus, we use the probability of the $(i + 2)$ th note occurring after the $(i + 1)$th and i th notes, $P(i + 2|i, i + 1)$, as a feature for estimating the starting tone.

The distribution of $P(i + 2|i, i + 1)$ changes depending on how the random variable is determined. For example, when determining the transition probability of a melody, the pitch is generally used as a random variable. However, when the pitch is used as a random variable, the probability distribution after learning is likely to be sparse. To avoid this, we consider two random variables, pitch interval and qualitative pitch interval. Because pitch intervals are divided into two values, i.e., S (small) and L (large), in I-R analysis, we define qualitative pitch as a binary expression of n or less semitones and more than n semitones.

2.4   Beat Structure

We use the beat structure for symbol assignment. The beat structure is known to affect group formation when listening to a melody. Fraisse reported that when presented with a sequence of sounds that occur in the same time span, people divide these sounds into two or three repetitive groups [3]. We hypothesize that the I-R symbols are also a type of group, and that symbols are assigned on the basis of the beat. For beat strength, we use the value obtained from Music21Object.beatStrength implemented in the Python library music21 [2] as a feature value. In the beatStrength object, beat strength is expressed as a relative value, such as 1.0 for the first beat of a measure, 0.5 for downbeats, and 0.25 for upbeats.

2.5   Feature Integration

We estimate starting tones from closure, pitch-transition pattern, and beat structure. The search range for estimating the starting tone is the interval from one closure to the next. We integrate pitch-transition pattern and beat structure within this interval. Integration refers to standardizing each value then calculating the sum. Because the sum of values indicates how likely it is to be a starting tone, we assign the symbols in order, starting with the highest value.

3   Symbol Assignment

3.1   Previous Symbol-Assignment Method and Actual Data

There are ambiguities with current method of the I-R symbol assignment. Basically, we can make rules from the PID and PRD proposed by Narmour on how to assign symbols to a triplet of notes. However, we also need to determine a threshold for determining the S or L pitch interval as a hyperparameter. Figure 3 shows the assignment map of the I-R symbol when S is six or less semitones and L is more than six semitones [11], indicating that different symbols are being assigned after the threshold. Nothing is written to the coordinates corresponding to triplets that do not assign I-R symbols. Figure 4 shows the map of the I-R symbol observed from Narmour's manual analysis. These figures show the correspondence between the symbols observed from Narmour's analysis and the pitches of the triplets, with the size of each point proportional to the number of times it was observed. We did not observe any example of "other" symbol assigned to a triplet. The intricacy of each symbol's region concerning the axial direction suggests that the threshold for determining the I-R symbol to be assigned is not fixed.

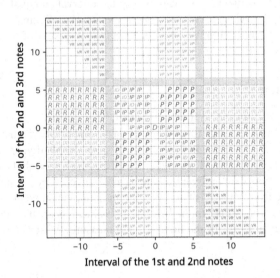

Fig. 3. The assignment map of the I-R symbol as defined in the previous study. No symbols are defined for triplets containing six semitones because the interval is neither S nor L.

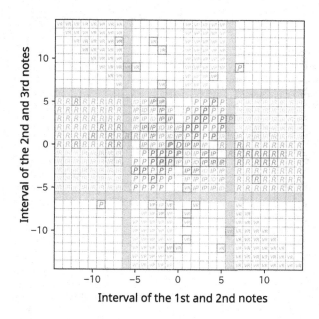

Fig. 4. I-R symbols that appeared in Narmour's analysis are enclosed in a square.

We propose a symbol assignment method that uses the map created by repeatedly fixing I-R symbols in undefined areas with varying the threshold for determining the boundary between small and large intervals. As shown in Fig. 4, the symbols in Narmour's analysis cannot be covered by the previous method using a fixed threshold. Therefore, we take a strategy to reduce the number of residuals by changing the threshold in multiple trials. Here, we denote a set of symbols not covered by trial i as A_i, a set of symbols defined by trial i as B_i, and a set of symbols defined by rules from the PID and PRD with threshold th as C_{th}. These sets have $triplet_{xy}$ as elements. The x corresponds to the number of semitones in the first and second notes, and the y corresponds second and third ones. For example, the symbols defined in Fig. 3 are denoted as $triplet_{00} = D, triplet_{11} = P$, and $triplet_{-11} = P$. It should be noted that the result of Narmour's analysis can be denoted as A_0 and the A_0 that cannot be covered by Fig. 3 is A_1.

The purpose of the proposed method is to reduce the residuals in each trial. The residual refers to the elemtents of A_i that are not coverd by B_i and it is denoted as $A_{i+1} = A_i - (A_i \cap B_i)$. To minimize the number of elements in A_{i+1}, we take the strategy of substitution undifined $triplet_{xy}$ in B_{i-1} for $triplet_{xy}$ in a certain C_{th}. Thereby, the method fills the undefined symbol region by searching for C_{th} that minimizes the residuals in each trial i.

Figure 5 shows the assignment map of the I-R symbol defined when using threshold values $th = [7, 0, 3, 11, 1, 2, 4, 5, 6, 8, 9, \ldots]$ that minimizes the residual for each trial. This map can assign any symbols to all triplets except a symbol not defined with any S or L. Its symbol is not defined in the I-R model, but if one were to name it, it would

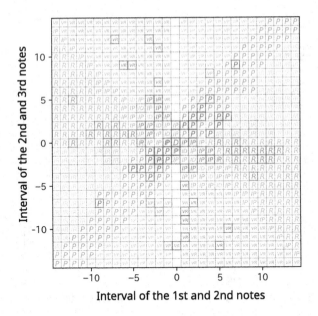

Fig. 5. The assignment map of the I-R symbol defined by the proposed method.

be VD (Triplets, where the first and second notes have the same pitch and the second and third interval is L). The coverage of the proposed method for Narmour's analysis is 88.2%. This is higher than the coverage rate of 69.3% for the conventional method, which fixed the threshold at six semitones.

3.2   Detailed Rules for the I-R Symbol Assignment

To conduct the I-R analysis for an actual melody, we need to determine the number of symbols to be assigned to each note. For example, if we allow three symbols to be assigned to any note, the operation is the same as the I-R analysis for a tri-gram. We conducted the I-R analysis with two and three maximum symbol assignments and compared the results.

The I-R symbol is usually assigned to a triplet, but four or more notes may be assigned symbols P or D. These symbols have the characteristic of repeating similar pitches in the same direction. Thus, the repetition of symbol P or D is thought to amplify the implication. Therefore, if symbols P and D are superimposed, they are merged and considered one symbol.

However, this is not the case if the implied attenuation occurs within symbols P and D, which consist of four or more notes. As already indicated, even when symbol P is consecutively, they may not be integrated (Fig. 2). This is thought to be due to the fact that closures occur between symbols. However, it is difficult to investigate all the possibilities of generating closures. Thus, we introduce a symbol-integration rule that focuses only on the beat structure, which can be understood intuitively.

4 Experiment

We conducted an evaluation experiment to investigate the accuracy of the proposed implementation method in estimating the symbol-start tone and the factors that contributed to the results. There were five evaluation categories, which include more detailed items (Table 1).

Table 1. Evaluation Categories and Items

Evaluation Categories	Evaluation Items
1. Features	1-1. Closure estimated from IOI
	1-2. Transition probability of triplet
	1-3. Beat strength
2. Random variable with transition probability of triplet	2-1. Pitch
	2-2. Interval
	2-3. Qualitative pitch interval
3. Maximum number of symbols assigned	3-1. Two
	3-2. Three
4. Division of symbols (Beat Strength)	4-1. No division
	4-2. First beat of measure (1.0)
	4-3. Downbeat (0.5)
	4-4. Downbeat and upbeat (0.25)
5. Threshold of symbol assignment	5-1. Previous method (Threshold is six semitones)
	5-2. Residual Method

4.1 Evaluation Values and Dataset

We used the results of the manual analysis by Narmour as the correct data. Because the rules of the I-R analysis are often ambiguous and the results are subjective, there is no large data set of I-R analysis results. Thus, we used 61 examples taken from Narmour's analysis examples [10] as the correct data. The melodies used as the correct data were selected on the basis of the following two criteria. The first criterion is the number of notes contained in the melody to be analyzed. If the number of notes is four or less, the results of the I-R analysis can be uniquely determined. Thus, we did not take into account melodies not considered as correct data. The second criterion is whether the three tones to be analyzed are adjacent to each other. In Narmour's analysis, there is an example in which similar sound sequences are considered as one cohesive unit, and the beginning of the unit is extracted and subjected to the I-R analysis. In these cases, we did not consider them as correct data because it is necessary to select three tones for the I-R analysis, which is beyond the scope of this study. The correct data were all created manually as MusicXML with the following information: pitch, duration, onset time, I-R symbol, and starting tone.

The input to the system is pitch, duration, beat strength, and the output is a binary value indicating whether the note is a starting tone. Thus, we used recall, precision, and F measure to evaluate the method.

4.2   Training Data

To calculate Feature 1-2. (Transition probability of triplet), we used 300 melodies from GTTM Database [5] as training data. As mentioned above, we did not label the training data because what we want is the conditional probability of three adjacent notes in the melody. Because the conditional probability will be zero if the pitch-transition pattern included in the target melody does not exist in the training data, we included the target melody in the training data.

4.3   Evaluation Results

As shown in Table 2, Case 1 yields the result of estimation with the three features, and Case 8 yields that without any features. The highest score was obtained when all the features were actually used.

Table 2. Combinations of Features

Features	Assignments of Features to Cases							
	Case1	Case2	Case3	Case4	Case5	Case6	Case7	Case8
1-1. Closure estimated by IOI	✓		✓	✓	✓			
1-2. Transition probability of triplet	✓	✓		✓			✓	
1-3. Beat strength	✓	✓	✓			✓		

Figure 6 presents the results for starting tone estimation when conditional probabilities are calculated using different random variables. The value of n in the graph represents the number of semitones used to determine the qualitative pitch interval. For example, if n = 3, all intervals appearing in the melody are represented as two values, one for intervals of three semitones or less, and one for intervals of four semitones or more. The highest evaluation values were obtained when n = 6, 7, and 8.

Figure 7 presents the results for starting tone estimation when comparing the maximum number of symbols assigned. When the maximum number of symbols assigned is three (3-1.), the analysis results are equivalent to the I-R analysis results for a tri-gram with the symbols that straddle the closure removed. We can see in Fig. 8 that when the maximum number of symbols is three (3-1.), recall is higher than when the maximum number of symbols is two (3-2.). This is because when the maximum number of symbols is three, our method estimates more starting tones. However, precision decreased. Therefore, Fig. 8 indicates that if we want to achieve a high F measure, it is better to use the maximum number of symbols of two.

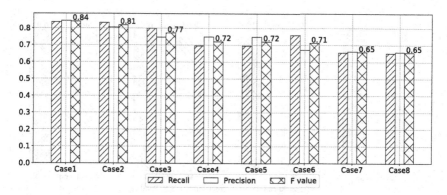

Fig. 6. Experimental results of evaluation category 1. Features under the conditions 2-3. Qualitative pitch interval, 3-2. Three, 4-2. The first beat of the measure, and 5-1. Previous method (N = 6)

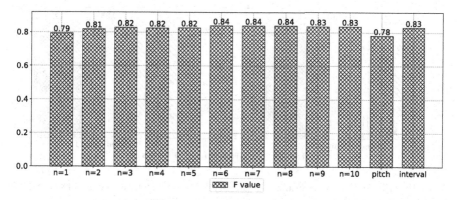

Fig. 7. Experimental results of evaluation category 2. Features under the conditions case1, Qualitative pitch interval, 3-2. Three, 4-2. The first beat of the measure, and 5-1. Previous method (N = 6)

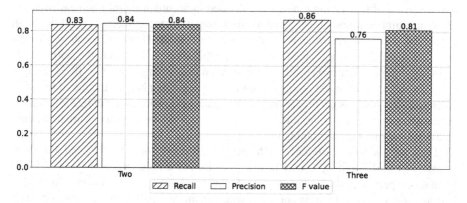

Fig. 8. Experimental results of evaluation category 3. Features under the conditions case1, 2-3. Qualitative pitch interval, 4-2. The first beat of the measure, and 5-1. Previous method (N = 6)

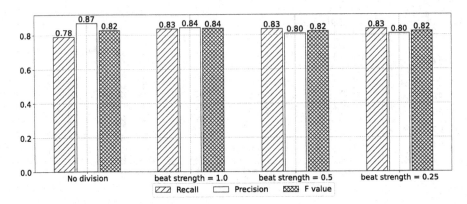

Fig. 9. Experimental results of evaluation category 4. Features under the conditions case1, 2-3. Qualitative pitch interval, 3-2. Three, and 5-1. Previous method (N = 6)

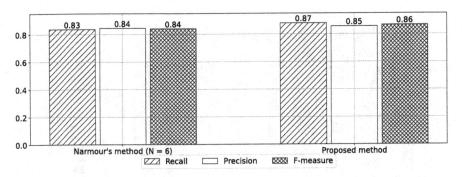

Fig. 10. Experimental results of evaluation category 5. Features under the conditions case1, 2-3. Qualitative pitch interval, 3-2. Three, 4-2. The first beat of the measure

Figure 9 presents the results for starting tone estimation when symbols P and D, which consist of four or more notes, are divided in accordance with the beat strength. Thus, the number of notes considered to be starting tones increased. The condition with the highest precision was when no splitting was carried out. However, recall was lowest among the four conditions, which indicates that the coverage in finding the starting tone is low. The highest F measure was obtained when beat strength was 4-1. (beat strength = 1.0), which is when the symbols are split at the beginning beat of the measure. Also, when splitting symbols on smaller beats (downbeat or downbeat and upbeat), precision decreased. Hence, if we want to increase the accuracy of starting tone estimation, only splitting symbols at the beginning of the measure is sufficient.

However, the small difference in the evaluation values for 4-1., 4-2., and 4-3. (beat strength = 1.0, 0.5, and 0.25) may be due to a bias in the appearance of symbols P and D. In this experiment, the best score was obtained by estimating the starting tone with a beat strength of 1.0, but we do not know whether similar results can be achieved when we conduct the I-R analysis on melodies with fast passages.

Figure 10 presents a comparison of the results of starting tone estimation with different symbol-assignment methods. The method of assigning these symbols conforms to the map shown in Fig. 3, 4, 5. Previous method (N = 6) corresponds to Fig. 3, and the proposed method corresponds to Fig. 5. The proposed method had a better score than previous method.

The difference between the two methods is in the handling of symbols that were considered as "other" with previous method. With this method, no symbol is assigned to the triplet corresponding to the "other", but with the proposed method, a symbol is assigned to the triplet. Thus, more notes will be inferred as starting tones with the proposed method.

5   Concluding Remarks

We presented an implementation method of a melodic analyzer based on the implication-realization (I-R) model, proposed by Eugene Narmour in 1990. We have tried several methods by switching the employed features and introduced new parameters (Table 1). Comparing with the analysis results shown in the Narmour's book [9], our melodic analyzer achieves an F measure of 0.86 regarding the starting tone estimation of the I-R symbols.

We think the demonstration of the usefulness of the I-R analysis is still not enough. For example, human usually acquire a melodic boundary using not only melodic features, but also the information of lyrics, syllables and neumes [1]. Using this information, there is room to improve the performance of the melodic analyzer and potentially increase its contribution to MIR. Future work includes to refined and add more features to the melodic analyzer.

Acknowledgment. This work has been supported by JSPS Kakenhi 16H01744.

References

1. Cornelissen, B., Zuidema, W., and Burgoyne, A.: Mode classification and natural units in plainchant. In: Proceedings of the 21th International Conference on Music Information Retrieval (ISMIR), Montréal, Canada (2020)
2. Cuthbert, M.S., Ariza, C.T.: music21: a Toolkit for computer-aided musicology and symbolic music data. In: Proceedings of 11th International Society for Music Information Retrieval Conference (ISMIR 2010), pp. 637–642 (2010)
3. Fraisse, P.: Rhythm and tempo. In: Deutsch, D. (Ed.), The Psychology of Music, pp. 149–180. Academic Press (1982)
4. Grachten, M., Arcos, J.L., de Mántaras, L.: Melody retrieval using the implication/realization model. Music Information Retrieval Evaluation (MIREX) (2005)
5. Hamanaka, M., Hirata, K., Tojo, S.: Musical structural analysis database based on GTTM. In: 15th International Society for Music Information Retrieval Conference (ISMIR), pp 325–330 (2014)
6. Koffka, K.: Principles of Gestalt Psychology. Routledge & Kegan Paul, London (1935)
7. Köhler, W.: Gestalt Psychology: An Introduction to New Concepts of Modern Psychology. Liveright, New York (1947)

8. Murao, T.: Cognition in musical analysis. In: Hatano, G. (Ed.), Music and Cognition, pp. 1–40. The University of Tokyo Press (1989). (in Japanese)
9. Narmour, E.: The Analysis and Cognition of Basic Melodic Structures. The University of Chicago Press (1990)
10. Narmour, E.: The Analysis and Cognition of Melodic Complexity. The University of Chicago Press (1992)
11. Schellenberg, E.G.: Expectancy in melody: tests of the implication-realization model. Cognition **58**(1), 75–125 (1996)
12. Yazawa, S., Hamanaka, M., Utsuro, T.: Subjective melodic similarity based on extended implication-realization model. Int. J. Affect. Eng. **15**(3), 249–257 (2016)
13. Yu, Y., Harscoët, F., Canales, S., Reddy, G.: Lyrics-conditioned neural melody generation. In: Proceedings of the 26th International Conference on MultiMedia Modeling, Part II, pp. 709–714 (2020)

Music and Performance Analysis

CROCUS: Dataset of Critique Documents of Musical Performance

Masaki Matsubara[1]([⊠]) [ID], Rina Kagawa[1] [ID], Takeshi Hirano[2], and Isao Tsuji[3,4,5]

[1] University of Tsukuba, Tsukuba, Japan
masaki@slis.tsukuba.ac.jp
[2] University of Electro-Communications, Chofu, Japan
[3] Senzoku Gakuen College of Music, Kawasaki, Japan
[4] Kunitachi College of Music, Tachikawa, Japan
[5] Nihon University College of Art, Tokyo, Japan

Abstract. In performance education, verbal as well as nonverbal information is used to convey knowledge. In the COVID-19 social situation, the demand for remote and asynchronous lessons is increasing, and it is unclear what kind of verbal information should be used. In this study, we collected 239 Japanese review texts from 12 teachers for a total of 90 orchestral studies performed by oboe players. We categorized the sentences of the critiques, and found that the content of the critiques varied more by teacher than by piece or student. We also found that the category of *giving practice strategy* played a significant role in the content of instruction that students found useful.

Keywords: Database · Music Lesson · Verbal Information

1 Introduction

[1] Playing music instruments has traditionally been taught face-to-face and was considered unsuitable for virtual learning environments. However, today, the COVID-19 pandemic has led to the increase of demand of online music lesson [1, 17]. In the field of musical performance lesson, knowledge is conveyed by using both non-verbal information such as singing melodies and making gestures, and verbal information such as pointing out mistakes [7, 12, 22]. Verbal information is essential for conveying how the learner's performance sounds, why he/she cannot play well, and how he/she should practice. An advantage of online music lesson is that space and time do not necessarily have to be shared, thus allowing for remote and asynchronous teaching. However, due to the low resolution of online video/audio communication, there is a limitation in the use of

---

M. Matsubara, R. Kagawa—Two authors equally contributed to this research.

[1] A part of this manuscript has been presented at the 15th International Symposium on Computer Music Multidisciplinary Research (CMMR 2021) [24], with additional results in "Evaluation of the validity of the classification" subsection in Sect. 3.2, parts of Sect. 4.3, Fig. 7, and regarding references.

© Springer Nature Switzerland AG 2023
M. Aramaki et al. (Eds.): CMMR 2021, LNCS 13770, pp. 253–266, 2023.
https://doi.org/10.1007/978-3-031-35382-6_20

nonverbal information as it is difficult to convey detailed body movements and high-quality sound performances. Therefore, it is expected that the importance of verbal information in music lesson, especially in critique documents of asynchronous online performance education, will increase in the future [10].

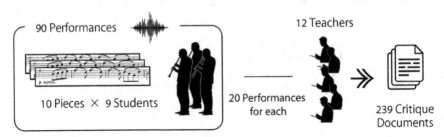

Fig. 1. Overview of the construction of the musical performance critique dataset.

However, it is not easy to teach by words. In our preliminary survey of nine music college students and 100 people who have musical performance experience, they had a good impression of their musical experience, while some of them were not satisfied with their teacher's instructions. We collected free-text responses about dissatisfaction with the instruction and categorized the results into the following three issues: (1) Content of performance instruction (e.g., "I would have preferred instruction based on facts", "Lack of concrete advice"), (2) Consistency of instruction over multiple lessons (e.g., "completely different or inconsistent attention from lesson to lesson"), (3) Wording of instruction not related to performance (e.g., "All he/she did was scold without much praise").

We believe that one of the reasons for these problems is the lack of teaching protocols in performance instruction and the lack of systematic clarification of what should be verbalized to benefit the learners. At present, however, the empirical knowledge of what kind of instruction is being given is not widely shared, even among students who aspire to become professionals.

This paper introduces an open dataset of musical performance critiques in Japanese, called *CROCUS* (CRitique dOCUmentS of musical performance), to promote music education through the study of verbal information in performance instruction. In this paper, we define critique documents as several text sentences written by teachers to give the feedback for the performance. We collected 239 critique documents from 12 teachers for 90 performances of the same 10 pieces by nine students (Fig. 1). Since music college classes are nowadays conducted online, we collected recordings and critique documents in a similar manner to asynchronous classes. This dataset allows us to compare critiques in each piece, student, and teacher. In this paper, we examined what kind of critique structure is perceived as useful instruction by the performers. Specifically, we analyzed the types of verbal information and measured the perceived utility of critique, and examined whether there were differences in utility scores among teachers, students, and pieces.

Table 1. List of Pieces

ID	Composer	Piece
p01	L. v. Beethoven	Symphony No. 3 in E flat Major 'Eroica', Op. 55
p02	G. A. Rossini	'La Scala di seta' Overture
p03	F. Schubert	Symphony No. 8 in B Minor D.759 'Unfinished'
p04	J. Brahms	Violin Concerto in D Major, Op. 77
p05	P. I. Tchaikovsky	Symphony No. 4 in F minor, Op. 36
p06	P. I. Tchaikovsky	"Swan Lake", Ballet Suite, Op.20a
p07	N. Rimsky-Korsakov	"Scheherazade", Symphonic Suite, Op. 35
p08	R. Strauss	"Don Juan", Symphonic Poem, Op. 20
p09	M. Ravel	Le Tombeau de Couperin I.Prelude
p10	S. Prokofiev	"Peter and the Wolf", Symphonic Tale, Op. 67

Our contributions are as follows.

- We constructed an open dataset of 239 critique documents of 90 musical performances of 10 oboe orchestral studies[2].
- We showed quantitatively that the content of the critique document varies more by teacher than by piece or student.
- We collected evaluations of the critique documents from people who have musical experience and examined the types of verbal information to find out what was described in the critique documents with high utility and what was not described in the critique documents with low utility.

2   Related Work

2.1   Music Database for Research

Music databases have been published with various perspectives, e.g., performance recordings data [14], metadata (genre, composer, lyrics, etc. [15, 29, 33]), musical scores (MIDI [20], piano notation [11, 34]), information associated with scores (fingering [25], music analysis [16]), and other multimodal information [23, 35]. There are also databases about the human aspect involved in music that include emotions [5, 37], listening history [27], and performer's interpretation [18, 19, 26], but to the best of our knowledge, there is no database that shares critiques in performance education.

2.2   Teaching Behavior on Musical Performance Lesson

Teaching behavior on musical performance lesson has been studied in music education field, e.g., comparison of teacher levels [13], analysis on time allocation [4], comparison [36] and categorization [30, 31] between verbal and non-verbal information, and

---

[2] Dataset is public on https://doi.org/10.5281/zenodo.4748243.

teacher-student interaction [9]. These studies target the transcription of speech in interactive instruction. Our study focused on critique documents that can be used for the asynchronous education.

Table 2. Types of verbal information used in this study

	Types	Definition
Adopted and adapted from Carlin, 1997 [3]; Zhukov, 2004 [38]; Simones, 2015 [31]	Giving Subjective Information (GSI)[a]	Teacher providing general and/or specific conceptual information based on teacher's subjectivity
	Giving Objective Information (GOI) (See footnote 2)	Teacher providing general and/or specific conceptual information based on objectively referable events or concepts
	Asking Question (AQ)	Enquiring
	Giving Feedback (GF)	Teacher evaluation of a student's applied and/or conceptual knowledge
	Giving Practice (GP)	Providing suggestions of ways to practice a particular passage or discussing a practicing schedule
	Giving Advice (GA)	Giving a specific opinion or recommendation to guide the student's action towards the achievement of certain specific musical aims, without demonstration or modelling

[a]Original is "Giving Information". Divided by authors.

For the utility of instruction, one study compared verbal and non-verbal instruction [6] and another study summarized the evaluation of the usefulness [8]. These studies were based on five or less performances. We conducted large-scale experiment and clarified relationship between the verbal information and the utility.

3 Method

We construct CROCUS (CRitique dOCUmentS of musical performance) dataset by collecting performance recordings and critique documents. Then, all sentences in the documents were annotated. Finally, perceived utility of every document was evaluated. All collecting procedures have been approved by the ethical review board of University of Tsukuba, Senzoku Gakuen College of Music, and Kunitachi College of Music.

3.1 Constructing CROCUS Dataset

A Total of 90 performances (10 orchestral studies by nine music college students majoring in oboe) were recorded. As online lessons have become the norm in the music colleges due to COVID-19, a similar situation to the lessons was adopted in our method. Each student played in a less reverberant and less noisy environment at home, about one meter away from the recording device (Roland R-07). Tuning and recording level were adjusted at the beginning of the recording. From the oboe orchestra study, we selected the 10 pieces of Table 1 considering balance of difficulty, style, form, and era.

3.2 Annotating Types of Sentences in CROCUS

Considering an asynchronous lesson with critique documents, we adopted and adapted the types in Simones' definition [31] as shown in the Table 2[3]. One of these six types was annotated to each sentence. Sentence breaks were period or exclamation marks. When it was judged that one sentence consisted of descriptions meaning multiple kinds of types, it was separated by a comma. Each two annotators annotated all 239 documents. If the annotations did not match, the final annotation was decided through discussion. The Cohen's Kappa coefficient was 0.96.

Evaluation of the Validity of the Classification: In order to confirm that the six types shown in Table 2 include the contents that the readers of performance reviews actually find useful, an experiment was conducted to collect and aggregate the types of review contents that the readers of critical documents find useful.

First, we collected information that the readers found useful. Seventy people with musical experience outside of school compared two critique documents for the same performance, and responded to each critique document with a free response in the form of "This document is useful in (that) __." and "This document is not clear in (that) __." for the points that would be useful for future performances and for questions to the author, respectively. Each participant worked on 40 randomly selected pairs of two critique documents, with a reward of 990 yen per participant. Among the obtained results, we extracted the "__" of the descriptions that complied with the description style of "This document is useful in (that) __." and "This document is not clear in (that) __," and obtained a total of 4,513 (unique number) descriptions (3,255 useful points and 1,258 questions). These are called candidate features.

Next, by aggregating the candidate features based on similarity, we would like to identify the contents that are considered useful in performance instruction. However, it is not easy to automatically determine the similarity between "It reminds me that I need to play more carefully with the dynamics because it lacks emotion" and "It explains specific performance techniques to enrich the expression." Therefore, we manually evaluated the similarity of candidate features and decided by majority vote whether or not a pair of candidate features are similar.

The following experiment was conducted on 300 randomly selected candidate features. For one randomly selected candidate feature, 30 randomly selected other candidate

---

[3] Types of "Demonstrating", "Modelling", and "Listening/Observing" were omitted because these actions are not observed in textual critique.

features were shown, and all similar ones were selected. A total of 200 participants performed this task with 60 questions each. A graph network was then created by using each candidate feature as a node and placing edges on pairs of candidate features that were judged to be similar by three or more participants. The Louvain method was applied to this network to extract communities, and five communities were extracted. Each community was interpreted as the content that should be included in the critique document.

In addition, from among the candidate features comprising each community, one candidate feature was determined by majority vote (or randomly selected in case of a tie) to be the most representative of that community. The candidate feature selected for each community was determined to be the name of the element required for a useful performance critique document. 102 participants were recruited, and they worked on all five communities. Given the intent of the experiment, the authors reorganized the names of the elements into noun forms, and the elements required for a useful performance review document were organized into "Expression", "Technique", "Specific points to be aware of", "Good and bad points", and "Future practice".

These can be interpreted as corresponding to GSI, GOI, GOI, GF, and GP, in that order. Based on these results, it was determined that the contents that readers of the CRITIQUE DOCUMENTS would actually find useful are contained in the 6 types listed in Table 2.

3.3 Evaluating Perceived Utility of Critique Documents

We examined the perceived utility by performers who read the collected critiques. A total of 200 people who have musical experience answered the question "Do you think that this document is useful for future performances?" with 11-point Likert (10: useful – 0: useless). Participants responded to 25 randomly selected critique documents. This question is called Q1 in this paper.

Detailed Analysis of the Utility: The utility perceived by the reader has various perspectives other than whether it is useful for future performance. Therefore, similar investigations were conducted for the other eight items, referring to the usefulness perspective used in software requirement specifications (IEEE Std830–1998 [21]) and accounting documents [32]. The questions we used were as follows. All questions were asked in the form of "Do you think that this document —?" Q1: is useful, Q2: is readable, Q3: is understandable, Q4: has description not related to future performances, Q5: is not ambiguous, Q6: contains all the statements related to the future performances, Q7: is consistent, Q8: can be verified by listening to the performance, and Q9: allows you to refer to the relevant part in the score from the contents described.

4 Results

4.1 Constructing CROCUS Dataset

A total of 239 critique documents[4] were collected by 12 teachers who are currently or formerly belonged to well-known music colleges, orchestras, and brass bands in Japan. Each teacher wrote critique documents assuming the usual lessons for a total of 20

---

[4] For one critique was missed during collecting process.

performance recording. The 20 performances were selected in counterbalanced manner by following constraints; each piece was reviewed by at least two teachers, and each student was reviewed by every teacher evenly. Due to today's social situation, the critique documents were also written at the teacher's home. An example of critique document is as follows.

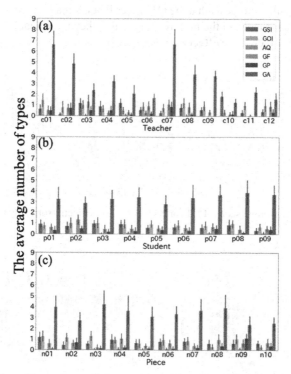

Fig. 2. The number of types for each document per (a) teacher, (b) student, and (c) piece. The error bar indicates the standard deviation.

> *The difficult passages are performed well here. If I were to ask for more, the sound is almost "too" fulfilling—it feels like a pancake with slightly too much syrup on. That may not be the best comparison...*

4.2 Annotating Types of Sentences in CROCUS

The percentages of documents containing each of GSI, GOI, AQ, GF, GP, and GA were 47.28%, 54.81%, 3.34%, 39.33%, 22.18%, and 93.72%, respectively. The average (and standard deviation) of the number of each category per document was, 0.70 (0.90), 0.85 (1.00), 0.03 (0.18), 0.61 (0.88), 0.33 (0.70), and 3.33 (2.50), respectively. Figure 2 shows that the differences in the contents of documents were larger among teachers than among songs or students.

4.3 Evaluating Perceived Utility of Critique Documents

Our results showed that critique documents had a variety of utility score, and there were documents that the reader perceived less useful (Fig. 3). Since the null hypotheses that the distribution of Q1 values for each teacher, student, and piece (Fig. 4) was a normal distribution were rejected by the Shapiro-Wilk test, the Kruskal-Wallis test was performed. The null hypothesis that the Q1 values that the reader perceived useful were equal among all teachers and the null hypothesis that they were equal among all pieces were rejected ($p \leq 0.001$, the effect size was small).

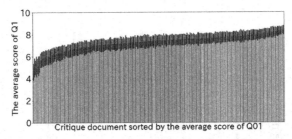

Fig. 3. The average score of Q1 for each critique document (sorted by Q1 score).

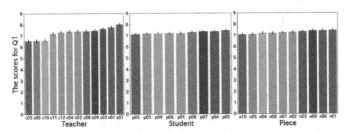

Fig. 4. The average scores of Q1 in teacher, student, and piece (sorted by Q1 score).

Table 3. The p-value and effect size of the Kruskal-Wallis test conducted for each question item for each teacher, student, and piece. * meant $p \leq 0.05$, ** meant $p \leq 0.01$, *** meant $p \leq 0.001$. m, s, and vs meant moderate, small, and very small, respectively.

	Q1	Q2	Q3	Q4	Q5	Q6	Q7	Q8	Q9
Teacher	***(s)	***(m)	***(s)	***(s)	***(m)	***(m)	***(s)	***(s)	***(m)
Student	**(vs)	***(vs)	***(vs)	***(vs)	***(vs)	***(vs)	*(vs)	***(vs)	***(vs)
Piece	***(vs)	***(vs)	– (vs)	– (vs)	***(vs)	***(vs)	*(vs)	***(vs)	***(s)

Detailed Analysis of the Utility: Table 3 showed the results of the Kruskal-Wallis test performed for the average score of each question (Fig. 5). The difference between the teachers was more remarkable than ones between the students or the pieces in all questions. This result was consistent with the previous research showing that the usage of words differed depending on the teachers [22]. It was suggested that there were particularly large differences among the teachers whether the commentary document is easy to read (Q2), not ambiguous (Q5), contains all the descriptions related to future performances (Q6), and can refer to the relevant part in the score (Q9).

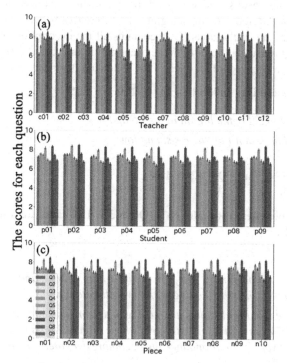

Fig. 5. The scores of each question for each document per teacher, student, and piece.

The critique document with the highest average value of Q1 and that with the lowest average value are shown below.

The Highest Rated Critique (n09-p04-c03) (Q1: 8.41 ± 1.44).

I feel that this performance is very good, and it leaves a very favorable impression. Because of this, I would like you to be a little more careful regarding the nuances of the performance. Please practice the grace notes in bars 2 and 4 again by themselves. The same for bar 10. There is always a mistake in the E-H transition in bar 11. Perhaps it is a problem with the tuning of the instrument. Please perform this part slowly and check carefully. If it is not a tuning problem, then I believe it is a fingering or breathing problem. Please practice carefully and check if the breathing and fingering are both coordinated properly. In the second half, there is tenuto on the high E and D notes. Please endeavour to perform each note carefully with nuance.

The Lowest Rated Critique (n04-p06-c05) (Q1: 4.63 ± 2.61).

The melodies are performed beautifully and vibrantly, almost as if I could hear an orchestra performing. The phrasings are well expressed for the piece, and it was lovely.

We checked the results, and we found that the documents rated higher (or lower) by each indicator differed. The most significant differences between the teachers were easy to read (Q2), not ambiguous (Q5), contains all the descriptions related to future performances (Q6), and can refer to the relevant part in the score (Q9). The documents with the highest average score for each of the following items are shown below.

The Highest Readability (n06-p05-c11) (Q2: 9.1 ± 1.29).

Be careful not to delay the breath in bars 5 and 6.
In the second half, don't let the cis sound low.

The Most Unambiguous (Q5: 8.5 ± 1.44).
same as the highest in Q1.

The Most Completeness (n03-p08-c07) (Q6: 8.3 ± 1.68) and the Most Traceability (Q9: 8.6 ± 1.42).

First movement

Counting from the beginning, the phrases are 2 bars, 2 bars, and 4 bars, so think about how to play them by looking at the overall balance.

Also, be aware that the clarinets are moving in unison, and add vibrato and other expressions. The clarinet is an instrument whose pronunciation sounds softer than the oboe, so if you do not pronounce the beginning delicately, it will not fit at that point.

In bars 17 through 20, be aware of a long phrase with the crescendo diminuendo in bar 18 as the apex of the phrase. This apex is also the natural, striking note, so it should feel "special". This is the same in every piece, so don't forget to savor the accidentals.

The first beat of measure 20 should not be strong.

Second movement.

The first and third bars should be blown with just a drifting sound, and the accented notes in the second and fourth bars should be used to add expression. I believe the accents in this case were written with the intention of adding expression to the notes rather than blasting them.

It would be nice to have more expression in the pp throughout.

There needs to be more crescendo towards bar 7.

Make sure to count the beats of the F note extension in the eighth and ninth bars. Also, the harmony changes from measure 8 to 9, so feel it as you extend the note.

When you go from the 14th bar to the 15th bar, it is better to move a little more carefully than to go immediately. It looks like the same note pattern continues before that, and there is a dim, but if you prepare to go to the next note at the last time, it will be realized and musical.

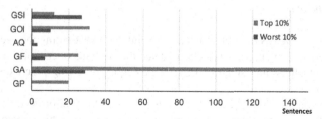

Fig. 6. Histogram of types in top 10% & Worst 10% Critique Document.

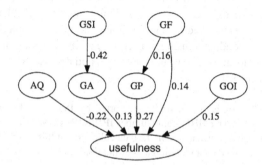

Fig. 7. The estimated causal network.

5 Discussion

Figure 3, Fig. 4, and Table 3 showed that the utility scores differed for each critique for each teacher rather than for each piece or each student. Teachers who got high utility scores (e.g., c07, c01, and c03) gave the information where the performance were not well based on objective evidence (GOI), indicated the direction that the student should aim for (GA), and suggested ways to practice strategy (GP).

Figure 6 shows histogram of types in top 10% and worst 10% rated critique documents in terms of Q1 score. As a result of the comparison, giving practice strategies (GP) was observed in top 10% whereas not in worst 10%. There are more giving advises (GA), providing information based on objective facts (GOI), and giving feedback (GF) in top 10%.

Finally, we discuss the impact on usefulness of the number of sentences that imply the six types of content shown in Table 2. We applied DirectLiNGAM [28] as a method that allows causal discovery on the data of the number of sentences that signify the six types of content and the usefulness scores for each document. Python 3.9.0 and

LiNGAM 1.5.4 were used, and the result was shown in Fig. 7. The results suggest that the usefulness of critique sentences increases as the number of GP, GOI, GF, and GA increases, and the usefulness of critique sentences decreases as the number of sentences implying GSI and AQ increases.

6   Conclusion

We published CROCUS dataset as a starting point for investigating the use of words in the critique document. This dataset clarified that the contents of critiques were different between the teachers, and suggested that the category of giving practice strategy was substantial for students.

Since this dataset was constructed as an early stage of the project, the instrument was limited to the oboe. Whether the findings can be generalizable remains as an open question. We would like to explore more instruments and discuss whether there is a common characteristic of a good critique document structure. The target students in this study were limited to music college students, thus we would like to explore at various levels of experience, such as professional and amateur students. In this study, the experiments were conducted using only Japanese. In the future, it will be necessary to conduct comparisons among multiple languages and discuss the differences between languages and cultures [2].

Acknowledgment. This study was partially supported by JST-Mirai Program Grant Number JPMJMI19G8, and JSPS KAKENHI Grant Number JP19K19347. We would like to thank all the performers and teachers who participated in the data collection of this study. We would also thank to those who helped us with data annotation and evaluation.

References

1. Bayley, J.G., Waldron, J.: "It's never too late": adult students and music learning in one online and offline convergent community music school. Int. J. Music. Educ. **38**(1), 36–51 (2020)
2. Campbell, P.S.: Lessons from the world: A Cross-Cultural Guide to Music Teaching and Learning. MacMillan Publishing Company, New York (1991)
3. Carlin, K.D.: Piano pedagogue perception of teaching effectiveness in the preadolescent elementary level applied piano lesson as a function of teacher behavior, PhD Thesis, Indiana University (1997)
4. Cavitt, M.E.: A descriptive analysis of error correction in instrumental music rehearsals. J. Res. Music. Educ. **51**(3), 218–230 (2003)
5. Chen, Y.-A., Yang, Y.-H., Wang, J.-C., Chen, H.: The AMG1608 dataset for music emotion recognition. In: ICASSP, pp. 693–697 (2015)
6. Dickey, M.R.: A comparison of verbal instruction and nonverbal teacher-student modeling in instrumental ensembles. J. Res. Music. Educ. **39**(2), 132–142 (1991)
7. Dorman, P.E.: A review of research on observational systems in the analysis of music teaching. Bull. Counc. Res. Music. Educ. 35–44 (1978)
8. Duke, R. A.: Measures of instructional effectiveness in music research. Bull. Counc. Res. Music. Educ. 1–48 (1999)

9. Duke, R.A. Simmons, A.L.: The nature of expertise: narrative descriptions of 19 common elements observed in the lessons of three renowned artist-teachers. Bull. Counc. Res. Music. Educ. 7–19 (2006)

10. Dye, K.: Student and instructor behaviors in online music lessons: an exploratory study. Int. J. Music. Educ. **34**(2), 161–170 (2016)

11. Foscarin, F., McLeod, A., Rigaux, P., Jacquemard, F., Sakai, M.: ASAP: a dataset of aligned scores and performances for piano transcription. In: ISMIR, pp. 534–541 (2020)

12. Froehlich, H.: Measurement dependability in the systematic observation of music instruction: a review, some questions, and possibilities for a (new?) approach. Psychomusicology **14**(1–2), 182 (1995)

13. Goolsby, T.W.: Verbal instruction in instrumental rehearsals: a comparison of three career levels and preservice teachers. J. Res. Music. Educ. **45**(1), 21–40 (1997)

14. Goto, M., Hashiguchi, H., Nishimura, T., Oka, R.: RWC Music Database: Popular, pp. 287–288. Classical and Jazz Music Databases, ISMIR (2002)

15. Goto, M., Hashiguchi, H., Nishimura, T., Oka, R.: RWC music database: music genre database and musical instrument sound database. In: ISMIR, pp. 229–230 (2003)

16. Hamanaka, M., Hirata, K., Tojo, S.: GTTM database and manual time-span tree generation tool. In: SMC, pp. 462–467 (2018)

17. Hash, P.M.: Remote learning in school bands during the COVID-19 shutdown. J. Res. Music. Educ. **68**(4), 381–397 (2021)

18. Hashida, M., Matsui, T., Katayose, H.: A new music database describing deviation information of performance expressions. In: ISMIR, pp. 489–494 (2008)

19. Hashida, M., Nakamura, E., Katayose, H.: Constructing PEDB 2nd Edition: a music performance database with phrase information. In: SMC, pp. 359–364 (2017)

20. Hawthorne, C., et al.: Enabling factorized piano music modeling and generation with the MAESTRO dataset. In: ICLR (2019)

21. IEEE: Recommended Practice for Software Requirements Specifications. IEEE Std 830–1998, pp. 1–40 (1998)

22. Lehmann, A.C., Sloboda, J.A., Woody, R.H., Woody, R.H., et al.: Psychology for Musicians: Understanding and Acquiring the Skills. Oxford University Press, Oxford (2007)

23. Li, B., Liu, X., Dinesh, K., Duan, Z., Sharma, G.: Creating a multitrack classical music performance dataset for multimodal music analysis: challenges, insights, and applications. IEEE Tran. Multimed. **21**(2), 522–535 (2018)

24. Matsubara, M., Kagawa, R., Hirano, T., Tsuji, I.: CROCUS: dataset of musical performance critiques: relationship between critique content and its utility. In: CMMR, pp. 279–288 (2021)

25. Nakamura, E., Saito, Y., Yoshii, K.: Statistical learning and estimation of piano fingering. Inf. Sci. **517**, 68–85 (2020)

26. Sapp, C.S.: Comparative analysis of multiple musical performances. In: ISMIR, pp. 497–500 (2007)

27. Schedl, M.: The LFM-1b dataset for music retrieval and recommendation. In: ICMR, pp. 103–110 (2016)

28. Shimizu, S., et al.: DirectLiNGAM: a direct method for learning a linear non-Gaussian structural equation model. J. Mach. Learn. Res. **12**, 1225–1248 (2011)

29. Silla Jr, C. N., Koerich, A. L. and Kaestner, C. A.: The Latin Music Database. In: ISMIR, pp. 451–456 (2008)

30. Simones, L., Schroeder, F., Rodger, M.: Categorizations of physical gesture in piano teaching: a preliminary enquiry. Psychol. Music **43**(1), 103–121 (2015)

31. Simones, L.L., Rodger, M., Schroeder, F.: Communicating musical knowledge throughgesture: Piano teachers' gestural behaviours across different levels of student proficiency. Psychol. Music **43**(5), 723–735 (2015)

32. Smith, M., Taffler, R.: Readability and understandability: different measures of the textual complexity of accounting narrative. Account. Audit. Accountability J. **5**(4), 84–98 (1992)
33. Sturm, B.L.: An analysis of the GTZAN music genre dataset. In: ACM Workshop MIRUM, MIRUM 2012, pp. 7–12 (2012)
34. Wang, Z., et al.: POP909: a pop-song dataset for music arrangement generation. In: ISMIR (2020)
35. Weiß, C., et al.: Schubert winterreise dataset: a multimodal scenario for music analysis. J. Comp. Cult. Herit. **14**(2), 1–18 (2021)
36. Whitaker, J.A.: High school band students' and directors' perceptions of verbal and nonverbal teaching behaviors. J. Res. Music. Educ. **59**(3), 290–309 (2011)
37. Zhang, K., Zhang, H., Li, S., Yang, C., Sun, L.: The PMEmo dataset for music emotion recognition. In: ICMR, pp. 135–142 (2018)
38. Zhukov, K.: Teaching styles and student behaviour in instrumental music lessons in Australian conservatoriums, PhD Thesis, University of New South Wales (2005)

A Psychoacoustic-Based Methodology for Sound Mass Music Analysis

Micael Antunes[1]([⊠])[iD], Guilherme Feulo do Espirito Santo[2][iD],
Jônatas Manzolli[1][iD], and Marcelo Queiroz[2][iD]

[1] Interdisciplinary Nucleus for Sound Communication/Arts institute,
University of Campinas, Campinas, SP, Brazil
micael.antunes@nics.unicamp.br
[2] Computer Science Department, University of São Paulo, São Paulo, SP, Brazil

Abstract. A *sound mass* is a specific state of the musical texture corresponding to a large number of sound events concentrated within a short time and/or frequency interval. Conceptually, it is associated with the work of György Ligeti, Krzysztof Penderecki, and Iannis Xenakis, among others. Recent studies have investigated *sound masses* via perceptual models, such as *Gestalt* models of perception and *auditory scene analysis*, and also from a more acoustic and psychoacoustic perspective obtained through audio recordings. The main goal of this paper is to propose a methodology for the musical analysis of *sound mass* music through audio recordings combined with other research sources from music theory, musical analysis and psychoacoustics. We apply this method in the analysis of a recording of the first movement of Ligeti's *Ten Pieces for Wind Quintet* (1968), and explore relationships between the obtained audio descriptors and Ligeti's concepts of *timbre of movement* and *permeability*, in order to reveal Ligeti's strategies when dealing with musical texture and *sound masses*.

Keywords: Sound Mass Music · Musical Analysis · Psychoacoustics

1 Introduction

This paper introduces a computer aided musical analysis methodology anchored on audio descriptors. Specifically, psychoacoustic models are applied to study *sound mass* composition. *Sound mass* composition emerges in the context of discussions about perception and 20th century serial music [22]. Noticeably, these discussions were part of the *Darmstädter Ferienkurse*, where composers attended classes and lectures on psychoacoustics, phonetics, information theory, and sound synthesis [6]. Some well-known examples of *sound mass* compositions are the large number of attacks in Ligeti's *Continuum* (1968), the micropolyphony and cluster techniques in his *Chamber Concerto* (1961), and the mass created by *glissandi* and extended techniques of the string orchestra in Xenakis' *Aroura* (1971).

© Springer Nature Switzerland AG 2023
M. Aramaki et al. (Eds.): CMMR 2021, LNCS 13770, pp. 267–281, 2023.
https://doi.org/10.1007/978-3-031-35382-6_21

The central idea in *sound mass* composition is to emphasize perceptual features of sound, by exploring the continuum of time and frequency domains to produce sound textures with a high level of fusion and inner movement. Perception of *sound masses* is often linked with the limits of sound integration by the ear [22] and *microtime* perception [4]. *Sound mass* music is also associated with Huron's perceptual principles of *minimum masking, pitch proximity and limited density*, which are anchored in the *critical bandwidth* psychoacoustic model [20,30].

Previous works have studied Ligeti's *sound mass* composition from a perceptual perspective, mainly through the *symbolic analysis* of the score. Clendinning explored such a perceptual approach in the study of Ligeti's compositional techniques such as *pattern-meccanico* [11] and *micropolyphony* [10]. Cambouropoulos [9] used *Gestalt* theory to investigate links between Ligeti's techniques and their perceptual outcomes, an approach already explored by Ferraz [16]. More recently, Douglas et al. [14] investigated *Continuum* (1968) within the context of Bregman's *auditory scene analysis* [7].

Methodologies anchored in audio descriptors with a psychoacoustic approach, which emerged in the context of computational and systematic musicology [24,26,42], have also been used to study Ligeti's works [2,3,24]. To get a broader view of musical analysis, the present study seeks to integrate several sources, such as musicological texts, psychoacoustic knowledge, symbolic information from the score, and audio descriptor representations. In this paper, we propose a methodology for musical analysis [42] focused on perceptual concepts that motivate *sound mass* music composition, associating them with descriptors derived from audio recordings. Specifically, we study Ligeti's viewpoint on *sound mass* composition through the concept of *timbre of movement* [22], associating it with *loudness* [15] and *roughness* [37]. Due to the correlation between spectral information and the perception of pitches and individual voices [20], we also investigate the use of *spectral entropy* [29] and *spectral irregularity* [8], associating them with Ligeti's concept of *permeability* [2–4,22]. We present an musical analysis of the first movement of Ligeti's *Ten Pieces for Wind Quintet* (1968), using score-based information alongside the audio signal of a particular performance of this piece. We also derive representations based on audio descriptors that allow us to discuss Ligeti's compositional strategies and their perceptual aspects, as well as the formal development of the piece from the viewpoints of *timbre of movement* and *permeability*.

In Sect. 2, we lay out the theoretical background for this study, starting with an exposition of the concepts of *timbre of movement* and *permeability*. Then, we give an overview of the first movement of the *Ten Pieces for Wind Quintet*, followed by a review of the audio descriptors used in this work. In Sect. 3, we outline the analytical methodology proposed, and in Sect. 4 we present and discuss the results of our study. Finally, in Sect. 5, we present our conclusions.

2   Theoretical Background

2.1   Ligeti's Concepts of *Timbre of Movement* and *Permeability*

Two relevant György Ligeti's concepts associated with *sound mass* music composition are *timbre of movement*, which is linked with his knowledge of electronic music and psychoacoustics, and *permeability*, related to his point of view on the perception of pitches within a polyphonic texture.

The concept of *timbre of movement*[1] refers to the achievement of fusion in musical texture by mixing a large number of sound events [22, p. 169]. Ligeti associates this concept with his collaboration with Gottfried Michael Koenig in the electronic studio of the Westdeutscher Rundfunk (WDR) in Cologne [22]. Regarding the relationship between Ligeti's concepts and electroacoustic technology, Sabbe [34, p. 1091] says that, "electronic technology makes it possible to work at the limit of discrete perception, between the discrete and the continuous, in this field of transition where rhythm turns into timbre". To him, the possibility of playing with the listener's perception is an important feature of sound synthesis that will impact Ligeti's compositional strategies.

To Ligeti, the most meaningful knowledge acquired in the studio was the observation that sound samples or synthesis components merge into a single texture when the number of sounds surpasses a certain threshold of our perception. This occurs when our auditory system can no longer discern the individual components of a musical texture, leading our attention to the global features and inner movements of *sound masses* [22, p. 169]. Ligeti used this concept of *timbre of movement* in his instrumental compositions with the *micropoliphony* technique [10], which allows achieving dense textures by overlapping a large number of melodies with short notes.

The concept of *permeability* refers to a state in which we are unable to distinguish pitches and individual voices. According to Ligeti: *"The loss of sensitivity to intervals is at the source of a state that could be called permeability"* [22, p. 123].

To Ligeti, the concept of permeability is linked to the perception of the interval in its musical context. Thus, he says that the contrapuntal technique of Giovanni Pierluigi da Palestrina (1525–1594) is the best example of impermeability. The reasoning is that in Palestrina's counterpoint there is a small degree of freedom for changing notes without causing perceptual changes in the musical texture [22, p. 124]. Following his argument, he says that the large number of voices in Johann Sebastian Bach's Brandenburg Concertos (1685–1750) corresponds to a more permeable musical texture [22, p. 124]. Regarding this logic, the music of sound masses thus exhibits a high level of permeability.

The concept of permeability is mainly associated with the use of *tone clusters* in his works, such as *Lux Aeterna* (1966). According to Ligeti, the tone cluster *"is somewhere between sound and noise and consists of several voices stratified and*

---

[1] In the original, Ligeti uses *timbre du mouvement* in French and *Bewegungsfarbe* in German [22, p. 169].

interwoven in semitones, which thereby give up their individuality and become completely dissolved into the resultant overriding complex" [23, p. 165].

2.2   First Movement of the Ten Pieces for Wind Quintet

Ten Pieces for Wind Quintet was composed in 1968, and dedicated to the Wind Quintet of the Royal Stockholm Philharmonic Orchestra. Each movement was conceived as a *micro concerto* with *tutti* odd movements and *solo* even movements, each solo being dedicated to one of the performers [39]. We choose as analytical corpus, for all feature extraction and section division, the version of the piece performed by *London Winds* in the album *Ligeti Edition 7: Chamber Music*, recorded in 1998.

Previous studies about the *Ten pieces*[2] may be considered from two points of view:

1. the *semantic* point of view, by exploring the relationship between Ligeti's discourse and his music [18];
2. the *symbolic* point of view, by examining the musical organization through the score information [39].

Of course, these two points of view are interrelated and this division in the sequel is done only for didactic purposes.

The Semantic Level - Floros and Bernhardt draw attention to the semantic aspect of György Ligeti's music. [18, p. 51]. In this context, it is Ligeti himself who builds the connections between sound and meaning through the idea of *gestures*. We can examine this question in the composer's creative drafts, texts and interviews. According to Ligeti:

> *I had made a list of all these types of "gestures" - I can't remember the exact number, there must have been about thirty of them. The ten movements of this composition were developed from these types, but the distribution of types changed from movement to movement.* [28, p. 198].

One of these documented *gestures* is important to the understanding of the first movement of *Ten pieces*: the *cystoscopy*. Ligeti uses the word, which consists of an uncomfortable medical procedure, to refer to the ninth of the *Ten pieces* [18, p. 51]. This movement consists of only one musical texture, with a high-register cluster played in fortissimo by the trio of piccolo flute, oboe and clarinet, affording the emergence of phenomena such as roughness, beats and differential tones. This excerpt is remarkably similar to the musical texture of bars 16–22 of the first movement, allowing us to infer that this excerpt is a unique musical gesture. This information, combined with an analysis of the score, will allow us to understand the formal development of the piece and its possible segmentation.

---

[2] From this point onwards this abbreviation will be used instead of *Ten Pieces for Wind Quintet*.

Table 1. Score segmentation for the *Ten pieces* and respective recording times.

	Section 1	Section 2	Apendix
Score bar	1–16	16–22	22–25
Record Time	0:00.000–1:32.367	1:32.367–1:58.390	1:58.390–2:17.04

The Symbolic Level - Vitale [39] presents a thorough score-based analysis of this work, and highlights the gradual processes appearing in the piece, based on micropolyphonic strategies to generate the musical texture, where the musical material is articulated with slow modifications in pitch, timbre, density, and rhythm [39, p. 2]. Using pitch register and dynamics as criteria, this author proposes a division of the score of the first movement of the *Ten Pieces for Wind Quintet* (1968) in two main sections (Sect. 1: measures 1–16; Sect. 2: measures 16–22) followed by an appendix (measures 22–25). The segmentation and segment recording times are displayed in Table 1. Figure 1 provides a piano-roll-like visualization of the score, clarifying the reasoning for this segmentation. Section 1 is marked by medium-low register pitches between C2 and C3, with complex rhythm and dynamics. Section 2 starts with a unison that becomes a high-pitched cluster with very intense dynamics, linked with the *cystoscopy* gesture, and the appendix consists only of a minor second in pianissimo. The proposed segmentation is also clearly visible in the recording, for instance in the CQT representation of Fig. 2.

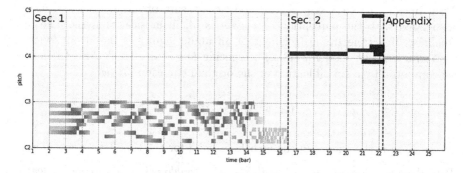

Fig. 1. Symbolic information from the score of *Ten pieces*. Pitches are represented in the vertical axis and bars are shown in the horizontal axis. Color intensity represents the integrated dynamics for the pitches. The dashed lines represent the proposed segmentation. Section 2 is associated with *cystoscopy* gesture.

2.3 Audio Descriptors

The use of audio descriptors in the context of musical analysis is a multidisciplinary task [42] which admits a multiplicity of approaches depending on the

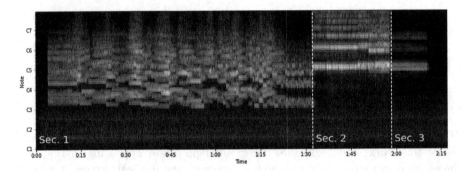

Fig. 2. CQT representation from the audio of *Ten pieces*. Pitches are represented in the vertical axis and recording time is represented by the horizontal axis. The dashed lines represent the proposed segmentation.

context in which it is applied [24,26,42]. In this work, we design the analytical methodology anchored in audio descriptors for two main reasons: 1. audio descriptors provide a perspective (in our case, a perceptual perspective) on the musical sound data, allowing a better understanding of the musical composition [26]; 2. graphical representations of audio descriptors guide the listening throughout the analysis and facilitates the observation of related perceptual concepts [12]. As detailed in Sect. 3, we associate the concepts of *timbre of movement* and *permeability* with four audio descriptors: *loudness*, *roughness*, *spectral irregularity* and *spectral entropy*.

Loudness - *Loudness* is a psychoacoustic measure of sound intensity, usually associated with the perception of *dynamics* [4] in musical analysis. The total *loudness* of a time frame (segment of an audio signal) is based on Zwicker's *critical bandwidth* model [8,43]. The specific *loudness* of each *Bark*[3] band can be computed by a simplification of the original equation [31] as

$$\text{Loudness} = \sum_{z=1}^{N} E(z)^{0.23} \qquad (1)$$

where $E(z)$ is the energy in the z-th *bark* band for the time frame considered.

Roughness - According to Vassilakis [37], *roughness* is a perceptual feature related with the sense of very fast amplitude variations in the sound and it is partially conditioned by both the sound stimulus and the properties of the basilar membrane. The *roughness* value of a time frame is based on an approximation, proposed in [36], of the Plomp & Levelt experimental dissonance curve[4] [32]. For complex sounds, the *roughness* value can be computed using a formulation by

---

[3] *Bark* is the unit of Zwicker's *critical bandwidth* model [43].

[4] For a full revision on *roughness* curves, see [37].

Vassilakis, which embodies the physical and psychoacoustic mechanisms involved in its perception, as

$$\text{Roughness} = \sum_{i=1}^{N}\sum_{j=i}^{N} \frac{(a_i * a_j)^{0.1}}{2} \left(\frac{2a_j}{a_i + a_j}\right)^{3.11} \left(e^{\frac{0.84|f_j-f_i|}{0.0207f_i+18.96}} - e^{\frac{1.38|f_j-f_i|}{0.0207f_i+18.96}}\right) \quad (2)$$

where f_i is the i-th partial of the sound and a_i its corresponding amplitude.

Spectral Irregularity - The *spectral irregularity* feature used in this work was proposed by Krimphoff et al. [21] as a measure of the noise content of the spectrum [8, p. 60]. It is usually computed for each time frame in the magnitude spectrum as

$$\text{Irregularity} = \sum_{k=2}^{N-1} \left|a_k - \frac{a_{k-1} + a_k + a_{k+1}}{3}\right| \quad (3)$$

where a_k is the value in the k-th magnitude coefficient and N is the total number of frequency bins in the spectrum.

A low *irregularity* value denotes a spectrum whose energy is concentrated in few frequency bins, associated with distinguishable components in the sound. In contrast, a high *irregularity* value implies a more regular energy distribution across all frequencies, associated with a more noisy content [8].

Spectral Entropy - *Spectral entropy* is an audio feature used for estimating signal information and complexity in the Time-Frequency Plane [17]. Higher *entropy* values are usually associated with higher spectral activity along all frequencies, and lower values are related to a concentration of spectral energy on few components.

The *Spectral Entropy* descriptor is derived from Shannon's information theory equation through an analogy between signal energy densities and probability densities [40], as

$$\text{Entropy} = -\sum_{k=1}^{N} P(E_k) \ln(P(E_k)) \quad (4)$$

where $P(E_k)$ denotes the relative frequency of the energy present in the k-th bin.

3   Methodology

In order to shed light on the musicological dimensions of this study, we disclose the methodological description in three steps: 1 - The description of the whole workflow; 2 - The significance of the audio descriptors we choose for the musical analysis; 3 - The technical parameters we use to the audio analysis.

The musical analysis methodology presented here is an interdisciplinary task [13], that seeks to integrate various musicological sources [26], such as theoretical and aesthetic texts, interviews, symbolic information from the score, and audio descriptor representations. We should emphasize that the authors' interpretation, anchored in the musicological information available, is a key element of the musical analysis, as different scholars may produce different interpretations of the same piece [1]. Thus, the criteria for choosing the audio descriptors and the graphic representations derived from them are anchored in the congruence between the perceptual features to be highlighted, Ligeti's creative process, and the musicological body of knowledge.

3.1   The Workflow

The workflow comprises three main tasks: 1 - Musicological research, whose results have already been exposed in Sects. 1 and 2; 2 - Audio analysis; and 3 - Musicological validation. The workflow substeps are detailed as follows:

1. **Musicological research and review of literature**
    (a) Review of texts about Ligeti and his compositional processes on *Ten pieces* (Interviews, theoretical and historiographical texts)
    (b) Music theory, Audio descriptors and Psychoacoustic references
    (c) Compilation of previous analyses of the *Ten Pieces*
2. **Audio analysis**
    (a) Choice of the audio descriptors anchored in the musicological findings of step (1)
    (b) Manual segmentation of the audio signal according to musicological research outcomes
    (c) Computation of the selected time-varying audio descriptors, their corresponding graphical representations, mean and standard deviation values, as well as scatter plots to illustrate their correlations
3. **Musicological evaluation/validation**
    (a) Musicological analysis of the piece to establish the relationships between musical content of the different sections and the obtained descriptor values
    (b) Musicological validation through the assessment of the results of audio analysis vis-à-vis the musicological context.

3.2   The Musicological Significance of the Chosen Audio Descriptors

Sound mass music, as already pointed, is intrinsically related to the perceptual outcome of the musical events [4,14,30]. Therefore, any musical analysis focused only on the score would not provide all relevant information for the understanding of *sound mass* features [4]. It is our aim to devise an appropriate approach to *sound mass* music analysis, based on information extracted from a musical performance through derived audio features. In order to do that, we propose a methodology for *sound mass* music analysis using audio descriptors and psychoacoustic features associated with Ligeti's musical concepts, aligned with score-based information.

The concept of *timbre of movement* is associated with the dynamic perception of the global behavior of musical texture and its *microtime* manifestation [2,33]. The *loudness* descriptor is used as a measure for *global perceptual dynamics* [4] and the *roughness* descriptor was used to describe the *microtime behavior* of *sound masses* [2,37].

According to the principles of *minimum masking* and *limited density* [20], the higher the level of spectral information in the auditory nerves, the lower our ability to perceive musical pitches and intervals. Therefore, the concept of *permeability* is represented by the *textural information level* of the *sound mass*, associated with *spectral entropy* [5], and the *noise content*, associated with *spectral irregularity* [8].

3.3 Technical Audio Analysis Parameters

Feature extraction was done using Python[5] and the Jupyter[6] environment. *Loudness, irregularity* and *entropy* were computed from the magnitude spectrogram obtained using Librosa [27], with a window size of 4096 samples and hop length of 1024 samples. The *roughness* descriptor was obtained from the reassigned spectrogram [19] (with the same parameters described above), as it depends on precise frequency and amplitude values. All the code used to extract and plot the audio features is available at a Gitlab repository[7].

4   Results and Discussion

Figure 3 corresponds to the graphical representations of the descriptors obtained from the audio analysis as functions of time. Each different color represents one of the three sections of the score: blue is the first section, orange the second section and green the appendix. Mean and standard deviation values for each descriptor and section are presented in Table 2. The analysis was conducted in 2 stages: first we explore the characteristics associated with *timbre of movement*, followed by the behavior associated with *permeability*.

Timbre of Movement - According to the methodology proposed (Sect. 3), the psychoacoustic descriptors of *loudness* and *roughness* are associated with the concept of *timbre of movement*. Each section of the piece displays a different behavior in terms of this concept.

The first section displays a somewhat regular fluctuation of *loudness* values (blue line in the upper left corner of Fig. 3). Within the same section, *roughness* (blue line in the upper right corner of Fig. 3) displays low values with low variation. The corresponding statistics can be seen in Table 2.

In evident contrast with the first section, the second section of the piece displays the highest values of *loudness*. We highlight that, although the standard deviation values for these two sections are not very different, by inspection of the *loudness* curve, we can see that the first section has an oscillatory behavior while the second section displays an ascending pattern. Also, in the second section we observe the highest values of *roughness* with a complex oscillatory pattern, with spikes that go upwards towards the end of this section. Finally, the appendix presents low values and low variation for both *loudness* and *roughness*.

---

[5] https://www.python.org/.

[6] https://jupyter.org/.

[7] https://gitlab.com/Feulo/ligetis-wind-quintet-analysis.

Table 2. Mean and standard deviation values for *Loudness, Roughness, Irregularity, Entropy* on each section.

Section	Loudness	Roughness	Irregularity	Entropy
1	41.87 ± 14.49	9.96 ± 5.86	63.54 ± 40.72	0.42 ± 0.13
2	66.36 ± 12.52	103.12 ± 62.44	171.63 ± 58.37	0.74 ± 0.15
3	13.36 ± 5.29	0.55 ± 0.56	9.98 ± 6.58	0.10 ± 0.03

Permeability - Ligeti's concept of *permeability* is linked to the audio descriptors of *spectral irregularity* and *spectral entropy*. By observing the two curves at the lower half of Fig. 3, we can also observe a distinct profile within each one of the sections of the piece.

In the first section, a regular fluctuation of the values is observed in both descriptors, but *entropy* displays a lower range of variation relative to the mean ($\sigma/\mu = 0.64$ for *irregularity* and $\sigma/\mu = 0.31$ for *entropy*, according to the values in Table 2). In the second section, we can observe an ascending pattern in both features, similarly to what was observed for *loudness* and *roughness*, with increasing spikes in the *spectral entropy* profile. The same observation can be made here for the relative variation of both features, with $\sigma/\mu = 0.34$ for *irregularity* and $\sigma/\mu = 0.20$ for *entropy*. Finally, the appendix displays once again the lowest values in both descriptors, as observed with *loudness* and *roughness*, with smaller relative *entropy* variation ($\sigma/\mu = 0.30$) with respect to irregularity ($\sigma/\mu = 0.66$).

By observing all descriptors taken together, we see that the three sections of the piece have very different behaviors from the perspective of their perceptual features. The psychoacoustic difference between the sections is illustrated in the first plot of Fig. 4, which represents the relationship between *loudness* and *roughness*, and in the correspondence between *spectral irregularity* and *spectral entropy*, shown in the second plot of Fig. 4. In both graphs, the spatial placement of the three section clusters, as well as their geometrical arrangement, make the exploration of *timbre of movement* and *permeability* relatively explicit, allowing us to observe a link between the formal division of the composition and the different perceptual feature aspects of the sound material.

It is interesting to observe that, with respect to the first section, we see the blue cluster lying horizontally on the scatter plot, where the large variations in *loudness* emphasize the global dynamic perception. In contrast, the second section (orange) corresponds to a highly scattered cluster in both *roughness* and *loudness* axes, but concentrating on high values of *loudness*, thus bringing the *microtime* behavior (variation of *roughness*) to the forefront.

In terms of *permeability*, we can observe in Fig. 4 that the *spectral irregularity* and *spectral entropy* fluctuations in all sections are highly correlated, producing a log-like, quasi-diagonal shape in the scatter plot, which correspond to constant changes of pitch perception in the musical texture. This might be associated with the harmonic technique of *blurring* [9, p. 122], used by Ligeti to manipulate the

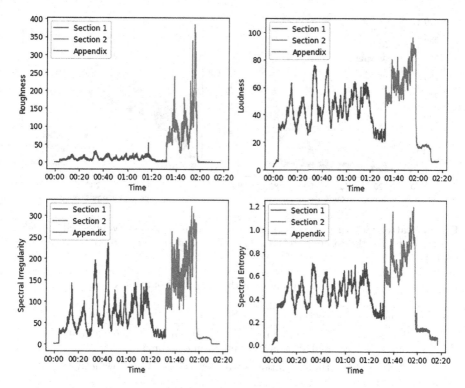

Fig. 3. *Roughness* (upper left), *Loudness* (upper right), *Spectral Irregularity* (lower left) and *Spectral Entropy* (lower right) for the 3 sections of the piece.

musical texture. Especially in the second section (orange), the higher values of *loudness* and the large variation of the spectral descriptors obliterate the perception of individual events, turning our attention to the mass behavior of the composition.

Thus, to summarize the analytical outcomes, as illustrated in Table 3: Sect. 1 has a focus on the global behavior of the musical texture in terms of *timbre of movement*, with a high variation of *permeability*. This is interpreted as a sound mass with different levels of global intensity that affords different levels of pitch perception. Section 2 emphasizes *timbre of movement* with a focus on the *microtime* behavior, while at the same time reaching the highest levels of *permeability*. This is interpreted as a sound mass which allows a very stable perception of dynamics and pitches, affording several psychoacoustic effects, like roughness, beats and differential tones. The appendix displays a low level of activity in terms of both *timbre of movement* and *permeability* which is interpreted as a stable musical texture without movement or direction.

By confronting the audio descriptor representations with the score contents we may notice that particular polyphonic strategies were used to achieve different perceptual features. In the first segment, the chromatic texture is composed of

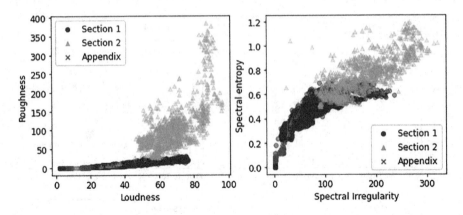

Fig. 4. Scatter plot with the *loudness* (x-axis) and *roughness* (y-axis) values (left). Scatter plot with the *spectral irregularity* (x-axis) and *spectral entropy* (y-axis) values (right).

Table 3. Summary of the analytical outcomes.

Concept	Section 1	Section 2	Section 3
Timbre of movement	Emphasis on global behavior	Emphasis on microtime features	Low activity
Permeability	High variation	Highest values	Low activity

several changes in dynamics and the complexity of polymetric rhythms into a medium-low-pitch register. In the second segment, the texture is composed of a simple rhythmic metric and a narrowband pitch organisation in a high-pitched register.

By looking at the audio features and the score information, we may infer that Ligeti draws on distinct polyphonic strategies in order to achieve different sound mass sensorial qualities. The sensorial singularity of the sound masses may be one of the sources of Ligeti's notion of *gesture*. Finally, it is interesting to notice that the low level of all descriptors in the third part could be the reason why Vitale [39] described this section as an appendix of the piece.

5   Conclusion

In this paper we presented a methodology for the musical analysis of *sound mass* compositions, based on audio descriptors associated with Ligeti's concepts of *timbre of movement* and *permeability*. Our approach sought to get a broader understanding of the *Ten pieces* by combining an analysis of the piece's audio recording with the score and musicological information, thus joining three levels of information: the symbolic, the semantic and the audio representation. In terms of the musicological interest in audio analysis techniques focused on *sound mass* composition, the proposed method reinforces the idea that the perceptual features associated with the performance of a musical work bring important elements that help understanding the formal development of a work, without reducing the importance of symbolic analyses based on the musical score. By analyzing the psychoacoustic features of each section of this particular piece, we may argue that the most important perceptual characteristics of the work do not depend heavily on specific choice of pitches, rhythms or harmonies, but are highly anchored on the perceptual qualities of the *sound masses*. Also, audio descriptors could expand the *gradual process* approach [38], enriching the symbolic analysis with performative characteristics of the piece.

Future work may focus on investigating other timbre-related psychoacoustic descriptors in the context of the proposed analysis, to verify whether they contribute to a better understanding of the perception of similarity of *sound masses* [25]. The study of other audio descriptors in the context of *sound mass music* could also foment applications in the field of creative processes, particularly in computer-aided composition and musical modeling. Exploration of perceptual features of a musical work through comparative analysis of different recordings of the same piece is also an interesting avenue for future work. It would be useful to investigate how the interpretative choices in different performances could reveal the invariant properties of a musical work [41], as expressed in the score.

Finally, musical analysis with audio descriptors might help in empirical studies with musical excerpts [14], offering exploratory ways to represent perception attributes of non-expert listeners. If, on the one hand, it is difficult to derive general assumptions about sound semantics through the musical analysis of a single work, on the other hand, this approach applied to a broader corpus could provide insights into the investigation of the link between timbre semantics [35] and the sensorial level of hearing.

Acknowledgments. Micael Antunes is supported by FAPESP Grant 2019/09734-3 and 2021/11880-8, Jônatas Manzolli is supported by CNPq Grant 304431/2018-4 and 429620/2018-7 and Marcelo Queiroz is supported by CNPq Grant 307389/2019-7.

References

1. Pople, A.: Modeling musical structure. In: Clarke, E.F., Cook, N. (eds.) Empirical Musicology: Aims, Methods, Prospects, pp. 127–156. Oxford University Press, Oxford, New York (2004)
2. Antunes, M., Feulo, G., Manzolli, J.: A perceptual approach to Ligeti's Continuum with a Roughness descriptor. In: Livro de Resumos do II EINEM Encontro Internacional de Investigação de Estudantes em Música e Musicologia, pp. 18–19. Évora (2020)
3. Antunes, M., Manzolli, J.: A psychoacoustical approach to Ligeti's concept of permeability. In: Livro de Resumos do II EINEM Encontro Internacional de Investigação de Estudantes em Música e Musicologia, pp. 20–21. Évora (2020)
4. Antunes, M., Rossetti, D., Manzolli, J.: Emerging structures within micro-time of Ligeti's Continuum. In: Proceedings of the 2021 International Computer Music Conference, pp. 271–274. Santiago, Chile (2021)

5. Baraniuk, R.G., Flandrin, P., Janssen, A.J., Michel, O.J.: Measuring time-frequency information content using the rényi entropies. IEEE Trans. Inf. Theory **47**(4), 1391–1409 (2001)
6. Borio, G., Danuser, H.: Die Internationalen Ferienkurse für Neue Musik Darmstadt 1946–1966. Concert program, lectures, masterclasses, tutors. In: Geschichte und Dokumentation in vier Bänden., vol. 3. Rombach (1997)
7. Bregman, A.S.: Auditory Scene Analysis: The Perceptual Organization of Sound. MIT Press, Cambridge (1994)
8. Bullock, J.: Implementing audio feature extraction in live electronic music. Ph.D. thesis, Birmingham City University (2008)
9. Cambouropoulos, E., Tsougras, C.: Auditory streams in ligeti's continuum: a theoretical and perceptual approach. J. Interdiscip. Music Stud. **3**(1–2), 119–137 (2009)
10. Clendinning, J.P.: Contrapuntal techniques in the music of Gyorgy Ligeti. Ph.D. thesis, Yale University (1990)
11. Clendinning, J.P.: The pattern-meccanico compositions of György Ligeti. Perspect. New Music **31**(1), 192 (1993). https://doi.org/10.2307/833050
12. Couprie, P.: Graphical representation: an analytical and publication tool for electroacoustic music. Organ. Sound **9**(1), 109–113 (2004)
13. Couprie, P.: Quelques propos sur les outils et les méthodes audionumériques en musicologie. L'interdisciplinarité comme rupture épistémologique. Revue musicale OICRM **6**(2), 25–44 (2020). https://doi.org/10.7202/1068384ar
14. Douglas, C., Noble, J., McAdams, S.: Auditory scene analysis and the perception of sound mass in ligetis continuum. Music Percept. **33**, 287–305 (2016). https://doi.org/10.1525/mp.2016.33.3.287
15. Fastl, H., Zwicker, E.: Psychoacoustics: Facts and Models. No. 22 in Springer series in information sciences, 3rd edn. Springer, Berlin, New York (2007). https://doi.org/10.1007/978-3-540-68888-4
16. Ferraz, S.: Análise e Percepção Textural: Peça VII, de 10 peças para Gyorgy Ligeti. Cadernos de Estudos: Análise Musical **3**, 68–79 (1990)
17. Figueiredo, N.S.: Efficient adaptive multiresolution representation of music signals. Master dissetation, University of São Paulo (2020)
18. Floros, C.: György Ligeti: beyond avant-garde and postmodernism. PL Academic Research, Frankfurt am Main (2014)
19. Fulop, S.A., Fitz, K.: Algorithms for computing the time-corrected instantaneous frequency (reassigned) spectrogram, with applications. J. Acoust. Soc. Am. **119**(1), 360–371 (2006)
20. Huron, D.: Tone and voice: a derivation of the rules of voice-leading from perceptual principles. Music Percept. Interdiscip. J. **19**(1), 1–64 (2001)
21. Krimphoff, J., McAdams, S., Winsberg, S.: Caractérisation du timbre des sons complexes.II. Analyses acoustiques et quantification psychophysique. Le Journal de Physique IV **04**(C5), C5–625-C5-628 (1994). https://doi.org/10.1051/jp4:19945134
22. Ligeti, G.: Neuf essais sur la musique. Éditions Contrechamps, Genève - Suisse (2010)
23. Ligeti, G., Bernard, J.W., Ligeti, G.: States, events, transformations. Perspect. New Music **31**(1), 164 (1993). https://doi.org/10.2307/833047
24. Malloch, S.N.: Timbre and Technology. PhD Thesis, The University of Edinburgh, Edinburgh (1997)
25. McAdams, S.: Timbre as a structuring force in music. In: Siedenburg, K., Saitis, C., McAdams, S., Popper, A.N., Fay, R.R. (eds.) Timbre: Acoustics, Perception,

and Cognition. SHAR, vol. 69, pp. 211–243. Springer, Cham (2019). https://doi.org/10.1007/978-3-030-14832-4_8

26. McAdams, S., Depalle, P., Clarke, E.: Analyzing musical sound. In: Empirical Musicology: Aims, Methods, Prospects, pp. 157–196. Oxford University Press, New York (2004)

27. McFee, B., et al.: librosa: audio and music signal analysis in python. In: 14th Python in Science Conference, pp. 18–24. Austin, Texas (2015). https://doi.org/10.25080/Majora-7b98e3ed-003

28. Michel, P.: György Ligeti. Minerve, Paris (1995)

29. Misra, H., Ikbal, S., Bourlard, H., Hermansky, H.: Spectral entropy based feature for robust ASR. In: 2004 IEEE International Conference on Acoustics, Speech, and Signal Processing, vol. 1, pp. I-193 (2004). https://doi.org/10.1109/ICASSP.2004.1325955

30. Noble, J., McAdams, S.: Sound mass, auditory perception, and 'post-tone' music. J. New Music Res. 49(3), 231–251 (2020). https://doi.org/10.1080/09298215.2020.1749673

31. Peeters, G.: A large set of audio features for sound description (similarity and classification) in the CUIDADO project. CUIDADO IST Proj. Rep. 54, 1–25 (2004)

32. Plomp, R., Levelt, W.J.M.: Tonal consonance and critical bandwidth. J. Acoust. Soc. Am. 38(4), 548–560 (1965)

33. Roads, C.: Microsound. MIT Press, Cambridge, Mass (2001)

34. Sabbe, H.: György Ligeti. In: Donin, N., Feneyrou, L. (eds.) Théories de la composition musicale au XXe siècle, vol. 2. Symétrie, Lyon (2013)

35. Saitis, C., Weinzierl, S.: The semantics of timbre. In: Siedenburg, K., Saitis, C., McAdams, S., Popper, A.N., Fay, R.R. (eds.) Timbre: Acoustics, Perception, and Cognition. SHAR, vol. 69, pp. 119–149. Springer, Cham (2019). https://doi.org/10.1007/978-3-030-14832-4_5

36. Sethares, W.A.: Tuning, Timbre, Spectrum, Scale. Springer Science & Business Media, Berlin (1998). https://doi.org/10.1007/978-1-4471-4177-8

37. Vassilakis, P.N.: Perceptual and physical properties of amplitude fluctuation and their musical significance. PhD Thesis, University of California, Los Angeles, Califórnia (2001)

38. Vitale, C.: A gradação nas peças 5 e 6 das Dez peças para quinteto de sopros de György Ligeti. In: Anais do I Encontro Internacional de Teoria e Análise Musical, pp. 1–8. São Paulo, Brasil (2009)

39. Vitale, C.H.: Dez peças para quinteto de sopros de György Ligeti: a gradação como uma ferramenta para a construção do discurso musical. PhD Thesis, Universidade de São Paulo, São Paulo, Brasil (2008)

40. Williams, W.J., Brown, M.L., Hero III, A.O.: Uncertainty, information, and time-frequency distributions. In: Advanced Signal Processing Algorithms, Architectures, and Implementations II, vol. 1566, pp. 144–156. International Society for Optics and Photonics (1991)

41. Ystad, S., Aramaki, M., Kronland-Martinet, R.: Timbre from sound synthesis and high-level control perspectives. In: Siedenburg, K., Saitis, C., McAdams, S., Popper, A.N., Fay, R.R. (eds.) Timbre: Acoustics, Perception, and Cognition. SHAR, vol. 69, pp. 361–389. Springer, Cham (2019). https://doi.org/10.1007/978-3-030-14832-4_13

42. Zattra, L.: Analysis and analyses of electroacoustic music. In: Proceedings of the Sound and Music Computing 2005, p. 10. Salermo, Italy (2005)

43. Zwicker, E., Flottorp, G., Stevens, S.S.: Critical band width in loudness summation. J. Acoust. Soc. Am. 29(5), 548–557 (1957). https://doi.org/10.1121/1.1908963

Musical Structure Analysis and Generation Through Abstraction Trees

Filippo Carnovalini[1]([⊠]), Nicholas Harley[2], Steven T. Homer[2], Antonio Rodà[1], and Geraint A. Wiggins[2,3]

[1] University of Padova, Padua, Italy
`filippo.carnovalini@dei.unipd.it`
[2] Vrije Universiteit Brussel, Brussels, Belgium
[3] Queen Mary University of London, London, UK

Abstract. "Structure" is a somewhat elusive concept in music, despite being of extreme importance in a variety of applications. Being inherently a hidden feature, it is not always explicitly considered in algorithms and representations of music. We propose a hierarchical approach to the study of musical structures, that builds upon tree representations of music like Schenkerian analysis, and adds additional layers of abstraction introducing pairwise comparisons between these trees. Finally, these representations can be joined into probabilistic representations of a music corpus. The probability distributions contained in these representation allow us to use concepts from Information Theory to show how the structures we introduce can be applied to musicological, music information retrieval applications and structure-aware music generation.

Keywords: structure · Schenkerian analysis · music representations · music generation

1 Introduction

"Structure" is a term that, even only considering music, can assume a variety of meanings. One common use of this term relates to form: the chaining of different sections to create a longer musical piece where some sections are repeated, with or without variations. Another use is more related to shorter melodic fragments, and relates to how a melody can be divided into periods, phrases, and motifs. In this latter case, a musicologist who wishes to analyze structure will try to divide the music into smaller segments and to find similarities, repetitions, inversions, parallel movements or otherwise links between these segments.

Despite the variety of information that can be gathered by such a process, this kind of analysis is often overlooked in algorithms and representation for computational musicology or music information retrieval. This becomes especially evident when computational systems try to generate novel music after learning some features of music from a given dataset of human compositions [3]. However complex or elegant the model used for the generation, we are still

© Springer Nature Switzerland AG 2023
M. Aramaki et al. (Eds.): CMMR 2021, LNCS 13770, pp. 282–300, 2023.
https://doi.org/10.1007/978-3-031-35382-6_22

far from obtaining results that are on a par with the starting material. This is generally due to the fact that while these models can capture some aspects of the music they analyze, e.g., typical melodic motifs, they fail to capture the entirety of the hierarchical, structural aspects of music. In many cases, this leads to algorithms that generate music that sounds reasonable for a short time, but seems to "wander off" as the length of the generated piece increases [4, 7, 11].

In the present work we aim to propose a novel solution to this, using a representation that builds upon existing hierarchical representations of music inspired by Schenkerian Analysis, but that goes further by operating pairwise comparisons between trees reducing small segments of music. These comparisons allow to find the kind of reuse of melodic material that we mentioned before. These structured comparisons are then further abstracted, by considering the comparisons operated on a variety of pieces rather than a single piece. These new representations describe structural regularities within a corpus, and use approaches from Information Theory to allow us to isolate more interesting features within the representation and to operate comparisons with other pieces. These regularities descriptors will then serve as guidance for music generation that considers structural aspects of music in a genetic approach.

1.1   Related Work

This work is linked to a variety of computational musicology applications. The basis for many such applications are music theory frameworks, such a Schenkerian Analysis [41] or the Generative Theory of Tonal Music [30]. These kinds of approaches form tree representations of the analyzed musical pieces, describing how different parts are linked together thorugh reductions. Other theories, such as the one proposed by Nattiez [37], follow a syntagmatic approach, where the piece is seen as a series of syntagms, basilar melodic units that can be grouped according to their resemblance.

A commonality among all these approaches is the fact that the musical piece is divided into smaller segments, which can be categorized to group similar segments and differentiate segments that have different roles within the piece [1]. Algorithms for segmenting melodies in this fashion can be directly based on music theories such as those inspired by Grouping Preference Rules from GTTM [18] which are mainly based on distance between notes and changes in duration or articulation within the local melodic context, or other theories like Temperley's Grouper model [44] which also incorporates the concept of parallelism and considers that phrases within a certain piece should have roughly the same length.

One especially successful model for segmentation is the Local Boundary Detection Model (LBDM) by Camburopoulos [6], which is based on the degree of variation between features like pitch, duration and inter-onset-interval of notes in a local context. Finding significant relationships between the segments is just as important as finding the segments themselves. The first and foremost relationship between melodic segments is that of similarity, i.e., repetition of melodic patterns, but also variations that do not alter the link between the segments [45].

The easiest approach is that of finding exact repetitions. This can be achieved by means of efficient string-based algorithms applied to textual encodings of melodies [5,25]. One way to consider non-exact repetitions as well is to take into account sub-segments, for example by using prefix-trees which allow to describe different hierarchical levels of repetition [29]. Another method is to use geometric representations of musical content, and use geometric tools to describe possible transformations between melodic segments. This approach is at the base of SIA and SIATEC [36]. which can also deal elegantly with poliphonic music, unlike most other algorithms covered above. Given the success of these algorithms, other algorithms that derive from these two can be found in literature [16,35].

Instead of focusing on the segments of a musical piece, other systems can directly implement structural and hierarchical theories, trying to give appropriate representations with ad-hoc algorithms and data structures [33].

Some researchers have applied grammar-based approaches to the computation of Schenkerian reductions, as grammars naturally allow the description of tree-like structures [27,34]. One limit to this approach is the complexity and aboundance of the rules needed to guide the process, which results in non-feasible computations [31,33]. Some researchers overcome this problem by employing markovian approaches to filter the rules [19], dynamic programming [32], or other kinds or pre-processing of the melodic material [28]. Another approach to making reduction more manageable is to use heuristic approaches. Orio and Rodà [38] perform melodic reductions by assigning weights to notes in a melody based on melodic and harmonic features and iteratively eliminating the notes with the lower weights. While the results are not actual Schenkerian analyses, the obtained reductions can be useful to other applications.

GTTM is another well-known hierarchical theory of music. One early example of using some of the rules from GTTM in a computational manner is the software Melisma Music Analyzer [44]. In order to implement the entirety of GTTM instead, it is necessary to resolve some ambiguities that are reasonable for a musicological theory but cannot be allowed in a computational system. Hamanaka et al. [20] proposed an extended version of GTTM (exGTTM) which was later implemented in software for computer assisted analysis (ATTA) or even for fully automated analysis (FATTA) [21]. More recently, deep learning was applied to learn the rules for grouping required by GTTM rather than explicitly implementing them [22].

Since the goal of this work is describing structure for music generation, it is useful to cite some relevant proposals that come from that field. GEDMAS [2] uses a top-down approach for structured generation, using Markov chains to generate the overall structure of a piece, but the melodic content itself is not part of this hierarchical structure and is generated at a later time. Other works use the opposite approach of generating melody through Markov chain and then imposing structural aspects through user-interaction [12,13]. MorpheuS [24] applies a structure to imitate a given piece, but there, structure is related to perceived tension, rather than repetition and reuse of melodic content. Deep learning techniques are often applied to melodic generation, and some researchers have given proposals on specific network topologies that can allow for more structured output [15,48], but the main downside of these approaches, besides the high computational requirements, is the fact that the learnt structures are not easily interpretable by humans and reusable in other contexts. Herremans et al. [23] propose explicit modelling of structural patterns for Ethiopian bagana songs (although the method could certainly be applied to other musical styles), and use markov chains along with optimization techniques to generate music that follows the given structural patterns. This proposal is the most similar to the one described here, but the main difference is that structure is imposed with top-down patterns instead of emerging from the analysis of a corpus, as proposed here. Finally, Wiggins [46] provides an in-depth theoretical base for the relevance of this approach to music analysis and generation, but does not provide any practical approach to perform the proposed analyses.

2 Representations

The algorithms we describe require the input corpus to be made of mono-phonic melodies with chord annotations over the melody (lead sheets). We used MusicXML format, but other formats could be appropriate as well.

The first step of the process is to segment the input pieces into segments of equal duration. Depending on the level of detail that is being investigated, a length of one or two measures can be appropriate.

Each segment is then individually analyzed, and from each a tree representing melodic reductions is built, following the algorithm described in [9,38,43]. This approach uses a sliding window that passes over the notes in the segment, and every time the window contains two or more notes, one of these is deemed the most important according to the tonality, the metric position, and the current chord. This note is kept and the others are eliminated, and the remaining note is made longer to fill the void left by the other notes. At the end of each iteration a new simplified melody is created, and the window is enlarged. At the end of the last iteration, only one note should be left. By stacking the obtained simplifications, a tree similar to those created by analyses such as the ones contained in GTTM [30] or in Schenkerian Analysis [41] is obtained. For this reason we call this tree *Schenkerian Tree* or simply *Sk_tree*.

Once the Sk_trees are built, it is possible to operate pairwise comparisons between them, comparing their roots and recursively comparing the child nodes. In particular, each node in a Sk_tree either represents a note that is present in the original melody (a leaf node) or a note that was created in the process of iterative simplification described above. In the latter case, this node has two or more children, representing the notes that were present in the previous simplification, one of which is kept and the others are eliminated, and it is possible to consider the musical interval of these children. The comparison between nodes of different Sk_trees depends on the content of this interval. The comparable features of these intervals include difference in number of child nodes, difference in pitch intervals between the children, difference in the direction of the children's intervals, or differences in the way that the Schenkerian reduction was performed (for example if the note that was saved was to the left or to the right of the child interval). Since this new structure is based on differences between different sections, we call it *Difference Tree* or *Diff_tree* Fig. 1 shows how a Diff_tree can be built from the comparison of two Sk_trees.

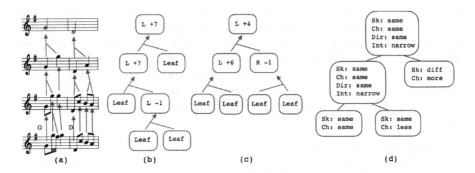

Fig. 1. One example of a simplified diff_tree (d), constructed from two sk_trees (b and c), each representing one of the two measures of the excerpt (a).

For each input piece, a set of $\frac{(n-1)(n)}{2}$ Diff_trees are produced, where n is the number of segments the input piece is divided into. This number is due to the fact that the segments are not compared with themselves nor the segments prior to them, but only with segments that come later in the musical piece, so not all the n^2 possible comparisons are performed. Each Diff_tree is then labelled to indicate which segments are compared in that tree (e.g. if the first and fourth segments are compared, the tree is labeled '0–3'). Once the Diff_trees for a set of pieces are produced, the Diff_trees that share the same label (i.e., that refer to segments in the same position but coming from different pieces) can be joined together into a single tree, that abstracts the general development of that particular comparison. For this reason, we call this representation an *Abstraction Tree* or *Abs_tree*. The procedure works as follows: a new node which will be the root of the Abs_tree is created. Starting from the root of all considered Diff_trees, for each of the possible features, the new node annotates all the possible values that the feature assumes in all the given Diff_trees and the number of occurrences of those values. The new node also annotates how many children the roots of the given Diff_trees have, as a new separate feature. Then the algorithm repeats recursively as long as at least one Diff_tree node has at least one child node. Once the recursion process is complete, it is possible to compute the probability of each value v for each feature in each node, using the following Bayes Estimator [42]:

$$p(v) = \frac{occ(v) + \beta}{tot + \beta * size} \tag{1}$$

where $occ(v)$ is the number of occurrences of the value v, while *tot* and *size* are respectively the total of samples for that feature and the number of possible

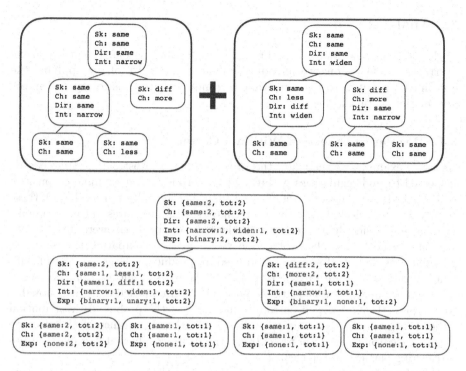

Fig. 2. A simplified Abs_tree built from the two Diff_trees on top. For readability, the tree reports frequencies of occurrence and the total number of observation rather than the probabilities that need to be computed with the Bayesian Estimator. The colors represent the tree from which each value for each feature comes: blue for left-side tree, red for the right-side one, and purple for those values that are found in both. (Color figure online)

distinct values for that feature. β was set to 1. All the features for which *tot* is less than a certain threshold (we used 5 in the experiments described below) can be removed as those features would entail too little information about the corpus. The nodes that remain empty because of this can be removed as well. Figure 2 shows a simplified example of an Abs_tree built from two Diff_trees. This process basically creates a probability distribution for each node, consisting of a set of stochastic variables depending on the features present in the Diff_trees. Because of this the Abs_tree is similar to a Markov Model, but rather than having the probability distributions vary in time depending only on the previous state, the only feature that determines the distribution is the position on the tree. For this reason, it would be misleading to think of an Abs_tree as a chain or an automaton, and it is best to only view it as a static probabilistic description of a musical corpus.

3   Analysis

In this section, we demonstrate, through example applications, the utility of the abstract representations we introduced as an analytical tool, by applying the explained structures to tasks relevant to computational musicology and music information retrieval.

3.1   Regularity Detection Within a Corpus

As a first example, we show how the above introduced Abstraction Trees can be inspected to find regularities within a given corpus. As an example corpus, we will use the Leone dataset, a set of twenty-four baroque allemandes [14]. Of these twenty-four we selected the twenty that have sixteen measures in total, to make comparisons easier thanks to the equal length. All the pieces were divided into two-bar segments and the abstraction trees pairwise comparing the segments were built as described above. The procedure produces a large amount of data which is difficult to interpret on its own, but the tools of information theory can help find the most relevant features. For each feature in each node, it is possible to compute the normalized entropy (efficiency) of the probability distribution it describes, which gives a useful indication of the importance of that feature within the corpus. The lower the entropy, the more strictly that feature describes a recurring element in the corpus.

For example, as can be seen in Fig. 3, looking at the mean normalized entropy of all the constructed abstraction trees, it becomes evident that the tree comparing segments 0 and 2 (shown in figure) and the one comparing segments 4 and 6 are the most regular ones. In those trees, almost each feature is set to "same", meaning that there are little or no differences between the above mentioned pairs of segments. Indeed, the phrases in this corpus tend to repeat after 4 measures (the distance between the start of segments 0 and 2), and that is captured by the abstraction tree. Moreover, while the phrases repeat, their ending is varied to make for more definitive phrase endings. This is captured in the abstraction tree comparing segments 1 and 7 (shown in figure) where the left side of the tree shows a repetition like the one described above, but in the right side of the tree the most relevant feature is the one describing the ending grade, which is usually the tonic, as expected from the closing of a musical period.

3.2   Genre Discrimination

The following example uses another metric commonly used in Information Theory. While entropy is related to regularity in a probability distribution, Information Content gives an indication of how unexpected a certain outcome is with respect to a given probability distribution. Since musical cognition is strongly related to expectation [26], this metric becomes a relevant indicator when analyzing musical pieces [39]. In this experiment, we learnt a set of abstraction trees from the 20 allemandes taken from the corpus mentioned above, and the difference trees from a set of 20 reels from the Nottingham Dataset [17], and from

Fig. 3. A table summing up the mean entropy of each abstraction tree derived from the corpus, and some examples of abstraction trees as a text output of the software. Only the first three levels were kept for readability. The labels of the tree represent the compared segments: for example "0–1" means that the first two bars of a piece are compared to measures 3 and 4, since in this case each segment was two measures long.

20 jazz pieces composed between 1921 and 1930 taken from the EWLD corpus [43]. The abstraction trees contain probability distributions for each feature in each node, while difference trees can be considered as outcomes for the same features. This means that for each feature it is possible to compute the information content. To give a single measure of the total information content of a difference tree compared to an abstraction tree, the mean of all the features in a node is computed to give the information content of a single node, and the mean of all the information contents across nodes is computed to give the general information content of a tree. This latter mean is also weighted by the mean entropy of the nodes, and by an added coefficient that makes nodes lower in the tree less important than nodes in the upper part of the tree ($depth\_k$ in the formula below). The total formula is described below, where $p(diff\_tree\_feature)$ represents the probability $p(v)$ (computed according to the estimator 1) of the value v found for the considered feature f in the diff_tree node.

$$ic(tree) = \frac{\sum_{node \in tree} ic(node) \frac{1}{ent(node)} * depth\_k(node)}{\sum_{node \in tree} \frac{1}{ent(node)} * depth\_k(node)} \tag{2}$$

$$ic(node) = \sum_{f \in node} \frac{-\log_2(p(diff\_tree\_feature))}{ent(f)} \tag{3}$$

Information Content comparison between corpora

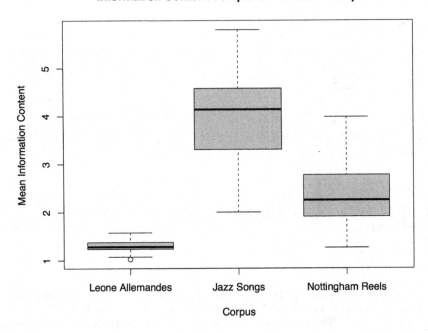

Fig. 4. Comparison of the mean information content computed from each of the three sets of twenty musical pieces. Mean refers to the mean of the trees of a single piece, rather than the mean of an entire corpus.

$$ent(node) = \frac{\sum_{f \in node} ent(f)}{number\_of\_features\_in\_node} \qquad (4)$$

$$ent(f) = \sum_{v \in alphabet(f)} -\log_2(p(v))p(v) \qquad (5)$$

Figure 4 shows the results of the comparisons. Since computing the information content of a piece included in the abstraction tree would be an unfair advantage, similarly to the bias one would get by evaluating a machine learning model using the same dataset that was used for learning the model, an approach similar to a k-fold validation was used. The allemande corpus was split into four parts of 5 pieces, and the information content of each piece was computed with respect to the abstraction trees built solely on the 15 pieces outside the considered allemande's group. This means that there were actually four sets of abstraction trees built each on a different subset of 15 pieces. The values for the other two groups (Jazz and Nottingham) were computed on all the four sets and the mean is reported.

The results clearly show that this approach is capable of detecting the structural differences between the corpora. The allemandes show a strong structural regularity, that is not found in the other pieces. As expected, the reels from the Nottingham dataset are less unexpected than the jazz pieces, since they too have some structural regularities that are not always found in jazz pieces. It is worth noting that being based on difference trees, what this system captures is the general structure of the piece and how much reuse of melodic material is present, rather than comparing for instance the regularities in the melodies and how typical they are for each genre, possibly making this metric a complementary indicator that could be used in combination with other approaches in genre detection, and possibly for the goal of estimating how well a generation system respects a given style [8].

4 Generation

The representations described above only serve as an analysis tool. They cannot be immediately employed as a generation tool since most of the information that is represented is related to structure and do not prescribe ways in which a melody can be constructed. Yet, its analytical power can be used to discriminate typical structures within a certain genre, as shown in the Genre Distinction task explained above. The music generation approach described here uses the same idea of using Information Content to find typicality of structures, but embedded within a genetic algorithm. This algorithm first generates some melodies, and then uses Information Content as the fitness function to choose those melodies that are more fit to be a continuation of the starting melodies given the genre of the analyzed corpus, so that the final generated piece will show a satisfactory long-term structure.

The generation process functions as follows:

Step Zero: Construct the required data structures from a given corpus.
Step One: One starting segment lasting two bars is generated.
   Other segments are generated with the following steps, until the specified length is reached.
Step Two: Generate some segments using the same procedure as the one above, to create a pool of candidates. Add to the candidates pool all the segments that constitute the piece so far.
Step Three: Mutate the pieces in the candidates pool. For each of the candidates, 5 mutations are generated, by selecting at random the operations: note deletion, note insertion, change of rhythm, change of pitch.
Step Four: Evaluate the Information Content of all the candidates. If for one continuation the information content is below a certain threshold, a winner is found. Otherwise, the pool is reinitialized with the 5 best results and 5 new segments, and the process repeats from Step Three.

The following sections will describe the above points in more detail.

4.1   Corpus Analysis and Generation of Melodic Beginning

Step Zero. For this process to function, it is necessary to have an input corpus that must be analyzed following the process described in Sect. 2. Each piece in the given corpus is divided into segments lasting two measures, and a Sk_tree is built for each segment. For each piece a set of Diff_trees are constructed, and finally the Abs_trees that represent the entire corpus can be computed. In addition to those structures, that only deal with structural representations, this algorithm extracts some additional data for the construction of melodies.

The first of such structures is a first-order Markov chain learnt from the notes at the topmost layer of the reductions operated on the segmented corpus. After the reduction process for the construction of Sk_trees, each segment is reduced to only one note, and thus the piece is reduced to a sequence of N notes where N is the number of segments in the piece. A first order Markov chain is built to replicate this sequence, that is needed as input for the following operations. We can call this chain the `Top_chain`. The Top_chain also saves the probability for each of the symbols in the chain to be found as the reduction of the first segment of a piece, by counting how many times each symbol is found in the first segment's reduction.

Additionally, a set of first-order Markov chains is constructed by analyzing the pitch sequences in each of the segments. Instead of learning just one chain for these melodies, a chain for each of the symbols found in the Top_chain is built. This is done to preserve the fact that melodies can have different developments depending on the underlying structure of the piece, represented here by the reduced note. Notice that prior to the segmentation, as required by the algorithms for the construction of the tree structures, all the pieces are transposed to the key of C Major/A minor, so that the reduced note is significantly comparable across all pieces. Additionally, the surface chains also save the probability for each symbol in the chain to be found at the start of the melody, by simply counting the occurrences of each note at the beginning of a segment. We can call these chains `Surface_chain`, and, for example, we can refer to the one built for those segments that are reduced to the note C by writing `Surface_chain[C]`.

The above Markov chains only consider pitch in their alphabets. This is fine for the Top_chain, that describes abstract notes, but for the construction of melodies it is necessary to consider rhythmic aspects as well [10]. In this work, a list of all the rhythmic sequences found in the segments of the corpus were collected, so that it is possible to select one at random when adding a rhythm to a melody.

Step One. All of the above chains and representations can be computed beforehand, and the resulting model can be used to generate any number of pieces. Once such a model is available, the generation process starts by creating a sequence of notes via the Top_chain. The resulting piece will have twice as many measures as the notes generated in this sequence. The resulting sequence is called the Top_sequence The first note from which to start the Top_sequence can be chosen beforehand (C is a reasonable choice) or it can be chosen at random using the saved probability for the beginning symbol.

The first segment is then generated. To do so, a rhythmic pattern is chosen at random from the rhythmic list. Then the surface chain is used to generate an appropriate amount of notes, starting from a note chosen at random using the probabilities saved for the beginning note. For this operation the surface chain labelled with the first note of the Top_sequence is used:

```
Surface_chain[Top_sequence[0]].
```

4.2   Generation of a Pool of Continuations

Step Two. Each of the segments beyond the first one are generated via a Genetic algorithm. A pool of candidates is built for this process, and a winner is selected within this pool. The pool is initialised with five segments that are generated using the same process described above, i.e., by choosing a rhythm from the model's rhythmic list and generating pitches selected with the appropriate Surface_chain. Notice that the selection of the chain depends on the note found in the Top_sequence in the position that corresponds to the segment that is being generated. Additionally, all of the segments that were already included in the piece are added to the pool, as well as a transposed version of the same in the case where the note in the Top_sequence differs. For example, if the third segment is being generated, and the Top_sequence looks like this: [C4, D4, C4], both the first and the second segments are added to the candidates pool, but a copy of the second segment transposed down by 2 semitones (the interval between D4 and C4) is added as well. This allows the algorithm to create melodic progressions (should this copy be chosen as a winner).

Step Three. For each of the candidates in the pool, 5 mutated segments are generated. The possible operations performed to mutate the segments are:

Note deletion: randomly select one note from the segment and delete it. The length of the previous note (or the following, if the deleted note was the first) increases by the length of the deleted note.

Note Insertion: randomly select one note from the segment. That note's length is halved, and a new note is generated (using the appropriate Surface_chain) to fill the void.

Change of Pitch: randomly select one note from the segment and delete it. A new note is generated to fill the void, using the appropriate Surface_chain if there is a preceding note or using the probability for the beginning note if the deleted note was the first.

Change of Rhythm: a new rhythm is chosen from the rhythmic list. If the previous rhythm had more notes, delete the last notes that would not be used. If the previous rhythm had less notes, add notes to fill the void by using the appropriate Surface_chain.

The amount of mutation operations applied to one segments varies with the number of the mutations that were already generated. That means that the first mutation for the segment has one operation, the following two, and so on until the last one that undergoes five operations.

4.3   Genetic Approach to Select Continuation

Step Four. Evaluate the Information Content of all the candidates. To do so, a diff_tree between the candidate and all the segments in the piece so far must be constructed, and those diff_trees are evaluated against the abs_trees learnt on the corpus (see Fig. 5). If the average information content is below a certain threshold, a winner is found.

Otherwise, the 5 best results are kept in the candidate pool and the others are eliminated. Five additional new segments are generated with the process described above, and are added to the pool. The process repeats from Step Three, meaning that each of the candidates in the new pool gets mutated five times before the evaluation restarts.

After ten generations, if the desired threshold is not reached, the computation is halted to avoid plateaus.

4.4   Example Results

Figure 6 shows one example of what the generation system described above is capable of creating. It is possible to see that the system managed to create a tune with a similar structure to the corpus of allemandes [14]. For example, the first two measures are repeated in the fifth and sixth measures (segment 3), as is the case for many pieces from the corpus. The ending of measure 8 and 16 fall on the tonic, variating from the previous segments. We can also see that the second part of the allemande is somewhat more free than the first part, with measure thirteen and fourteen being rather different from the rest. This reflects the fact that in the corpus the second section of the tunes is less regular than the first half.

The main shortcoming of this generated allemande is the presence of large melodic intervals, which are indeed present in the corpus (otherwise those could not have been generated by the Markovian approach), but are usually justified by melodic progressions leading to those intervals, or happen with longer notes that allow the player to move the hand the required amount in time. These intervals make the generated allemande rather unfriendly for a beginner player, which is not the case for the ones in the corpus. The use of an extremely simple algorithm for melodic generation (first order Markov chains) may be the cause of the unfitting melodies, and this could possibly be solved by using more refined algorithm in the segment generation phase, as well as in the mutation phase. On the bright side, the fact that the final output is reasonable despite the use of such a simple approach to melodic generation shows the potential of the structural fitness system.

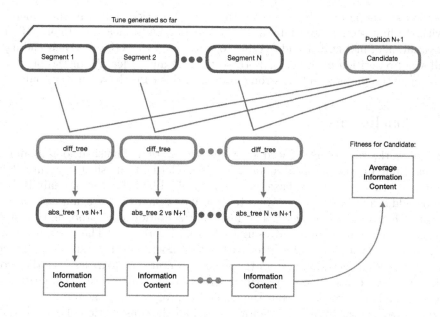

Fig. 5. The process of the construction of the fitness for a new candidate. For each of the already generated segments, a diff_tree must be constructed which will be used to compute the information content with respect to the relative abstraction tree.

Fig. 6. One allemande generated with the system.

Fig. 7. One reel generated with the system.

Figure 7 shows one additional example. In this case, the system was primed with reels from the Nottingham Dataset [17]. In this example it is possible to clearly distinguish and A and a B sections. As customary in this style, the B section shows more embellishments than the A section, but remains coherent with the first section especially in how the period ends: measures 15 and 16 are a variation of measures 7 and 8, tying together the two sections in their endings, allowing repetition of either or both sections in any order. As in the previous example, the phrases end on strong grades, in this case always on the tonic.

5   Conclusions

In this work, we have introduced a novel representation of musical content aimed at encoding in a hierarchical manner features relating to musical structure. The approach builds upon tree-based methods inspired by Schenkerian analysis, but adds additional abstraction layers to describe regularities in a musical corpus rather than in a single piece. The final representation uses probability distributions, that can be analyzed using tools from Information Theory as we show through two examples in the latter part of the paper, and that can be applied to guide a music generation system to impose structural regularities over the produced pieces. The system as described here is capable of detecting regularities in a simple allemande corpus, but the general approach can be adapted to a variety of specific algorithms: the algorithm used for the construction of Schenkerian trees could be changed, as well as the set of features used to compare them and build the Difference trees, potentially adapting to different kinds of music and different analysis needs. One drawback of the current implementation is that it is based by design choice on a fixed window length, making it harder to capture smaller structural features. An algorithm for segmentation could be embedded in the system to detect the best subdivision of a piece, but the general algorithm would need to be modified to adapt to segments of unequal length.

The representation system was applied to the goal of Music Generation, to create folk music showing convincing structure. The limits of this representation, that does not consider harmony, rhythm, and other key features of music, required the use of additional algorithms and knowledge representations, taken from literature. While these additional methods were not particularly innovative nor sophisticated, the use of information content applied to the structural representations allowed for convincing results. A genetic approach to generation was used, where the information content was at the basis of the fitness function, to select continuations to a generated melody that resulted in a plausible structure given the learnt corpus. Genetic algorithms are not commonly used in recent literature for music generation, and some question their usefulness within this context [11,40,47]. Yet, this work exemplifies how this approach can be useful when dealing with complex features (such as information content) that cannot be easily imposed by construction on a given melody.

While this work is not meant to give a comprehensive descriptor of all musical aspects of a corpus, we believe that this contribution might help formalizing some facets of music that are sometimes overlooked in favour of more prominent features such as melody, rhythm, and harmony.

Acknowledgments. FC received funding from the University of Padova, from Fondazione Ing. Aldo Gini, and from the Department of Information Engineering of the University of Padova. NH, ST and GW received funding from the Flemish Government under the "Onderzoeksprogramma Artificiële Intelligentie (AI) Vlaanderen" programme.

References

1. Abdallah, S., Gold, N., Marsden, A.: Analysing symbolic music with probabilistic grammars. In: Computational Music Analysis, pp. 157–189. Springer, Cham (2016). https://doi.org/10.1007/978-3-319-25931-4_7
2. Anderson, C., Eigenfeldt, A., Pasquier, P.: The generative electronic dance music algorithmic system (GEDMAS). In: Proceedings of the Artificial Intelligence and Interactive Digital Entertainment (AIIDE'13) Conference, p. 4. AAAI Press, Boston, MA (2013)
3. Briot, J.P., Hadjeres, G., Pachet, F.D.: Deep Learning Techniques for Music Generation. Computational Synthesis and Creative Systems. Springer International Publishing, New York, NY (2020). https://doi.org/10.1007/978-3-319-70163-9, https://www.springer.com/gp/book/9783319701622
4. Briot, J.-P., Pachet, F.: Deep learning for music generation: challenges and directions. Neural Comput. Appl. **32**(4), 981–993 (2018). https://doi.org/10.1007/s00521-018-3813-6
5. Cambouropoulos, E.: Towards a general computational theory of musical structure. Ph.D. thesis, Ph.D. thesis, University of Edinburgh (1998)
6. Cambouropoulos, E.: The local boundary detection model (LBDM) and its application in the study of expressive timing. In: ICMC, p. 8 (2001)
7. Carnovalini, F.: Open challenges in musical metacreation. In: Proceedings of the 5th EAI International Conference on Smart Objects and Technologies for Social Good, pp. 124–125. ACM, Valencia Spain, September 2019. https://doi.org/10.1145/3342428.3342678, http://dl.acm.org/doi/10.1145/3342428.3342678
8. Carnovalini, F., Harley, N., Homer, S.T., Rodà, A., Wiggins, G.A.: Meta-evaluating quantitative internal evaluation: a practical approach for developers. In: Proceedings of the 12th International Conference on Computational Creativity, p. 5. Association for Computational Creativity, México Virtual, September 2021. https://computationalcreativity.net/iccc21/wp-content/uploads/2021/09/ICCC_2021_paper_98.pdf
9. Carnovalini, F., Rodà, A.: A multilayered approach to automatic music generation and expressive performance. In: 2019 International Workshop on Multilayer Music Representation and Processing (MMRP), pp. 41–48. IEEE, Milano, Italy, January 2019. https://doi.org/10.1109/MMRP.2019.00016, https://ieeexplore.ieee.org/document/8665367/
10. Carnovalini, F., Rodà, A.: A real-time tempo and meter tracking system for rhythmic improvisation. In: Proceedings of the 14th International Audio Mostly Conference: A Journey in Sound, pp. 24–31. ACM, Nottingham United Kingdom, September 2019. https://doi.org/10.1145/3356590.3356596, https://dl.acm.org/doi/10.1145/3356590.3356596
11. Carnovalini, F., Rodà, A.: Computational creativity and music generation systems: an introduction to the state of the art. Front. Artif. Intell. **3**, 14 (2020). https://doi.org/10.3389/frai.2020.00014, https://www.frontiersin.org/article/10.3389/frai.2020.00014/full

12. Carnovalini, F., Rodà, A., Caneva, P.: A musical serious game for social interaction through augmented rhythmic improvisation. In: Proceedings of the 5th EAI International Conference on Smart Objects and Technologies for Social Good, pp. 130–135. ACM, Valencia Spain, September 2019. https://doi.org/10.1145/3342428.3342683, http://dl.acm.org/doi/10.1145/3342428.3342683

13. Carnovalini, F., Rodà, A., Caneva, P.: A rhythm-aware serious game for social interaction. Multimed. Tools Appl. (2022). https://doi.org/10.1007/s11042-022-13372-3, https://link.springer.com/10.1007/s11042-022-13372-3

14. Carnovalini, F., Rodà, A., Harley, N., Homer, S.T., Wiggins, G.A.: A new corpus for computational music research and a novel method for musical structure analysis. In: Audio Mostly 2021 (AM 2021), p. 4. ACM, virtual/Trento Italy (2021). https://doi.org/10.1145/3478384.3478402

15. Chen, K., Zhang, W., Dubnov, S., Xia, G., Li, W.: The effect of explicit structure encoding of deep neural networks for symbolic music generation. In: 2019 International Workshop on Multilayer Music Representation and Processing (MMRP), pp. 77–84. IEEE (2019)

16. Forth, J., Wiggins, G.A.: An approach for identifying salient repetition in multidimensional representations of polyphonic music. In: London Algorithms 2008: Theory and Practice. College Publications (2009)

17. Foxley, E.: Nottingham Database (2011). https://ifdo.ca/seymour/nottingham/nottingham.html

18. Frankland, B.W., Cohen, A.J.: Parsing of melody: quantification and testing of the local grouping rules of Lerdahl and Jackendoff's a generative theory of tonal music. Music Percept. **21**, 499–543 (2004)

19. Gilbert, É., Conklin, D.: A probabilistic context-free grammar for melodic reduction. In: Proceedings of the International Workshop on Artificial Intelligence and Music, 20th International Joint Conference on Artificial Intelligence, pp. 83–94 (2007)

20. Hamanaka, M., Hirata, K., Tojo, S.: Implementing "A generative theory of tonal music". J. New Music Res. **35**(4), 249–277 (2006)

21. Hamanaka, M., Hirata, K., Tojo, S.: FATTA: full automatic time-span tree analyzer. In: ICMC, pp. 153–156. Citeseer (2007)

22. Hamanaka, M., Hirata, K., Tojo, S.: deepGTTM-III: multi-task learning with grouping and metrical structures. In: Aramaki, M., Davies, M.E.P., Kronland-Martinet, R., Ystad, S. (eds.) CMMR 2017. LNCS, vol. 11265, pp. 238–251. Springer, Cham (2018). https://doi.org/10.1007/978-3-030-01692-0_17

23. Herremans, D., Weisser, S., Sörensen, K., Conklin, D.: Generating structured music for bagana using quality metrics based on Markov models. Expert Syst. Appl. **42**(21), 7424–7435 (2015). https://doi.org/10.1016/j.eswa.2015.05.043, https://www.sciencedirect.com/science/article/pii/S0957417415003796

24. Herremans, D., Chew, E.: MorpheuS: generating structured music with constrained patterns and tension. IEEE Trans. Affect. Comput. **10**(4), 16 (2017). https://doi.org/10.1109/TAFFC.2017.2737984, http://ieeexplore.ieee.org/document/8007229/

25. Hsu, J.L., Chen, A.L.P., Liu, C.C.: Efficient repeating pattern finding in music databases. In: Proceedings of the Seventh International Conference on Information and Knowledge Management, pp. 281–288. CIKM 1998, Association for Computing Machinery, New York, NY, USA (1998). https://doi.org/10.1145/288627.288668, https://doi.org/10.1145/288627.288668

26. Huron, D.: Sweet Anticipation: Music and the Psychology of Expectation. MIT Press, Cambridge, January 2008

27. Kassler, M.: Proving musical theorems I: The middleground of Heinrich Schenker's theory of tonality. Basser Department of Computer Science, School of Physics, University of Sydney (1975)
28. Kirlin, P.B., Utgoff, P.E.: A framework for automated schenkerian analysis. In: ISMIR, pp. 363–368 (2008)
29. Lartillot, O.: Automated motivic analysis: an exhaustive approach based on closed and cyclic pattern mining in multidimensional parametric spaces. In: Computational Music Analysis, pp. 273–302. Springer, Cham (2016). https://doi.org/10.1007/978-3-319-25931-4_11
30. Lerdahl, F., Jackendoff, R.S.: A Generative Theory of Tonal Music. MIT Press, Cambridge, MA (1985)
31. Marsden, A.: Automatic derivation of musical structure: a tool for research on schenkerian analysis. In: ISMIR, pp. 55–58 (2007)
32. Marsden, A.: Schenkerian analysis by computer: a proof of concept. J. New Music Res. 39(3), 269–289 (2010). https://doi.org/10.1080/09298215.2010.503898, http://www.tandfonline.com/doi/abs/10.1080/09298215.2010.503898
33. Marsden, A., Hirata, K., Tojo, S.: Towards computable procedures for deriving tree structures in music: context dependency in GTTM and Schenkerian theory. In: Proceedings of the Sound and Music Computing Conference 2013, pp. 360–367. KTH Royal Institute of Technology, Stockholm, Sweden (2013)
34. Mavromatis, P., Brown, M.: Parsing context-free grammars for music: a computational model of schenkerian analysis. In: Proceedings of the 8th International Conference on Music Perception & Cognition, pp. 414–415 (2004)
35. Meredith, D.: Cosiatec and siateccompress: pattern discovery by geometric compression. In: Music Information Retrieval Evaluation eXchange (MIREX 2013). International Society for Music Information Retrieval (2013). international Society for Music Information Retrieval Conference, ISMIR 2013; Conference date: 04-11-2013 Through 08-11-2013
36. Meredith, D., Lemström, K., Wiggins, G.A.: Algorithms for discovering repeated patterns in multidimensional representations of polyphonic music. J. New Music Res. 31(4), 321–345 (2002). https://doi.org/10.1076/jnmr.31.4.321.14162
37. Nattiez, J.J.: Fondements d'une sémiologie de la Musique. Union Générale d'Editons (1975)
38. Orio, N., Roda, A.: A measure of melodic similarity based on a graph representation of the music structure. In: ISMIR, pp. 543–548. ISMIR, Kobe, Japan (2009)
39. Pearce, M., Wiggins, G.A.: Expectation in melody: the influence of context and learning. Music Percept. 23, 377–405 (2006)
40. Phon-Amnuaisuk, S., Tuson, A., Wiggins, G.: Evolving musical harmonisation. In: Dobnikar, A., Steele, N.C., Pearson, D.W., Albrecht, R.F. (eds.) Artificial Neural Nets and Genetic Algorithms, pp. 229–234. Springer, Vienna (1999). https://doi.org/10.1007/978-3-7091-6384-9_39
41. Schenker, H.: Free Composition (Der freie Satz). Longman Music Series, Longman, New York, NY, USA (1935)
42. Schürmann, T., Grassberger, P.: Entropy estimation of symbol sequences. Chaos Interdiscip. J. Nonlinear Sci. 6(3), 414–427 (1996). https://doi.org/10.1063/1.166191, http://aip.scitation.org/doi/10.1063/1.166191
43. Simonetta, F., Carnovalini, F., Orio, N., Rodà, A.: Symbolic music similarity through a graph-based representation. In: Proceedings of the Audio Mostly 2018 on Sound in Immersion and Emotion - AM 2018, pp. 1–7. ACM Press, Wrexham, United Kingdom (2018). https://doi.org/10.1145/3243274.3243301, http://dl.acm.org/citation.cfm?doid=3243274.3243301

44. Temperley, D.: The Cognition of Basic Musical Structures. MIT Press, Cambridge, Massachusetts (2004). 1. paperback ed edn. oCLC: 255948904

45. Wiggins, G.A.: Models of musical similarity. Musicae Scientiae **11**(1 suppl), 315–338 (2007). https://doi.org/10.1177/102986490701100112

46. Wiggins, G.A.: Structure, abstraction and reference in artificial musical intelligence. In: Miranda, E.R. (ed.) Handbook of Artificial Intelligence for Music, pp. 409–422. Springer, Cham (2021). https://doi.org/10.1007/978-3-030-72116-9_15

47. Wiggins, G.A., Papadopoulos, G., Phon-Amnuaisuk, S., Tuson, A.: Evolutionary methods for musical composition. University of Edinburgh, Department of Artificial Intelligence (1998)

48. Zixun, G., Makris, D., Herremans, D.: Hierarchical recurrent neural networks for conditional melody generation with long-term structure. In: 2021 International Joint Conference on Neural Networks (IJCNN), pp. 1–8 (2021). https://doi.org/10.1109/IJCNN52387.2021.9533493

Analysis of Musical Dynamics in Vocal Performances

Jyoti Narang[✉], Marius Miron, Xavier Lizarraga, and Xavier Serra

Universitat Pompeu Fabra, Barcelona, Spain
jyoti.narang@upf.edu

Abstract. Dynamics are one of the fundamental tools of expressivity in a performance. While the usage of this tool is highly subjective, a systematic methodology to derive loudness markings based on a performance can be highly beneficial. With this goal in mind, this paper is a first step towards developing a methodology to automatically transcribe dynamic markings from vocal rock and pop performances. To this end, we make use of commercial recordings of some popular songs followed by source separation and compare them to the karaoke versions of the same songs. The dynamic variations in the original commercial recordings are found to be structurally very similar to the aligned karaoke/multi-track versions of the same tracks. We compare and show the differences between tracks using statistical analysis, with an eventual goal to use the transcribed markings as guiding tools, to help students adapt with a specific interpretation of a given piece of music. We perform a qualitative analysis of the proposed methodology with the teachers in terms of informativeness and accuracy.

Keywords: Vocal Performance Assessment · Music Education · Loudness Measurement · Dynamics Transcription

1 Introduction

Musical expression is an integral part of any performance. The subjective nature of this term makes it difficult to identify "whether the expressive deviations measured are due to deliberate expressive strategies, musical structure, motor noise, imprecision of the performer, or even measurement errors" [15]. While the choice of expressions used may vary from performer to performer and also from performance to performance, deriving the expressions used in a specific interpretation of a performance can offer significant advances in the realm of music education. Not only can it help students learn from a specific musical piece, insights about the variations in expressions can add to possible set of choices that one can employ during a performance.

With the advent of online practice tools like music minus one, audio accompaniments, users have a wide variety of mediums to chose to practice with [7]. However, most of these tools are limited to pitch and rhythm correctness,

© Springer Nature Switzerland AG 2023
M. Aramaki et al. (Eds.): CMMR 2021, LNCS 13770, pp. 301–311, 2023.
https://doi.org/10.1007/978-3-031-35382-6_23

offering little or no insight about the expressive variations of the performance. In this work, we focus on deriving the dynamic variations of vocal rock and pop performances via loudness feature extracted from the audio recordings. The goal of this paper is to develop a methodology to extract and compare the dynamic variations of similar pieces of vocal performances that can lay the foundation of transcribing dynamic markings of vocal performances.

This overall idea can be broken down into a set of 2 questions that we intend to address through our work.

(i) Given a mix, is it possible to transcribe dynamics using the source separated voice signal with the same accuracy as would be achieved when the vocal stem of the mix is available?

(ii) Can we analyze the similarities and differences between two loudness curves in order to provide feedback on dynamics?

In order to address the first question, we use state of the art source separation algorithms to extract vocal tracks from mixes followed by loudness computation, and compare them to the loudness curves of the vocal stems available for the same mix. To address the second question, we have conducted a preliminary experiment comparing the loudness curves of the source separated commercial mixes with multi-track karaoke versions with vocal stems. Overall the structure of the paper is as follows. Section 2 presents some fundamental information about the kind of loudness scales and the study of dynamics in music information retrieval. In Sect. 3, we describe a methodology of the proposed approach followed by preliminary investigation of the comparison of loudness curves in Sect. 4. The influence of vocal source separation on loudness computation is also presented in Sect. 4.

In Sect. 5, we conduct a case study where the dynamic variations of the two versions (karaoke and commercial) have been analyzed by a teacher to give feedback followed by Sect. 6 with conclusions and future work.

2   Background and Related Work

Significant work has been done to model performance dynamics by measuring the loudness variations [2] with a conclusion that the variations in dynamics are not linear. Several measurement techniques have been defined to measure the loudness of signals.

2.1   Loudness Measurement Scales

Of the scales available for loudness measurement, some are inspired by the subjective psychoacoustic phenomenon of human ear, while others are objective in terms of measurement. The most commonly used measurement is the dBFS scale, or loudness unit full scale. The more recently adopted industry standard is the EBUR scale [6]. For our analysis, we make use of the sone scale, which is based on psychoacoustic model, and compare our results to RMS values computed from the signals directly.

Sone Scale. This scale is inspired by the psychoacoustic concept of equal loudness curves, with the measurement being linear i.e. doubling of the perceived loudness doubles the sone value [1]. While the phon scale is more closely associated with dB scale, a phon value of 40 translates to 1 sone. The relationship between phons and sons can be modelled using the equation:

$$S = \begin{cases} 2^{(L-40)/10}, & \text{if } P >= 40. \\ (L/40)^{2.642}, & P < 40. \end{cases} \tag{1}$$

RMS. RMS or root mean square is the square root of the mean square of the amplitude of the signal.

$$RMS = sqrt((x_1^2 + x_2^2 .... x_n^2)/N) \tag{2}$$

2.2   Dynamics in Music Information Retrieval

Work on measurement of dynamics has been typically centered around Western Classical piano performances, incorporating dynamics as an expressive performance parameter that can vary across performers/performances [19]. Kosta et al. [14] used change-point detection algorithm to measure dynamic variations from audio performances and compared them to the markings in the score. Further, they applied machine learning approaches like decision trees, support vector machines (SVM), artificial neural networks [12] to predict loudness levels corresponding to the dynamic markings in the score. They found that the loudness values can be predicted relatively well when trained across recordings of similar pieces, while failing when trained across pianists' other performances.

Another approach to model dynamics is using linear basis functions to encode structural information from the score [9]. Each of the "basis function" stand for one score marking like *stacatto, crescendo*, the active state being a representation of the expressive marking present in the score and vice-versa. Chacón et al. [5] carry out a large scale evaluation of expressive dynamics on piano and orchestral music using linear and non-linear models.

3   Methodology

A diagram of the proposed methodology is presented in Fig. 1. In case solely the mix is available, the input audio mix is passed to a source separation algorithm, U-Net [11] to get the separated vocal track. Thereafter, we extract the loudness from the separated vocal track or vocal stem using the sone scale and RMS as described earlier. The loudness extraction for the sone scale is carried out in the same way as proposed by Kosta et al. [14] in their analysis. Each of the loudness curves are normalized by dividing with the max value for the rendition in order to carry out a fair relative comparison between different renditions. This step makes sure that only the relative values are compared and not the absolute ones. Finally, we apply peak picking operation to get a range of overall dynamics that can be further processed to map to specific dynamics based on musicological knowledge. It is to be noted that we limit the current set of experiments to comparison of loudness curves, leaving the actual mapping of loudness values to musically meaningful values as future work.

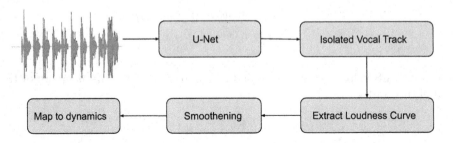

Fig. 1. Methodology for extracting loudness from a mix.

4   Experiments

4.1   Data Curation

We have primarily used three sources of data for our analysis:

(i) Commercial official recordings of rock and pop songs
(ii) Custom karaoke tracks from the site[1] exactly replicating the official tracks
(iii) Musdb dataset to validate the efficacy of source separation algorithm

To evaluate the impact of singing voice source separation we use the musdb dataset containing 150 multi-track songs. For the commercial recordings, we conducted a preliminary investigation with 7 popular tracks shown in Table 1. For the commercial popular recordings, only the mixes are available while for the karaoke versions, we have access to all the stems. This leads to 3 sources of data for the analysis of the same tracks - source separated vocals from the commercial mix (CSS), source separated vocals from the karaoke mix (KSS), vocal stems from the karaoke stems (KSV).

4.2   Experimental Setup

As mentioned above in the methodology, we first apply source separation using the spleeter implementation of UNet [10] to separate the mix into two stems - vocal track and the accompaniment. This step is skipped in case vocal stems are available for analysis. We use a block size of 512 samples or 11 ms with a hanning window, and a hop size of 256 samples or 5.5 ms. We follow the same block and hop size for the sone scale as well as RMS values. For loudness extraction using

---

[1] https://www.karaoke-version.com/.

the sone scale, we use ma_sone function in Elias Pampalk's Music Analysis toolbox [16] in Matlab. The RMS values are extracted using the essentia library [3]. We further apply smoothening operation using two methods - "loess" with *smooth* function in matlab (based on locally weighted non-parametric regression fitting using a 2nd order polynomial) and exponential moving average [8][EMA]. Based on experimental testing, we use a span of 5% for the loess method. With the exponential moving average smoothening, we use an attack of 2 ms and release time of 20 ms. In the current set of experiments, the RMS smoothening is carried out using EMA methodology, and sone scale is smoothened using loess method. This operation was followed by peak picking operation to get a sense of overall dynamics followed. The peak picking parameters were experimentally set to a threshold of 0.1, and a peak distance of 1.2 s. We used the madmom library [4] for peak picking operation with RMS, and findPeaks function in maltab with sone scale loudness extraction. Figure 2 and Fig. 3 show an example of computation of loudness value using Sone scale and RMS respectively, followed by smoothening operation and detected peaks for the song 'Don't know why' by Norah Jones.

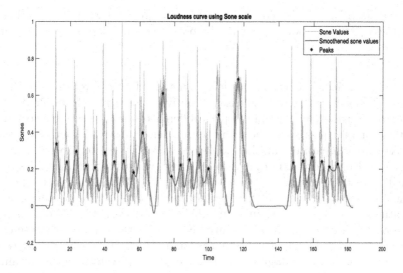

Fig. 2. Loudness using sone scale for Don't Know Why by Norah Jones

4.3   Results

Overall Loudness Comparison Between Renditions. In order to compare the structure similarity of the loudness curves, we computed Pearson Correlation Coefficient of the smoothened curves extracted from the audio signals. Table 1 shows the values observed for each of the 7 songs. As evident from the table, most values are greater than 0.8, and in the case of comparing source separated version

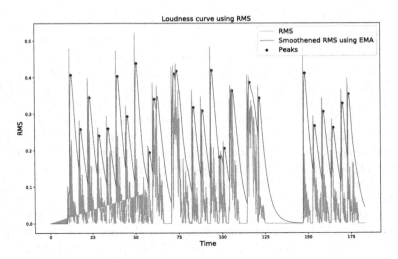

Fig. 3. Loudness using RMS values for Don't Know Why by Norah Jones

with the clean karaoke version, most values are greater than 0.9 indicating the robustness of the methodology with the pre-processing step of applying source separation.

Local Dynamics. To account for local dynamic changes, we compute the differences between consecutive peaks and derive a histogram from all the local differences. Further, the computed peak differences for each song are combined together for all songs from the same source i.e. commercial source separated, karaoke source separated and karaoke stem vocal. Thereafter, we use the nonparametric Kolmogorov-Smirnov 2 sample test which fits the properties of our data. This test is computed between each pair of the 3 histograms corresponding to the 3 sources. We find that for each of the comparisons, the p-value was 0.99 indicating no statistically significant differences between the histogram plots. These results are in line with our initial claim that the overall structure of the local dynamics changes as reflected in the loudness curves. These analysis results were the same for the histograms obtained using RMS values and sone values.

Global Dynamic Range. The global dynamic range of each of the songs is computed using difference in max peak and min peak extracted from the smoothened loudness curve. As indicated in Table 2, the observed global dynamic range based on peak values are mostly similar in the case of karaoke source separated version and the karaoke vocal stem version with the exception of the song 'Son of a preacher man' with RMS values, and 'Fade into you' with sone values.

Table 1. Chosen songs and Pearson Correlation Coefficients for smoothened loudness sone curves

Song Name	Artist	CSS, KSV	KSS, KSV	CSS, KSS
Skyfall	Adele	0.867	0.994	0.931
Torn	Natalie Imbruglia	0.701	0.946	0.800
Fade into you	Mazzy Star	0.943	0.887	0.897
Imagine	John Lennon	0.889	0.981	0.440
Say you won't let go	James Arthur	0.955	0.835	0.800
Don't know why	Norah Jones	0.866	0.997	0.870
Son of a preacher man	Dusty Springfield	0.701	0.957	0.669

Table 2. Observed dynamic range with RMS and sone values

Song Name	RMS			Sone		
	CSS	KSS	KSV	CSS	KSS	KSV
Skyfall	0.460	0.156	0.176	0.503	0.477	0.489
Torn	0.092	0.138	0.206	0.355	0.199	0.213
Fade into you	0.144	0.195	0.167	0.306	0.354	0.182
Imagine	0.172	0.149	0.171	0.320	0.287	0.271
Say you won't let go	0.187	0.138	0.142	0.272	0.190	0.199
Don't know why	0.256	0.222	0.217	0.526	0.489	0.462
Son of a preacher man	0.150	0.227	0.371	0.275	0.339	0.295

Outlier Analysis. With a deeper analysis of the song 'fade into you', we find that there is a guitar section in the original song that becomes an artifact in the source separation output. This leads to a peak being wrongly detected increasing the overall dynamic range for both CSS and KSS resulting from peak detection. A high value of Pearson Correlation Coefficient between CSS and KSS as compared to KSS and KSV reflects from the fact that both of them have source separation as a pre-processing step, and both the versions contain similar artifacts.

4.4   Influence of Voice Source Separation on Loudness Computation

In order to validate the efficacy of the source separation algorithm prior to using it for evaluating dynamics, we computed the Pearson Correlation of the smoothened loudness curves extracted from the mix with the smoothened loudness curves of the vocal stem tracks available with the musdb dataset [17].

As evident from the histogram in Fig. 4, 138 values of the 149 songs evaluated are greater than 0.90. There are 6 songs with values between 0.80 and 0.90, and only 1 song with a value less than 0.50. The mean of the values is 0.960 and the standard deviation is 0.081. These results look promising to be able to use source separation as a prior step for dynamics analysis.

Outliers. The song with the lowest value of correlation coefficient "PR-Happy Daze" contains a lot of instrumental music without much vocal component. Hence, the output of source separation algorithm is mostly artifacts. The song "Skelpolu - Resurrection" with a correlation coefficient of 0.58 has similar challenges.

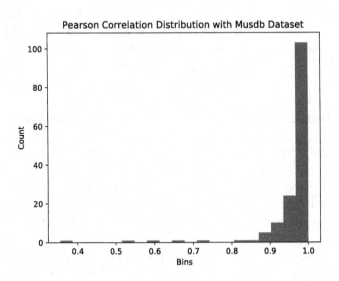

Fig. 4. Distribution of Pearson Correlation Coefficient applied to smoothened loudness curves of musdb dataset

5   Discussion

Work on transcription of dynamics is a challenging task for several reasons. One of the primary reasons being lack of sufficiently annotated data for singing voice to validate the efficacy of these algorithms.

Hence, in order to validate our approach, we conducted a case study with the song 'Don't know why by Norah Jones' where we asked a teacher with 6 years of Western singing teaching experience to compare the two tracks and provide feedback on the dynamic changes. Following is the feedback that we received from the teacher for some phrases of both tracks.

I waited 'til I saw the sun
For Norah's Version: "Norah's dynamics change over the line. "I've" is 'mp'. "Waited till" starts as 'mf', which gradually drops down to 'mp' as she ends the line, can be seen as a diminuendo." For the Backing Track Version: "Dynamically, the singer is 'mf' throughout. This sounds like the kind of vocal take where the original vocals have been compressed one too many times."

I don't know why I didn't come

For Norah's Version: "Dynamically between an 'mp' and 'mf'". For the Backing Track Version: "Once again at an 'mf'. Vocals have definitely been compressed to sound at the same level consistently".

Case Study Results. As evident from the first phrase, the teacher claimed that Norah Jones used a wider range of dynamics in her performance as compared to the cover version. Figure 5 shows the loudness curve of the cover version along with Norah Jones version using the sone scale. The classified dynamic markings for the two renditions are shown in the same plot. As compared to Norah's version of the same song, there is definitely a relatively very low difference between consecutive initial peaks in the cover version. The global dynamic range observed in the results section for this song is also in line with this observation. Similar results can be seen with RMS computation.

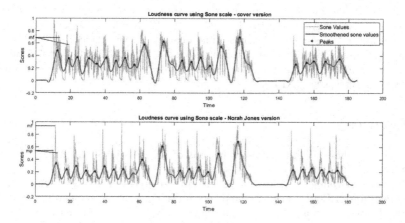

Fig. 5. Loudness using sone scale for Don't Know Why

Challenges. Despite having noisy artefacts and interferences from other instruments, state of the art source separation may be adequate for music analysis, when extracting dynamics. However, the peak detection method may not be robust enough to different performances and require calibration. Smoothing should be done w.r.t the tempo of the song.

While our initial case study showed some promising results, scaling such a system is still a very cumbersome task. Apart from the limitations with data and annotations, we are constrained by the knowledge that can help us realize the right granularity of transcription. For example, expressive markings like crescendo and diminuendo are associated with phrase boundaries [18], but the reverse might not be true. We would need collaborative efforts from multiple fronts in order to take advantage of the recent advances in the field of audio signal processing.

6   Conclusion and Future Work

We presented a methodology to extract dynamics from a performance using loudness as a feature. In the current investigation, we found that it is possible to use these loudness metrics to reach a level of relative changes that can in turn be mapped to dynamics. In future, we intend to discretise these relative values to map them to musically meaningful terms that can be used for providing the right feedback to students. Apart from that, in order to realize the overall goal of transcription, we intend to continue annotations of popular songs and further apply data driven approaches of machine learning to automatically derive the dynamic markings.

We also intend to apply the current methodology to student recordings to validate the efficacy of the system, and if the approach can be used to provide feedback on dynamics to students.

Acknowledgements. We would like to thank Ajay Srinivasmurthy and Divakar Nambiath for their invaluable contributions to this work. Part of this research is funded by the projects Musical AI (PID2019-111403GB-I00/AEI/10.13039/501100011033 funded by the Spanish Ministerio de Ciencia, Innovación y Universidades (MCIU) and the Agencia Estatal de Investigación (AEI)) and NextCore (RTC2019-007248-7 funded by the Spanish Ministerio de Ciencia, Innovación y Universidades (MCIU) and the Agencia Estatal de Investigación (AEI)).

References

1. Beck, J., Shaw, W.A.: Ratio-estimations of loudness-intervals. Am. J. Psychol. **80**(1), 59–65 (1967)
2. Berndt, A., Hahnel, T.: Modelling musical dynamics. In: Proceedings of the 5th Audio Mostly Conference: A Conference on Interaction with Sound (2010)
3. Bogdanov, D., et al.: Essentia: an audio analysis library for music information retrieval. In: Britto, A., Gouyon, F., Dixon, S., (eds.) 14th Conference of the International Society for Music Information Retrieval (ISMIR); 4–8 November 2013; Curitiba, Brazil.[place unknown]: ISMIR; 2013, pp. 493–8. International Society for Music Information Retrieval (ISMIR) (2013)
4. Böck, S., et al.: Madmom: a new python audio and music signal processing library. In: Proceedings of the 24th ACM International Conference on Multimedia (2016)
5. Cancino-Chacón, C.E., Gadermaier, T., Widmer, G., Grachten, M.: An evaluation of linear and non-linear models of expressive dynamics in classical piano and symphonic music. Mach. Learn. **106**(6), 887–909 (2017). https://doi.org/10.1007/s10994-017-5631-y
6. EBU-Recommendation, R.: Loudness normalisation and permitted maximum level of audio signals (2011)
7. Eremenko, V., et al.: Performance assessment technologies for the support of musical instrument learning (2020)
8. Giannoulis, D., Massberg, M., Reiss, J.D.: Digital dynamic range compressor design-A tutorial and analysis. J. Audio Eng. Soc. **60**(6), 399–408 (2012)
9. Grachten, M., Widmer, G.: Linear basis models for prediction and analysis of musical expression. J. New Music Res. **41**(4), 311–322 (2012)

10. Hennequin, R., et al.: Spleeter: a fast and efficient music source separation tool with pre-trained models. J. Open Source Softw. **5**(50), 2154 (2020)
11. Jansson, A., et al.: Singing voice separation with deep u-net convolutional networks (2017)
12. Kosta, K., et al.: Mapping between dynamic markings and performed loudness: a machine learning approach. J. Math. Music **10**(2), 149–172 (2016)
13. Kosta, K.: Computational Modelling and Quantitative Analysis of Dynamics in Performed Music. Diss. Queen Mary University of London (2017)
14. Kosta, K., Bandtlow, O.F., Chew, E.: Dynamics and relativity: practical implications of dynamic markings in the score. J. New Music Res. **47**(5), 438–461 (2018)
15. Langner, J., Goebl, W.: Visualizing expressive performance in tempo-loudness space. Comput. Music J. **27**(4), 69–83 (2003)
16. Pampalk, E.: A Matlab toolbox to compute music similarity from audio. ISMIR (2004)
17. Rafii, Z., et al.: MUSDB18-a corpus for music separation (2017)
18. Smith, J.C.: Correlation analyses of encoded music performance. Stanford University (2013)
19. Widmer, G., Goebl, W.: Computational models of expressive music performance: the state of the art. J. New Music Res. **33**(3), 203–216 (2004)

With Love: Electroacoustic, Audiovisual, and Telematic Music

Paulo C. Chagas[1]([⊠]) [ID] and Cássia Carrascoza Bomfim[2] [ID]

[1] University of California, Riverside, USA
paulo.chagas@ucr.edu
[2] University of São Paulo, Ribeirão Preto, Brazil
cassiacarrascozabomfim@usp.br

Abstract. This article discusses different approaches of music composition and performance with electroacoustic, audiovisual and telematics media. It provides different points of view for understanding the so-called electroacoustic paradigm which emerges from the use of apparatuses in the sound creation and production. From within electroacoustic music paradigm, we examine tendencies and visions of audiovisual and telematic music composition and performance. As illustrations we examine the pieces *Vega_S* (2019) by Kefalidis and *Mojave* (2021) by Chagas/Carrascoza. The telematic communication has the potential do convert discursive thinking into dialog and opens up new possibilities of artistic collaboration. The holistic potentiality of telematic art supports Ascott's metaphor of love in the telematic embrace.

Keywords: Electroacoustic Music · Audiovisual Music · Telematic Music · Composition · Performance · Artistic Collaboration · Flusser · Ascott

1 Electroacoustic Music

What is electroacoustic? And what is electroacoustic music? From an evolutionary perspective, electroacoustic music represents a new paradigm in the history of music that carries on the tradition of vocal and instrumental music and extends it to include the use of apparatuses to produce and move sound around in spaces. From this historical point of view, it has emerged in a period of crisis represented by the disruption of the fundamental role tonal harmony has played as the established disciplinary matrix of music composition. This crisis triggered different responses leading to non-tonal textures in the music of composers such as Schoenberg, Webern, Stravinsky, Debussy, Bartok, Messiaen, and others. Moreover, it pushed composers to explore other constructive principles of musical organization focused on the physical reality of sound phenomena, and to emphasize sound qualities such as timbre and noise. Within the crisis of tonality as foundation, electroacoustic music was able to meet the demands of an aesthetic sensibility focused on this expanded consciousness of sound phenomena. We find three different orientations in the development of electroacoustic music: *musique concrète, elektronische Musik,* and computer music.[1]

---

[1] For an account of the development of electroacoustic music see [2, 103–158].

© Springer Nature Switzerland AG 2023
M. Aramaki et al. (Eds.): CMMR 2021, LNCS 13770, pp. 312–330, 2023.
https://doi.org/10.1007/978-3-031-35382-6_24

The *musique concrète* that came into existence in Paris after World War II, began with Pierre Schaeffer's experiments in recording techniques for capturing sounds of the acoustic environment. This approach engaged the persistent myth that the world is the primary acoustic space of music extending from the earth to the whole universe. The acoustic myth allows sound phenomenon to be isolated from the physical environment, be heard as a unique object and event, and eventually be disconnected from its material source and origin. Released from its cultural references, sound becomes a self-referential paradigm for composing new audible forms. At this point, composition took advantage of new technology for recording, manipulating, and reproducing sound. Drawing ideas from Edmund Husserl's phenomenology of time consciousness [10], the aesthetics of *musique concrète* developed notions such as *sound object* and *reduced listening*. These categories emerged through the interaction of sound material with technical apparatuses, most notably, the tape recorder. *Musique concrète* provided electroacoustic composition with analytical and synthetic approaches to sound perception and composition.

The *elektronische Musik*, most closely associated with the electronic music studio of Cologne, pioneered the creation of sounds whose models are neither found in nature nor possess the qualities of instrumental or vocal sounds. Methods adopted by Karlheinz Stockhausen and other composers of *elektronische Musik* were used to invent new sounds building from the simple elements of technical apparatuses. The signal generator and the noise generator became the prototypes of electronic sound devices despite being designed to test equipment and not for making music. These apparatuses are both mathematical constructs; the signal generator explores the simplicity of a single harmonic motion such as the sine wave, while the noise generator explores the statistical model of all possible vibrations occurring randomly in auditive space. The aesthetics of *elektronische Musik* took advantage of electroacoustic technologies developed during the German Third Reich, which radically transformed the experience of listening while creating new logics to frame political activity. Radio broadcasting and sound amplification were interconnected technologies used for acoustic landscape control and organic synchronization of masses. Radio in particular activated the sonic experience of private intimacy and transformed the universe of telematic paradigm. However, radio also preserves the ancient magic of mythical worlds. As McLuhan [12, 299] notes, "The subliminal depths of radio are charged with the resonating echoes of tribal horns and antique drums."

The historical opposition between *musique concrète* and *elektronische Musik* is emblematic of the diversity of the electroacoustic paradigm. After World War II, the activity of cultural institutions such as the radio studios of Paris and Cologne, promoted a shift of consciousness in electroacoustic music composition. *Musique concrète* developed a poetics of *detachment* from the previous vocal and instrumental paradigms and *attachment* to the sound phenomenon; it disengaged sound consciousness from the models of traditional vocal and instrumental music while at the same time, moved toward interactions with sound that revealed cultural values and identities. Meanwhile, *elektronische Musik* developed a poetics of *detachment* from the sound and *attachment* to the paradigm of music composition. By carrying on the compositional path of the previous vocal and instrumental paradigms, it disentangled consciousness from the representative background of sound as a meaningful artifact and focused on the musical relevance of sound phenomenon. *Elektronische Musik* explores differentiations of acoustical agency in the vibration-centered model of sensitivity.

The *heterogeneity* of sound material is an aesthetic foundation of electroacoustic composition. The opposition between recorded sounds (*musique concrete*) and synthetic sounds (*elektronische Musik*), quickly dissipated as any kind of sound could become the object of musical composition. The electroacoustic paradigm not only integrated the musical puzzles of the previous vocal and instrumental paradigms but provided new ways for representing and manipulating sound. As the prototype of a reproduction apparatus, the tape machine was able to radically transform and manipulate recorded sound despite the fact that electromagnetic tape symbolizes linear thinking. On the other hand, digital systems of audio recording introduced non-linear representation in which sound is broken down into an atomic dot-like structures that disintegrate into a mosaic of numbers as the bond with temporal sound tissue dissolves. The fragmented granular structure of the sound, which can be manipulated by computers and artificial intelligences, replaces linear thinking and promotes a consciousness of the microstructure of any given sound.

Digital systems such as samplers, programs, and storage devices stand as proto-types with the potential to project sound artificially, and thus, reinvent it. As Pousseur observed, electroacoustic music articulates a continuous interaction between different levels of sound organization, so that it becomes difficult "to draw a precise boundary between internal composition of sound and higher levels of composition" [13, 82]. A myriad of sound poetics emerged within the electroacoustic paradigm such as soundscape composition, deep listening, live-electronics, and other musical distinctions involving vocal, instrumental, or electronic sounds. The electroacoustic paradigm extended sound perception and consciousness, especially in the way it relates to microscopic and macro-scopic levels of sonic composition. The opposition of macro/micro sound, along with the methodic use of music apparatuses, is a signature of the electroacoustic paradigm symbolizing a desire for intensification of the living experience.

2   Electroacoustic Music Composition

Do composers of electroacoustic music imagine a certain sound when composing or do they conceive of a musical structure to be filled with sounds? Is electroacoustic music composition the same as sound composition according to Varèse's definition of music as "organized sound?" If not, what is the difference and what distinguishes electroacoustic music from a work of sound art? These questions can be addressed within the broader context of electroacoustic music that cultivates intersections with other artistic forms that use sound as a primary medium of expression while paving the way for creativity within forms that take advantage of modern technology such as visual art. The term "multimedia" refers to forms of communication combining different media such as text, audio, and images. Multimedia is thus a kind of interdisciplinary matrix encompassing both acoustic and visual forms. However, we have to carefully consider the application of this concept to artistic works, as the manifold forms of artistic communication accomplish different functions in society.

First, we must consider the best way to analyze the form of an electroacoustic com-position and how a composer uses individual sounds to create a sound structure that corresponds to the entire piece. We must examine how individual sounds constituting the structure of the work are defined. Alternately, we could also consider electroacoustic composition from a more traditional point of view, simply as a specific musical form to be analyzed with the traditional tools of music theory. In this case, we would emphasize the connections between the electroacoustic composition and the models of vocal and instrumental composition. From the starting point of sound not being an isolated object, we are able to understand it only within a compositional context. For it is not possible to speak of sound phenomenon without considering its connections to other sounds that create the sense of temporality. The world is not silent or mute. Our sense of temporality is closely related to our ability to perceive sounds in the acoustic environment, as the acoustics provide the temporal experience with sound objects and events. In the course of human history, music has been produced mainly with human voices and instruments. That is, until the development of apparatuses became capable of recording, manipulating, and reproducing sound for the purpose of creating new synthetic sounds. The electroacoustic sound is no longer attached to the body, whether by voice or instrument, but is the output of an apparatus. However, the universe of the electroacoustic music is not limited to all possible sounds that we are able to produce and listen to; it must include all perceptions and experiences that the work of art can offer.

Is the composer of electroacoustic music the person who drafts ideas or the one who produces the sounds? Can a single human being accomplish these two tasks? In fact, electroacoustic music has generated new fields of professional endeavors in classical and popular music, and in film and audiovisual creation. Alongside traditional artists such as singers, instrumentalists, conductors, composers, and lyricists—there have emerged new kinds of creators with artistic and bureaucratic functions. For example, the sound designer who creates new sound environments in film, the sound programmer who creates new synthesizers and sound creation platforms (DAW), and the sound producer who fulfills both administrative and business functions directly influencing the creative process, especially as seen in popular music. In fact, if we consider electroacoustic music in a broad sense as a multiplicity of categories, genres, and artistic forms, we see that musical creation depends on a network of ideas that require the use of apparatuses. The multiple agents involved in the creative process develop specific competencies so that the continuous dialogue is the basis of the creative process. The dialogue involves the manipulation of apparatuses and the systematic exploration of their possibilities. The creation of electroacoustic music is a playful game with apparatuses in which human beings and intelligent tools continuously interact with each other. This idea of creation challenges the traditional question of authorship. Creation emerges not from a mythical author, but from the incessant dialog taking place in different stages of the process. The crucial question of artistic collaboration determines the transformational power of art and creativity in the current society.

How does one critically appreciate the quality of electronic music in general or the quality of electroacoustic music of a particular composer? What are the parameters for evaluating electroacoustic music in relation to vocal and instrumental music and how can we investigate the truth of the work for its authenticity and historical meaning? According to Heidegger [9] the creative preserving of truth in a work of art is what allows it to articulate a style within a culture. The search for the answers to these questions is driven by the fact that electroacoustic music has become a fertile field of artistic and technological exploration and innovation affecting practically everything that is understood as music or sound art including the collective perceptions of listeners, composers, performers, and musicologists. The electroacoustic paradigm is one very particular form of life, as it concerns the whole of communication with sound and music in the society. It has exponentially increased the music information available to us, including the music of the past, and has radically transformed sound and music perception and consciousness. In this sense, it is a propitious field for exercising cultural criticism of the present.

3   Language, Speech, and Electroacoustic Sound

As analog systems of communication, music and language elaborate forms in the medium of sound with sound being the primary layer of language and the main communication system of society. As Wittgenstein suggested, sound is the surface of music that allows access into meaningful depth. Music shows us that we must dive beyond the surface of sounds to understand its complexity:

> Music, with its few notes and rhythms, seems to some people a primitive art. But only its surface is simple, while the body which makes possible the interpretation of this manifest content has all the infinite complexity that is suggested in the external forms of other arts and which music conceals. In a certain sense it is the most sophisticated art of all [17, 11].

Language is built upon a very small number of sounds, or phonemes, that have no value in themselves but acquire value in relation to each other. The phoneme is a differential and connective element of language, which organizes sounds by means of phonological oppositions constituting the sound material of speech. Linguistic binary coding structures operate on the basis of a choice between a positive or a negative value. Moreover, the binary code of language constitutes a paradigm for other forms of communication. Speech is the act of using the language, which is linked to several factors that are not necessarily linguistic such as context, personality, history, culture, and society. Language is primarily a concept, a repertoire of possibilities viewed from the outside, while speech is associated with the ability to express thoughts and feelings by articulating sounds. Speech is not just the physical materiality of sound, but also the muscular effort and psychic imprint. Put another way, language is the realm of the virtual where nothing is yet said, while speech represents the embodiment of the individuation process bringing the personal and collective unconscious into the realm of the conscious. Using Tarasti's existential semiotics terminology, the distinction between language and speech represents the movement from the immanent to the manifest through which meaning emerges [16, 157–177].

For Wittgenstein, musical understanding is a prototype that can be used to understand language: "Understanding a sentence is much more akin to understanding a theme in music than one may think" [18, 151]. There is family resemblance between the verbal phrase, the melody, and the musical phrase. Both music and language are primally manifestations of a physical presence. Even sounds produced electronically need the vibration of objects such as the membranes of loudspeakers, to be perceived by the ear. However,

different than vocal and instrumental music, which are manifestations of a bodily presence, electroacoustic music encompasses sounds that are abstract and disconnected from
living organisms. This leads to the necessity of providing some organic foundation to the
sound in order to attribute musical meaning. One example is the research on phonetics.
A key figure in the early days of the Electronic Music Studio in Cologne was Werner
Meyer-Eppler—an experimental acoustician, information theorist, and phonetics expert
who introduced many concepts in electronic music composition that grew out of his
research on phonology. His ideas inspired the composition of Karlheinz Stockhausen's
Gesang der Jünglinge [*Song of the Youths*] (1955–56), a piece representing a great
evolution in the composition of electronic music as it integrated electronic sounds with
human voices and explored the similarities between phonemes and electronic sounds for
developing new compositional methods. Since the early 1950s, electroacoustic music
has been exploring the living quality of voice to create electronic imitations of phonemes
and other elements of spoken speech such as formants, articulation, and intonation. The
phonetic metaphor of sound inspired a new approach to electroacoustic material that
shared the acoustical characteristics of speech—vowels are associated with harmonic
sounds constructed from sine tones, fricative and sibilant consonants are related to filtered noises, and plosive consonants to impulses. The formants that shape the color of
different vowels are associated with bands of frequency and timbres.

4 Sound Embodiment and Sound Space

Human *embodiment* can be seen as a mediator between technology and the world. In
traditional acoustic music, gestures are made distinctive through specific features such
as articulations, dynamics, timing, rhythm, meter, texture, and timbre. In electroacoustic
music, the body's gestural interface – visual, acoustic, and tactile – facilitates new kinds
of interactive and intersubjective communication. For both acoustic and electroacoustic
music, gesture articulates not only the perception of nuance, cognition, and affect—
but also negotiates the understanding of higher sound and musical structuring through
internal synthesis and integration of elements.

Embodiment and *gestural* activity emerge as key concepts in discussions of space
in electroacoustic music, as for instance in Smalley [15]. The increasing focus on the
multiple connections between sound, body, and listening reaffirms the notion of space as
enacted experience. This represents a significant shift from the typological and morphological approaches of sound to new formulations based on more synthetic, phenomeno-
logical, and ecological categories. Nevertheless, a problem persists in the theoretical and
analytical discussion, namely the distinction between "internal" and "external" sound
space. The structural coupling of internal and external references, as pointed out by Luhmann [11] in the realm of his autopoietic theory of social systems, poses the question:
How do artistic objects articulate and combine perception and communication?

In Luhmann's response, sound space must be defined not in terms of sonic qualities, but as a *mode of operation of consciousness that gives form to the perception of
space within the acoustic environment*. Similar to the operation that produces polyphony,
sound space is the form of the difference between *self-reference* (internal world) and
hetero-reference (external world) in acoustic perception. This definition implies that

consciousness has to establish the boundaries that connect and disconnect the perception of sound phenomena to the perception of space. The definition of sound space is a particular embodiment based on the possibility of perceiving sounds as meaningful elements.

In opposition to instrumental and vocal sounds that are *tightly coupled* with the body and the objects that produced them, electroacoustic sounds can be seen as *loosely coupled* because they leave room for multiple combinations. The sound recording of a voice, instrument, or environment is an inscription and re-creation of sound waves that can be transformed in different ways and turned into something completely altered from the original sound. Luhmann introduced the opposition between *loose coupling* and *tight coupling* to account for the difference between media and form. Media is a loose coupling of elements, something more abstract and fluid—while form is a tight coupling of elements, something more stable and tangible. [11, 102–132]. Electroacoustic music is a disembodied entity as sound frees itself from the body. Therefore, electroacoustic composition requires a process of re-actualization of meaning in order to endow sounds with a bodily, spatial memory.

From the beginning, space has been a functional and operational category of electroacoustic composition. Sound space composition then became more fully realized with the introduction of multi-channel audio technology. Prototypes of multi-channel technology consist of the four-track tape recorder and the quadraphonic speaker system surrounding the listener: a stereo pair in the front and another in the back. Through the use of this technology in the late 1950s and 1960s, composers began to create pieces in which sounds were designed for specific positions in space. Once space became a parameter of composition, sound developed a "tactile" dimension. Similar to a body, it occupies a unique position in the space from which it can exclude other spaces.

5 Audiovisual Composition

Currently, the concept of audiovisual art is framed by the dominant role film and television play in our society, founded on technology of sound and image reproduction invented in the second half of the 19th Century. Cinematography, as an audiovisual art that emerged from the movement of technical images, elevated film to the most popular artistic form in human history. With the supremacy of the moving image, especially during the silent film era, it was possible to cross borders and establish patterns of transnational communication. As the sound film quickly prevailed as a product of mass consummation, cinema, and later television, shaped the perception of sound and image until the end of the 1980s when digital technology set the stage for radical transformation. The popularization of personal computers, mobile devices, and networks of information and communication, began to reframe the creativity of audiovisual art. Technology propelled convergences of sound, image, space, and performance to create new architectures of collaboration giving rise to new kinds of transnational dialogues. As the traditional structures of creation and production of audiovisual art underwent this enormous change, new artistic forms of audiovisual composition began to emerge.

In the universe of electronic music, there has been a growing interest in audiovisual composition with more electroacoustic works being coupled with video, and mixed works combining electroacoustic sounds, live performance, and visual projection. Audiovisual composition has the potential to bring electroacoustic music to a broader audience, as it addresses a multimodal perception and sensibility. It reveals two important components: the convergence of fields and perceptions as well as the creation of a diversity and differentiation of forms. Composers of audiovisual works have much to consider. Based on their initial motivation to create a new piece, they are faced with the question of which will be more important – the music, the visuals, or the combination of the two? They must consider how the sound and image relate to each other as they attempt to intensify the immersive, sensorial experience and try to raise the consciousness of the interconnection between hearing and listening as a mode of being in the world. If they fail to achieve these objectives, should the audiovisual composition be considered just another distraction reinforcing the patterns of entertainment and diversion? As a society inhabited with myriad trivial objects and gadgets of audiovisual technology taking a hold on our existence, we have become saturated by the torrent of audiovisual impressions. Faced with this flood of information that can lead to a state of entropy, it is important to develop a critical reflection on audiovisual communication. We need a comprehensive account of the relation between sound and image beyond the conventional form of cinema in order to understand its full creative potential. It is necessary to deconstruct the hegemonic discourses and point out the broad spectrum of possibilities and diversity of forms within audiovisual composition.

6   The Electronic Music Video

The music video, which emerged in tradition of electronic music, is a contemporary form of audiovisual composition coupling electronic sounds with image projection that enjoys growing interest and is developing into a sub-genre of electroacoustic music. The music can be "heard" and "seen" at the same time. The audiovisual merge seems to have the potential to make the music more accessible to a broader audience. But here one has to raise the following question: Does the multimedia intensify the sensorial experience and make it thus more attractive, or does it simply provide a distraction that reinforces the patterns of entertainment and diversion of the consume society? Whatever the answer may be, embedding the music into an audiovisual form provides the listener with an immersive experience that is functionally linked to the situation of the movie theater: the music is projected into the room through loudspeakers, the sound surrounds the bodies, while the image projected onto a screen—usually located in front of the audience—focuses the audience's attention on an illuminated surface.

The electroacoustic music video relating sound, image, and space is primarily an immersive experience that can be also integrated with other forms, such as the concert with live music performance (vocal, instrumental, and/or electroacoustic music); the performance with dance, acting, etc.; the installation; and so on. Traditionally, the audiovisual art is structurally coupled with the space both as physical and social medium. The immersive experience relates physical presence to social presence. By contrast, watching an electroacoustic music video on a computer, on internet, or on a mobile device is mainly an individual experience, in which the embodied experience is dispersed along a spectrum of possibilities emerging from the interaction with the technological environment.

As an illustration of audiovisual composition, we would like to examine the piece *Vega_S* (2019)[2] by the distinguished Russian composer Igor Kefalidis (b. 1941). Kefalidis' profound interest in electroacoustic music has resulted in a long period of composing pieces exclusively with electroacoustic sounds—most in combination with solo instruments, chamber music, and orchestra. His creativity reaches into the fields of dance and audiovisual composition and the relationship between sound and image plays a crucial role in his recent work, in which he has been collaborating with visual artists. Most recently, he has been adopting new tools to create synthetical images.

Vega_S (2019) – length 13′05″ – for electronic sounds and video is a remarkable piece that represents a mature stage of Kefalidis' audiovisual composition style. Here, the electroacoustic music seems to bring forth the imagery, as though the sounds are endowed with visual symbolism. The visual composition by Andrew Quinn takes advantage of the imaginative character of the music and seeks to create an organic relationship through the use of a thin white vertical line in the middle of the screen that varies in brightness according to the music. The line turns into a narrow dark space separating two walls that constitute the main element of the visual composition. The walls are curved with a translucent and pixelated structure in black and white that continuously rotate in opposite directions, changing speed according to the sonic variations of the music. Figures appear and disappear in the narrow space between the walls and the spaces and on their left and right sides and the pulsing activity of these intermittent elements are in sync with the music. At 5′20″, a strong beat punctuates the visual composition and the music speeds up and ascends in a pseudo–quotation of a short compelling rock guitar solo (8′35″ – 8′48″). As the musical energy increases, colorful strips are introduced in the wall landscape, rotating ever faster and disrupting the visual symmetry to create a fragmented, fast-moving kaleidoscopic image to accompany the rock guitar. The electronic music creates the impression of fluid space as the sound objects and events seem to move closer and then farther away. The visual composition explores the fluidity of the space by creating a kind of futuristic landscape that constantly moves without a clear direction. The audiovisual composition presents us with the ambiguity of experiencing a calculated universe while simultaneously allowing us the chance to move between the world of algorithms. Overall, it infuses us with energy and hope as it suggests the need to disrupt hegemonic structures of power to escape via beams of flight leading to unknown territories. *Vega_S* is an accomplished example of the synergy of sound and image. The multiplicity of connections between electroacoustic sounds and synthetic images portrays the massive potential of audiovisual composition.

7   From Soundscape to Telematic Immersion

Telematic music is an attempt to make a synthesis of two different types of communication: (1) The communication of chamber music, which occurs in the physical medium with bodies producing gestures that are translated into sounds; (2) the communication of electronic music, which occurs in the virtual medium with apparatuses producing programs that are translated into sounds or images. Unlike traditional chamber music,

---

[2] Available at <https://youtu.be/QLGKroHIpaA> (accessed June 7, 2023).

which is structured as a succession of linear events such as themes and variations, telematic music creates a dialog that "occurs in simultaneous time and space, and all players in all places make decisions relating to themes and their variations all at once" [4, 163]. Telematic music offers the possibility to reshape musical performance in virtual spaces by reconstructing the subjectivity with the *experience of presence*.

As an illustration of telematic music, we will discuss *Mojave* (2021)[3] – length 8:53″ – a collaborative work for flute, electronics and video that unfolds an aesthetics of audiovisual immersion with telematic performance. The work was developed on the basis of 3D video and ambisonics audio recordings on the desert of Mojave (California) in January 2020. Cássia Carrascoza created a performance for this specific site physically interacting with the landscape and improvising with sounds exploring extended techniques for flute and bass flute. Paulo C. Chagas composed a score for flute and live electronics exploring algorithms of delay and feedback, which create a universe oscillating between latencies and synchronies. Different versions of the piece were created for audiovisual media and live telematic performance. Mojave is a multilayered audiovisual composition that reflects on the presence and absence as vectorial forces of creativity. The contrast between the vast desert landscape and the confined telematic environment evokes the existential feelings of eternal and transitory, the finite and the infinite, and the anxiety we current experience between isolation and the opportunity to immerse ourselves into virtual worlds.

Conceptually, *Mojave* is part of the large-scale research project *Sound Imaginations*, which aims to investigate listening cultures and different categories of listening.[4] The emblematic notion of *soundscape* proposed by the Canadian composer and scholar Murray Schafer in the 1970s [14] is a key concept for observing the sonic environment, which includes not only the "natural" sounds but also the entire culture that characterizes the sonic environment of any specific space or object of study. Driven by Schafer's ideas, many scholars and artists have been pursuing the mapping of historical and contemporary soundscapes and observing the transformation of soundscapes in the industrial and digital societies. Many authors have criticized Schafer for having projected the problematic concept of "soundscape" borrowed from visual art into sound studies as it suggests a static perspective rather than the moving and surrounding characteristic of sound phenomena. Also, it implies a division between hearing and seeing, which is highly problematic in the contemporary world shaped by the connective reality of audiovisual and multimedia technology.

Feld [3], for instance, proposes the concept of acoustemology – the union of acoustics and epistemology – that investigates the primacy of sound as a modality of knowing and being in the world. Soundscapes are not just physical exteriors, they are perceived and interpreted by human actors and are invested with significance by those whose bodies and lives resonate with them in social time and space. As a cultural system, sound both emanate from and penetrates bodies; hearing and producing sound are thus embodied with competencies that situate actors and their agency in particular historical worlds.

---

[3] Available at <https://youtu.be/GB-KwDOImho> (accessed June 7, 2023).

[4] Sound Imaginations (2020) audiovisual immersive installation; available at <https://youtu.be/V_9VlC1sBgk> (accessed June 7, 2023).

The compositional concept of *Mojave* was elaborated on the basis of the semiotic square proposed by Hayles [7] that reconstructs the distinction between *randomness* and *pattern* in the so-called *posthuman* society while emphasizing the role of *embodiment* and *materiality* in the processes of constituting meaning. Hayles' semiotic square (Fig. 1) has two axes: the main axis is the distinction between *presence* and *absence*; the secondary axis is the distinction between *randomness* and *pattern*. Two diagonals that connect these two axes trigger a dynamics of signification. The diagonal connecting presence and pattern conveys *replication*; the diagonal connecting absence and randomness signals *disruption*. The interplay between presence and absence shapes materiality; the interplay between randomness and pattern gives rise to information [7, 247–251] (see Fig. 1).

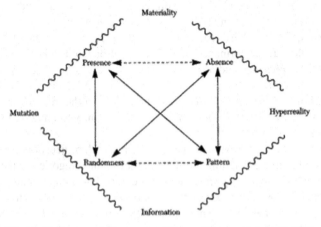

Fig. 1. Hayles' semiotic square of the posthuman society [7, 249].

On the site of the desert of Mojave, Cássia Carrascoza developed a performance with flute and bass flute that articulates a dialectics of presence/absence emerging from the auditory and visual perception of the soundscape/landscape. For instance, the presence the strong wind blowing through the vast space of the desert – which also autonomously activated flute sounds –, and the sounds produced by the crackling of small stones as one moves across the uneven desert ground, these are two elements that were integrated in the performance, along with long sounds and extended flute techniques. The 3D images move around Cássia as focal point, a central figure that captures the human presence in the emptiness of the desert landscape, which symbolizes void and absence. Starting from this focal point, the movements unfold edges, diagonals, curves, rotations, and circular movements that opens up a constant play of spiracle shapes, a vortex of 3D images that pushes things beyond the center, creating a path of decentering moving along both the axis of presence/absence and randomness/pattern. The musical composition associates visual imagery with the spherical sound perception of the ambisonics technology. It explores a vocabulary of sound shapes and colors, sound objects, events or movements that tease out the decentering of the listener, which is sometimes synchronized and sometimes out of sync with the visual.

Mojave is a collaborative work between a composer and a performer acting as equal partners that takes into account the new fields of creativity emerging through the convergence of sound, image, and the development of new architectures of collaboration. The work illustrated the method and practice of *telematic dialogue*, the creative process through which information is generated in the society of the future. Flusser tries to demystify the idea of the "artist", the individual author of creation, molded in the image of the divine Creator of the Judeo-Christian religion. For him, creation – or information – is a process of synthesis through which previous information is decomposed (analyzed) and recombined. Nature produces information at random; man, in turn, plays – plays and plays – intentionally with available information in order to produce new information [4, 98]. Flusser thus re-elaborated the mystique of creation through dialectics such as probability/improbability and chance/intention, which refer to Hayles' semiotic square. Information arises through improbable accidents and reproduces itself through probable accidents. Nature produces information in a non-methodical way, the human being in a methodical way.

Mojave addresses resources, approaches, and strategies of audiovisual composition in an environment where information is embedded in complex heterogenic and polyphonic structures of subjectivity. As pointed out by Guattari [5, 6], subjectivity is no longer restricted to human consciousness, but incorporates the body of technology through what he defines as "machinic assemblages". Creativity no longer depends on personal identity and subjectivity but on the particular assemblage that happens in connection with technological bodies that extend the framework of cognition and meaning. The structure of the "machinic assemblages" can be defined as "polyphonic, as it articulates a multiplicity of human and non-human subjects bringing several simultaneous and independent levels of perception and meaning" [2, 106].

There are different versions of *Mojave*, including two media versions – a long and a short video – and a video recorded from a real-time telematic performance.[5] The following sequence of screenshots taken from the long video version documents some aspects of the 3D visual composition (Figs. 2, 3, 4, 5, 6, 7, 8, 9, 10 and 11).

---

[5] Available at <https://youtu.be/onuWdf92KrI> (accessed June 7, 2023).

Fig. 2. *Mojave* – 00:38;03 (min:sec;frame) – panoramic view of the performance site in the Mojave desert; Cássia Carrascoza stands on the bottom right.

Fig. 3. *Mojave* – 02:00;11 – Panoramic view of the performance site from another angle; Cássia Carrascoza in the center and the hill in the background.

Fig. 4. *Mojave* – 03:19;27 – Spherical view; Cássia Carrascoza and the sound recording equipment on the center (ambisonics microphone, tripod and multichannel recorder).

Fig. 5. *Mojave* – 04:31;08 – Spherical view from another angle; sound recording equipment on the bottom; the hill appears on the left.

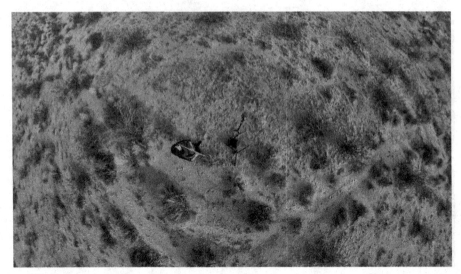

Fig. 6. *Mojave* – 05:21;20 – View from the top of the camera; Cássia and the sound recording equipment on the center.

Fig. 7. *Mojave* – 06:27;13 – Inverted image with the sky emerging from the center of the earth.

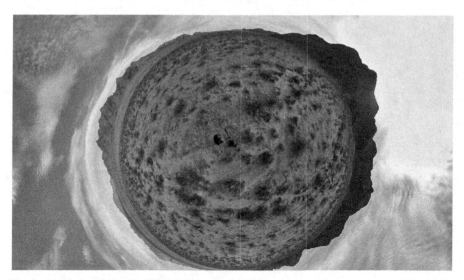

Fig. 8. *Mojave* – 07:02;20 – Spherical image with the earth on the center surrounded by the sky.

Fig. 9. *Mojave* – 07:44;22 – 3D transition from spherical to panoramic view.

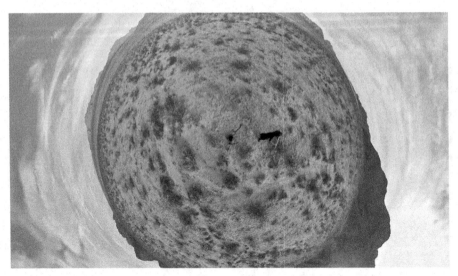

Fig. 10. *Mojave* – 08:27;03 – Another spherical image with the earth on the center surrounded by the sky and clouds, which creates a sensation of rotation.

Fig. 11. *Mojave* – 08:53;05 – Spherical view as a planet; Cássia and the sound recording equipment on the bottom.

8   Conclusion: Telematic Embrace

As Heidegger [8] argues, modern technology has changed our sense of the world as it tends to reduce everything into mere resources, including human beings. The programmatic magic of technical apparatuses, including artistic apparatuses that produce synthetic sounds and images, tends to eliminate critical thinking, replacing historical consciousness with a second-order magical consciousness that reduces culture to its lowest denominator. With the technical apparatus, relations of power move from physical objects to a symbolic level of programs and operators.

The telematic paradigm embraces the communicative complexity that emerges from the convergence of telecommunications and information processing in today's society. Flusser [4] believes that telematic communication has the potential to radically transform the way we communicate. Telematics can reverse the natural tendency of entropy – the state of randomness in which information is unpredictable and therefore impossible – by converting historical and discursive thinking into dialog. In Flusser's telematic dialog, man and apparatuses act as partners devoting themselves to the systematic generation of information through a playful game. The telematic dialog embodies Flusser's utopia of freedom as a struggle against entropy, which emancipates man from the controlling functionality of the machine.

The possibilities of artistic collaborations between participants in remote locations, interacting via electronic networks, can facilitate interactive art and interdisciplinary, as Ascott pointed out in his seminal writing of 1960s [1, 109–156]. The telematic paradigm involves not only the technology of interaction among human beings but between the human mind and artificial systems of intelligence and perception. It transcends the body, amplifies the mind into unpredictable configurations of thought and creativity, and can contribute to the emergence of a global consciousness. The holistic potentiality of telematic art supports Ascott's metaphor of love in the telematic embrace. Like gravity, passionate attraction draws together human beings an connects then. Global telematic embrace would constitute an "infrastructure for spiritual interchange that could lead to the harmonization and creative development of the whole planet" [1, 245].

References

1. Ascott, R.: Telematic Embrace: Visionary Theories of Art, Technology, and Consciousness. University of California Press, Berkeley (2003)
2. Chagas, P.C.: Unsayable Music: Six Essays on Musical Semiotics. Electroacoustic and Digital Music. Leuven University Press, Leuven (2014)
3. Feld, S.: A rainforest acoustemology. In: Bull, M., Back, L. (eds.) The Auditory Culture Reader, pp. 223–279. Berg, Oxford, New York (2003)
4. Flusser, V.: Into the Universe of Technical Images. University of Minnesota Press, Minneapolis (2011)
5. Guattari, F.: Chaosmosis. Galilée, Paris (1992)
6. Guattari, F.: Machinic heterogenesis. In: Rethinking Technologies, pp. 13–17. University of Minnesota Press, Minneapolis (1993)
7. Hayles, K.: How We Became Posthuman: Virtual Bodies in Cybernetics, Literature, and Informatics. University of Chicago Press, Chicago (1999)

8. Heidegger, M.: The question concerning technology. In: The Question Concerning Technology and Other Essays, pp. 3–35. Harper and Row, New York (1977). (trans. W., Lovitt)
9. Heidegger, M.: The origin of the work of art. In: Basic Writings, pp. 139–212. Harper Perennial, New York (2008)
10. Husserl, E.: Zur Phänomenologie des Inneren Zeitbewußtseins. M. Nijhoff, The Hague (1966)
11. Luhmann, N.: Art as Social Systems. Stanford University Press, Stanford (2000)
12. McLuhan, M.: Understanding Media: The Extensions of Man. The MIT Press, Cambridge (1994)
13. Pousseur, H.: Fragments théoriques I sur la musique expérimentale. Editions de l'Institut de Sociologie de l'Université Libre de Bruxelles, Brussels (1970)
14. Schafer, M.: The Soundscape: Our Sonic Environment and the Tuning of the World. Destiny Books, Rochester (1994)
15. Smalley, D.: Space-form and the acousmatic image. Organized Sound 12(1), 35–58 (2007)
16. Tarasti, E.: Signs of Music: A Guide to Musical Semiotics. Mouton de Gruyter, Berlin; New York (2002)
17. Wittgenstein, L.: Culture and Value, Revised, 2nd edn. Basil Blackwell, Oxford (1998)
18. Wittgenstein, L.: Philosophical Investigations [Philosophische Untersuchungen], 4th edn. Blackwell Publishing, Oxford (2009)

Author Index

© Springer Nature Switzerland AG 2023
M. Aramaki et al. (Eds.): CMMR 2021, LNCS 13770, pp. 331–332, 2023.
https://doi.org/10.1007/978-3-031-35382-6

Printed in the United States
by Baker & Taylor Publisher Services